Development Administration and Multi-Level Planning

Development Administration and Multi-Level Planning

Edited by
Rakesh Hooja
Sunil Dutt

KANISHKA PUBLISHERS, DISTRIBUTORS
NEW DELHI-110 002

KANISHKA PUBLISHERS, DISTRIBUTORS
4697/5-21A, Ansari Road, Daryaganj
New Delhi-110 002
Phones : 2327 0497, 2328 8285
Fax : 011-2328 8285
e-mail: kanishka_publishing@yahoo.co.in

First Published 2008

ISBN 978-81-8457-073-1

PRINTED IN INDIA

Published by Madan Sachdeva for Kanishka Publishers, Distributors, 4697/5-21A, Ansari Road, Daryaganj, New Delhi-110 002; Typeset by Sunshine Graphics, Delhi, and Printed at Nice Printing Press, Delhi.

Foreword

Countries all over the world have approached planning with a view to overcoming economic backwardness and facilitating the changeover to a modern economy. In the jargon of development administration the multi-level planning has come to be known as a technique, a methodology, and a system of planning where the lowest unit is allowed to plan and implement everything that can be performed most effectively at that level and only the residual is left to the higher levels. Thus, the task of planning for the development and optimal utilisation of resources of a nation is addressed to conceivable local agencies or units. This process also creates certain intermediary levels along the ladder for fulfilling the same task at increasing levels of spatial reference, perspectives, and appreciation of the environment. The success of such a concept depends on the optimal functioning of the supportive institutions.

Initial attempts at a centralized model of planning have brazenly criticized for having degenerated into uncoordinated, mutually exclusive schemes by various government departments that did not provide optimal utilization of resources. They were largely condemned for being bureaucratic that gave people no say in their formulation or execution and led to overlapping programmes, duplication and waste of resources, and laxness in monitoring. There was a bitter lesson to be learnt that market mediated economic growth as such cannot uphold balanced regional development in a country as spatially diverse as India. There emerged a compelling need to highlight the significance of bottom-up planning for "economic development and social justice" as has been laid down in Articles 243G and 243W of the Constitution.

By mandating the panchayats to prepare plans for economic development and social justice based on area planning, the

Constitution facilitates micro-plans that form the building blocks of a large part of macro-development plans at the state and national level. The cardinal consideration in the multi-layered federation like India is admittedly the well-known principle of subsidiarity, viz. that those functions which can be performed well at a particular level should be done at that level and not at a higher level. We have woefully failed in this task, with overlapping structures worse confounded. Experts are of the view that planning should be based on organized social knowledge rather than mechanistic reductionist methodology and favour a planning process that accommodates interacting macro, meso and micro factors.

Multi-level planning came into existence in India much before the 73rd and 74th Constitutional Amendments which were meant to usher in decentralised governance and, somehow, coincided with the introduction of the economic reform process in the country. In the recent years, of course, attempts have been made to evolve a pervading organisational plan that might be applied for effective implementation of multi-level planning in the Indian context.

Decentralized planning does not mean complete abandonment of higher level responsibilities. The ultimate goal is a substantial relaxation of central control and substantial community empowerment. The never ending debate on the nature of decentralized planning needs an in-depth analysis of the planning process and organizational characteristics at the specific levels—evaluation of their roles and effectiveness in their planning and developmental tasks—strengths and weaknesses vis-à-vis the multi-level planning process.

The articles in this volume take a closer look at the evolution of a normative structure of multi-level planning in India and analyses the role of multi-level planning as it has emerged through the various five-year plans. Various essays touch upon the structure and features of the Indian polity and the administrative and planning framework, make assessment of the historical and the current processes-need for multi-level planning process, and, emergence and relevance of the national, sub-national, regional and local planning and development organizations. They discuss many important issue relating to structure, implementation and sustenance of multi-level planning. The articles compiled in this volume have been culled from the treasure trove of Institute's prize publication. It is hoped the scholars, researchers, administrators and students will find it as one of their most valuable possessions.

S.P. Verma
Director
Indian Institution of
Public Administration
New Delhi

18th June, 2007

Contents

Introduction

When we talk of planning in the Governmental context in India, we are referring not only to techno-economic planning, but also to financial or budgetary planning, spatial or area planning, administrative planning, project planning, sector-by-sector planning, participatory and decentralized planning and the like. We also include in our ambit planning at levels lower than the national i.e. state, district, block, special project area, or village which are linked in a framework of multi-level planning generated by both 'top down' and 'bottom up' impulses, and systems for both vertical and horizontal coordination of planning including its implementation. In this context it is clear that planning is not viewed as simply a technical exercise, not only as a political, economic, social or administrative device but an integrated amalgam of all of these.

Planning at the state level is at least as old as the framing of the Indian Constitution which made 'social and economic planning' a concurrent subject. The history of attempts to introduce planning at sub-state levels is almost as old, since the First Five Year Plan had touted the idea of a village production council for agriculture planning; and village, block and district plans were required to be prepared on the eve of the formulation of the Second Five Year Plan. At least from the Fourth Five Year Plan period in 1969 (when D. R. Gadgil was Deputy Chairman of the Planning Commission) India has been focusing on a system of multi-level planning with the Central and State levels being supplemented and complemented by decentralized planning where, after an initial debate between the merits and demerits of the district and the block, the district was accepted as the basic unit of decentralized planning.

Notwithstanding the Planning Commission's Working Group on Block Level Planning (Dantwala Committee Report of 1978) which left a significant impact; it is the Planning Commission Guidelines for Formulation of District Plans, 1969, the Report of the Working Group on District Planning (Hanumantha Rao Report, 1984), and the 73rd and 74th Constitutional Amendments of 1993-94 that have been major landmarks in providing further impetus to district and multi-level planning in the country. The latest in the line, the Planning Commission Report of the Working Group on Decentralized Planning and Panchayati Raj Institutions for Tenth Five Year Plan (2002-07) of November 2001, expounds on planning efforts that should be made at the three levels of panchayati raj—the district, the intermediate level or block and the village—and its relationship with planning at the state level.

The 74th Constitution Amendment Act provides for the setting up at the district level of a District Planning Committee (DPC) to consolidate the plans prepared by the Panchayats and municipalities in the district and to prepare a draft district development plan for the district as a whole. Many states have constituted such DPCs. Thus, district planning, which has been talked about, debated, and tried out in various ways to a lesser or greater extent, for the last few decades, is now getting better institutionalized.

This has imparted a sense of both urgency and importance to the need for a better understanding of, and reflections upon, issues such as the relationship between the national and state level as well as district plans; planning structures and the administrative organization of planning and related procedures at the state and especially the district levels; funding arrangements; planning functions more appropriate for each of the levels—state, district, block; methodologies of spatial and areal planning and for planning for infrastructure development, provision of services and production and income generation (poverty alleviation) using resources optimally and how district planners can integrate these with techniques of participative planning, as well as with techniques of techno-economic planning; training of state and district-level personnel and Panchayat representatives in planning; the various experiments and experiences over time in different parts of the country at district, block or micro-area planning; the various government reports and related literature on the issues; and the like.

One of the editors of this volume had in 1978 raised the issues in an article as to whether district planning should be physical (involving land-use, communication, services and utilities); economic (involving production and distribution of goods and services and overall productivity), administrative (involving creation of organizational structures, procedures and rules; fixing targets and norms, etc.); fiscal (arranging for and providing funds); or socio-political (and participatory). In subsequent writings following the publication of the Hanumantha Rao Report in 1984, he added the question whether the district plan should be more spatial and temporal, or client group based, or sectoral in character. These issues appear to be equally relevant today.

In the late 1960s Gadgil's ideas first expressed in his Kale Memorial Lecture of 1966 greatly influenced Indian thinking about 'district development planning'. In the early 1970s it was V.K.R.V. Rao's writings that moved forward thinking about 'district planning concept'. This was also the time when Lalit K. Sen was writing on Micro-level Planning and Rural Growth Centres and Integrated Area Development. So much so that in 1973 *Indian Journal of Public Administration* had found it fit to bring out a special annual number on Multi Level Planning, and Y. Venugopal Reddy brought out a book on *Multi Level Planning in India* in 1977.

As regards block-level planning, a project focusing on the rural growth centre approach conducted by Council for Social Development Delhi had resulted in the publication of Pradipto Roy and B.P. Patil's *Manual for Block Level Planning* in 1977 shortly before the Dantwala Report of the Working Group on Block Level Planning had come out.

The Planning Commission had constituted a Working Group on District Planning under Dr. C.H. Hanumantha Rao whose recommendations, made in 1984, were accepted by the Government of India as part of the Seventh Plan.

The functions of the district planning body as suggested by the Working Group are: (*a*) crystallization of local needs and objectives within the broad framework of national and state-level objectives, (*b*) taking stock of the natural and human endowments of the district and the regions within the district as well as the level and pattern of development attained so far, (*c*) listing and mapping of amenities at the village, block and district levels, (*d*) formulation of district plans in their socio-economic, temporal and spatial dimensions along with their linkages with the rest of the economy, (*e*) formulating of policies, programmes and priorities relevant for the district, (*f*) coordination and implementation of the district plan, and (*g*) monitoring and review of implementation of the district plan and programmes with due regard to their linkages and dependencies.

The Working Group had suggested the following steps for the planning exercise: (*i*) formulation of the major objectives of district planning; (*ii*) compilation of data; (*iii*) bringing out the profile of the district in relation to the basic objectives; (*iv*) formulating the main strategy and thrust, (*v*) analysing existing programmes and projects regarding (*a*) modifications of ongoing schemes/projects, (*b*) removal of inter-block disparities, (*c*) assessment of unemployment/underemployment and proposals regarding manpower planning/budgeting, (*d*) inclusion of new projects and plan, (*e*) interlinkages between various projects/programmes, (*f*) organization and management to eliminate gap in implementation, and (*g*) the relationship and links between the district plan and the state development plans; (*vi*) assessment of resources for allocation to various programmes/projects, and (*vii*) preparing a statement of physical and financial components of the plan.

For each local level scheme the minimum details required as suggested by the Hanumantha Rao Report are: (*a*) description of the scheme and its significance to the area, (*b*) location, (*c*) raw material and inputs requirements and linkages, (*d*) volume and value of likely resultant output, (*e*) number of beneficiaries, (*f*) likely employment generation, and (*g*) (for some select schemes only) simple cost-benefit calculation.

It was further suggested by the Hanumantha Rao Working Group that the district planner would also need to dovetail in an integrated manner, resources available from: (*a*) State Plan for particular projects, (*b*) State Plan for schemes of general nature not tied to specific projects, (*c*) local bodies, (*d*) credit institutions, and (*e*) raised by voluntary agencies and other local sources.

The Hanumantha Rao report led to experiments in district planning in many states and inspired much analysis on district and decentralized planning over the succeeding decade with R.P. Mishra, K.V. Sundaram, Amitabh Mukherjee, B.N. Yugandhar, Rakesh Hooja and Kamta Prasad being amongst those who wrote repeatedly and copiously on the various aspects of multi-level, regional, micro-level, decentralized and district planning.

Panchayati Raj-based planning had been receiving much attention of scholars since 1959 and the introduction of Panchayati Raj in the country. The 73rd and 74th Constitutional Amendments resulted in a spate of writings on decentralized and panchayati raj planning. Writers on this theme are too numerous to enumerate individually and many of them have emphasized democratic decentralization aspects rather than decentralized planning.

The report of the Working Group on Decentralized Planning and PRIs for the Tenth Five Year Plan 2002-07, which came out in November 2001 states that "while preparing draft development plan, the DPC should keep in view the matters of common interest between panchayats and the municipalities including social planning, sharing of water, other physical and natural resources, the integrated development of infrastructure, environment conservation, and the extent and type of resources available in the district." The Working Group Report adds that "the important aspect of decentralized planning is identifying ingredients of (*a*) a strategy of rural development, (*b*) determination of spatial and temporal references of activities and their coordination, (*c*) infrastructure for essential services, and (*d*) social institutional framework." Further, "another important aspect of the rural development strategy and decentralized planning is to maintain coordination not only among different sets of functionaries but also among different sectors of the rural economy."

Many writers have expressed views about what should be the nature of decentralized planning that should evolve in India. For example, Abdul Aziz and P.V. Shenoy in *Journal of Rural Development* (1997) have suggested that decentralized planning should be (*i*) people's need and local resource based, (*ii*) people directed, (*iii*) its focus should be on developing backward sub-regions and weaker sections, (*iv*) project implementation and monitoring should be cost-effective, (*v*) the development targeted should be sustainable, and (*vi*) an integrated area development framework should be used for such planning.

Multi-level planning, particularly at sub-state levels can take many forms depending upon the level and planning unit involved, but unlike at central and to some extent state levels it normally does not involve macro-planning.

Some of the deficiencies noted over the years in district-level plans, as also in the plans emanating from the three tiers of panchayati raj, have been (*i*) the plans have often been a mere collection of felt needs of people and resultant demands for financial provisions without taking into account their local resources and infrastructure, (*ii*) so-called district/block plans have been purely rural plans, not taking into account plans for urban areas—thus showing an absence of integrated rural-urban spatial planning, (*iii*) the plans have tended to be a mere collection, without much integration, of various departmental or sub-departmental proposals and plans which are often indicated or influenced by the state headquarters, (*iv*) each lower administrative or panchayat unit and planning body has been reluctant to muster any resources at its own level, but has tended to depend upon funds and functionaries being passed down from higher levels, thus limiting its own flexibility while planning.

Government reports and governmental policies have continually for the last 50 odd years tried to grapple with the issues as well as shortcomings as listed above. So, as we have noted, have many scholars and observers through analysis and suggestions set forth in their writings.

In this volume we have picked out articles published over the last half century in *Indian Journal of Public Administration*. We are deliberately ensuring that the articles retain the flavour of the period when they were written. In that way the evolution of thinking about multi-level planning; state district and block planning; and decentralized planning in the country after independence can be seen and understood, as can the various experiments tried out over time in various states in this regard including the problems faced, overcome, or still persisting. It is hoped that all relevant issues pertaining to multi-level planning in India and its changing contours since independence would stand out in all their ramifications and facets through the articles selected for this volume.

In a country of India's size and diversity, planning can only work through a multi-level framework—particularly when Panchayati Raj Institutions appear to be moving in the direction of becoming a genuine third tier of federalism and governance, and the district continues to remain important as a planning and implementational unit—a fact attested to by numerous demands for the creation of new districts.

Rakesh Hooja
Sunil Dutt

1

The Administration of Planning

A.H. HANSON

Today most countries in the world are making at least an attempt to plan their economies and there are very few that have not established a central planning agency of one kind or another. The place which is occupied by this body in the constitutional structure, its composition, internal organization, and relationships with other governmental agencies have become matters of great interest and importance to all who are concerned with the study of administration.

I therefore propose to ask what are the various possibilities in this field and to suggest some principles which might determine the choice to be made among them.

We must define the functions that a planning agency is called upon to perform, because these must be quite clear in the minds of those responsible for organizing it. The first thing to realize is that effective planning cannot be done by a planning agency alone. In a sense, planning is the responsibility of the whole nation. It is of direct and immediate concern to the legislature, the chief executive, the ministries, the public enterprises and other specialized governmental agencies, and of course, to all lower governmental formations such as local authorities. Furthermore, it requires the advice and if possible the consent of a whole host of representative institutions, such as chambers of commerce and manufacturers' associations, trade unions and co-operatives. Indeed, there are some who would regard it as the main duty of a central planning agency to criticize and co-ordinate the sectoral and local plans which have been drawn up initially by others. That, however, would be to go much too far, and it is certainly not an assertion which I myself would make. 'Planning from below', although necessary to ensure that plans are realistic and that there is a widespread interest in their success, is subject to severe limitations. If the plan is to be a genuinely national plan, then some initial guidance must be given to the lower units so that they are fully informed of the general framework into which their individual plans must be fitted and the resources which are likely to be available to them. In other words, they have to be presented with a draft which is drawn up by the central planning agency and at least provisionally approved by the highest political authorities.

In practice, of course, this draft will not be formulated in a vacuum by the planning agencies. It will incorporate at least some of the ideas and objectives put up by the various executive bodies whose relations with the planners must be close and continuous. Although macro-planning has logical priority, the actual drafting process will inevitably involve a rather complicated interplay between the macro and the micro. Nevertheless, unless the general targets are centrally indicated at an early stage, the available resources estimated and provisionally allocated, and sectoral balances at least roughed out, 'planning from below' will get nowhere in particular, and may come to be regarded by the people who take part in it as a somewhat superfluous exercise. I think India had some experience of that sort during the course of the preparations for the Second Five Year Plan, an experience which caused the planners to make certain rather important changes in their methods and approaches when the Third Five Year Plan was being formulated.

When the discussions on the draft plan are completed and the final document has been sent up to political authorities for approval and implementation, the duties of the central planning agency are of course by no means over. Indeed in some respects they have only just begun. If the plan is a middle-term one, that is a four- or five-year one, as most of them are, the planners will have to advise on its breaking down into yearly plans and the translation of the relevant parts of these yearly plans into budgetary terms. They will have to watch and record the movements of the economy, detect deviations from expected behaviour and recommend remedial action. Such action, of course, in extreme cases, may involve very substantial modifications of the original plan itself. Moreover, long before the end of the current planning period, they will be busy recording and discovering the reasons for the achievements and shortfalls in order that they may more adequately define the tasks for the ensuing period and make the next round of planning a more realistic exercise than the last.

If it has to perform all these duties, such an agency needs to have on its staff, not only people who are familiar with the various sectors of the economy, but a hard core of technicians who are skilled in the science of economic analysis at the so-called macro level. Without these, planning is liable to be very little more than a somewhat indiscriminate gathering together of projects and the arbitrary cutting down of these to fit the estimated available resources. I think I can say without fear of contradiction that the First Five Year Plan in India was rather like that. I am not suggesting for one moment that it is a futile procedure. The First Five Year Plan was anything but futile, and I believe that valuable results have accrued from such 'rule of thumb' methods, particularly in countries which are at a comparatively early stage of economic development, when statistics are rudimentary and technicians are extremely scarce. But I think I will be generally agreed that such methods need to be transcended as soon as possible. It is also clear that the relationship between the backroom boys and the planning agency as a whole need to be very carefully regulated. The same applies to the relationships between the agency itself and the people who are responsible for asking the ultimate political decisions. We have a saying in England that the specialist must always be on tap but never on top. The technician, in fact, cannot be allowed to prescribe, but his voice, nevertheless, must be clearly heard so that the decision-maker who chooses to disregard his advice knows exactly what risk is being taken, and if he chooses to take that risk what the consequences are likely to be. The difficulty is always to preserve a just balance between technical considerations and political considerations, because neither of them can be disregarded. Normally, as the politician always has the last word, it is usually important to tip the existing balance somewhat in the technician's favour; and that is an action not always to the politician's taste. So the status of the planning agency and the relationships which it establishes with the other agencies of government, upwards, downwards, and sideways, are of vital concern.

I think it can be safely said that the status and therefore the influence of the planning agency is likely to be highest when it is under the chairmanship of a Prime Minister or Chief Executive (according to the constitutional system) and when it numbers among its members some of the leading ministers concerned with the formulation and execution of economic policy. This is quite clearly the case with the Indian Planning Commission which, as you know, is chaired by the Prime Minister and contains three other ministerial members, one of whom, appropriately enough, is the Minister of Finance. The Turks, who have taken to economic planning very recently, have adopted a similar type of organization. In this case, however, a formal distinction is made between a Planning Board which is mainly ministerial in composition, and a planning organization, which is responsible for supplying the board with technical advice. In practice, the organization draws up the plan according to the terms of reference given to it by the Board.

This intimate association of leading politicians with the preparation of a plan is said by some to have serious disadvantages. The Estimates Committee of the Lok Sabha, for instance, had certain things to say on this subject. The status of the planning body as a staff agency, it argued, is undermined by having ministers on it; it becomes something more than advisory but less than executive, inhabiting a sort of unhappy half-world. Moreover, the recommendations which emerge from the labours of that kind of body—recommendations which inevitably become the subject of wide discussion—tend to reflect an economic rationality which has already become considerably deflected by political pressures. Consequently, the interested public never has a chance to consider the draft plan which the macro-analyst would regard as ideally adapted to the terms of reference which have been given. Those are the criticisms made and I am not suggesting that they are trivial. But most experience to date suggests that they are not decisive. To my mind, they are overborne by the fact that this type of planning organization continuously exposes the leading politicians who are its members to technical considerations which otherwise they might be inclined to ignore—and, what is even more important, commits them much more firmly to the implementation of the plan than they would otherwise be committed.

These desiderata, of course, are no necessarily achieved by a mere form of organization. Their realization will also depend on the characters of the politicians concerned, on the pressures to which they are subject and on the general political situation. When these are unfavourable, as they are in Turkey, for instance, at the present moment, any planning agency, however well-organised, will be just left high and dry. But that is no excuse for failing to organize a planning agency in such a way that, other things being equal, the maximum amount of political drive will be imparted to the emergent plans. Certainly there is a great deal of evidence to suggest that in some countries planning has suffered from the adoption of forms of organization which have relegated the planning agency to a comparatively humble and so-called non-political status. In the Philippines, for instance, the Office of National Planning has never been able to compete in political influence with such powerful bodies as the Central Bank and the Ministry of Finance. The result is that the Office of National Planning in the Philippines draws up beautiful plans but nobody takes much notice of them. It is a purely academic exercise. The so-called Ministry of Co-ordination in Greece engages in exercises of the same kind.

At the same time, dogmatism on the subject of the organization of a planning agency and its constitutional position is extremely unwise, because our experience is yet very limited, and what works well in one country works badly in another. France, for instance, which probably offers the best example of a planned economy outside the Communist orbit, uses a non-ministerial Commissariat General du Plan. Pakistan, which has certainly begun to take planning seriously since the political changes of 1958, has a Planning Commission consisting of a Chairman, a Deputy Chairman, and two other members, none of whom are of ministerial status. On the other hand, Thailand has the Prime Minister as Chairman of the Planning Commission, and the Deputy Prime Minister as Vice-Chairman; but nobody can say that Thailand is planning its economy particularly well. Nor can they say that Nepal is particularly successful in the field of planning, although the King himself is the Chairman of the Planning Commission, and the Minister of Finance is Vice-Chairman, and various cabinet ministers sit *ex officio*. So one has to use the saving phrase, 'other things being equal'. One does not necessarily put political drive into one's planning by having the Prime Minister or the King as the Chairman of the planning agency and a number of other prominent ministers as its members. Hence any conclusions or recommendations on the subject of planning organization must be very tentative. The most that one can safely say is that, in the less developed countries, the Indian type of planning organization, suitably adapted to national needs, would appear more likely than most others to give economic planning the sort of political impetus it requires to achieve any measure of success.

When a country has adopted the Indian type of planning organization, there can be no doubt about the location of the technical planning machinery (irrespective of whether it is given a distinct identity as in Turkey, or functions as an arm of the board or commission). But when this form of organization has not been adopted, there are several alternative schemes, each with its merits and demerits, which are open to adoption. One of the simplest, and perhaps the best in these circumstances, is to locate the function of technical planning in the office of the Prime Minister or the Chief Executive. This gives it direct access to the man who takes the ultimate decisions, whether on his own individual responsibility or as an expression of the collective responsibility of the cabinet. Some argue that the burden thus placed on his shoulders is too great for him to bear when it is added to all the other burdens that he carries; but while it is true that every Prime Minister or Chief Executive with any sense of duty to his country is persistently overworked, one cannot rightly regard planning as a sort of extra burden; for he cannot escape being held responsible for the success or failure of the economic plans with which his name will be inevitably identified. The solution to the problem of overwork, which is a very real one, is not to take the technical planning machinery out of the Prime Minister's or the Chief Executive's office but to ensure that the head of that machinery is a man in whom the Prime Minister or the Chief Executive can feel complete confidence and to whom he can delegate all planning decisions, save those of the greatest political importance. Indeed, in many countries, this type of solution has been adopted; for instance, Burma, Ceylon, Malaya, Venezuela and Mexico—a very mixed bag.

Another possible solution, which has found favour in some countries, is to appoint a Minister of Planning and to locate the technical planning machinery in his office. There are obvious advantages here. You can be reasonably certain that at least one person of ministerial status is giving more or less undivided and continuous attention to planning problems. But the disadvantage, which can be very grave, is that the Minister of Planning, although possessing an overall, if ill-defined, responsibility for his country's economic future, is only one among many cabinet ministers and liable to be outvoted by his colleagues or overruled by the Prime Minister; the question is then bound to arise whether he is executive or advisory, or something of both. It is difficult to define precisely what kind of authority he is authorized to wield. This does not mean that a Minister of Planning should never be appointed but simply that it is highly dangerous to 'contract out' the planning function to someone who holds a rather ambiguous position. In India, of course, there is a Minister of Planning who, as Vice-Chairman of the Planning Commission, has a general responsibility under the Prime Minister for the efficient organization and functioning of that body. But the planning decisions are not taken by him, but by the whole commission, which is headed by the Prime Minister himself; and I do not think it is an exaggeration to say that once that has happened, ratification by the cabinet becomes almost if not quite automatic.

What about the Finance Minister? In some countries and in some of the Indian States the function of planning is located in the Ministry of Finance. In Singapore, for instance, the Ministry of Finance has an economic development division headed by a permanent secretary. It is possible that this arrangement reflects the British influence. In Britain, before the very recent establishment of the National Economic Development Council, such economic planning as was attempted fell within the province of the Treasury. This did not work particularly well, and I think it is likely to be even less satisfactory in a country which is lower in the scale of economic development. There are arguments in its favour, of course. One can argue that the planning function is naturally associated with the framing of the budget, the raising of taxation, and the control of national outlay on public account. One might argue furthermore that the Finance Ministry contains much of the necessary technical expertise, and that it is the most senior of departments with which all other departments and governmental agencies have to maintain close, and in many respects, subordinate relationships. But I think it would be quite wrong to imagine that the Finance Ministry possesses any special competence in the field of planning as we now understand it. The experts needed by the planning agency are different in qualifications and outlook from those employed by the Ministry of Finance to prepare the budge, to collect the taxes, to control expenditure, raise public loans, and supervise the central banking system and the various other things that the Ministry of Finance does. Indeed, I might almost go so far as to say that years of experience in this ministry might actually disqualify a man for the exercise of the planning function. For planning is essentially dynamic and forward-looking. Heavy expenditures need to be undertaken in the expectation of comparatively distant and indirect and sometimes problematical returns. By contrast, you often find that a cautious and conservative spirit tends to prevail in the Finance Ministries. They are ideologically oriented towards prevention rather than towards an encouragement of expenditure. Admittedly a dynamic Finance Minister can sometimes change these attitudes. But I am inclined to doubt whether he should attempt to do so because, after all, there is a vital part to be played in any governmental system by an agency which thinks consistently in terms of economy. But that agency is not the agency which ought to do the planning. Moreover, when a dynamic minister is replaced by someone of the average qualities, it is more than likely that the ministry will revert to its usual routine. Consequently, the Finance Ministry is usually an unsuitable location for a technical planning agency. Its place in the planning structure, so to speak, is operational rather than creative and dynamic.

There are various other locations which have been tried from time to time in various countries. Sometimes planning has been given to the Central Bank. Sometimes it has even been contracted out to the universities. But we need take little notice of these eccentricities.

I have already emphasized that dogmatism in this field is very ill-advised, but it could seem to me that the two alternative systems most likely to yield favourable results, at least in the less developed countries are: (1) the system where the technical planning agency is attached to a Planning Commission, containing strong political representation, and working under the chairmanship of a Prime Minister or Chief Executive; and (2) the system where it is attached to the Prime Minister's or Chief Executive's own office.

If there are circumstances, political or otherwise, which seem to suggest another kind of arrangement, I think they ought to be scrutinized with the greatest possible care.

II

I want to turn now from the problems of administrative construction involved in the creation and the composition and the location of a planning agency to the much more serious administrative problems which arise in respect of plan implementation. These have been discussed at great length in India and I want to select just one or two which seem to be particularly important, or perhaps unduly neglected. But first let us have a brief look at the general administrative problems involved in plan implementation. It is the merest commonplace to say that the planning sets the administrator new and difficult tasks. Take the following passage, which I think is fairly well-known, from Pakistan's First Five Year Plan:

> "So far as law and order, administration of justice and collection of revenues are concerned, the system (that is the system handed down to Pakistan by the British) continues to serve the country reasonably well. However, its efficiency in these essential fields tends to invest it with a fictitious appearance of adequacy for all purposes, including the new and supremely important task of planned development. This, on the one hand, creates a psychological atmosphere of complacency unfavourable to growth; and on the other, increases the inertia of the system, its power of resisting change. The result is an inner conflict in the business of government. While government policies have a clear and definite bias in favour of development, the administrative system, wedded as it is to the status quo in its approach, organization and procedures, tends to pull in a different direction."

That was written about Pakistan. It might be written about almost any country which is attempting to develop from a comparatively low level by means of economic planning.

The remedies for these administrative deficiencies are now well-known. The administrator, we are told, quite correctly, needs training of a different kind from that traditionally given, a training which emphasizes the art of management rather than the mere knowledge of the law and regulations. Within the administration, there must be greater delegation of responsibilities to reduce congestion and delay at the centre and to enable the official to react swiftly to changing circumstances and exercise his initiative in the solution of problems. In most cases, this involves a greater preparedness on the part of ministers to trust their civil servants and to ensure that only matters of really prime importance come to rest on the ministerial desk, and not the petty-fogging day-to-day decisions. It also demands—and there has been an enormous amount of discussion about this in India—a revamping of the traditional methods of financial control through the abandonment of that meticulous checking of estimates and control of disbursements which is suitable to more leisurely age and more negative type of administration.

I am not suggesting that these reforms can be effected by a stroke of the pen. On the contrary, they involve the most continuous struggle against ingrained habits. Even in India, where considerable progress has been made towards the accomplishment of these things, the Third Five Year Plan emphasized very much the same administrative deficiencies emphasized in the First Plan, as is evident in the following extract from the Third Five Year Plan report:

> "Our slow pace of execution in many fields; the problems involved in the planning, construction, and operation of large projects, difficulties in training men on a large enough scale, and securing personnel with the requisite calibre and experience."

Generalizing about these things the authors of the Third Five year Plan say:

> "As large burdens are thrown on the administrative structure,

it grows in size. As its size increases, it becomes slower in its functioning. Delays occur and affect operations in every stage and the expected outputs are further deferred. New tasks become difficult to accomplish if the management is open to criticism. In these circumstances, there is need for far-reaching changes in procedures and approach and for re-examination of the prevalent methods and attitudes."

This is one set of problems. Then there is the problem of administrative co-ordination, which is of the very essence of planning. To break down the Five Year Plan into a series of yearly plans, to translate these into budgetary plans, to ensure that every agency, not only understands its commitments but is determined to fulfill them; to bring about continuous co-operation between the various agencies involved; all these things demand very considerable degree of administrative sophistication, a readiness to subordinate personal ambitions to the common good and an *esprit de corps* at the top level of the kind that has given the British administrative class its world-wide reputation. Even more, it requires a government sufficiently authoritative and sufficiently determined to be able to resist all the pressures both from within and without the official hierarchy, each one aiming at deflecting the course of the plan in its own favour. Failure at that governmental level is undoubtedly responsible for the fact that Pakistan's First Five Year Plan never really go off the ground, and that the moral of hose who were supposed to be implementing it was so thoroughly undermined. This, of course, is an extreme example, because the government did not give the Plan its firm endorsement and made no serious effort to enforce its discipline. I believe they are doing better now.

These, however, are what might be called straight-line administrative problems. They are problems of a kind which can be solved if there is the will to solve them, together with the necessary energy and intelligence. (A certain amount of ruthlessness may be required also, particularly in the highest political levels.) The really daunting difficulties of planning, in a mixed economy, arise at the points where the administrator, in order to be effective, has to enlist the co-operation of private groups and individuals. It is here in a very real sense that the administrator is on his own. The authority which the Government has vested in him can win passive obedience—at least we hope it can—but not the active support which is needed.

Take the district officer confronted with an apathetic municipal council, or a block development officer confronted with a community of peasants which obstinately refuses to alter its traditional methods of cultivation. Of such gentlemen, one may truly say, in the words of President Truman: "The buck stops here." The problem is one of attitude, of personal relationships, of sociological insights. At this point, the manuals of procedures have become almost worse than useless.

It is with the agriculturist that the worst difficulties are experienced; for it is a thousand times easier to restrain the exuberance of the private businessman, if that is what is required, than to dispel the apathy of the peasant. Nevertheless, I would say that relations with private business are rarely as well-adjusted from the administrative end as they might be. Obviously, the businessman must not be allowed to dominate the economy, to run it in his own exclusive interests, particularly as, in most underdeveloped countries, that interest is often an extremely short-sighted one. But no more, on the other hand, must he be treated as a parish. I think the first danger sometimes materializes in countries committed to a free enterprise pattern, and the second in countries where the emphasis is on the public sector, and where the Government has assumed a political commitment to socialism of one kind or another. In the early stages of economic development, and perhaps in the later stages as well, controls of private business are, of course, essential, if only because every kind of resource, with the exception of unskilled labour, is in short supply. If these controls are exercised in effect by the businessmen themselves, they will degenerate into a racket, and if they are operated by bureaucrats who invariably think they 'know better' than businessmen, they will become stultifying and invite almost universal evasion. In either case he plan, at least as far as the private industrial sector is concerned, comes badly unstuck. What is needed is that they should be exercised with fairness, intelligence and flexibility, and furthermore, that they should be seen to be so exercised. This, in my view, is well-nigh impossible unless the business community itself is drawn in an advisory capacity into the whole business of formulating and executing the plan, as is being done in France through the Commissions de Modernization and as is being attempted in England through the network of advisory bodies which are now capped by the newly-created National Economic Development Council. The same considerations apply with equal force to the trade union movement in those countries where it is sufficiently well-organized and sufficiently articulate to make a coherent contribution. One of the difficulties is that, in many underdeveloped countries, neither the business nor the trade union community has adequately representative organs. In some of them, moreover, the prestige of business is low, and in some cases justifiably so in view of the anti-social practices in which many businessmen engage. Nevertheless, I am convinced that the attempt to enlist the businessmen's co-operation must be made, because a mixed economy, without effective business participation in the taking of important decisions, is really a contradiction in terms.

By the same token, effective peasant participation is equally essential—in fact more so, because the whole future of the economy rests upon the development of its agricultural base. But the difficulties here are absolutely appalling. For, while administrators and businessmen at least speak in mutually comprehensible terms—they may abuse each other, but they understand the abuse—administrators and peasants might even be members of different nations. The administrator all too often appears to the peasant as the emissary of an alien urban civilization, to be treated with circumspection and suspicion, even when he comes bearing gifts, and perhaps especially then. The approach adopted by the administrator, therefore, becomes of decisive importance. He must be able, first of all, to give expression to national objectives through the formulation and the operation of a multitude of small-scale schemes and projects which are meaningful to his constituents in terms of their own experiences and aspirations; and this is not easy. For, as the Third Five Year Plan says, "the line of communication between planning for the country as a whole and for each district, block and village, is a long one and to be able to preserve broad national priorities, while seeking to adapt the plan in its myriad forms to the conditions and needs in each area and each community, is no small objective". But even more than this, the administrator has to be willing to pocket his pride as a government servant. He has to be prepared to learn from those whom he is administering, because these not only have a fund of traditional wisdom which is not always to be despised, and inevitably a far more intimate knowledge of the local situation than he, as an outsider, can ever hope to acquire. Only if he is capable of projecting himself imaginatively into the mentality of the unlettered peasant will he be able to induce and guide the healthy growth of those self-governing institutions such as village councils and co-operatives upon which the realization of the plan objectives of the country ultimately depends.

What I want to emphasize is that, fundamentally, this is a question of attitudes rather than of organization. I think that you in India are realizing that more and more. You have changed the organizational pattern of your community projects several times, and it has become fairly evident that a mere change in organizational pattern is not in itself going to produce the results which are required. The administrator has, in fact, to adopt the unfamiliar role of persuader, demonstrator and indeed listener rather than the familiar one of giver of orders. This demands an enormous effort of psychological adjustment—so enormous that, except with most unusual individuals, it can be induced only by an elaborate course of training and indoctrination. This is generally recognized in most countries although it is not so generally acted upon. What is less generally recognized, and I am afraid hardly ever acted upon, is that the rural administrator, the man who is responsible for carrying the plan to the rural community, needs to be selected from the very best of the administrative corps. Special qualities are required and the rewards and prestige need to be commensurate with those qualities. For the present, there are very few countries where a man is going to make a reputation or even a reasonable competence for himself by becoming an administrator in a rural area. The plums are all at the centre, in the secretariats, the departments, and the public enterprises, and the big town is inevitably a Mecca for the able administrator, as indeed it is for anyone else of more than average ability. Rural life is so 'dull' and so 'uncultured'. These are no playhouses, cinemas or lectures, and little possibility of sharing one's experiences with people of a similar educational background. Naturally, people do not want to go there if they can avoid it. To change his situation, which can be wholly disastrous for the cause of agricultural development and rural uplift and therefore in the long run for planning, a positive revolution in government's administrative policies is called for.

As yet there has been no such revolution anywhere, and I think that is one of the main reasons why agriculture, which is everywhere the most vital sector in developmental policies, is usually the least successful of all sectors. I would suggest that if more attention be given to these and similar problems and perhaps less to such comparatively overworked subjects—and I am responsible for a great deal of overwork myself—as the conduct and organization of public enterprises, there would probably be very much better results to record in the field of planning.

I hope I have not sounded too dogmatic. I am certainly not attempting to give any advice to this country because I am not in a position to do so. I am simply retailing some of the conclusions I have provisionally and tentatively come to—and I underline those words 'provisionally and tentatively'—as a result of looking at the administration of planning in a fair number of countries.

2

Promise and Prospect of Local Level Planning in India

KULDEEP MATHUR

The need to decentralize planning and strengthen organizational capabilities at the local-level to formulate and implement plans for development has been expressed in various ways in India. The Five Year Plans have pointed to the need for local level planning but have not been uniform in developing its meaning in concrete terms. Both the contents of local level planning and its scope have assumed different meanings in different government documents and statements. Partly as a consequence few effective steps have been taken to make it an integral part of the planning process in India. The purpose of this chapter is to briefly review the emphasis given to local level planning in the planning process in the country and to assess the attempts made to create or strengthen institutional capability for the purpose.

THE PROMISE

The First Five Year Plan itself set the ball rolling by proposing that village production councils should be set up "to provide an effective base for the entire structure of agricultural planning. It will be through this machinery that targets of production will be proposed by the people in the villages and their implementation ensured."[1] Specific tasks were envisaged by the planners for these councils and it was hoped that they would virtually become village level planning bodies.

The Second Plan while continuing to emphasise that "vigorous local planning is essential if the aims of local planning along democratic lines are to be realized",[2] showed its preference for the district as the pivot of the structure of democratic planning. It argued that "district planning represents an area of common action significant for the welfare of mass of people in which differences in views and affiliation are of relatively small consequence."[3] The aim of district of planning would be "to make these plans a means for solving the pressing practical problems of each local area and through local community participation and cooperative self-help, to augment the total effort and provide greater scope for local initiative and leadership,"[4] Significantly, the Second Plan shifted the attention to the district away from the village as envisaged in the First Plan. This shift was significant in another sense too. District provided much better technological and bureaucratic infrastructural support with clear links with the Centre. It would be easier at this level to translate Central policies into action and thus this proposition appeared to be a preparation for the strategy to be adopted later, wherein the role of public participation received relatively less emphasis.

By the time the Third Plan (1961-66) was finalized the scheme of democratic decentralization or panchayati raj had been accepted and was being implemented with vigour by various States. The Third Plan recognized the importance of this scheme for institutionalizing decentralized planning and declared that "responsibility and initiative in the development of rural areas will rest increasingly with village panchayats, panchayat samitis and zilla parishads." [5]

The Fourth Plan took shape in an environment of shortages and scarcities. The country was going through a period of drought and the Indo-Pak war had added to the balance of payments difficulties. For the planners and policy-makers, increased agricultural production appeared as the primary objective of the entire planning process. The Intensive Agriculture District Programme (IADP) had been initiated in areas which provided the maximum potential for agricultural growth. National targets for use of high yielding varieties of seeds, chemical fertilisers, etc., were being established and the technical machinery at the local level was translating them into local targets by helping cultivators prepare farm production plans. Thus, local level plans were sought to be seen as instruments of achievement of national level plans.

The emergence of the instrumental view of local level planning supported by the focus on the district as a unit of local planning marked the major shift in conceptualizations regarding the relationships between local and national level planning process and the objectives of decentralized policy making. Stress on participatory mechanisms receded and it became increasingly important to improve the efficiency of the local planning processes and implementation. The lessening of the importance of the role of the people's participation in local planning was logically derived from the increasing technological bias in the intensive agricultural strategy which relied on the bureaucracy and the prevalent administrative system to fulfill the developmental goals.

In view of increasing disparities arising from intensive agricultural strategy and the inability of the existing district set-up to tackle this problem and to perform many other tasks of local development, the Fourth Plan sought to establish separate agencies at the local level to cater to the needs of specific areas and specific groups of people. Specialized agencies serving the needs of small and marginal farmers, of command areas of irrigation projects or of drought prone areas were set up. It was envisioned that these agencies would develop coordinated plans of local development and help fulfill the aims of national development.

The Fifth Plan took the above emphasis further and noted that "a serious defect in the Fourth Plan was that many schemes remained as paper proposals for a long time and the process of working out detailed contents of a programme was sometimes not tackled. All this emphasises the need for detailed formulation of projects and programmes."[6] It chose to emphasise the role and relevance of administrative hierarchy in formulating and implementing area development programmes.

In addition, the Fifth Plan laid great emphasis on the concept of a project and its efficient execution. This was partly a consequence of increase in external aid coming in for rural development programmes during this time. The World Bank and other aid agencies preferred to give project linked credit which could show directly visible results and also could be monitored better. The Plan emphasis due to such reasons also led to what came to be known as 'project based approach to development'. It proposed that in area development schemes an area development authority with suitable administrative and financial powers should be established to implement programmes at the local levels. Because such an authority was not to be part of the existing administrative machinery, it was hoped that the task of project formulation and implementation would be facilitated. Most Centrally sponsored area and target group oriented schemes are being implemented within this suggested organizational structure. The responsibility for preparing projects and implementing them has been given to these agencies and the effort to strengthen their capability for this purpose has received greater attention of the government in recent times.

The Plan 1978-83 sought to strengthen the organizational working of these agencies and proposed that "(the plan) will require creation of a full time professional planning machinery at the block and district-level and will call for a great deal more of public paricipation."[7] Having said this, the Plan enunciated that "the bulk of investment on agriculture, minor irrigation, animal husbandry, fishing, forestry, marketing or processing cottage and small scale industries and local infrastructure and social services including water supply, housing, health, education, sanitation, local transport, etc., are clearly amenable to planning at local level."[8]

There is no doubt, therefore, that the successive plans have emphasized the role of local level planning in the entire planning process. Both professional expertise as well as popular participation have figured in their visions but little operational requirements in terms of institutions or linkages have been spelt out. All too often expressions of the need of decentralized planning have not had much practical significance. In fact, it has been argued that "there is no conceptual advancement since 1951...Certain inferences are implicit in the First Plan arguments. Subsequent plans make them explicit, shift emphasis, rarely elaborate concepts, but do not in any substantial way refine either the methodology or the inherent logic."[9]

However, an attempt to refine methodology and operationalise institutional strategy was made through the guidelines for district planning issued by the Planning Commission in 1969. But the guidelines did not succeed adequately in either delineating the procedures or institutions needed for planning at that level.[10] The guidelines also offered few suggestions regarding the development of professional expertise needed to perform planning functions.

In 1977, the Planning Commission appointed a working group to prepare guidelines to initiate block level planning in the country. At the outset itself, the working group emphasized that "the issue whether a district or block is more appropriate for the purpose of planning need not be viewed with rigidity."[11] It is not an 'either'-'or' choice and the group viewed block level planning as a link in the multi-level planning process. In terms of availability of expertise the group accepted that "no serious attempt to induct technical skills in planning" has yet been made. Identifying such inadequacies, the group recommended the inclusion of a minimum group of professionals in the proposed district planning cells with well-defined functions.[12]

The working group tended to symbolize the emergence of a consensus on the critical importance of decentralized planning. It attempted to shift the focus away from the districts to lower units of administration and emphasized the need to look at planning at the block-level as a link in 'a hierarchy of levels'. In addition, it was the working group that made the clear recommendation regarding the need of professional expertise at the district level and block level to perform the planning functions.

Despite all emphasis laid in the plans and preparation of guidelines for planning for district as well as block levels, planning at the local level has not taken roots. There appear to be several factors responsible for this state of affairs.

CENTRALISING FEATURES OF THE CONSTITUTIONAL FRAME

One of the striking features of Indian federal system is that it has a bias towards centralization. The Central Government enjoys wide powers for formulating policies both in the general area of economic and social planning and in the individual sectors of the economy. Even where matters are squarely under the jurisdiction of the States, the Centre has exercised its overriding influence. This has happened because the way the federal system works depends to a great extent on the way the political forces operate in the country. So long as there has been a single party rule in both the Centre and the States, power has tended to shift towards the Centre.

The centralization tendency has been further strengthened through the way the financial resources are distributed between the Centre and the States. While grants-in-aid to different States are determined by a finance commission appointed every five years under a constitutional provision, the Central Government can make use of another constitutional provision for discretionary transfer of resources from the Union to the States. Much of the funds for implementation of five year plans has been transferred under this provision. The result is that many programmes are implemented at the local level because the Centre provides funds for them. Centrally sponsored schemes have become a common feature of the local development scene. Provision of funds leads to the determination of how hey should be spent and what is the criterion of programme effectiveness. Such a concern of the Central agencies providing funds at least reduces local level initiative if it does not eliminate it completely. Quite often, local interest in a scheme exists only till the time Central funds are available. In addition, with the collector or the project officer being part of the administrative hierarchy which reaches to the top, there is far greater concern for monitoring the progress of the Centrally sponsored schemes. Both the State as well as the district administrators are quite anxious to see that little shortfall occurs in the expenditure of centrally allocated funds. Fulfilment of financial targets helps the State to demand more and also brings credit to the officials concerned.

DISTRIBUTION OF POWERS

The use of this discretionary method of distributing funds has also to be seen within the wider framework of devolution of powers under the Constitution. The federal system provides for distribution of legislative or financial powers between the Centre and the States only. The village, block or the district considered as the three-strata of what is broadly termed as local level, have not been recipients of any shared power. The Constituent Assembly chose to ignore the issue because, as B.N. Rau pointed out, the proposition "that our Constitution should start from the village and work upwards towards the provinces and the centre was at variance with the basic features of a modern constitution which dealt with state and central Governments.[13] Rau further asserted that "...if we do this, not merely for the district but down to the village, the Constitution will be of inordinate length and will be even more rigid than at present."[14]

Apparently, then, delegation of policy-making powers through the Constitution to any of the strata of the local level was given up both on constitutional as well as administrative grounds. Decentralization was understood only upto the level of States and the levels below were assumed to be beyond the conceptual framework of the Constitution. Ambedkar added strength to this view of the Constitution with his famous comment in the Constituent Assembly about the backward environment of villages from which no progress can be made. The constitution-makers including Nehru asserted that India could not emerge as a modern nation if its developmental edifice was based on the concepts of village self-reliance or sufficiency.

However, as a concession to those who were strongly supporting the cause of making villages the building blocks of new India's development, the Constitution enjoined in this Directive Principals of State Policy that "The State shall take steps to organize village panchayats and enable them to function as units of self-government." Thus panchayati raj emerged as a product of an ideological debate in which the view of the villages emerged tarnished. It is probably this image that has continued to shape the perceptions of the policy-makers towards rural institutions and local level planning particularly.

PANCHAYATI RAJ

Panchayati raj with its elective institutions was aimed at providing popular support to rural development programmes of the government. The Balvant Ray Mehta Committee suggested a three-tier structure from the village to the district level in which the elected bodies had interlocking membership with only one entry point at the base level.

The institutional framework of panchayati raj followed the pattern of community development scheme. The basic roles of the district collector, block development officer, extension officer and village level worker were unaltered. In addition, these development officials were now expected to work with non-officials. Thus, essentially, the vertical hierarchical pattern of bureaucracy was maintained while a new set of people and institutions was introduced to legitimise, to a great extent, the Centrally linked administrative action being taken at the local level.

A consequence of this interlocking web of relationships between the officials and non-officials was the emergence of friction between the two and their lack of ability to work as a homogenous team. Without much responsibility for planning or utilizing resources available in the area or ability to design schemes for local development, the non-officials took the opportunity of using their new found power to maximize benefits flowing out of the implementation of programmes and schemes being implemented in their area for themselves. The administrators, on their part, resented the injection of this type of leadership in rural administration and perceived it as a threat to their own power and influence. This led to a relationship of hostility which often resulted in lack of concern for achievement of targets and inability to relate programmes to the good of all people.

In this struggle for cornering benefits, panchayati raj institutions began to be seen as arenas of petty politics where the power of local elites found sustenance. Several studies pointed to the fact that the propertied and the privileged groups in the villages used these institutions to further their own narrow ends. Much of this happened because from the very beginning these institutions were not given adequate opportunity to take up planning and implementations work on a sizable scale.[15] All developmental activities did not flow through them and the government continued to choose its own bureaucratic agencies to plan and implement major programmes in the rural areas. This further led to blurring of responsibilities and achievement of programmes suffered. In addition, giving greater responsibilities to bureaucratic agencies had even further implications. As the Mehta Committee Report[16] has pointed out, "Bureaucracy had probably its own role in dissociating Panchayati Raj Institutions (PRIs) from the development process. Several factors seem to have conditioned their perception. The system of line-hierarchy would find favour with them as an organizational principle. The officers would feel that they are primarily accountable for results and financial proprieties to the State Government. The officials "knew no better than to trust their own fraternity."

The government further demonstrated its disinterest in these institutions by frequently postponing elections for them on one plea or another. Some States even superseded one tier or the other of panchayati raj in the interest of better programme implementation. For most detractors of local planning and decentralized policy making, events in panchayati raj presented a self-fulfilling prophecy. It was indicted for faults that are endemic in the Indian social-political scene. Singling out local institutions was an evidence of persistence of perceptions cited earlier. Thus, without a clear concept of how panchayati raj institutions were supposed to function as local planning institutions and without a clear indication of the kind of professional and administrative support necessary to make local level planning successful, the government entered a new phase of development through special schemes and Centrally sponsored projects.

SPECIAL SCHEMES

Citing the need of greater expertise in planning and implementation of development, numerous specialized agencies have been established in the districts. All of them are set up to serve the needs of a specific area or a target group.

At the present moment, out of 392 districts in the country, only 62 districts have not been covered by one programme or the other. The distribution is as follows:

Distribution of Special Schemes Among Districts

Programme	*No. of Districts Covered*
Small Farmers and Development Agency/ Marginal Farmers and Agricultural Labourers	198
Drought Prone Area Programme	74
Integrated Rural Development	20
Command Area Development	124
Tribal Area Development	5
Integrated Tribal Development	64
Hill Area Development	3

Source: J.P. Sharma and D.S. Mehra, *Rural Development: Choice of the Programme and Strategy*, IIPA, New Delhi (mimeo), 1978, p. 3.

What is interesting is that there is more than one programme operating in all the above 330 districts. Thus, each programme demarcates its own area of interest and formulates and implements its projects. Establishment of these schemes has further tended to diffuse the concept of local level planning and planning has become confined to individual schemes or projects.

The emphasis on special schemes has led to great emphasis on the need to build expertise in project formulation and implementation. Wider concerns of spatial units like a district or a block have tended to give place to the narrower though vital need of making projects capable of successful implementation. Efficient project formulation and execution has gradually emerged as the corner stone of the development effort as the special schemes at the district level have multiplied.

THE PROSPECT

Two other striking but related features of the context in which local planning is sought to be implemented need to be mentioned. In the usual discussions of planning at the local level, there have been advocates for either establishing the district or the block as the unit of local planning. Some of the discussion has sought to make out that there is an 'either-or' choice. The Dantwala Working Group Report[17] has argued that below the State or divisional level, "the issue whether a district or a block is more appropriate for the purpose of planning need no be viewed with rigidity." The Working Group has advocated that district and block should be assumed to be part of the same exercise where "block level planning is to be viewed no as an isolated exercise but as a link in a hierarchy of levels from a cluster of villages below the block level to the district, regional and state level."[18] This proposition leads towards the important conclusion that the determination of the scope of functions of local planning will depend upon the level of decision-making one is referring to. Thus, while planning is desirable at each level, its scope will differ. What is being advocated, therefore, is not concentrating the planning function at a single level below the State but spreading it to each level of decision-making from village up.

If one were to accept the hierarchical levels of planning and the concept of linkages the other issue is concerned with the question of determination of the scope of planning activities at each level. By and large, planning has been equated with decision-making function of choosing the direction of development based upon identification of local resources. This included setting of targets and optimum utilization of financial resources available. It was for this reason that devolution of powers was demanded to enable the local planning agencies to take decisions of allocation and mobilization of resources effectively. It has been assumed that if such powers were not delegated then the concept of local planning will be vitiated and made ineffective.

As we have seen from the above review, little such delegation has occurred. The centralizing tendency has continued to be strengthened and the planning strategy has not adequately taken into account what it intended about local planning. The plan approach is still target oriented wherein the districts are expected to follow formulae established at the State or Central level in order to arrive at their production goals or targets. Financial outlays are determined on the basis of these production targets. Most target setting is at the sectoral level, the needs of the area as a whole are not necessarily taken into account.

The administrative system supports this process with sectoral departments being represented at the district and the district collector performing the role of coordination among them. His coordination function is essentially confined to facilitating the achievement of sectoral targets and the concern for the spatial unit, the district, is not necessarily taken into account. The facilitative role of the district collector is also not provided to all sectoral schemes or individual schemes. His choice of which projects to monitor and give the weight of his influence for effective implementation is decided either at the State or Central level or depends on his personal whims. In any case, his concerns may not always be reflective of district needs. The result is that both planning as well as the administrative strategy have not brought about adequate changes in their own methods to support local level planning. The failure of not bringing about changes is of two kinds. One is at the level of strategy itself which demands changes in the planning, budgetary and administrative procedures. These are changes broadly in the sphere of delegation of authority and power. The other is at the level of the inability to establish planning institutions at the district and block level. There have been several efforts at identifying the composition of planning machinery at the district level including that by the Dantwala Working Group but few institutions have been established.

It appears now that changes in planning, budgetary and administrative machinery and procedures are difficult to come by. The experience of administrative reforms since independence does not give us much hope of immediate modification. What can possibly be remedied is the second type of failure where additional planning cells need to be created. However, the inability of planning institutions to take shape at the district level is intimately tied to the identification of activities that should fall within the scope of planning at that level. With this identification, it also needs to be demonstrated that any new set-up will not pose a threat to the power and authority of the districts administration including that of the sectoral department.

Therefore, the first task is to reconceptualize the tasks of planning at the district level. In the course of an action-research project on district planning*, we found that the cornerstone of special schemes was project formulation and execution. The officials prepared their projects within the framework of guidelines that came from the Central ministries concerned. To meet financial targets, there is always a sense of urgency which places great pressure on the achievements of actual expenditure rather than on the goals of a programme. So either projects remain on paper and are not implemented at all or are implemented but without being properly formulated. Some of the members of our team in the district have attempted to help out individual officials in preparing projects on a scientific basis. The members of the team have also prepared projects where new programmes are being attempted like *antyoday*. But, by and large, the team has not been able to provide enough support because there have to be as many subject matter specialists in the team as in the district to formulate projects in all the areas. However, successful implementation of Central schemes depends on how well projects are formulated and executed. Thus, currently, the greatest need at local level is

* District project planning cells—An action-oriented research project conducted under the coordination of the Indian Institute of Public Administration, New Delhi, in six districts, *viz.*, Jodhpur, Kurnool, Mahendragarh, Panchmahals, Purulia and Ramanathapuram (1978-81)

identification of projects relevant to the area or target groups, formulating them and executing them effectively.

Secondly, we have found that still there is little systematic effort at looking at the district as a whole. As already mentioned, the district collector acted as a facilitator so that sectoral schemes are implemented effectively. He rarely sought to perform the planning function. In any case, he did not have adequate staff support even to examine the suitability of a scheme with the needs of the district. What became the major planning function was in relation to locational planning. This aspect of local planning has been emphasized by the Manual on Integrated Rural Developemnt[19] when it justifies the need of a block level plan because "it serves as a guide for appropriate locational decisions." However, in the face of paucity of systematic data, decisions on location have tended to be based on local knowledge and experience or influence rather than on any systematic resource analysis or data base.

Thus, within the tasks being performed at the district level, the following appear to be the major requirements:

(*a*) Professional expertise in order to formulate projects so that schemes are executed effectively.
(*b*) An adequate data base that can feed systematized information for planning purposes to both the district as well as levels higher up.
(*c*) A systematic monitoring system that can make the district authorities take corrective action.
(*d*) An evaluation system that can assess whether the location, identification of beneficiary groups and operational processes of project implementation are fulfilling the goals of the programme or not.

Preparation of projects will continue to be the responsibility of the implementing agencies and hence what needs to be done is to enhance the capability of district officials in project planning, in locating projects spatially and in implementation. This has to be done through training programmes and the Dantwala Working Group has gone in detail in prescribing the content of these programmes.

Strengthening of skills of the officials at the district level stems from the argument that the essential element of the special schemes is that the goals and procedures of these schemes are still being determined at the Central level. Only disaggregation of schemes into specific projects is envisaged at the district/agency level. In order to do so, project formulation and analysis techniques become an important part of the administrative equipment.

The other more important function to be performed is that of monitoring the progress of projects being implemented at the district level. Monitoring becomes all the more important because with so many projects being implemented, links among them have to be identified so that projects mutually support each other. In addition, the purpose of monitoring has to shift from reporting of financial progress to providing support to the emergence of an integrated view of the development of an area. For this purpose, a more systematized view of monitoring has to be adopted. Secondly, monitoring of projects and their linkages cannot be left to the vagaries of the district collector. That would continue to damage the concept of integration and lead to an unbalanced approach towards district development. Therefore, monitoring has to be done of certain crucial projects so that the overall interests are taken care of. Finally, a distinction will have to be made between monitoring and the current system of submission of reports. A mass of data collected through elaborately designed proformas make their journeys from the village level to the top. Such a movement of data may not be entirely functional to any level of decision-making. Therefore, a system of sifting data is required which processes information and makes it relevant for each level of operation so that corrective action can be taken. At the same time, there is a need for rationalization of data collection to meet functional requirements.

To undertake the above mentioned tasks, professional skills are required at the local level. But, because monitoring is essentially an implementation function, as it allows the managers to take corrective action in time, these skills cannot be placed in an agency set outside the executive system. Such a separation, for example, may not help the collector unless these professional skills act to provide him staff support to help him perform his role as facilitator and coordinator more effectively.

The tasks of evaluation, on the other hand, can be located outside the district administrative set-up particularly if they are concerned with impact evaluation.

Thus, if the scope of planning at the local level is restricted to monitoring, evaluation and review and preparation of a systematic data base necessary to improve the planning of schemes at the State or Central level and locating projects at the local level, then there are two-fold requirements: (*a*) steps have to be taken to improve local implementation machinery through changes in procedures of work, system of reporting, evaluation of personnel, etc., and (*b*) establishment of a cell consisting of a few professionals at the district level who help support the implementing agencies perform these tasks better.

Even though we had identified that the establishment of district cells would be easier than bringing about changes in the overall administrative, budgetary and planning system, such an assertion is rather premature. For even in terms of staffing, he IRD Manual (1980) mentioned above, has diluted the recommendation of the Dantwala Working Group and commended only a three-member team consisting of an economist/statistician, a credit planning officer and a small/cottage industry officer.[20] Together with this, the status of these cells in relation to the implementing agencies has yet to be clearly defined. Our experience in the study mentioned above has been that the cells have not been able to appropriate for themselves the necessary prestige to influence the district administrative machinery. Among the many reasons, the office in which they are located has an important bearing. The collector's office continues to command high prestige and not only has this cell to be part of its outfit but also has to be seen to be used by him. Together with this the cell must have links with the planning agency at least at the State level which can demonstrate the acceptance of its role and also influence the relevant local agencies to utilize the data and expertise provided by it. Thus, a district cell can be functional only if the above factors are taken into account.

An additional but important factor to make planning at local level effective is the nature and extent of public participation at that level. If a local democratic institution is aware of its responsibilities, it alone can effectively utilize the data generated by the district cell but also provide for a feedback channel necessary both for implementation and formulation of local programmes and projects. Specific efforts in this direction have been lacking. Even the Dantwala Working Group has not been able to come up with concrete suggestions. In face, the Group has cautioned: "If we wish to plan for the weak the plan may have to be imposed from above and cannot be (simply) a product from below, in which below, is dominated by the rich and the strong."[21] It has done so because, as Dantwala himself in a later article has pointed out "public participation often develops into a lobby of vested interest."[22] Therefore, most observers of the rural scene have come to the disconcerting conclusion that public participation cannot be meaningful unless effective steps are undertaken to promote more egalitarian structure of ownership of assets. Because, this opens up many more issues, public participation has usually remained at the level of respectable rhetoric.

FINAL CONSIDERATIONS

What needs to be emphasized is that with the acceptance of the proposition that the district is only a link in a hierarchy of planning decisions, it is possible to designate the scope of planning at various levels differently. For various constitutional, ideological and administrative reasons, it has not been possible to accept district as a unit of planning in the strict sense of the term. Therefore, it is necessary to parcel out the planning functions in such a way that the district performs such functions that are most appropriate in the overall framework. This cannot be done, however, without adapting the local administrative system to the new needs. Establishment of a district cell can only provide support to this change. By itself, it may be quickly sucked into the usual administrative funnel. Local level planning cannot also succeed without effective public participation.

Therefore, it depends on the extent of will existing in the policy-makers and planners to operationalize and institutionalize planning at the local level. The development strategy is the product of socio-political forces a work and the processes and institutions of planning further reflect his interaction. Well established methods of work have to be transformed and these require something more than hopes expresses in the plans and guidelines.

The Technology of Human Cooperation

Because we have lived from birth in a society with an advanced technology of cooperation and have learned so much of this technology without awareness, we accept the miracles of human cooperation all about us as though they were natural or indeed inevitable. But they are not. Far from it. This technology was achieved through incalculable human industry, much systematic thought, and the flashes of inspiration of occasional geniuses. The technology of human cooperation must be learned afresh with each generation. Still fuller achievement of human purposes depends upon its extension by study and invention.

—*The Study of Public Administration,*
DWIGHT WALDO, 1955

REFERENCES

1. Government of India, *First Five Year Plan,* New Delhi, p. 89.
2. Government of India, *Second Five Year Plan,* New Delhi, p. 58.
3. *Ibid.*
4. *Second Five Year Plan, op cit.*
5. Government of India, *Third Five Year Plan, Summary,* 1962, p. 18.
6. Government of India, *Draft Fifth Five Year Plan,* New Delhi, 1974, p. 102.
7. Government of India, *Five Year Plan 1978-83,* New Delhi, p. 184.
8. *Ibid.,* p. 188.
9. S. Sambrani, "Mythology of Area Planning", *Economic and Political Weekly,* XII. 51-52, p. A 138.
10. Sudipto Mundle, *District Planning in India,* IIPA, New Delhi, 1977, pp. 24-38.
11. *Report of the Working Group on Block Level Planning,* Planning Commission, New Delhi, 1978, p. 2.
12. *Ibid.,* p. 12.
13. Shiviah M., *et. al., Panchayati Raj: An Analytical Survey,* NICD, Hyderabad, 1976, p. 53.
14. *Ibid.*
15. *Report of the Committee on Panchayati Raj Institutions,* Ministry of Agriculture and Irrigation, Deptt. of Rural Development, New Delhi, 1978, p. 4.
16. *Ibid.,* pp. 5-6.
17. *Report of the Working Group on Block Level Planning,* Planning Commission, New Delhi, 1978. p. 2.
18. *Ibid.*
19. *Manual on Integrated Rural Development Programme,* Ministry of Rural Reconstruction, New Delhi, p. 6.

20. *IRD Manual, op cit.*, p. 39.
21. *Dantwala Working Group Report, op cit.*, p. 12.
22. M.L. Dantwala, "Block Level Planning Revisited" *Economic and Political Weekly*, Vol. XV, No. 30, p. 1280.

3

Role of Area Development in Multi-Level Planning

LALIT K. SEN

Multi-level planning, as the term indicates, is integration of planning at various levels. Our past planning efforts were primarily sectoral in nature and were focussed at the national and state levels. Budgets were prepared with specific allocations for various sectors of the economy, such as agriculture, industry, education, health, family planning and so on. These schematics budgets reflected national priorities as well as the availability of funds. The same procedure was adopted at the state level.

We have, by now, acquired enough knowledge about the efficacy of this system of planning over the past 20 years and it is almost universally agreed that balance has to be maintained between national priorities and local needs[1]. Sectoral planning at the national and state levels with the help of schematic budgets has shown some modest overall gains but at the local level the impact, if at all visible, has been uneven. This uneven impact in the current socio-political context, has created problems for backward regions as well as for backward classes. While new wealth has been concentrated in a few regions and in a few hands, unemployment has also increased steadily.

Obviously, our past planning efforts at the national and state levels were not enough and now more and more attention is being given to planning at the local levels. The Planning Commission, for example, has recommended the district as the unit of planning and development.[2] Regional planners would rather have a homogenous region as the unit of planning.[3] Experiments have been attempted in Tamil Nadu to identify regions by regrouping taluks.[4] Whatever the unit of planning may be, the idea is not to prepare schematic budgets for units smaller than the Sate, but to prepare area development plans based on the needs and potentialities of the smaller units. Targets of achievement in this case will be dictated by the needs and potentialities of an area rather than by sectoral allocations.

There is also a danger in making area plans the sole basis of all our planning endeavours. The needs of our rural areas are many and plans based only on these may require astronomical amounts of money. Moreover, priorities have to be considered before finalizing these plans. Multi-level planning provides an approach by which local plans can be fitted into the matrix of sectoral plans based on national priorities and the availability of funds. Our five-year plans at the national and the state levels are sectoral plans. We now need a consensus on the methodology for preparing area-development plans which can be fitted into the framework of these sectoral plans.

The main purpose of his article is to raise some issues which the area planner faces while planning for specific areas, such as a region or a district or even a taluk, within the framework of sectoral plans.

CONCEPT OF INTEGRATED AREA DEVELOPMENT

Area development is, by definition, based on an integrated approach. Very briefly, it refers to two types of integration—functional and spatial—which are themselves interrelated. Functional integration refers to the integration of all economic and social activities which influence the life of a people. Thus, health, education, agriculture, industries and several other aspects of our day-to-day living overlap. A change in one sector almost invariably brings about a change in another. This point is generally understood and needs no elaboration here. It is also understood that any policy for development must try to utilize these interrelationships. What puzzles administrators who are responsible for implementing policies, and social workers is how to use this knowledge.

The community development programme in India tried to achieve functional integration by establishing an integrated staffing pattern. Specialists from different departments of government representing health, education, agriculture, industry, etc., were brought together as a team at the block level and it was expected that the daily interaction among such an interdisciplinary team will also lead to an integrated development of the rural areas. By and large, this has not happened.

There are many reasons for this failure which have been discussed at length in hundreds of publications and in public forums. However, one of the reasons which has not been discussed often enough and which has never been fully understood is the spatial nature of functional integration.

The interrelationships among various socio-economic activities depend a great deal on where they are located. If spatial relationships among existing activities are observed, it will be noticed that there is a definite pattern in the dispersal or concentration of activities in space. The actual location of a specific activity in relationship to other activities depends on several factors. Some of the important factors are the general level of development, demand for specific services and their supply, accessibility of these services in terms of roads and transporation, time and distance of travel, level of income of the people, cost of obtaining these services, and so on. Large portions of our rural areas are deprived of many basic amenities of life due to one or a combination of such factors. On the other hand, there are areas where there is a concentration of such amenities and services due, again, to similar reasons.

Thus, in the context of development, when new activities or services are proposed, the location of such services becomes extremely important. An appropriate location of a new activity may start a chain reaction of development with far-reaching effects. An understanding of functional interrelationships in space, therefore, goes a long way toward the development of an area. Integrated area development, thus, refers to the appropriate location of social and economic activities over a physical space for the balanced development of a region.

The idea of an appropriate location is, by definition, selective. In other words, each and every settlement cannot have each and every activity or service. It has been observed by location theorists that there is a hierarchy of settlements, based on availability of services of various degrees of specialization and also on area and population served by a settlement. Services of various degrees of specialization, therefore, need to be located in the most appropriate places. It must be pointed out that this selective location is by no means discriminatory. Higher-order settlements have their own hinterlands, which include those of the lower-order settlements. The location of a specific activity in a specific settlement is meant not only for the centre but also for its dependent territory. The pattern of linkages between the centre and its territory may need strengthening but the appropriate location of activities will necessarily be in the central place itself.

The idea of selective and appropriate location is most relevant under our present economic conditions. We do not have enough resources to provide all services and all developmental programmes to all settlements. Furthermore, we need quick returns for all our investments to build up our capital supply for further investments. Selectivity should, therefore, be our guiding principle in any future investment.

Integrated area development is also concerned with the development of backward areas. If only the existing hierarchy of settlements in a particular region is utilized for formulating a developmental plan, then areas far away from important centres of economic activity may remain permanently underdeveloped. Some inducement for growth is, therefore, necessary in backward areas in the form of overheads and infrastructures in selective locations. The decentralization of investments of this kind will, of course, depend on the potential resources of the backward area and on the expected multiplier effects of the investment.

Integrated area development is thus based on the ideas of selectivity on the one hand and decentralization on the other. Decentralization of development is seen here on a regional level between the rich and the poor areas. But the actual location of developmental programmes in both the rich and the poor areas is selective.

Decentralization and actual location of activities need to be done within the framework of a region encompassing both urban and rural sectors. In the past, the development of these two sectors has been kept separate and towns could not be utilized for the development of rural areas. It is needless to say that the separation of the urban from the rural is arbitrary and harmful from the point of view of development of a region.

The concept of integrated area development suggests a framework for decentralizing economic and social activities by locating specific functions in appropriate places. The network thus created provides a meaningful infrastructure which can attract and sustain a diversified but a growing economy.

MICRO-LEVEL PLANNING AND INTEGRATED AREA DEVELOPMENT

The term micro-level planning remains rather vague unless the actual level of planning is defined. At the lowest level, each village provides the raw material for planning. However, the village with its small population base and meagre resources is too small a unit for development. With rare exceptions, our villages are not economically viable for developmental investments. Past researches have indicated a very strong possibility of the presence of functional units, consisting of clusters of villages with close functional ties which, for all practical purposes, constitute a community.[5]

It is postulated that a central village among the constituent villages of such a functional community will provide some of the higher-order services needed by the people. These services will, of necessity, be those which can be supported by the total population of the functional community. It is also postulated that a number of these functional communities will constitute a sub-region which also will have a focal point. This sup-regional focal point may be called a service centre which will be of higher order than the central villager. In addition to the services provided by the central village, the service centre will also provide a set of more complex activities.[6]

Following this logic one can visualize several such sub-regions on a hierarchies scale with progressively increasing geographical area and population base and with service centres (or growth centres) of increasing functional complexity as one goes upward from the functional community toward a region. The final level, one step short of the national level, is a region with perhaps a metropolitan city as its centre. The central villages, service centres, growth centres and the regional cities will be interconnected with roads, fast-moving transport, telegraph and telephone lines and other means of communication. It is essential to keep this hierarchic picture in mind for any area planning. With the use of available theories and methods, one can prepare guidelines for the location of services and for economic investments at various levels of this hierarchy. Micro-level planning is not limited to any particular level of settlement. It takes a whole hierarchy of central places and its hinterland as its focus. The emphasis in micro-level planning is on planning from the lowest level (in this case, the functional community) upward to a clearly defined region. In many cases, this region may be coterminous with the district. In doing this, the needs of the local areas, as well as the purpose of regional development, are served. The location of specific socio-economic activities and their interlinkages over a region are major concerns of micro-level planning.

Macro-level planning, on the other hand, starts at the national level and is broken down into segments suitable for regions. This is generally in the nature of budgetary allocations, indicating national or state level priorities and without any guidelines for locations.

It is obvious that these two methods of planning must complement each other. Without national or state level priorities, no micro-level planning is possible. The national and state plans provide a broad framework within which detailed planning can be done. On the other hand, micro-level plans can help fix priorities for different regions depending on their specific needs. Also, without micro-level planning, no national plan can be properly implemented. In India, we have gone through the exercises of macro-level planning without evolving micro-level plans for implementation. The dilemmas and contradictions of half-planned development are already with us.

DISTRICT-LEVEL PLANNING

As indicated earlier, micro-level planning cannot be done for each village separately. It takes into account the interlinkages and the hierarchies of a whole range of settlements. Yet, one has to draw a boundary around such a system or systems which will provide a unit for planning and development. Ideally, this unit should be a region based on a certain amount of homogeneity. Criteria, such as agroclimatic characteristics, ecological conditions, common resources, cultural ties, etc., have been used in the past for delineating a region. In India, attempts at identifying such regions have just begun.[7] In the current socio-political context, however, planning for such regions may be difficult as these regions are bound to cut across the boundaries of various states. Our past experience in inter-state planning has not been very encouraging. One practical difficulty will be the non-availability of inter-state data. Secondary data maintained in the various official records on agriculture, industry, etc., are all aggregated at the existing administrative levels. To collect data for a region which overlaps some of these units will mean a near-impossible task of reclassification and collation of masses of data.

District, on the other hand, provides a large enough area for planning although it may not necessarily be identical with a region. In most cases, a district will form a sub-region or a combination of a few sub-regions belonging to different regions. Yet, the practical advantages of selecting a district as a unit of micro-level planning will definitely outweigh its drawbacks. In the long run, if all districts are studied and planned, regions will emerge from contiguous districts. The added advantage of the district is that it has a well-integrated administrative structure for implementing micro-level plans.[8] Planning and implementation in a district can, therefore, be easily coordinated. This was definitely one of the considerations which the Planning Commission had in mind in recommending the district as a unit of planning and development.

Two considerations need to enter into micro-level planning at the district level. First, the funds available under the various subjects are very limited and it is not possible to give individual attention to each village. It is necessary, therefore, to be selective in allocating funds over a large area. Second, even if funds were available for developing each village separately, it is doubtful whether it would be an economically viable proposition to put higher-order functions in smaller villages. For example, not all villages will be able to make use of a hospital, a high school or a rice mill.

A more realistic way of looking at allocation of funds is to select appropriate locations for specific investments. Two points must be kept in mind before such a selection is made: (1) a settlement selected for a specific investment must be able to absorb and sustain it, and (2) the benefits of the newly located function must filter down to the surrounding settlements which were not selected for such investment. The question, therefore, is of optimum location of services, such as education, health, etc., on the one hand, and inputs of development, on the other. The locations are optimum in the sense that maximum impact is obtained by putting investments in specific places for the development of an entire region.

THE GROWTH CENTRE CONCEPT

This concept takes into account the considerations mentioned above and provides the basic tool for micro-level planning in rural India. The growth centre concept is not new in India, though in the past not enough attention was given to it. It has been revived only during the last two years as an important strategy of rural development. In the early fifties, the Narielwala Commission recommended planning for rural-urban communities with a small town at the centre and a number of villages at the periphery. The economic relationship between the town and the surrounding villages was suggested to be one of mutual dependence. The villages would produce raw materials and food for the town. In return, the town will process these materials and send them back to the village in finished form. Machinery and their servicing would also be provided by the town. However, the Narielwala Commission did not foresee the use of such a concept for planning purposes. For example, the linkages between the rural-urban communities themselves and the hierarchical arrangement of these in terms of progressively specialized services and functions were not defined in the Commission's report.

The available theories and methods for identifying growth centres of various orders and their hinterlands could be utilized for planning of our rural areas. One that may suit our purposes very well is the Central Place Theory. There are alternative theories also which need to be tested under Indian conditions. To save space, we would like to state briefly the main theme of the central-place theory and its methods.

The concept of central place is mainly a contribution of a German geographer, Christaller and has been refined and improved upon by Losch and other.[9] The theory is deductive but was tested by Christaller in southern Germany and by others in different parts of the word. The gist of Christaller's theory, stripped of details and elaboration, is as follows:

1. A central place (usually a city, a town or a large village, depending on the specific area or region under study) which provides functions and services to its tributary area, is located at the centre of minimum aggregate travel, providing minimum cost to the customers and maximum profit to the sellers.
2. There is a hierarchy of such central places. Higher-order places provide functions in addition to what the lower-order places have.
3. Functions which are unique to higher-order places have a wider hinterland than those which are common to both higher- and lower-order places.
4. It follows that higher-order places also command a larger tributary area than lower-order places. In other words, their degree of centrality is higher than that of lower-order places.
5. The higher-order places are fewer in number and more widely spaced than the lower-order places.

According to Christaller, the centrality of a place is a measure of its importance. He recognizes population size as an associative factor but the major emphasis is placed on the functional importance of a place in terms of the nature of services offered.

Role of Growth Centres in Integrated Area Development

The concept of growth centres provides a methodology for a balanced programme of rural development. If the central-place theory, as formulated by Christaller and refined by others, is utilized, field investigations will indicate a hierarchy of settlements and their hinterlands based on the progressive specialization of functions in each settlement. In our previous discussion on the problems of development in India, we have pointed out the following major handicaps in our efforts: (1) lack of enough resources and need for consolidation of resources in selected places, and (2) lack of scientific guidelines for selecting places which are ideally located for regenerating the entire countryside.

We had also discussed the need for decentralizing economic activities so that benefits of economic development can be shared by all groups and all regions.

The scientifically selected growth centres at various levels would provide such locations. Empirical research could easily provide guidelines for: (1) location of different orders of services and investments; (2) delineation of viable communities, sub-regions and regions; and (3) planning for future growth centres, which will be needed in a rapidly changing agricultural scene.

Planning for Integrated Area Development

The basic idea behind the growth centre concept is to select larger villages and towns which could service hinterlands of various sizes. Depending on agricultural potentiality of the area, growth centres will provide services, such as agricultural input distribution, marketing, storage, nodal points for a transportation network and various types of agro-based industries. The reason for selecting a few places rather than providing these functions in every village is based on a scientific assessment of the situation. It has been proved in several research studies that not all functions can be sustained in all settlements. There is a hierarchy of functions based on the degree of complexity or the degree of specialization. Very highly specialized functions can be sustained in only a few large places. On the other hand, functions with low specialization can be found in a large number of places of all sizes.

To start with, a thorough inventory of the existing and potential resources of an area has to be undertaken. Depending on the predominant resource, such as land and water, mineral deposits, livestock, forestry, etc., a proper projection should be made about future production; it should be based not only on existing resources but potential resources as well. These projections will provide future production goals. Secondly, in order to attain these production goals, proper inputs have to be provided. With the higher production, storage, marketing, distribution and processing of the produce have also to be done. Within this framework, one can think of introducing new programmes, such as intensive farming with the help of high-yielding varieties of seeds, fertilizers, etc., credit to small and marginal farmers, land development, irrigation, and drainage, road-building, agro-based industries and so on.

A growth centre will provide the location for introducing various programmes for receiving marketable produce and for processing them. The scheme will only work if the growth centres are linked with their hinterlands by roads and other communication facilities. The growth centres can be seen at various levels. At a very low level, they could performs only a few functions, such as input distribution and collection of produce. At a higher level, the produce can be scored, marketed and processed. From here, the processed goods can be transported to still higher level growth centres. Along with these, services, such as education and health, can also be located in various growth centres in increasing order of specialization.

The contribution of the growth centres to the development of an area depends upon the fact that all productive forces in a unit area can be integrated within a spatial framework. The community development programmes emphasize the aspect of functional integration in the development process. But at the time of implementation, this idea could not be operationalized because no model was available to bring about this functional integration. A spatial plan indicating the location of various functions, their geographical as well as functional relationships can correct this deficiency. The growth centres by providing stimulus for improved agriculture or development of the basic resources will help raise production. By providing marketing, storage and transport facilities, it will provide the basic infrastructure for a commercialized agriculture. At the same time, several agricultural and non-agricultural jobs will be created. The higher level growth centres, by providing processing and other agro-based industries, will create more jobs. The growth centres, in short, combine both agricultural and industrial development within one framework, and improvement in agriculture, according to this scheme, directly affects the prospect of rural industrialization. At the end, the development of the tertiary sector consisting of trade and commerce, transport, construction and services will also come in the wake of commercialization and industrialization creating even more jobs.

PLAN IMPLEMENTATION

A realistic planner tries to keep the cost of such a plan within reason. Major limitations are budgetary allocations made under various subjects at the macro-level. Another constraining factor is the investment already committed to by the Government which does not fit into the plan. One way out of these difficulties is to phase the plan over a number of years so that the investment in the first or second year can be made within budgetary restrictions. The phasing is done on the basis of a careful analysis of the interrelationships of the various investments. For example, if a large mineral-based industry is planned, the initial investment may consist only of power supply and a network of roads. New demands for funds for the plant may be made simultaneously for the next year.

A careful cost-benefit analysis will indicate the return of the investments in terms of more service facilities, higher production and above all more employment. A well integrated plan for the entire planning area, conveniently phased over a number of years and based on local needs and resources, should be an ideal exercise in micro-level planning.

One important factor in the success of a plan of this nature is its acceptance by the Government and local leaders. It has been the experience of the present author that in the case of a well-formulated plan these difficulties can be easily overcome. If the plan is priced within the framework of budgetary allocations, the government or governments are willing to consider it. Local leaders may provide strong political support, if they are involved at various stages of plan formulation. Sometimes, their sound commonsense may be a welcome relief for the planner whose success depends, to a great extent, on how realistic the plan is.

REFERENCES

1. Planning Commission, *Approach Paper to the Fifth Five-Yare Plan,* New Delhi, Manager of Publications (Government of India), 1972.
2. Planning Commission, *Guidelines for the Formulation of District Plans,* New Delhi, Manager of Publications (Government of India), 1969.
3. See, for example, Lalit K. Sen (ed.), *Readings on Micro-Level Planning and Rural Growth Centres,* Hyderabad, National Institute of Community Development, 1972; and R.P. Misra (ed.) *Regional Planning: Concepts, Techniques, Policies and Case Studies,* Bangalore, University of Mysore, 1969.
4. A.V. Krishna Murthi, "Regional Planning in Tamil Nadu" in Lalit J, Sen, *op. cit.*

5. F.C. Fliegel, *et al*, *Agricultural Innovations in Indian Villages*, Hyderabad, National Institute Community Development 1968.
6. Several nomenclatures for naming centers at different hierarchic levels are available. See, for example, Lalit K. Sen (ed.), *op. cit.*, and R.P. Misra (ed.), *op. cit.*
7. The notable examples are the work done by the SIET Institute, Hyderabad; the Institute of Development Studies, University of Mysore; Wardha Institute, Wardha, Maharashtra; the Town and Planning Organization, Ministry of Works and Housing, Government of India, and the Town and Country Planning Department, Government of Tamil Nadu.
8. Y. Raghavaiah, "District Planning and Development Administration—A Case for Unified and Integrated Approach", *The Indian Journal of Public Administration* Vol. XIII, No. 4 (1967); also Planning Commission, *Guidelines for the Formulation of District Plans*, *op. cit.*
9. W. Christaller, *The Central Places of Southern Germany*, Englewood Cliffs (NS), Prentice Hall, 1966; and A. Losch, *The Economics of Location*, New Haven, Yale University Press, 1954.

4

Multi-Level Planning for Industry

RAM K. VEPA

Although planning has become a familiar exercise in India for almost two decades, there has been a growing feeling that the pattern of planning adopted so far has not yielded the expected results. In spite of the impressive increase in industrial production recorded in many sectors, planning has not somehow contributed to a real increase in the standard of living of the common people. It is this disillusionment that makes many wonder whether commonly used economic indices, such as per capita income or Gross National Product (GNP) have any real meaning for developing countries and whether a more down-to-earth approach in regard to helping the weaker sections of the population and backward regions of the country might not be more fruitful. The Fifth Plan will undoubtedly provide an indication of this changes attitude, both of the public and the Government, towards the whole process of planning.

The Four Five Year Plans that have so far been implemented have significantly raised the industrial production in a number of sectors, although the increase has not been as great as was anticipated or expected at one time. In fact, when planning began, in 1950, it was expected that by the end of the Fifth Five Year Plan, there would a doubling of the per capita income (in real terms) as also a complete independence from foreign aid. Today, as the Fifth Plan is about to begin, both these objectives seem far from fulfilment.

In addition, the problem of unemployment has become increasingly significant from the Third Five Year Plan onwards.

The number of the unemployed at the end of each plan has been consistently larger than at the beginning; at the end of the First Plan, it was estimated to be 5.5 million, at the end of the Second 7.5 million, at the end of the Third 9.5 million and, perhaps, around 17 million today. The Expert Committee on Unemployment has estimated the figure to be 18.7 million, including 16.1 million in the rural area. By the end of the Fourth Plan period, at least 20 million persons are expected to be without meaningful jobs. This does not take into account the vast under-employment that is a perennial feature of the Indian economic scene and the fact that a significant proportion of the unemployed are educated persons with technical qualifications which, one may normally expect, would be a scarce commodity in a developing country.

Another important deficiency of the plans has been the regional imbalances created in the country. Even the limited increase in prosperity that has taken place has not been evenly spread out; some states, such as Maharashtra, Gujarat, Tamil Nadu, Punjab and Haryana, are forging ahead more rapidly while some others, such as Bihar, Assam, Madhya Pradesh, Orissa, Rajasthan and U.P., seem to be falling behind. Even within the so-called advanced states, the pockets of prosperity are all too few and the prosperity itself is somewhat artificial. Even the 'Green Revolution' which was expected to transform the rural scene has also tended to make the cleavages in the agrarian society more pronounced. The rich and more efficient peasant and the landlords are able to obtain larger yields from land because of the increased inputs which only they can afford.

All these factors have made many ask whether the pattern of planning, so far implemented in this country, is indeed the most appropriate. On the one hand, there are examples within Asia itself of countries, like Japan, Korea and Taiwan (not to mention the island states of Hong Kong and Singapore), which seem to have found out a magic formula for rapid economic growth. On the other hand, China in Asia and many east European countries seem to be advancing quite rapidly with a completely different political and social framework. India's own planning effort has tended to fall between the two ideologies and, while bravely attempting to promote 'growth with justice', there seems to be, in the opinion of some, little of either. There is, therefore, need to look at the planning process afresh so that the full benefits of planning may permeate all parts of the country and all sections of the population.

Planning as conceived today is more a macro-process, where Plans are formulated at national and state levels and then broken up into various component parts for field operations. Although ever since planning began, considerable lip service has been paid to the concept of 'planning from below', little of it has so far been practiced. All plans tend to start with broad projections and desirable growth rates and are then broken down into individual sectoral and regional plans. Though State Planning Boards have been constituted in many states, there is, as yet, insufficient appreciation of the need for initiating planning genuinely from below so as to arrive at a national picture.

II

Planning for industrial growth forms an important segment of the total national plan. Although agriculture is, and will continue to remain, the most important activity of the country's population, a significant proportion of the national surplus must increasingly come from industry. Further, increased employment opportunities will have to be provided in this sector so as to relieve the pressure on the land. Industry, therefore, provides an important avenue of national growth which can contribute to increasing GNP as well as individual wage level.

However, industrial planning has largely tended to be looked at only form the national and state levels. At the national level, the public sector projects in important areas, such as steel, fertilizers, oil, machine tools, electrical, etc., have been based on broad national considerations, as they must be. In spite of the somewhat disappointing performance of most of these projects, there is little doubt, in the long run, they will contribute significantly to the total industrial capability of the country and will yield the expected dividends. In any case, these are areas in which the private sector at that time (and perhaps even now) has hardly the resources or the skills to manage projects of this magnitude. The planning of industries at the national level has, therefore, been justifiably based on total considerations of long-term needs of the country.

At the state-level, there has hardly been any industrial planning. Most of the states have only concentrated on vying with each other to provide the incentives for the location of the major public sector projects within their states. Sometimes, these incentives have been given at 'sacrificial' rates and it is doubtful whether the states themselves have benefited as much from these projects as they had anticipated. Many of the large-scale projects, obtained with so much effort, have not had the 'diffusion' effect that was expected of them and have tended to operate in isolation with little impact on the environment around them. Only in Maharashtra, there has been an appreciation of the need for a balanced development of the various regions within the state; for this purpose, Area Development Corporations have been set up in western Maharashtra, Konkan, Vidharbha and Marathwada. The concept of undertaking the total development of a region through the application of all inputs—both scientific and technical—has not yet been taken up by most of the states in any meaningful manner.

Planning for industry, therefore, hardly exists except at the national and, to some extent, the state levels. The need for generating a new entrepreneurship within the state which would utilize the opportunities available for setting up medium and small units at important locations has not been tapped as yet. Although, sporadic efforts are made in isolated districts or in a few states, there is still no adequate awareness of the need for looking at planning for industry *within* a state in an integrated manner so that the full potentialities of an area could be utilized for generating a momentum of growth. The belief, wide-spread at one time—that once the large industries are established within an area, there would automatically take place a 'diffusion' of the industrial growth to the tires below—has not, in fact, been realized. On the contrary, the larger urban centres have tended to become conglomerations attracting more industry, while the relatively backward areas have tended to remain where they are.

Even the growth of the small-scale sector, which at one time was expected to provide the impetus for the push into the interior, has not really been up to expectations. Although the growth of the sector as a whole has been creditable, 80 per cent of the new units set up in the small-scale sector have been in the five or six large metropolitan towns, such as Delhi, Bombay, Calcutta, Madras, Bangalore and Hyderabad. The financing institutions which have been established by the Government have also tended to provide industrial credit to the units in a few states with the result that industrial growth has been more or less localized to isolated regions in four or five states.

It is true that some attempts have been made in last ten years to remedy the situation. Rural Industries Projects have been set up in 50 districts with additional funds at their disposal so as to promote the growth of industries in rural areas but the impact of this programme has been uneven and limited, except in a few areas where it is largely due to the enthusiasm of those in charge of the programme. The rest of the projects have become more or less stagnant, and what was expected to be a catalyst in the growth of industries in rural areas has in practice, become, merely a channel for subsidies and grants to institutions and individuals that could not fully utilize them. The same has been the case with the Khadi and Village Industries Commission that was set up in the mid '50s to operate an elaborate programme of assistance to cottage industries as well as to spinning and weaving of Khadi. In spite of the idealism and enthusiasms of many of those who had participated in this programme, the work of the Commission itself has not made the impact on the rural scene as was expected of it at one time.

The basic defect in the planning for industry in the country has been that each of the sectors—large, medium, small and 'tiny'—have been looked upon as separate entities and not as a continuum. There has been inadequate meshing between one sector and the other and between one level and the next. Thus, there is hardly any point of contract between the rural and the small-scale industries and very inadequate contact between the small and the large industries. Government policies have tended to be mutually conflicting and since the agencies looking after these areas are different, there has been very little coordination in the policies and the plans for the three sectors. What is, in fact, a continuous spectrum of activity has, for administrative and other reasons, been broken up into three separate sectors that do not always see eye to eye with each other and at times seem to compete, rather than supplement, each other's efforts.

If one were to look at planning from below, one would have to start with the village as the basic unit for all planning. However, in the case of industry, the village—as is commonly understood in India—with a population of about 500 persons may be too small a unit for any industrial planning. There is, therefore, need for taking a wider region as the basic unit for such planning and the Community Development Block which has now come to be recognized as the unit for development planning could be taken as such a unit. A block is roughly abut one-tenth of a district and, on an average, has a population of about one lakh person. It has a team of officers from several departments who are primarily concerned with the development programmes and there is some degree of coordination, both at official and non-official level. A block may, therefore, be taken as the basic unit for industrial planning at the lowest tier.

Within the block, it should be possible to identify one or two growth centres which have potential for industrial growth. These growth centres should be those which are traditional *Mandi* or market towns and which have close linkages with the rural neighbourhood. They are usually towns with a population of at least 10,000 and have the basic infrastructural facilities, such as roads, water, powers and communications. These growth centres, which can hardly be more than one or two in each block, could be identified and used as the focal points for new industries at the block levels. Such industries will need to be woven round the raw materials available in that area. These could be processing of grains and cereals and also simple servicing facilities for the machinery which is increasingly in use in the country-side. Agro-service centres can be located at these growth centres so as to serve the entire block. It is at the growth centre in the block that the initial industrial planning has to begin and full use made of the resources—both human and material—available in the country-side. Entrepreneurs must be encouraged to set up simple industries, with investment normally not exceeding rupees one to two lakhs and adequate technical support given for such persons to operate these centres.

The next tier for industrial planning is the district where larger industries, both agro as well as of consumer type, could be set up. Here again, the emphasis should be on the full utilization of skills available within the district and an identification of suitable entrepreneurs to take up new industries. The Zilla Parishad, which is the District Development council under the Panchayati Raj System, should be the body to undertake a comprehensive economic survey of the entire district and ensure that the industries that can be set up in this area have the necessary support, both financial and technical.

The economic surveys so far conducted by many agencies have tended to be largely pedestrian and give no indication of the strength and the weakness of a particular region. What is required is a more imaginative approach to the problem of industrial growth in the district and a greater use of modern innovations and technologies which could make many of the processes economically viable. The State Small Industries Corporations which have been set up in almost every state would need to take more active interest in the development of industries at the district level and the State Financial Corporations should allot to each district adequate funds out of which new entrepreneurs could be assisted. At the moment, these two bodies are largely concerned with providing financial and technical assistance to persons at the state level and industrial growth at the district level has been sporadic and dependent on the enthusiasms of a few person, both official and non-official. What is now needed is a more systematic approach to the growth of industries at the district level and below.

The practice of holding district level industries seminars and formulation of district industrial plans has been done in some states, such as Tamil Nadu, Wes Bengal, and Andhra Pradesh. But even this is not enough; there should be concrete district level plans which are fully worked out both as regards men, materials and money and which are 'action' programmes accepted for implementation rather than vague indications of good intentions.

From the technology point of view, there is already a considerable amount of knowledge at the national and regional laboratories for utilization of agricultural raw materials for industrial products. Quite often, these processes are still at the laboratory stage and there is justifiable apprehension that their industrial utilization may not be lucrative. The State Small Industries Development Corporations have a duty in this regard to set up demonstration plants for such processes so as to assure potential entrepreneurs of the feasibility of these new processes. Where the demonstration plant has failed, it would be a warning signal to other entrepreneurs, who want to enter into these areas. The considerable resources available in the forest areas of the country also need to be fully tapped through such new processes. Though a number of states have set up Forest and Tribal

Development Corporations, they have largely undertaken trading activities for the tribal and forest people. A new approach is now required to look upon the development of these areas, not in the old-fashioned terms of mere trading but in setting up small viable industries which can tap the resources of these regions and also provide meaningful employment to the people living in them.

At the state and at the national levels, some degree of industrial planning already exists and no basic change is required in this regard. Certainly, the anxiety of the states to obtain large public sector projects within the state is commendable but there is, one fears, an insufficient appreciation of the 'home work' the state itself has to do before such projects can yield the benefits expected of them. All too often, there is a naïve feeling that a large public sector project, whose investment may run into crores of rupees will somehow transform the economy of the environment in which it is situated but it is being realized more and more that this does not happen automatically and a deliberate attempt is required on the part of the State Government to develop linkages with the public sector project and providing suitable facilities and amenities to entrepreneurs to act as sub-contractors for the big public sector projects. This requires close coordination between the local Industries Department of the State Governments and the management of the public sector projects so that various parts are identified which can be farmed out to local entrepreneurs, while the State Government on their part would have to ensure that adequate facilities are provided to enable the manufacture of these parts to the required degree of appreciation.

Similarly, there is a pathetic belief that a mere announcement of a 'package of incentives' would automatically attract a swarm of private industrialists to the state. A few years back, it was quite the fashion for the Minister of Industries of a state to announce such a 'package' with great fanfare, preferably at a lunch or dinner at a fashionable hotel in Bombay or Calcutta. In fact, such 'gimmicks' do not yield much results; hard-boiled industrialists are fully aware that a mere package programme means little unless backed up by an efficient administrative infrastructure. The speed with which decisions are taken and the attitude of helpfulness displayed by the key figures at the state level—both official and non-official—are more attractive incentives than any 'package programme' which often remains a paper programme.

Another important lacuna in the planning for industries at the district and sub-district level is the lack of adequate technical back-up to potential entrepreneurs. The District Industries Officers have often tended to view there role as merely regulatory; they also do not have the aptitude to undertake promotional work in a meaningful fashion. Even the local technical institutions have often no specific expertise to help the entrepreneur with his problems. There is need for a high level industrial consultant in each district, who could advise the entrepreneurs in the district on the type of industries they can undertake. The national and state-level organizations can provide the basic formats of schemes but, in each case, these will have to be adapted to the conditions obtaining in a district. The District Industries Officer can hardly be expected to do this job and a high level industrial consultant could be employed by the Zila Parishad to perform this task. Even his salary could be party paid by Zila Parishad and partly through consultancy fees which could be charge from potential entrepreneurs.

There is also need for scientific agencies to look upon the development planning in the district as part of their own effort. It is, therefore, gratifying to note that the CSIR, under the dynamic leadership of Dr. Nayudamma, has undertaken a pilot project in Karimnagar District of Andhra Pradesh so as to bring in all the scientific and technological inputs which are available to it for the development of the district as a whole. It is this type of focusing of the scientific and technological capability available within the state that would make ultimately the planning of industry at the district and block level a reality.

Adequate funds, earmarked for each district would also need to be provided so that these could be utilized for the specific purpose of generating new industrial growth. For this purpose, there could be a District Industrial Development agency with the District Collector as the Chairman and the Chairman, Zila Parishad and representatives of Industries Department, Development Corporations and local Industries' Associations as members. Such an agency could be provided with funds of about rupees one crore for each district so as to undertake several tasks in the identification of entrepreneurs, selection of projects, preparation of meaningful techno-economic surveys and also to provide 'seed capital' for the industrial schemes when they are ultimately implemented. Unless such specific funds are made available to each district, there is a tendency even within a state for a few districts to monopolise the resources meant for industrial growth of the state as a whole.

For too long, planning in industry has tended to rely on the large-scale unit as the central piece of the picture and even if considerable support has been given to small-scale sector, it has been more in pronouncements rather than in practice. One suspects that there is still an inadequate appreciation of the full potentialities of the small and medium units in generation a new climate for growth. Unless the priorities are altered so as to make them the primary elements in the new strategy for industrial growth, one fears that such growth will continue to be confined to a few urban locations without making that broad-based impact which alone makes industry meaningful to the economy as a whole.

III

The experience in China, since the Communist Revolution, in this regard needs to be more closely studied. There has been in recent years a significant movement into the interior regions for setting up small and medium industries in large numbers. After the Soviet advisers left in 1957, China has followed a policy of what they call 'walking on two legs'; one 'leg' is represented by heavy industrial concentration around Shanghai, Wuhan, Canton and Nanking and the other 'leg' is represented by industries in rural areas into which a large number of personnel have moved in during the last 10 years. From Shanghai alone, it is estimated that one million people (out of its total population of 10 millions) have left in the last 20 years to work in the 'less developed' regions of China. More and more industries have been pushed into he backward regions of the country so that they can generate a new growth in those areas.

Again, the pattern of industrial development has been a multi-tiered one. At the Commune level, simple processing industries are taken up by the Commune, so as to cater to the requirements of those living in it. At the Hung Chiao Commune (near Shanghai), which produces 240 tons of vegetables per day, there are five factories allied to farming—farm tool production, insecticides, repair shops as well as a major paint shop for spraying electronic equipment. At the next higher level, the 'Hsien' (corresponding to the district) are industries which are consumer-oriented and also based on agricultural raw materials. At the national level are the large and heavy industries which are geared to the total national and strategic requirements of the country. Thus, China is operating its industries at three tiers with considerable benefit to the economy as a whole. Targets are set by each of the units for themselves and there is a certain amount of linkages between one-tier and the other. There is, however, still insufficient knowledge as to how these linkages are able to operate in practice, but there is no doubt that considerable success has been achieved in meshing the three-tiered industrial economy successfully to provide considerable increases in industrial production in the last 15 years.

IV

Multi-level planning for industry ultimately should have the objective to carry forward industrial growth to the district and the sub-district levels. The present concentration of industrial growth at the state and the national levels should give way to a greater attention being paid to industrial progress at the lower levels. The new industrial effort should be woven round agriculture and allied activities so that in rural and semi-urban areas, there is a genuine 'agro-industrial' society with agriculture providing in industry the raw material, and industry furnishing the processed foods and articles for consumption by the peasant. It is only then that industrial planning will have an impact on the lives of the common people and industry as a whole will be able to generate the type of surpluses that can contribute significantly a national prosperity.

5

Gaps in the Indian Process of Planning: Importance of Regional Planning

P.R. DUBHASHI

Though planning in India has been going on for the last 22 years, it could be characterized as one with apoplexy at the centre and anaemia at the periphery. There is a big machine of planning at the Centre—the Planning Commission with many experts assisted by a huge staff and advisory bodies. They indulge in sophisticated and esoteric exercises and processes of planning. But the base on which the planners at the apex operate is not always very strong. It is only now that the State machineries of planning are expanding beyond the rather limited capabilities of the Planning Department doing mostly the function of compilation of various schemes. At the district level, the burden of planning is borne by the overworked Deputy Commissioner though he is now being assisted by the Development and Planning Assistant. At the block-level, the block itself was expected to be the machinery of planning and development. But, in the beginning, it never went beyond the community development programmes and, later, the specific development schemes entrusted to it. A the village level, though farm and village plans have been attempted from time-to-time, they are more the result of compliance with instructions of higher authorities than serious attempts of planning based on scientific compilation and analysis of data which lie beyond the capacity of most of the village level workers and organizations.

The weaknesses in the different horizontal levels in the various sectors of planning are equally serious. Sectors, like agriculture, industry, and trade, and infrastructure activities are ultimately reduced to the activities of various departments and the strength of overall planning ultimately depends on the strength of departmental planning. Sophistication in overall planning leads to no results if there is chaos in intra-departmental planning. Unfortunately, this seems to be the case. After all, there could be no planning unless it becomes an essential feature of the working of each department, handling specific aspects of development. Planning must enter into the warp and woof of departmental activity and indeed should be the normal method of its functioning. Unfortunately, planning still remains as something of an appendage externally attached by the planning department to a substantive department. The process of planning has been reduced to a fine ritual of filling up numerous *pro formae* and the job of the Planning Departments in a State is to compile data from the *pro formae* filled up by various departments and send them on to the Planning Commission. This *pro forma* filling exercise takes place at the centre also. The very core of planning process consisting of an integrated, inter-linked and synchronized system of operations or programmes seems to be missing. Even a single activity handled by a single department is not governed by the method of planning, *viz.* that of analysis of the present prognostication of the future, determination and specification of objectives and orderly arrangements of programmes and mobilization of resources to reach desirable results. There is no overriding common concept of planning in several departments. The best indication of this is that the function of planning (which means filling up prescribed *pro formae*) is entrusted to a minor functionary in the department called the Planning Officer, when, in fact, it should be the direct special function of the head of the department or an organization or the district head. But these heads are all the time involved in a whirl of administrative activities of all sorts which do not seem to include planning. These administrative actions are governed by expediencies of all sorts, including various pulls and pressures. In the normal method of administration, pulls and pressures prevail over everything else. Thus, while these constitute the normal stuff of administration, planning has become some sort of an independent exercise for the satisfaction of higher authorities.

There could be no more telling example of the absence of planning in the normal departmental activities that our failure in spite of planning for the last 25 years to ensure timely supply of seeds, fertilizers and credit to the farmer. It is more important that normal administration is informed with the logic and method of planning than the fact that we ensure preparation of plan documents of various degrees of reliability.

The absence of regional planning is a gap of a peculiar sort in our planning mechanism. Planning in our country has been sectoral rather than spatial. As a result, spatial, regional or area planning in the scientific sense of the term has never been introduced in our country so far. Of course, we have plans at the state, district, block and village levels. More often than not, they are no more than break-ups of sectoral programmes or more accurately, schemes of departments. Regional science is itself a somewhat new discipline and has yet to be assimilated in our academic studies, and more so in our administrative system. Our units of administration, like the district or the taluka, are not necessarily rational units of planning and yet for planning purposes we use them because they are administratively convenient. However, planning regions run across the traditional administrative boundaries. These have to be co-related with certain natural or economic homogeneities, *e.g.*, metropolitan regions or river valley areas—such as those looked after by Tennessee Valley Authority (TVA) in the United States of America or Deodar Valley Corporation (DVC) in India. These are the more appropriate regions of planning. The identification of such homogeneous units for planning has yet to be attempted in a serious manner in our country. One of the great contributions of Khruschev to Soviet planning was to create new units of planning called 'Sovnarkhozis', different from the republics of the Union.

Regional planning differs from normal planning not only in respect of the boundaries of units but also in respect of the fact that it looks at planning from spatial rather than a sectoral point of view. This involves not just coordination of various sectors of the economy in the region. It visualizes the planning as a dynamic process of development emanating from certain growth centres or central places. In this view, there is a hierarchy of such central places or growth centres, each linked up with another.

During the Fourth Five Year Plan, with the help of Ford Foundation funds, such an approach was attempted to be evolved in the pilot projects on growth centres. However, the work of these projects has been going on slowly, like the proverbial 'Birbal's Khichadi', and its product is not available for consumption even though we are already finalizing the Fifth Plan in whose formulation the regional approach should have been integrated.

II

In what follows, an attempt is made to describe the various aspects of regional planning for integrated area development under the river valley projects.

Integrated regional planning for development of areas under major river valley projects has received special attention in recent years. It is identified as a programme needing special attention during the Fifth Five Year Plan. An allocation of Rs. 150 crore has been made in the Fifth Plan for command area development under 50 major irrigation projects in the country. Though planning in India has always accorded priority to expansion of irrigation potential, equal attention was not paid to the problem of full and speedy utilization of irrigation potential. The irrigation projects were looked at more from the engineering point of view than the irrigation development point of view. This led to the time lag between the creation of irrigation potential and its utilization. It is this time lag and the causes of this time lag which led the Irrigation Commission to identify *ayacui* development as an important concept and programme in its own right and the commission devoted a special chapter to the subject in its report. The task force under Dr. B.S. Minhas, appointed by the Planning Commission, has also recognized irrigation project command area development as a special case of integrated area development in the country. The National Commission on Agriculture considered the programme of integrated area development and modernization of irrigation system as of such importance that they too have brought out a special interim report on the subject. Finally, recently a Committee of Ministers, appointed by the Union Government, has comprehensively gone into the subject and made a number of recommendations. They have pointed out that, since inception, Rs. 2,400 crore have been spent on major irrigation projects creating an irrigation potential of 9.6 million hectares, costing Rs. 2,500 per hectare. Of this potential, 1.6 million hectares are yet to be developed which means that an investment of Rs. 400 crore has remained entirely infructuous. We talk of under-utilization of plant and machinery as an important problem, the major cause of under production and rise in prices. Under-utilization of irrigation projects is also an equally significant factor. The Minister's Committee has, therefore, forcefully pointed out that the nation cannot afford anything less than the quickest possible use of investment in irrigation projects. They have given examples of Tungabhadra, Kosi and Chambal projects, which were started years back and have yet to yield full results. They have felt that the only way to remove shortages of agricultural commodities in our country is to ensure fullest utilization or irrigation potential under every major irrigation project within 3 to 5 years. They have suggested plans for command area development on this basis for every major irrigation project in the country.

OBJECTIVES OF COMMAND AREA DEVELOPMENT

Immediate Objectives

The objective of the *ayacut* development is to utilize the *irrigation potential,* described above, as speedily and effectively as possible and, to this end, initiate a process of *ayacut* development involving the following items:

1. Formation and implementation, year after year, of a coordinated and integrated development plan, involving the *conjoint efforts* of the Departments of Public Works, Agriculture, Horticulture, Animal Husbandry, Fisheries, Cooperation, Marketing and Town and Country Planning as well as the work of development Blocks and Institutions like the District Cooperative Banks, Primary Cooperative Credit Societies, Primary Land Development Banks, State Land Development Bank and Marketing Societies, and Agro-Industries Corporation.
2. Undertaking *conjoint operation for developing soil and water resources* consisting of water distribution and management system, land leveling and reshaping, drainage, and consolidation of holdings, and crop planning.

3. Providing *agricultural inputs* like hybrid seeds, fertilizers and implements, commensurate with the requirements of modern irrigated agriculture.
4. Setting up a number of agro-processing units mainly on a cooperative basis.
5. Developing villages and towns in the *ayacut* area as modern communities.

Ultimate Objectives

In the ultimate analysis, the objective is nothing less than to usher in an economic and social revolution in the project area in order to raise the level of living of the people and make it richer, fuller and better.

It is to provide permanent protection and insurance against droughts. Throughout the centuries, the areas under many projects have suffered from severe famine once in 10 years and acute scarcity once in five years.

The project is protective but it is also productive and would additionally produce 3.08 lack tones of foodgrains like jowar, sweet corn (maize), wheat—0.95 lakh tones of oil seeds, and 1.89 lack tones of cotton, in addition to pulses, fruits and vegetables.

The objective is also to develop supplementary occupations, like dairies, poultry and fisheries.

Tasks of Development

The specific tasks of various departments, as a part of integrated development, would be as follows:

1. *Tasks of the P.W.D.* are as follows: (*i*) developing distribution system; (*ii*) developing system of *ayacut* roads; (*iii*) providing general drainage system; (*iv*) maintaining a proper system of water management; and (*v*) localization of crops.
2. *Tasks of Agricultural Department* are as follow: (*i*) providing field drainage; (*ii*) providing technical guidance to farmers and, wherever possible, directly undertake land shaping, through a scheme of land shaping and land development; (*iii*) undertaking a massive demonstration programme to

educate the farmers is soil and water management; and (*iv*) providing inputs, like hybrid seeds and fertilizers.

3. *Tasks of Agro-Industries Corporation* are as follows: (*i*) setting up sufficient number of Agro-Industries service centres; and (*ii*) providing machinery and services for undertaking task of land-levelling and reshaping.
4. *The Task of Land Development Banks* is to provide necessary long-term credit to farmers for land development.
5. *The Task of D.C.C. Bank* is to provide necessary short-term and medium-term credit to farmers for agricultural operations and subsidiary activities.
6. *The Task of Cooperation Department* is to promote formation/ rejuvenation of cooperative societies to ensure adequate and smooth flow of credit and inputs for agricultural development marketing and processing facilities.
7. *The Role of the Block Organization* is to undertake extension and development activity at the grassroot for rapid utilization of irrigation potential. [For this tasks the job charts of the Extension Officers and Village Level Workers (Gramsevaks) and indeed of the organization as a whole, have to be redefined. Block Development Officers have to function as irrigation development officers.]
8. *The Role of Animal Husbandry Department* is as follows: (*i*) providing and developing better breed of cattle through intensive cattle development scheme; (*ii*) providing veterinary services; (*iii*) developing grass and fodder for animals; (*iv*) undertaking marketing and processing of milk; and (*v*) stepping up production and marketing of poultry products.
9. *Tasks of Fisheries Department* are: (*i*) developing fisheries in the lake; (*ii*) establishing fish farms to exploit the fish; and (*iii*) organizing fishermen to undertake processing and marketing of fish.
10. *The Tasks of the Horticulture Department* is to promote cultivation of fruits and vegetables.
11. *Tasks of the Marking Department* are: (*i*) providing adequate marketing facilities by establishing new regulated markets or developing existing ones; and (*ii*) arranging for adequate ware-housing capacity.

12. *Tasks of Directorate of Industries and Commerce* is to promote establishment of agro-processing industries on modern lines, such as oil-extraction plants, cotton ginning and pressing units, etc.
13. *The Tasks of Town and Country Planning* is preparing physical plans for villages and towns and growth centres in the *ayacut* area.
14. *The Role of Farmers* is as given below: (*i*) using water economically according to technical advice of the Department of Agriculture; (*ii*) undertaking land shaping on their land; (iii) using hybrid seeds, fertilizers and modern agricultural practices; (*iv*) following localized cropping pattern; (*v*) not using water unauthorizedly; (*vi*) deriving full advantage of credit and marketing cooperatives by joining as members; and (*vii*) taking full advantage of demonstration and training facilities to get educated in irrigation agricultural practices.
15. *Tasks of Project Administration* are coordinating activities of the foregoing departments and ensuring timely realization of the objectives set out above.

SETTING UP PROJECT AUTHORITY IN PROJECT AREA

The Project Authority has to take up comprehensive area development programme. It has to undertake responsibility for all activities in the command area, including maintenance and operation of the irrigation system.

The normal departmental structure and their administrative jurisdictions and methods are not entirely appropriate for a change-oriented and innovative, and yet a time-bound and speedy area development programme for the following reasons:

1. The jurisdictions of departmental officers are not coterminous with the project area since the project area extends beyond the normal administrative jurisdiction of the officers. They work in terms of the whole district or the whole taluka and are unable to think in terms of project area. They are used to district plans and block plans and not project plans. Their statistical and information system are in terms talukas and districts and not in terms of the

project. Nor do they find it easy to exhibit data for the project area.

2. The departments are hierarchy bound. Their normal means of communication and the whole system of command and compliance runs along vertical lines. Departmental Officers look to the departmental authority at higher level in the hierarchy for issue of instructions. Their tour programmes are to fulfill departmental obligations and not the project development effort. In other words, their loyalty is to the departments rather than to the project. As a result, it becomes difficult for officers of various departments to work together and continuously as a project team though this is what is essential for the successful fulfillment of the project plan. This traditional fragmentation on departmental lines is not conducive to unified area development since it scatters responsibility, creates chances for buck-passing and alibis which prevent fixing responsibility and frustrates accomplishment in term of projects goals.
3. This impedes the tasks of unified and cohesive area development. The departmental officers are unable to provide necessary intensive attention to the task of area development. This delays formulation of programmes. Moreover, timely achievements of targets in the project area becomes almost impossible. This may be illustrated by examples. It is found that seeds are not available in adequate quantities on time. Demonstrations are delayed. The technical sanctions of departmental officers for approving programmes do not come in time.

It is for these reasons that the comprehensive area development can be satisfactorily accomplished only by setting up a *horizontal rather than a vertical authority,* an agency for the area than for a department. Such a horizontal authority should have three characteristics.

1. Firstly, it should be *multi-purpose agency* cutting across the traditional functional lines of the departmental agencies.
2. Secondly, it should be a regional agency with adequate *decentralization of authority* to take all final decisions for regional area development.

3. Thirdly, it should be able to undertake area development as a large *business type operation.* In other words, the authorities should not be bound by the rigid rules of the department, but must have a necessary degree of managerial flexibility.

All the three desiderata could be fulfilled by setting up a River Valley Authority as an independent agency under a corporate form, deriving its administrative status from a broadly conceived statutory charter. A corporation, registered under the Companies Act or an autonomous body, set up under an administrative order of Government, could be alternatives to the statutory corporation suggested above. Such a body should be clothed with powers of Government but possess all flexibility and initiative of private enterprise.

Tasks and Structure

The River Valley Authority may be entrusted with the following tasks:

1. Construction of the dams and the irrigation system *i.e.,* rebuilding river and maintenance and operation of irrigation system;
2. Levelling of land;
3. Drainage;
4. Land consolidation;
5. Arrangements for supply of agricultural inputs and agricultural credit;
6. Crop planning;
7. Infrastructural development;
8. Agricultural extension and adaptive research;
9. Marketing and processing of agricultural produces; and
10. Town and country planning and development.

The Project Authority may be composed of three Directors. The Administrator could be the Chairman-Director while of the other two, one should be an expert Chief Engineer and another a specialist in agricultural science with high level experience of successful conduct of agricultural development programmes.

The authority may appoint such additional technical and managerial staff as may be necessary. It should have full freedom to appoint staff entirely on merit and efficiency free from all traditional administrative considerations (*i.e.,* mere seniority) or political pressures.

It is only with such an organization that the plan of area development can be accomplished within a specific period of time.

6

Future Role of Planning Under New Perspectives

KAMTA PRASAD

Ever since 1951, more particularly since 1956 when the Second Five Year Plan was launched, centralized planning has occupied a dominating position in the Indian economy. Any discussion with respect to development of any sector, sub-sector or region is often coloured by the approach, strategy and content of the five year plans. During this period, the National Planning Commission, even though a non-statutory body, established through an administrative order, emerged as the most powerful single institution influencing the economic life of its people. This resulted from the philosophy of a controlled or semi-controlled economy which the nation adopted after Independence and the centralizing provisions of the Indian Constitution which flourished on the bedrock of centralized administrative tradition inherited from the British. During the last three years, however, a number of significant changes in the direction of removal of economic controls have already been introduced in the country and more are expected in future. During the same period, changes have also been made in India's Constitution through the 73rd and 74th Amendments, resulting in a more decentralized framework of government. Thus, serious erosions have already taken place in the base of Indian planning resulting in questions like: What will be the role of planning in the new set-up? Will planning in India, as evolved so far, survive? If so, in what form? It is proposed to examine such questions in this article and indicate probable outcomes.

Is Planning Needed in a Market Economy?

The new economic policy initiated since the middle of 1991 has three components: first, measures to augment foreign exchange reserves; second, changes in monetary and fiscal policies designed to remove fiscal imbalances and contain the inflationary pressures; and third, measures to reorient the economy towards liberalization. Of these, the first two can hardly be termed as new policies as such; these signify a determination to implement in line of thinking which has always been advocated not only by the academic economists but also by the Government itself. It is the third component which represents a fundamental change in the policies pursued earlier. This comprises several measures designed to remove or relax government control over the private sector's investment decisions. Changes have been introduced in industrial, trade, foreign exchange and fiscal policies dismantling or relaxing the control mechanism, encouraging competition, including that from abroad, and moving towards globalization of the economy. More such change designed to strengthen the market forces in the Indian economy are expected in future.

But, as every Economics textbook points out, a market economy is its own planner. Answers to the basic questions like, what to produce, how much to produce, how to produce and for whom to produce, are provided by the price mechanism. The need for planning, thereby gets reduced. This is supported by other factors also. During the period since 1951, when planning was introduced, the private sector has grown enough in size to continue the process of development on its own. The rate of saving too has gone up from about five per cent in 1951 to over 22 per cent now. The considerable infrastructural, institutional and technological developments that have taken place during the preceding four decades would also help the private sector to carry on the process of development on its own. Private sector is now in a position to invest even in such infrastructural projects as power and telecommunication. The gap in domestic savings can be bridged by inflow of foreign capital for which several new incentives have already been offered and more may be offered in future depending upon needs. It may, therefore, be said that some of the factors which had necessitated introduction of planning in 1951 are no longer as important as they were at that time. It may also be said that removal of controls, which results in more competition, would promote efficiency and thereby raise the growth rate.

The prospect of a higher growth by itself, however, would not be enough to dispense with planning altogether. The real test is whether the resulting growth rate would be high enough to eradicate in near future the problem of massive poverty from which India suffers. Poverty eradication has been an avowed objective of the nation. No responsible government would like to be a moot spectator of the economic system so long as a sizeable proportion of its citizens remain below the poverty line. The persistence of poverty in India thus puts it on a somewhat different footing from those of several other countries.

Can a market economy eradicate India's poverty in the near future, say the next ten years? The answer is in the negative. A free enterprise system is usually not considered appropriate for promoting the growth of poor people, backward areas or depressed regions. What is likely to happen in the immediate future is that foreign as well as low cost domestic enterprises located in advanced areas within the country would grow at the cost of enterprises located in backward areas. The inter-regional disparities, already quite marked, would become more accentuated. The accent on modern technology alone, without safeguards, would, therefore, have an adverse effect on the objective of removal of poverty and unemployment. Creation of full employment, comprising both self- and wage-employment and offering a wage rate or earning level at least equal to the minimum wage rate, is essential for poverty alleviation. According to the Eighth Five Year Plan, the number of persons requiring employment would be 58 million during 1992-97 and 94 million during 1992-2002.[1] It has also been pointed out that employment should grow at the rate of four per cent per annum if full employment is to be achieved in five years by the end of the Eighth Plan period and at three per cent per annum if it is to be achieved in 10 years by the end of the Ninth Plan period.[2] Let us explore the implications of the less ambitious target of 10 rather than five years for attainment of full employment. The employment elasticity of output is estimated to have fallen down to 0.30 during 1983 to 1977-78 from 0.54 during 1977-78 to 1983.[3] In view of the prevailing trend towards capital intensity in the economy, which would be further accentuated due to inflow of more capital intensive foreign technology, this elasticity for the current period can be assumed to be lower than 0.30, say between 0.25 and 0.20. As a result, output would need to grow at the rate of 12 to 15 per cent per annum to ensure employment growth at the rate of three per cent per annum. As against this, the target rates of growth determined by the Government for the Eighth and Ninth Plan periods are 5.6 and 6.02 per cent respectively. This falls much short of the full employment target. Poverty, therefore, cannot be eliminated by market forces in the near future.

Poverty alleviation through generation of full employment would be possible only if the employment elasticity of output is raised adequately. This can be achieved by: (*i*) raising the labour intensity of the mix of technology, (*ii*) raising the proportion of labour intensive products and investment in national output and investment, and/or (*iii*) increasing exports of labour-intensive products. Can the market forces by themselves bring these about? The first alternative is ruled out in view of the prevailing trend towards increasing capital intensity of technology. It is the second and third alternatives resulting in changes in product-mix for: (*i*) domestic use, and/or (*ii*) exports which provide some scope. Here, it may be noted that the outstanding success of Indonesia, Malaysia and Thailand in reducing poverty in recent years lies in the fact that these countries not only had a sustained annual growth of more than six per cent but the growth was also relatively labour-intensive.[4]

Given the limited scope for growth of agriculture in backward or poverty concentration drought-prone, flood-prone and hilly areas of our country, the main reliance has to be on small-scale and rural industries for providing income-generating opportunities to the poor. Productivity in these industries, however, is very low and their product cost is too high to compete with the large and medium enterprises in the market. Hence, an element of direct governmental involvement in the form of protection or subsidy or promotional measures, like marketing support, input delivery, credit availability, technological upgradation and training, etc., would be needed. Such an approach might go against relying exclusively on the market. But there is no alternative. It is better to pay some subsidy and keep the labour engaged on productive activities rather than give them unemployment doles and force them to be a drag on the society.

Poverty alleviation in India, therefore, is not possible without governmental intervention. This has been accepted by the Government of India despite its recent emphasis on market-orientation. The Eighth Five Year Plan approved in May 1992 makes an explicit statement that "State intervention will have to continue, in fact, on an expanded scale so as to protect the poor and the vulnerable sections from some of the burdens of structural adjustments."[5] Even the IMF and World Bank combine call for a system of "transfers and safety nets" which, however, is less efficient than having a development strategy appropriate to generation of full-employment and removal of poverty. Planning would be needed for this.

Apart from the above mentioned consideration, which is related to the specific stage of India's economic development, planning would also be needed for a longer period to take care of some of the permanent weaknesses of the market mechanism. Economic theory teaches us how the market is not capable of allocating resources efficiently in certain cases, like natural monopolies, external economies or the production of public goods. Another weakness is short-sightedness; markets are not always the best guides for decision-making with a long-term impact. The need for planning would be further strengthened on grounds of environmental protection which receives a raw deal in a market-dominated economy. Besides, planning has some advantages other than the allocative one as the experience of planning in market dominated economies, notably France, points out. The voluminous information provided in the plan documents as well as that made available during the process of plan formulation, if it is reliable, would be of help to the private sector in reducing uncertainties associated with the market. This might also help in reducing production bottlenecks in specific industries, promoting higher investment and smoothening industrial fluctuations. The information would also help the government in knowing the possible effects of a change in economic policies on the entire economy thereby facilitating adoption of more rational and coherent economic policies. The information provided is expected to be cost efficient in view of economies of scale involved in its collection, compilation and dissemination.

Thus, in my view, planning is likely to continue despite a switchover to a market economy. But its nature and scope might not be the same as before. The important changes which I expect to take place are explained in the next section. These changes have been suggested by theoretical plausibility as well as insights derived from my continuing study of the French planning system which has been functioning in a market-dominated economy for a long time.[6]

Liberalisation Induced Expected Changes in Nature and Scope of Planning

First, planning would no longer be comprehensive but only partial. Government's share in total investment is likely to decline and the range of sectors/sub-sectors directly under public outlay might shrink. Some indications of this are already emerging. Prime Minister Narashimha Rao has declared on more than one occasion, that his government would redirect resources from sectors like large-scale industry and power to those related to rural and social development. Government may also dispense with price and wage controls, import quotas, consumer rationing and allocation of raw materials and capital.

Second, planning would be indicative rather than imperative. Government might be content to provide broad indications for development of different sectors but might not compel the private sector to follow the same. After sometime, as the private sector becomes more strong and competitive, even this might change. Instead of detailed indications, planning might only provide indicators or a set of rules and guides concerning production, prices, etc., so as to improve the functioning of the economy and correct market's short-sightedness.

Third, planning would be based on consent and inducement rather than on directive and coercion. Its aim would be to reduce constraints for the market rather than to increase them. The role of planning would thus change from one of controller of the market to that of its facilitator. This, however, is best achieved when there is a near perfect harmony between planning and the market. This is ensured when the emphasis is on modernization, efficiency, competition and expansion. Rather than putting any restriction on the expansion of big business, the plans may take measures to facilitate their expansion so as to encourage a group of dynamic entrepreneurs to raise productivity and face international competition. Thus, apart from being planning in a market economy, planning might also turn out to be for the benefit of the market economy. It may be said that other objectives, like poverty alleviation, equity, employment generation and regional development, are likely to suffer in this process. But, rather than controlling the market to take care of the adverse distributional effects, the government may take up direct measures on its own to promote equity related objectives. One such measure could be promotion of small and village industries as has already been indicated earlier. This might be supplemented by indirect measures designed to influence the behaviour of the private sector as explained below.

Fourth, there would be much greater reliance on the use of the policy instruments of the nature of incentives or disincentives to influence the market trends and thereby help the basic planning objective of resource allocation. Another mechanism for this purpose might be provided by projections of macro-aggregates if these form part of the plan document as they usually do. In order to perform the allocative function, these planned projections should be different from mere forecasts in the ordinary sense of the term; these should carry an element of normative judgement in the light of set objectives. In this way, the information contained in a plan would induce firms to manage their output as per information provided by the plan. Plan projections, of course, might fail to influence the actual behaviour if enterprises choose to ignore them as it would not be obligatory for them to follow these projections. This would suggest the need for a different planning machinery as indicated below.

Fifth, it is likely that the planning machinery may be made broader to provide for adequate representation of the business enterprises as is the case in France. The advantage would be that the formulation of a plan would take into account the information supplied and the views expressed by the private sector. This would make it easier for the plan projections to influence the production decisions of private enterprises. Thus, the chance of businessmen ignoring the plan projections would become less. But it cannot be eliminated altogether. The mere fact that the consultation processes takes into account the plans and projects of the private sector enterprises need not guarantee that they obey the plan. They may agree on something in the meeting, but may opt out of it later on specially if the circumstances change as they do.

Sixth, there may be a change in the methodology of planning on account of the declared policy of the Government of India to open the Indian economy to external competition and integrate it with the world economy. Considerable pressure is already being generated to bring even agriculture in India under the gaze of international competition. Opening of the Indian economy to the outside world is sure to increase uncertainties to a considerable extent. External developments are beyond the control of national planning agencies. Long-term forecasting would become increasingly difficult in an unpredictable international situation— as can be inferred from the experiences of other countries. It might be useful here to throw light on what happened to French planning under similar circumstances. The increasing uncertainty on account of the international factor and the planners' inability to predict them correctly showed the futility of having precise targets. Hence, target fixation was given up. In its place, the Revised Seventh Plan (1976-80) as well as subsequent plans indicated strategies expressed in qualitative terms only. Planning there is now mainly in terms of scenario analysis rather than precise quantitative targets. A similar approach may be adopted in India in case most restrictions on foreign trade are removed and the economy becomes completely open.

Recent Constitutional Amendments and Their Implications for Planning

Two major amendments to the Constitution of India were passed by the Parliament in the second half of 1992. Thereupon these were ratified by the legislatures of the required number of states and came into force in April 1993 after receiving the assent of the

President of India. The one-year period given to states to enact sporting state legislations is also over. Both of these amendments aim at decentralization of administration below the state level. They have similar philosophy and similar provisions. The Constitution (Seventy-Third Amendment) Act, 1992 deals with rural areas and provides the constitutional framework for the establishment of a three-tier Panchayat structure. The Constitution (Seventy-Fourth Amendment) Act, 1992 deals with urban areas and provides the constitutional framework for elected urban authorities briefly known as municipalities.

The enactments are significant because these make the local authorities for both rural and urban areas as essential and indispensable part of the administrative set-up of the country for the first time. They are also significant because of the reservations of seats for women, SCs and STs in the composition of the elected bodies. We need not go into the details of these aspects as well as the issues related to the strengths and weaknesses of these enactments. We will concentrate only on provisions related to planning these enactments. We will concentrate only on provisions related to planning.

Taken together, these amendments are designed to strengthen decentralized planning. On contrast to the purely administrative status of the existing planning machinery at the national and state levels, the Constitution (Seventy-Fourth Amendment) Act creates constitutional bodies for planning at the district and metropolitan levels, Article 243ZD and 243ZE which contain the provisions are reproduced in the Appendix.

According to Article 243ZD, "there shall be constituted in every State at the district level, a District Planning Committee to consolidate the plans prepared by the panchayats and the Municipalities in the district and to prepare a draft development plan for the district as a whole." And, according to Article 243ZE, "There shall be constituted in every Metropolitan area a Metropolitan Planning Committee to prepare a draft development plan for the Metropolitan area as a whole". This plan would take into account "the plans prepared by Municipalities and Panchayats in the Metropolitan area", The amendments refer to several other factors to be taken into account by both the plans namely, (*i*) matters of common interest between Panchayats and Municipalities, including spatial planning;

(*ii*) sharing of water and other physical and natural resources; (*iii*) integrated development of infrastructure; (*iv*) environmental conservation; and (*v*) extent and type of available resources whether financial or otherwise. The plans prepared by these committees would be sent to the State Government. The amendments empower the state legislatures to make provisions with respect to composition and other details of these committees, subject to certain restrictions imposed.

Planning has been decentralized even below the district and metropolitan area level. All levels of Panchayats and Municipalities would be involved in planning in their respective sphere of activities. However, the constitutional provisions related to this aspect are not very clear and definite. Article 243G of the Seventy Third Amendment and Article 243W of the Seventy-Fourth Amendment provide for the legislature of a state to give power to Panchayats and Municipalities respectively with regard to "the preparation of plans for economic development and social justice." Two new schedules, one each for rural and urban areas, have also been added. Schedule 11 gives a list of 29 items, work on which can be taken up by Panchayats and Schedule 12 gives a similar list of 18 items for the municipalities. Both the lists are quite comprehensive and cover almost all items of relevance and importance to the rural and urban population respectively.

The above mentioned framework, however, suffers from three deficiencies. First, the provisions are recommendatory rather than mandatory. It is left to the legislatures of different states to make the necessary enactments. Second, while the list of items under the Schedules 11 and 12 is quite comprehensive, not a single item has been allotted exclusively to Panchayats or Municipalities. The State Government has got the overriding powers on each of them. This cannot be regarded as a satisfactory allocation of power and responsibility. Given the past tradition as well as experience, this provides considerable scope for imposition of restriction by higher authorities on lower ones. Third, the position regarding finance remains vague. Lack of financial autonomy would be an obstacle in development of local planning capabilities. The later two difficulties would be applicable even for planning at the district and metropolitan area committee levels. Moreover, the plans prepared by them are mere recommendations. These would be sent to the State Government for approval. In view of the above, there has been only a partial and half-hearted attempt at decentralized planning.

Nevertheless, a large number of planning centres at village, intermediary, district panchayat, municipality, district and metropolitan area levels would come into existence as a combined result of Articles 243G, 243W, 243ZD and 243ZE. In view of the overlapping jurisdictions at all levels, this type of planning exercise will raise serious problems of consistency resulting in disequilibrium between demand and supply of marketable products or conflicts over utilization of non-marketable products.[7] There will, therefore, be need for centralized planning to coordinate planning at different levels so that overall consistency is maintained. This consideration, therefore, provides one more reason why planning in India is likely to continue in future.

Consistency in decentralized multi-level planning set-up, as per the new Constitutional provisions, would imply a change in methodology of planning followed so far in India wherein the plan at the higher level is prepared first and those at lower levels are worked out within the framework already decided at the higher levels. In its place, an iterative procedure is likely to emerge. Here planning units at different levels would participate, each giving information on its plan and programme and making revisions in the light of information received from the lower and the higher units. "As compared to purely centralized planning, this process may be expensive, time-consuming and administratively problematic. Conflicts between different regions may arise, and if not properly handled, they may vitiate the developmental atmosphere. There is also the risk that iterative planning may degenerate into a more bargaining process for extracting maximum benefits to themselves by the planning units at various levels. However, ultimately a consistent plan should emerge if the planning agencies at various levels of the hierarchy: (*a*) adopt a flexible approach, with more than one variant of their plans to start with (which, incidentally, is a desirable feature of any planning exercise), and (*b*) respect the right of others to make certain decisions, if such decisions are better made at a higher or lower level."[8]

Articles 243ZD and 243ZE, which provide for the constitution of statutory planning committees at district and metropolitan area levels respectively, also give a list of factors to be taken into account while preparing the plans. An analysis of these factors mentioned earlier makes it quite clear that the intention is to prepare integrated area plans embracing both horizontal and vertical integration. This is an extremely good feature of the constitutional provisions. It captures the real meaning and import of planning. Such a planning results in more efficient utilization of resources and raises productivity. However, it is also more difficult. There is dearth of personnel and complete lack of experience in the government departments. Operationalisation of integrated planning approach would, therefore, require creation of an appropriate planning organization at those levels with a nucleus of well-trained staff. From where to get such people? It appears that availability of right personnel would pose a real problem for planning under the new set-up. Meeting the gap would require the government to launch a massive training programme on integrated planning, preparation of a large number of model plans for different parts of the country and also creation of a cadre of planners with adequate avenue for promotion, etc. It may, however, take time before the government becomes aware of these considerations. For the time being, authorities at all levels, seem to be completely unconcerned with these issues.

To sum up, despite limitations, the new constitutional measures tend to strengthen planning at the grassroot levels and thereby a higher levels also.

REFERENCES

1. A study, made by the Reserve Bank of India projects an even higher figure of growth of labour force, *i.e.*, 106 million by the year 2000 (See *Business Standard*, October 29, 1993).
2. Government of India, *Planning Commission*, New Delhi, *Eighth Five Year Plan*, p. 120.
3. Government of India, Planning Commission, *Directional Paper on the Objectives, Thrusts and Macro-Dimensions of the English Plan, 1992-97*, New Delhi, December 1991.
4. The World Bank, *World Development Report 1990*, New York, Oxford University Press, 1990, p. 45.

5. Government of India, Planning Commission, *Eighth Five Year Plan, op. cit.*
6. Kamta Prasad, *Planning in a Market Economy, A Study of the French Planning System*, New Delhi, IIPA, 1985: and Commissariat General Due Plan (French Planning Office). *The French Mixed Economy Experience*, Paris, March 1991.
7. This aspect is examined in detail in one of my papers see. Kamta Prasad, "Area Planning Approach to Rural Development and the Problem of Consistency between National and Local Planning" in *Rural Challenge*, published by the Gower Co., (UK) on behalf of the International Association of Agricultural Economists, 1981.
8. Kamta Prasad, "Planning in India: Some Basic Issues Relating to Operational Strategic Aspects". *The Indian Economic Journal*, Vol. 31, No. 4, April-June 1981, p. 11.

Appendix

EXTRACT FROM THE CONSTITUTION SEVENTY-FOURTH AMENDMENT ACT, 1992 ON MUNICIPALITIES

Committee for District Planning

243ZD (*i*) There shall be constituted in every State at the district level a District Planning Committee to consolidate the plans prepared by the Panchayats and the Municipalities in the districts and to prepare a draft development plan for the district at a whole.

(2) The Legislature of a State may, by law, make provision with respect to:

(*a*) the composition of the District Planning Committees;

(*b*) the manner in which the seats in such Committee shall be filled:
Provided that not less than four-fifth of the total number of members of such Committee shall be elected by, and from amongst the elected members of the Panchayat at the district level and of the Municipalities in the district in proportion to the ratio between the population of the rural areas and of the urban areas in the district;

(*c*) the functions relating to district planning which may be assigned to such Committees;

(*d*) the manner in which the Chairpersons of such Committees shall be chosen.

(3) Every District Planning Committee shall, in preparing the draft development plan:

(*a*) have regard to:

(*i*) matters of common interest between the Panchayats and the Municipalities including spatial planning, sharing of water and other physical and natural resources the integrated development of infrastructure and environmental conservation;

(*ii*) the extent and type of available resources whether financial or otherwise;

(*b*) Consult such institutions and organizations as the Governor may, by order, specify.

(4) The Chairperson of every District Planning Committee shall forward the development plan, as recommended by such Committee, to the Government of the Sate.

Committee for Metropolitan Planning

243ZE (1) There shall be constituted in every Metropolitan area a Metropolitan Planning Committee to prepare a draft development plan for the Metropolitan area as a whole.

(2) The Legislature of a State may, by law, make provisions with respect to:

(*a*) the composition of the Metropolitan Planning Committees;

(*b*) the manner in which the seats in such Committees shall be filled:
Provided that not less than two-thirds of the members of such Committee shall be elected by, and from amongst, the elected members of the Municipalities and Chairpersons of the Panchayats in the Metropolitan area in proportion to the ratio between the population of the Municipalities and of the Panchayats in that area;

(*c*) the representation of such Committees of the Government of India and the Government of the State and of such organizations and institutions as may be deemed necessary for carrying out of functions assigned to such Committees;

(*d*) the functions relating to planning and coordination for the Metropolitan area which may be assigned to such Committees:

(*e*) the manner in which the Chairpersons of such Committees shall be chosen.

(3) Every Metropolitan Planning Committee shall, in preparing the draft development plan,

(*a*) have regard to:
(*i*) the plans prepared by the Municipalities and the Panchayats in the Metropolitan area;
(*ii*) matters of common interest between the Municipalities and the Panchayats, including coordinated spatial planning of the area, sharing of water and other physical and natural resources, the integrated development of infrastructure and environmental conservation;
(*iii*) the overall objectives and priorities set by the Government of India and the Government of the State;
(*iv*) the extent and nature of investments likely to be made in Metropolitan area by agencies of the Government of India and of the Government of the State and other available resources whether financial or otherwise;
(*b*) consult such institutions and organizations as the Governor may, by order, specify.

(4) The Chairperson of every Metropolitan Planning Committee shall forward the development plan, as recommended by such Committee, to the Government of the State.

7

Good Governance at District Level: A Case Study of District Planning

RAJESH SHARMA

India's experience of governance since Independence has one constant feature: while its Constitution, resolutions of objectives and plans formulated at the macro-level have, by and large, been lauded, those elected to implement them have been, with few exceptions, rejected at the hustings. Apart from the left front in selected areas, none of the incumbent rightist, centrists or socialists parties or those espousing serious concern for "social justice" have received broad or viable electoral endorsement for what they have done to implement their pledges to the people. Neither the pledge of socialist pattern nor of *garibi hatao*; neither the pledge of liberal democratization nor of globalization nor of social justice has resulted in good governance in larger parts of the country. No doubt, some states have been better governed than others; but states like Bihar, Orissa and Assam, through their continued status of under-development quality to acquire the position of belonging to the "fourth world". It is not difficult to find out the cause of their under-development.

Implementation of Programmes and Schemes

According to P.P. Agrawal, effective implementation of a plan really begins at the formulation stage where various decision-making groups in the public and private sectors are drawn into the process of preparing the plan.[1] It is a continuing procedure beginning with consultations, leading to emergence of consensus and ending with agreed decision.[2] What Agrawal says may be true, but it needs to be added that the crux of implementation process starts after a plan is put into action. In implementation of some developmental schemes—like rural development, agriculture, irrigation, fodder distribution, coaltar use for construction of roads, or distribution of medicines, vaccines, family planning pills or condoms through health centres, or distribution of provisions like sugar, kerosene etc., in far-flung areas/peripheries of the country—Bihar's case is particularly problematic because of being more prone to misuse and disuse of funds[3] due to rampant political and administrative corruption.

It is a truism that plan implementation is the Achilles' Heel of Indian planning. Most needed and hankered after implementation, *i.e.*, delivery of goods and services to the target groups, particularly the weaker sections in rural areas, has been the weakest aspect of Indian planning. When the district plan scheme was introduced, following the guidelines prescribed by the Planning Commission of 1969, which were modified by V.K.R.V. Rao and D.R. Gadgil's recommendations, its implementation raised both academicians' and people's hope for better implementation and through it, better governance. We shall examine in this article whether and how far these hopes have been realized.

Implementation of district plan involved greater responsibility for putting the decided strategies into action. Whereas specialized ministries of the Centre and States are called upon to implement their respective plans, and the Planning Commission watches, advises and reports on their implementation,[4] district level planning institutions, it may be hypothesized, are less specialized and more politicized and less coordinated with those they were called upon to work in cooperation and with those they were supposed to deliver. District planning requires the support of not only the state and local political elites and bureaucracy but also people's active involvement and genuine participation at all levels—district, block and village—in both selection and implementation of schemes. It is to be seen, through this article, whether the entrenched political-administrative elites, operating in collusion with the vested interests within the district, have allowed common and needy men and women, who are the shoe-bearers having full and even articulated views about where the shoe pinches to have a say in improving their lot.

We may not be wide out of the mark in suggesting that the implementation process including that of district planning appears to be quite depressing in Bihar because the administrative and work culture there is in bad shape.

Evolving Indices of Good Governance through Implementation Process

Let us, therefore, try to develop indices of good governance, like evolving sound principles and processes for selecting the schemes, choosing the agencies which execute the scheme or plan, obtaining technical and administrative approval, upkeep of resources, physical ratification, etc. Patna district was chosen for the study as it represents varied economic and social situations with a mix for rural and urban areas; and is one of the comparatively developed districts in the otherwise "backward" state of Bihar where economy's mainstay continues to be agriculture. But since the district headquarters of Patna is located in the capital city of Bihar, it may be hypothesized that it is perceptibly more prone to intense pulls and pressures generated from above and beyond (by-passing the bottom) negatively and dysfunctional affecting administrative, planning and developmental processes. The interface between state-level politicians, people's representatives and bureaucrats is more vividly visible here. That makes Patna district a representative sample for studying actual governance at district level in Bihar.

To begin with, an illustration to elaborate the point made above, we notice that more often than not, it is neither the district officers (DDE or DPO or any other) nor the Panchayat authorities who select the agencies which execute the schemes but the MPs, MLAs and MLCs of the area rule the roost and their recommendations, favouring their henchmen or electoral allies, like contractors and even criminals court most and, in fact, are respected most by the highest officers of the district, including the District Magistrate who is invariably the CM's man or woman. The planning process, thus become a farce.

So far as the formal details go, every department has to send the District Sector Schemes plan-wise for their specific areas to the Planning Department in the manner as prescribed (in D.P. 2/3) till the 25th of April every year. These particulars are examined by the Planning Department and on the basis of this, district plan is prepared. Accepted list of the District Sector Schemes and district-wise expenditure is sent to the district till the 15th of May every year by the concerned departments. Then district office goes into action.

Norms and actual implementation of district plan as indices of good governance are being discussed here.

PROCESS OF DISTRICT PLANNING

Selection of Schemes

District officer is entitled to select agencies for implementation of the available untied fund under district plan. For decentralized planning process, it has been decided by the government that for the implementation of plans under JRY, etc., Panchayati Raj Institutions (PRIs), voluntary institutions and their representatives and workers' committees are to be given priority. For implementation of plans and use of available resources under untied fund of district plan, guidelines issued by Rural Development Department for the selection of execution agencies is accepted.

Since untied fund is allotted as complementary to development plans, there is no question of constitution an independent agency to execute the plans undertaken to utilize the fund. Since district officer is responsible for coordinating and formulating plans to utilize untied fund, it is his responsibility to ensure that available administrative and technical capacity is made use of in the implementation of such schemes. For instance, road construction schemes may be implemented by the engineers of the REO or NREP. Likewise, school building construction or construction of health centre is to be done by the PWD. Officers of the administrative divisions are under strict orders that the approval of DPDC in the selection of sites for schemes under district sector is essential, and in the monitoring and implementation of district level schemes, only the available agencies at the district level should be used.

Technical and Administrative Approval

It is the responsibility of the district officer to see that the scheme taken up under district plan is technically sound and it is properly supervised and implemented. Like Jawahar Rojgar Yojna schemes, schemes under district planning should also be implemented by administrative officers. Where it is not possible, the relevant departmental procedures may be followed in getting the schemes executed by contractors or by any other agency.

In technical supervision of roads, guidelines issued by the REO are to be followed. In the same way, in the schemes of house construction, water supply and minor irrigation, technical guidelines of concerned departments are to be followed. The expenditure incurred on every item and unit is to be according to the approved scheme of the administrative department. For different kinds of buildings for primary schools, health centres, sub-centre and hospitals, guidelines relating to surface area standards decided by the administrative division are to be followed. Secretaries of administrative divisions are expected to send relevant guidelines to districts for implementation of district plan schemes. State Government, according to these guidelines, does not want schemes to be revised under any circumstances and wants schemes to be completed within a financial year. If there is any difficulty, the approval of DPDC is to be taken for extension for three months. This extension in no case is to extend beyond six months.

Districts are also allotted optional funds to be used for rendering benefits directly to the residents. These funds are to be used for schemes which are locally important and which involve expenditure within allotted amount and which can be completed within a year or two. It should be used for such locally important schemes which contribute to production and increase in productivity. It should be used for schemes which create resources for the community. The current schemes should be followed by supplementary/complementary schemes so that current schemes may render maximum benefits. Such schemes should be used to remove defects in the structure of district planning. The amount of this optional fund, in no case, is to be used for subsidies or for other purposes like expenditure on material used by the office, office expenses or sale/repair of vehicles. The dividends created by local institutions may, however, be added so that the scheme may be more fruitful.

Untied Fund and Its Use

The untied fund is not to be treated as substitute for departmental fund. It should not be used for such schemes for which funds are made available generally to administrative divisions. Since untied fund is a part of the plan, hence, it should be used for creation of new resources. Though the importance of local roads is undisputed, yet a maximum amount of 30 per cent should be earmarked for rural roads. A minimum amount of 50 per cent of untied fund is to be earmarked for irrigation purposes. Such schemes which contribute to the use of available irreparable capacity or contribute to its production needs to be taken up. A maximum of 15 per cent can be spent on schemes related to the urban area if such schemes contribute to alleviation of poverty and environmental upgradation. The available funds are to be spent on completing the current schemes on a priority basis. The new schemes can be approved to the extent of 10 per cent of the allotted amount for any year. The rest of the amount is to be used for completing the incomplete schemes under district plan. After these two allocations are made, new schemes can be taken under explicit instructions from the stage government and with the approval of the DPDC. The BDOs have to pull on well with the cooperation of the *Mukhiyas* in the BDC bargain. It is seen that BDOs tend to oblige the *Mukhiyas* by allotting some schemes to be executed by them. This has become source of their income. Hence, BDOs find it better to allot local schemes to the *Mukhiyas* then to contractors because the former have greater accountability to the people.

In view of the importance of people's cooperation in the implementation of district plan schemes, priority is to be accorded to schemes taken up by local agencies and PRIs particularly if local agencies or PRIs are able to collect 15 per cent fund by way of labour or money.

The State Government had decided that the schemes under district plan must contribute to development of scheduled castes residing in the district in proportion to their population. Hence, a minimum amount out of the total allotted amount under district plan must be allocated for schemes which contribute to development of Scheduled Castes. The description of such schemes should be sent to planning and development department and welfare department of state government. The District Officer is personally responsible to see that the rules in this regard are strictly followed and actually benefit the targeted section of the society. Because of the nexus between the officials and executing agencies, these norms are not maintained leading to paper work only.

The executive agency should be given an advance of only 10 to 25 per cent of the estimated amount at the first instance. The next instalment is to be paid only after the amount of the first instalment is actually spent. The schemes are not to be revised under any condition. For execution of plans, wages to labourers are not to be paid in the form of cereals but in cash. No scheme should be taken up under district plan which involves expenditure of an amount exceeding 15 lakh.

It is the function of the DPDC to review all the schemes under district plan. Hence, for constant review of the schemes, meetings of DPDC are to be arranged on a regular basis. The departmental heads of all the district plan units in the district will collate all important information related to the scheme, like objects of the scheme, approved expenditure, items of expenditure, physical objects, sites of implementation, proposed date of completion and number of beneficiaries so that DPDC may have full view of the things. DPDC may state the reasons for continuance of such schemes and any suggestion regarding the mode of implementation and send it to the concerned administrative department and planning department.

District planning units are to maintain a register in which all the schemes could be divided and their separate accounts and progress maintained so that adequate monitoring could be done. Agencies responsible for implementation of the schemes will send progress report of financial and physical progress to the DPDC periodically. The executive committee of the DPDC is to make a review of the progress every month and apprise the DPDC of its results.

Allocation of Schemes

State Government has instructed districts that allocation of schemes under district plan has to be done according to the Directive Principles of State Policy. All such schemes are to be properly monitored, and their progress is to be sent every month to the planning department. The Divisional Commissioner has been asked to review implementation of schemes and inspect sites from time to time.

The competent authority to accord technical approval to completion of schemes is the executive engineer of the concerned department, who certifies completion of DM or DDC attests and documents these. The list of schemes completed under district plan is to be placed before the DPDC at the end of the year, and a copy of it is to be sent to the concerned department.

PROBLEMS AND PITFALLS IN IMPLEMENTATION OF SCHEMES: AN EMPIRICAL OVERVIEW

Selection of Agency for Plan Execution and Sites of Execution

Though the power of selecting the agencies for execution of district planning schemes belongs to the district officer, the recommendations of the elected representatives regarding selection of particular agency are constantly received by the DM and the DDC. Sometimes, past performance of the concerned agencies is lost sight of by elected representatives for the Vidhan Sabha of the State in making such recommendations. The MLAs and MPs try to help their political supporters. This consideration is of greater importance to them than the suitability of the agencies and its past record. Pressures exerted upon District Officers have the effect of influencing them to curry favour of the elected representative, ignoring even the guidelines of the rural development department regarding selection of agencies. There is no concrete development in direction of minimizing the process of execution of schemes by administrative department.

Administrative departments often ignore recommendation that the district planning unit should be treated as a nodal agency for the development and for implementing of all the schemes in an integrated manner. This strikes at the root of good governance, and those who stand for good governance must see to it that such practices are dispensed with as quickly as possible.

Approval of DPDC is essential for selecting the sites for the schemes for administrative divisions. But this is also not always done. No procedure has been established for selection or sites scientifically and in a planned manner for district planning schemes. District planning unit is not even able to collate information on actual site of development works carried out in the district in the past.

We may suggest that foolproof arrangement should be made to ensure that the DM does not grant new works to such an agency which has been blacklisted in the past or whose performance had been unsatisfactory and also to ensure that guidelines regarding selection of agencies issued by rural development department are not flouted. Penal action should be taken in cases of flagrant violation in these matters. Stringent action should also be taken if schemes are not completed on time. Only those district level schemes, it must be seen, are sponsored by district plan units where selection of sites under the schemes has been done in a systematic and scientific manner. Distinct plan units must maintain a record of sites on which work had been taken up in the past, and a map should show the sites undertaken in the past. Site selections have also political overtones because the elected representatives prefer the sites from where they get support in the election. In most of the cases, genuine claims are ignored and good governance becomes a casualty.

Multiplicity of Officials According Technical Approval

More than one officer is empowered to accord technical approval of schemes but schemes are not divided departmentwise, which adversely affects monitoring and physical verification. No report is procured about the process of site selection, approval of DPDC and assessment of socio-economic benefits to be obtained after completion of the scheme before according administrative approval. District planning office and its functionaries have not been given any role in according administrative and technical approval of the projects which is against the principles of district planning. A scheme entailing an expenditure up to Rs. 15 lakh can be taken up from the untied fund but rules have not been framed regarding according of technical and administrative approval of such projects.

It is suggested that scheme should be divided department-wise for according technical and administrative approval so that it may be convenient to make physical verification of the projects. Administrative approval should be granted only after obtaining report on the process of site selection and assessment of socio-economic benefits to be obtained after completion of the scheme. The consent of the district planning office and its functionaries must be obtained before granting administrative and technical approval so that work may be done according to the objectives of the district plan. Schemes involving an expenditure upto Rs. 15 lakh should be properly considered and the procedure of according administrative and technical approval of such projects be documented and made explicit and simple.

Technically Unsound Schemes and Delays

Effective steps have not been taken in the direction of finding out timely solution to the problem and finding ways and means to gradually minimize the role of departments in implementation of the schemes under district plan. No professional organization at the Panchayat and Block level or committee of proposed beneficiaries or any organization of unemployed community has been encouraged for the purpose. Often, many schemes are found to be not sound from technical point of view because of which they take longer than the time stipulated for completion and are not useful with a long-term perspective after their completion. Proper implementation and supervision of schemes are not done because these are not based on local resources and convenient techniques and repair work on institutional basis is also not made after the work is complete. No rules are framed regulating the process of selecting agents for implementation of schemes by departmental agencies. No priority is accorded to locally available resources and traditional good techniques, reliance is placed only on the concerned department's guidelines. Standards established by administrative departments in respect of surface areas are not adapted or changed keeping in view the local conditions and requirements. The complete abolition of the system of revision of schemes is not proper in the context of so many problems and creates many difficulties. Sometimes time-limit for completion of scheme is not maintained strictly which may mitigate the very purpose of the scheme for which it is launched and results into mal-governance or bad governance.

Minimising Departmental Role in Implementation

We may suggest that, in order to ensure good governance, priority should be accorded to village panchayats, voluntary organizations, committees of beneficiaries and organizations of unemployed men or women to minimize the role of departments in implementation of schemes. Techniques based on convenient and local resources should be used which do not undermine the technical aspects of the scheme. Work, which is qualitatively better, may be completed sooner; and may be repaired locally in future. Locally available traditional skills and techniques should be used on a priority basis. Rules should be determined about selection of agents and priority be accorded to the unemployed social workers. Provision should be made for bringing in unemployed social workers and introduce changes according to local conditions and requirements in standards of construction of buildings and in the surface areas. We are against abolition of the system of revision of schemes, though, to be sure, very few schemes should be revised and that too under special conditions; and an officer should be specifically authorized to see that there is no hanky-panky in the system of revision of schemes. Particular emphasis should be laid on maintaining the time schedule of completion of schemes.

Misuse of Untied Fund

It has been discovered during study that untied fund has been made on renovation and repairs in addition to taking up new schemes. Quite a few schemes taken up under the district plan had been outside the list of Minimum Needs Programme. Expenses were not incurred following areawise allocation of untied funds in the past. As importance of different districts in a state changes according to local conditions, similar provision for all the districts will not be proper. District-wise principles should be framed and adopted. The present system of receiving and spending grants is not based on area-wise division of districts and blocks. The distribution according to definite percentages for selection and implementation of new schemes is not proper. No rules are available about the allocation of funds within a district between old and new schemes. Allotments are made by the State Government to the districts twice a year and the amount fluctuates due to which implementation of schemes is adversely affected. If a scheme is not complete on time, expenses increase. Recommendations of MPs, MLAs, and MLCs (some of whom are also ministers) get high priority and rules are ignored.

Violation of Rules Governing Grant of Advances

The rule regarding granting advances to executive agents is also flouted. In this, recommendation of MPs, MLAs and MLCs (some of whom are also ministers and ex-ministers) get maximum importance. Some schemes remain pending and incomplete for years and are not taken up; and advances are not given in the absence of recommendations of people's representatives in the Vidhan Saba because of which funds spent in the past on the said schemes are wasted. Stopping such schemes in the midway and without cause results in their exclusion from district plan. Such fate generally befalls those schemes which had been recommended and taken up under the recommendations of ex-MPs or MLAs. This is not in keeping with the rules framed by the department and officers of the district level are much too ready to oblige the existing MPs or MLAs who are on the government side, and to sidetrack ex-MPs and MLAs.

Non-involving of SCs in Selection/Execution of Schemes for Them

The representation of the Scheduled Caste (SCs), particularly in the selection and execution of schemes for SCs, is recommended. The schemes meant for development of SCs must start on time. Steps should also be taken to elicit peoples' cooperation in collecting funds to start special programmes. Even awareness is not created to arouse local people to cooperate in a special programme. Although it is State Government's policy to provide incentives in the form of financial assistance to programmes for which land, house, etc., is locally available, yet no such programme has been initiated. Applications should be separately invited for such schemes at the time of selection of schemes. Such incomplete schemes, which can contribute to increase in production and employment opportunities and for which funds are not available from other sources, can be competed from the untied fund. The number of such schemes is quite large in the districts. Hence, it is suggested that efforts should be made to complete such schemes from the untied fund.

No Plan Information from HODs in the Field to District Office

Heads of departments at the district level do not gather information on schemes in their area, their objectives, estimated amount, actual site for implementation, date of completion, etc., in full. Therefore, they do not send information on these to district planning office. The departments at the district level do not respond to the request by the district planning office to send such information; even though district planning office is known as the secretariat of DPDC and has been declared nodal agency for development of the district. It is clear from perusal of the proceedings of the meetings of the DP.DC that the DPDC does neither make effort to collect such information from the departmental heads of the district level, nor does it send information about the reasons for continuance of such schemes and their information to the concerned administrative division and planning department. District planning office does neither collect nor send to the DPDC information about schemes which are not related to the untied fund. The executive committee of the DPDC is expected to make a monthly review of the progress of schemes but the executive committee does not meet on a regular basis and in some districts, does not meet at all.

Formulation of schemes and their approval by DPDC, implementation of schemes and sending of lists of such schemes with requisite information to the departments concerned is not done in full. A Systems Analyst in District Planning, Vaishali, in his typed monograph, succinctly mentions the following reasons to explain why these are not being done.[5]

Formulation of planning had been obstructed by political inference and departmental rules have been replaced by recommendations of elected representatives.

Violation of Procedures

The approval of DPDC is to be obtained after the schemes get approval of the Executive Committee of the DPDC but on several schemes, approval of the DPDC is received direct without even taking the matter to the Executive Committee of the DPDC. After implementation of schemes, approval of DPDC is to be secured but many schemes are implemented at that stage which is against the departmental rules. Review of implementation of schemes is done according to physical and financial progress reports of the concerned executive agencies and on-the-spot-inspection and minute checking of materials used in the scheme is not done on a regular basis. Inquiry is conducted only after receiving complaints regarding use of sub-standard materials, etc. The district administration does not extend the requisite cooperation in conducting inquiries in the schemes and does not extend the facilities of conveyance, etc., in conducting such enquiries usually. The DM is much too engaged in administrative activities and, therefore, does not pay personal attention in the conduct of inquiries. Divisional Commissioners hardly make as on the spot verification of implementation of schemes. Lastly, district planning office under the present system does not get proposals of new schemes directly. Proposals come through the instrumentality of DM and DDC which is against the objectives of district planning.

Need for Streamlining of Review of Schemes

A lot need to be done about the review of the schemes for which meetings of DPDC should be held on a regular basis. Heads of departments at the district level should send all necessary information on schemes of district plan to district planning office which should collate it. DPDC should be provided with up-to-date knowledge of the scheme by district planning office which should also send its suggestions. Departmental heads should provide information demanded by district planning office on a priority basis. In case of slackness or delay in sending such information, departmental heads should be held personally responsible. The role of executive committee of DPDC has to be taken much more seriously than it is being done at present. The system of DPDC not approving schemes, which have not been recommended by local representatives or of granting *post facto* approval of such schemes, without the approval of the executive committee of DPDC should be dispensed with. In no case *post facto* approval should be granted to the schemes being implemented against the departmental guidelines. Review of implementation should not be done on the basis of monthly financial and physical progress report. High priority should be accorded to regular verification of the quality of materials being used in the construction work. For this, sudden inspection be made by superior officials and monthly inspection reports should be sent to the departments. The system of inspection of schemes only when letters of complaint are received should be dispensed with and effective steps taken to elicit cooperation of district administration. Despite heavy preoccupation, DM and Divisional Commissioners should make on-the-spot inspection of schemes under implementation. The proposals for new schemes should be received by the DPO direct from local institutions. Only in special circumstances, DM and DD should recommend new proposals under the scheme.

Physical Verification of Works Done

Physical verification of works completed under schemes many years ago is pending in almost all the districts of Bihar, including Patna district, since long. Physical verification should be done only by officers who grant technical approval to the scheme, but this is not being done by an official. Although, work of physical verification should normally be done immediately after completion of the scheme, yet this is not being done. Schemes should be handed over for use only after physical verification but this is also not being done. The list of the completed schemes is sent to the DPDC and concerned departments without physical verification.

It is suggested that if good governance is to be ensured, physical verification of all completed schemes should be taken up on a priority basis in each district. Clear instructions should be sent for physical verifications to be made in an effective manner within a stipulated period. Instructions should also be issued that physical verification can be done only by an officer who grants technical approval to the scheme. Physical verification should be done within a definite period after completion of the scheme so that it can be determined whether the work has been done according to the estimate. Only after physical verification, a scheme should be sent to the administrative department for useful work done. And only after physical verification report, DPDC should certify its completion.

Delays Due to Loopholes at DPDC Level

Lags in implementation occupy most of the time of the DPDC. This point is illustrated by perusal of the proceedings of meetings of Patna DPDC. Implementation is bad also because many loopholes of implementation are not properly anticipated while making the plan, and lack of monitoring does not provide the planner adequate experience on loopholes of implementation which can be corrected; and a modified scheme pattern may be incorporated in the next district plan. Hence, integration of formulation and implementation of plan should be more seriously attended to in future; and genuine participation of people (as against the vested interests represented by the entrenched politicians at the state level and their local henchmen, brokers, contractors, criminals and normless band of people, old caste lords and rich *baniyas* and landowners, money-lenders, new brand of officials pressing for bribe for any governmental work done or promised to be done) must be institutionalized, encouraged and developed if good governance is an objective to be achieved. Similarly, women, particularly of low castes with low education, have to be encouraged to come up (as against the wives of those who had enjoyed or are yet enjoying power). The shackles of superstition, *purdah* and worship of the husband or *sarkar* (mother-in-law) is to be nationalized among women. Scheduled Castes have come up though not to a satisfactory extent. Much needs to be done to make Scheduled Tribes more effective citizens who can discriminate between fake and genuine leaders. Poor, as a whole, need to be objectively treated and organized. In fairness, good governance must be backed by rational, genuine and moral level of participation of citizens "up to the last"; and formulation and implementation of district plan must bear the imprint of that level of participation in concrete terms. Voluntary agencies, enlightened citizenry and activists for a better society must respond to this task of society building.

REFERENCES

1. P. P. Agrawal, "Some Aspects of Plan Implementation", *Indian Journal of Public Administration*, Vol. XIX, No. 1, January-March, 1973, p. 16.
2. *Ibid.*
3. As several 'scams' under CBI investigation which refer to misuse of funds. The secretaries of the Government of India have gone to the press to inform the public that the Government of Bihar has disused, *i.e.*, surrendered huge funds meant for development, etc.
4. R.K. Sapru emphasises this point in his *Development Administration*, Delhi, Deep and Deep Publications, 1986, p. 173.
5. Ram Nivas Prasad Singh "Zila Yojana Karykaram Kee Niyamawali: Samasyaen Avam Sujhav" (types monograph in Hindi), May 7, 1994, pp. 65-66.

8

Planning for Rural Development by Field Staff: A View from Rajasthan

RAKESH HOOJA

Much is often[1] written about the importance of intermediate and lower level planning so as to reduce the gap between the planning agency and the area of implementation and consequently to enable location, specific needs, and solution to be spelt out in the light of both local resource availability and national developmental priorities, keeping in view local socio-administrative practices and inter and intra local area economic linkages. Such local/intermediate plan documents would not only make sectoral financial outlays easier to decide, but also enable better coordination between the various sectoral allocations for an area and better physical, spatial and human (including individual beneficiary) planning. The lower the level of the plan, the smaller the plan area is likely to be, and thus, the more detailed the plan document, making its implementation easier. Also in case people closer to the implementation level do the planning then such plans are also likely to be much more practical and realistic from the implementation point of view. So the theory goes. And unless tried out in real earnest it can neither be proved nor disproved.

Such an approach if taken to its logical conclusion implies that the field level implementation staff should prepare its own village block/district plans as also its own special developmental micro-projects and then also implement them. Or at most that the local citizenry, or other experts specially placed at the local level, associate with the local implementation agency to undertake such plan and project formulation.

It is the purpose of this brief paper to examine existing trends (as are visible to this observer) in this direction in Rajasthan's rural development efforts to try and figure out whether such a trend is likely to continue until a situation is achieved in which local plan/projects can be prepared and implemented locally. This question can be phrased in another manner—whether the field implementation agencies shall ever be able to develop the capability to be able to undertake their own local planning/projectisation (on their own or with some assistance from local citizenry and locally situated experts). The question as to whether such an eventuality would be desirable can then be commented upon.

PANCHAYATI RAJ AND LOCAL PLANNING

It would be appropriate now to turn to the last two decades in Rajasthan and to provide a simplified account of the trends as visible to this observer.

For the third and fourth plans the panchayati raj structure (both panchayat officials and panchayat non-officials) were involved in what was called district planning.[2] However, what in effect occurred was that while the non-officials added more and more to the lists of demands and expressed felt needs, the officials tried to follow the lead of the district/state level officers from their departments and get district-wise break-up of the State plan approved. The resulting compromise documents were often forgotten after drafting. Even otherwise this effort should not be considered to be a true planning exercise because detailed resource and problem inventories were never conducted and only either political compilations of charters of demands or bureaucratic listing of district-wise break-ups of the State plan were properly attempted.

After that the entire arena of development administration in Rajasthan underwent a change. Panchayati raj started to lose its vitality as elections were put off. Special project agencies for Marginal Farmers and Agricultural Labourer (MFAL) development, Small Farmers Development (SFD), Command Area Development (CAD) and Drought Prone Areas Programme (DPAP) and tribal sub-plan area development were set up and they cut into the importance of both the panchayat structures and of the regular State Government departments. As the approach of the specialized schemes was different from the old community development—panchayati raj approach, the need for greater sophistication in project/scheme/action plan preparation also emerged. This was accentuated by greater use of institutional finance as financing agencies like the Reserve Bank of India (RBI), the Agriculture Refinance and Development Corporation (ARDC) and the World Bank, as well as commercial banks asked for better examination of schemes based on improved appraisal technique and their own norms of the bankability of a project/scheme.

Simultaneously the Planning Commission issued detailed guidelines in 1969[3] which envisaged techno-economic resource inventories before detailed analysis, which would lead to better district planning. Simultaneously academicians were also talking of more sophisticated planning based on, for example, the concept of rural growth centres.[4]

Hence, the old panchayati raj based attempt at local planning died a natural death.[8] What came instead was greater reliance on the preparation and sanctioning of institutional finance projects and an attempt at pilot studies on detailed district planning. The special project agencies and departments in the meantime continued turning out and implementing what can at best be called action plans which contained physical and financial targets and outlays based on prompting from above.

As project formulation for institutional finance assistance grew in importance a special schemes organization evolved in the State's secretariat agriculture department in 1971-72. This not only looked after the implementation of the special schemes of the Government of India mentioned above and State Government schemes like Antyodaya as the administrative secretariat department, and acted as its own executive department, but it also set up its own project formulation cell for formulating special district or block projects for, say, minor (well) irrigation, soil conservation supply of milch/drought, etc., animals, market yard development, fruit development, drought prone areas development and for getting them sanctioned and implemented. The cell contains experts from various government departments that are concerned with rural development who visit or correspond with the district level special project agencies to obtain data for their project formulation.[6]

Simultaneously by 1974 the State planning department was setting up district planning cells in four of Rajasthan's twenty-six districts to try and undertake detailed district planning as per the Government of India guidelines.[7] However, somehow the resource inventories and then plan drafting have dragged on till this year—especially since no clear decision about how these detailed district plans would be sanctioned and implemented has been taken and because government programme/scheme implementation has gone on as usual in the absence of these plans.

In 1978-79 the special schemes organization was also asked to undertake *Samagra* gram vikas[8] (whole village development) rural growth centre[9] planning, and comprehensive block planning[10] and, by 1979, district planning cells (with skeletal official staff and hardly any statistical or clerical assistance) were in position in all the districts. Such cells are under the administrative control of the special schemes organization and have been located in the SFDA/DDA (district development agency) which are the implementational special project agencies in each district so as to integrate the plan/project formulation and implementational wings at the district level. The residuary detailed pilot district planning work earlier being got done by the State planning department has also been transferred to these district planning cells as has work of the recently started Integrated Rural Development (IRD)[11] and of block credit project[12] formulation which is controlled by the special schemes organization at the State level. Special technical cells for the formulation and implementation for community lift irrigation from rivers and *dehs* have also been placed in the SFDA/DDAs.

Other special project works as for example UNICEF sponsored area development schemes or tribal mini-block development through the Modified Area Development Approach (MADA) are also entrusted to the special schemes organization and through it to the district planning cells.

Thus theoretically both at the State-level (special schemes organization) and the district level (district planning cells located in the SFDAs/DDAs) the area plan/project formulations and implementers are the same agency. Thus to hypothesize that in the coming decades such integration of planning/projectising and implementation is likely to go down to the village level (and that comprehensive block planning and preparation of block credit projects now have been initiated for all the 236 blocks in Rajasthan shall be followed by the spread of the formulation of pilot *Samagra* gram vikas village projects and rural growth centres—now being undertaken sparingly—to all 33,000 odd villages and 1,265 identified rural growth centres in Rajasthan) appears realistic.

However, the actual practice raises some doubts.

SHORTCOMINGS IN LOCAL PLANNING

While the SFDA/DDA with, or without its district planning cell is capable of preparing its own draft action plans in the light of previous action plans, it manages little more than that independently. Even where minor (well) irrigation schemes, already sanctioned by the ARDC, have to be rephrased the district staff normally has to be called to the Special Schemes Organization (SSO) for discussions before a supplementary minor irrigation scheme can be finalized. For *Samagra* gram vikas/rural growth centre projects the district planning cell prepares the first draft as per the SSO guidelines. Thereafter, this draft has to be got rewritten at least twice by SSO officers before it can be considered for appraisal at the SSO level. For block credit projects, the SSO officers are moving from district to district to ensure that the credit requirement projections being made at the district level prior to the drafting of the project report have been projected correctly. In the case of soil conservation watershed works under DPAP or DDP (desert development programme—also looked after SSO),[13] the watershed works proposal prepared at the field level by the technical staff of the DDA has to be technically got checked at the assistant/additional director soil conservation levels and still, when submitted to the SSO, may have faults. The above are only examples. In fact, the only programme where field level work plans, called 'chak files' of On Farm Development (OFD) catchments, do not need much revision at levels higher than that of the project, known to this observer, is the CAD project at Chambal and Rajasthan Canal. These exceptions prove the rule, especially because in these projects, officers of the levels of chief engineer/additional chief engineer have been placed at the local project level.[14]

But what is the reason why, in practice, local (in this case district) level plan/project formulation has shortcomings?

One reason is that at lower levels, the project area becomes smaller and detailed micro planning instead of aggregate planning becomes necessary. Most government servants are not used to such detailed planning which is possible only after sufficient field data is collected. This observer has seen examples where rough calculation on the basis of estimated size of the proposed work and a schedule of what are called Basic Standard Rates (BSRs) have been sent up to the SSO from the SFDA/DDA because that is what the government engineer has been accustomed to doing before getting a sanction. However, with smaller areas being planned in more detail, the SSO now requires actual field data about the availability and cost of raw material, labour costs, survey of land and actual measurements and design of the proposed work, as also the actual expected beneficiaries and incremental benefits of the proposed works to be worked out and cost rates compared with anticipated incremental benefits before sanctioning.

Another reason is that often personnel at the lower levels[15] lack technical knowledge of sufficient standard and also lack information about policies and decisions of the government (because being in the field they are too junior) as well as of financial institutions like banks. In fact, regarding banks, they even lack an idea of the culture, style and processes of commercial/cooperative bank working which can differ from bank to bank. They often also lack commercial information about rates and supply of goods, etc., required from outside the local area. And more than that they even usually lack the knowledge and orientation about what is the concept of a project or of a proper plan. Having worked all their life with Basic Standard Rates, or budgets based on establishment costs and rough work costs based on: (*a*) physical targets, and (*b*) the rough norms of cost per unit of physical target to be achieved, they find it difficult to adjust to a more detailed examination of proposals and the calculation of anticipated benefits required for projectisation. In fact, many persons in the field today refer to an action plan or rough schematic budget estimate as a project or detailed plan because they do not know otherwise. Even proper training to overcome this has only started being developed on a large enough scale in the last couple of years.

Other reasons are that the local officials are more easily swayed by vested interests and local political forces because they are more involved in the local milieu as also because, being junior, they cannot easily stand up to such pressures, and because often their mental horizons are not broad enough to see the need to resist such pressures. Nor are their service conditions such that better, more idealistic, knowledgeable, and courageous persons would man such posts.

Local officials are also often likely to press for lower targets or easier objectives so as to have less problem in implementation. They may also for the same reason, stress easier to perform rather than vital tasks while planning. Also they may not be able to work out the possible adverse consequences that can follow for areas outside their jurisdiction from proposals being made by them.

The fact that no local area is a closed system either economically or administratively also means that the local planner cannot plan only locally. He has to know the eternal supply points for benefit delivery and the likely supply bottlenecks (*i.e.*, for fertilizers which may have to be imported into the local area. For this he needs information from outside his area. And if he himself is responsible for obtaining and importing government benefit supplies into his area before they are got delivered by him, then he may not even have the time to plan anything except the immediate receipt and delivery of government benefit.

Another reason is that just as many government decisions and policies which could affect the nature of the plan/project being made are not known at the local level, similarly much data for example from the regular census, the agriculture and livestock censuses, compiled figures of the licensing of certain items, etc., is available only at the State level. Even the statistics department of the State often gets data collected through district statistical officers—but gets it compiled only at the State capital. Hence, the district planners have to obtain such data not from the field but from the State capital. The problem is further compounded when even at the State level data may be found compiled on a tehsil by tehsil basis and not block-wise. Not only is the data collected at field level compiled only at the State level, but often the sample size, as for example in crop cutting experiments to determine agricultural yield figures, is too small for reliable estimations at levels lower than that of the entire State. Also ground-water, soil and geological surveys (to name a few) are centrally managed at the State-level and this data is seldom available at the district or lower levels. Facilities like aerial photo interpretation laboratories are also located at most in one or two places in the State. Thus, the accessibility of adequate data, knowledge and skills is all lacking local and intermediate levels.

An additional problem is that even at the State-level many government departments have not yet started functioning at such higher qualitative standards of projectisation and detailed planning; they function as in days of yore on the basis of some scrutiny based on common sense and administrative experience. Even in these State departments where change is occurring (especially due to Government of India or international agency prodding) the change is usually at the highest or near summit levels. Thus, the gap between this level and the SFDA/DDA or the departmental district level officers in touch with the SFDA/DDA is huge. Hence the SFDA/DDA often cannot get sufficient guidance from some of the departments. At times due to this reason they try to copy projects prepared in other districts or circulated as model reports by the SSO in a blind manner or try to resist projectisation and press for a commonsense scrutiny of schemes instead.

In fact today even the State plan is not prepared in such a detailed manner in many departments as is now being conceived for the preparation of comprehensive block plans, because the State plan of the department often is a rough break-up of the plan outlay ceiling given from above to the department, with some details of old (committed) and newly proposed posts and establishment costs and old (committed) liability of works with the remainder being roughly calculated and ascribed to new proposed works.[17] When State level departmental plans are thus prepared after little economic or financial analysis, to expect junior officers of those departments to undertake economic, financial, technical, and administrative feasibility analysis of block/district/growth centre/village projects is perhaps expecting too much.

Further, as there is a tendency amongst Indians to look upwards for decisions, beliefs, etc., as is evident from the institution of the *karta* of the joint family system of some years ago, or the old tendency to look upto the zamidar/jagirdar/maharaja/company bahadur, most government servants also feel more comfortable when plans/projects are thrust down from above, than when they have to send up proposals on their own for examination at higher levels.

It may be added in an aside—that in Rajasthan the new breed of professionalized voluntary agencies are scarce and only the older variety of 'social worker' bodies inspired by the national movement exist and they do not possess the technical and professional expertise which could supplement at the local level, the planning efforts of the government planning workers. The expertise these older type voluntary agencies do possess is chiefly in the sphere of motivating and educating people, but these are more germane to implementation than to planning/projectisation.

SOPHISTICATED LOCAL-LEVEL PLANNING POSSIBLE

The above appears to paint a very gloomy picture. However, when the situation is compared to a few years ago, this observer feels that there is cause of optimism in view of the trend that is visible. As the general level of education increases, the level of education of junior local officers (as also of other persons in the local area who could possibly influence or contribute to local level planning) is also likely to increase leading to an overall improvement in their quality. Further, just as the style of functioning has changed in favour of more sophisticated analysis and projectisation/planning at the Government of India level and has started to change at the State level, similarly this is likely to spread downward to the district and intra district levels because that is how most administrative innovations have spread in India. It can also be assumed that as more and more sophisticated techniques of projectisation/planning are evolved by academicians, the academic-practising-administration-gap notwithstanding, some changes in government functioning are inevitable. Also, due to the influence of international financing agencies and the demonstration effect of foreign administrative systems which have already adopted more sophisticated techniques; as also due to communicational and technological break-through such as increased use of calculators and computers which both made data available at lower levels and its more rigorous analysis possible there; the trend in the coming decades is likely to be towards more sophisticated lower level planning. This is also likely to increase as technological changes raise the cost magnitude of investment decisions at all levels and thus necessitate more detailed investment planning.

Further, as more and more developmental activity is undertaken, the complexity of what is left to be done will increase, simpler and cheaper tasks having already been achieved earlier. This would also necessitate more detailed planning for the remaining complex problems of all regions/units of settlement.

Hence, this observer's intuitive feeling is that planning/projectising of smaller and smaller areas at lower levels is inevitable in the coming decades. Also the need for feedback from local areas and about local level implementational problems is likely to increase as such detailed planning/projectisation increases. Thus even if the local field staff itself does not do the planning, it is likely to be closely associated with it. And the most likely devise for this, as of today, is likely to be the placing of the local planner and the local implementor in the same local administrative agency. The only alternative is one mobile planning team being attached to 2-3-4 local implementing agencies which would mean almost the same in terms of the relative closeness and a stable relationship between the planner and the implementor.

The question now left is whether such an eventuality is desirable. Theoretically there can be no doubt that detailed planning for smaller and smaller units shall prove useful. The doubt is about the desirability of the planning and implementing functions being situated in the same local level agency, or being closely related. Western theories of administrative development[18] often follow the structural functional formulation that greater structural differentiation is a sign of development or modernization or rationality. The point raised earlier about the implementor trying to tone down the proposals so that he would end up with lower targets also seems to point towards the need for separation of the functions of implementing and planning in a manner similar to the arguments advocated in favour of the separation of powers theory in the field of constitutionalism.

However, if detailed local level plans are made, then keeping the two functions separate may not be possible both because the interaction between planner and implementor (where separate) is likely to be greater in local face-to-face communities and also because in very small communities reasons of economy are likely to cause the same person(s) to be made planner(s) and implementor(s). Another factor in this is the fact that planning at a given point of time has perforce to build on the results of previous implementation or the absence of it.

Only when projectising/planning has moved down to lower levels as envisaged in this paper is empirical data likely to become available which will either support or negate the structural differentiation thesis, at least in this context.

Effect of Deforestation

Deforestation increases food production in the Less Developed Countries (LDCs) wherever it leads to an increase in the arable land area. As the limits of arable land are approached, however, continued deforestation suppresses agricultural production. The negative effects include direct environmental processes, such as the situation of irrigation works, and indirect effects. As wood has become scarce in South Asia, for example, cattle dung and crop residues that once functioned to maintain soil fertility have been used for fuel. In India, Pakistan, Java, Madura, and in parts of Central America and West Africa, the negative effects of deforestation have already begun to constrain food production. It appears like that by the year 2000, the effects will be severe throughout the tropical regions. Both fuel and food shortages could result in increased LDC demands for aid, and suppression of the LDC economies may reduce markets for the products of the industrialized economies.

—The Global 2000, Report to the President,
Volume 2, Washington, 1980

REFERENCES

1. A recent example of such writing is the debate covered by: (1) Sandeep and Aruna Bagchee "The Dantwala Committee and After", *Economic and Political Weekly*, June 7, 1980, Vol. XV, No. 23, and M.L. Dantwala, "Block Level Planning Revisited", *EPW*, Vol. XV, No. 30, July 26, 1930.
2. For the third plan see: (1) D.K. Saxena, "Planning from Below in Rajasthan", *Political Science Review*, Vol. 1, No. 2, 1962, and (2)

Yoginder K. Alagh "Formulation of State Plan—Rajasthan—A Caste Study, *Economic Weekly*, 7 June, 1962. For the fourth plan see P.C. Mathur, "Multi Level Planning in Rajasthan—A Study of the Formulation of the Fourth Plan in Jaipur District", *Voluntary Action*, Vol. II. No. 4, 1966.

3. *Guidelines for the Formulation of District Plans*, Planning Commission, Delhi, September, 1969.
4. Examples of such thinking in India can be found in: (1) Lalit K. Sen (ed.) *Readings in Macro Level Planning and Rural Growth Centres*, NICD, Hyderabad, 1972, (2) Multi Level, Planning—A Special Issue of *Indian Journal of Public Administration*, Vol. XIX, No. 3, Aug-Sep. 1973, (3) Special Issue on District Planning, *Journal of LBS National Academy of Administration*, No. 1, 1975, (4) Venugopal Reddy, *Multi Level Planning in India*, Vikas, New Delhi, 1979, (5) R.P. Misra and K.V. Sunderam, *Multi Level Planning and Integrated Rural Development in India*, Heritage, Delhi, 1980. This author has trial to summarize prevailing conceptual thinking on district planning in articles in both the *Indian Journal of Public Administration* and *Journal of LBS National Academy of Administration*. Special issues mentioned above in this note. Also likely to be useful are the mimeographed documents of the UNIDS National Correspondence Seminar organized jointly by the Institute of Development Studies, University of Mysore, the Planning Commission, Delhi, and the United Nations Social Development Division.
5. For the Panchayati Raj based system of planning there prevalent see M.V. Mathur and Iqbal Narain (eds.), *Panchayati Raj Planning and Democracy*, Asia Publishing House, 1969. For the general decline of Panchayati Raj in Rajasthan, see P.C. Mathur, (1) "Performance of Panchayati Raj Institutions in Rajasthan, 1959-74—A Critical Survey", *Social Change*, Vol. VII, Nos. 3 & 4, September-Dec., 1979. (2) "Report from Rajasthan", *Seminar* No. 234, Symposium on Grassroots Democracy, February, 1979.
6. See *A Project Approach to Accelerated Agriculture Development in Rajasthan* (mimeo), Special Schemes Organization, Jaipur, January. 1978.
7. The State Government Planning Department issued its own mimeographed guidelines also.
8. *Samagra Gram Vikas—Whole Village Development—Guidelines for Identification Survey Formulation and Appraisal of Village Projects*, Special Schemes Organization, Jaipur, December, 1979.
9. S.S. Acharya, "Rural Growth Centres" (mimeo), training note circulated at the Workshop on Project Formulation (IRD/SGV/RGC) January 22-24, 1980, organized by Special Schemes Organization in Jaipur. This RGC (Rural Growth Centers) scheme is different from

Panjab's 'Focal Point' scheme because in Rajasthan an attempt is being made to scientifically identify each centre's hinterland, its resources and problems before planning and implementation are taken up for that centre.

10. *Guidelines for the Formulation of Comprehensive Block Development Plans* (mimeo), Special Schemes Organization, Jaipur, January 1980. These guidelines were developed independently of the *Guidelines for Block Level Planning*, Planning Commission, Government of India, December 1979 though both the State and national guidelines have drawn from *Report of the Working Group on Block Level Planning* (Dantawala Committee) Planning Commission, 1978. Also interesting to see for Block Planning is Prodipto Roy and B.R. Patil (ed.), *Manual for Block Level Planning*, Macmillan, 1977.
11. See, *Manual of Integrated Rural Development Programme*, Ministry of Rural Reconstruction, Government of India, January, 1980.
12. *Guidelines for Formulation of Block Level Credit Projects (Banking/Credit Plans) under Integrated Rural Development Programme*, Special Schemes Organization, Jaipur, May, 1980.
13. As a number of Government of India schemes have been mentioned in this paper interested readers may like to consult Rakesh Hooja, "Delivering Benefits to the Rural Poor—A View from Rajasthan" (mimeo), paper presented at the Government of India—UN ESCAP *Working Party on Public Service Delivery Systems for the Rural Poor*, organized at Delhi, 8-12 November 1979, which contains a list of Government programmes and of the various parts of the government delivery system which contribute to the implementation of these programmes. For details about these programmes, see *Rural Development in India—Some Facets*, NIRD, Hyderabad, 1979.
14. For the organizational chart of CAD Chambal Rajasthan Project, see Rakesh Hooja, B.N. Maheshwari and S.R. Mittal, "CAD and On Farm Development in Chambal Rajasthan Project" forthcoming in Satish Batra (ed.). *Administration in Indian State*, Associated, Delhi, 1980.
15. Some articles which give an Idea of the nature of implementation of rural development programme in India, and thus of the nature of the implementors also which can profitably be consulted are: (1) D. Aurora, "Adaptation of Administration for Rural Development with Special Reference to Poor", *Behavioural Sciences and Rural Development*, Vol. II, No. 1, January, 1979. (2) Bhupendra Hooja "Functional Approach to Pachayat Development—A Post Ashok Mehta Perspective", *Administrative Change*, Vol. VI, Nos. 1 & 2, July, 1978—June, 1979, (3) Mohit Bhattacharya, "Administrative and Organizational Issues on Rural Development", Proceedings of the *22nd Annual Conference of Members of IIPA*, IIPA, Delhi, 1979, (4) P.C. Mathur, "Administrative Realignments for Rural Development: Some

Policy Issues in the Context of India", *Indian Journal of Political Sciences*, Vol. XL, No. 1, 1979, (5) V.R. Gaekwad, "Management of Rural Development Programme: Organizational Deficiencies and Strategy for Improvements", *Indian Journal of Public Administration*, Vol. XXI, No. 4, Oct.-Dec. 1975, and (6) Rakesh Hooja, *op. cit.*, note 13.

16. Notably the Training Division of the Department of Personnel, Ministry of Home Affairs, Government of India is sponsoring a number of such courses all over the country.
17. For a description of how State Planning is currently undertaken in Rajasthan *vis-à-vis* theoretically approaches, see: (1) Kanta Ahuja (ed), *District Planning in Rajasthan* (HCM SIPA, Jaipur 1977), (2) Rakesh Hooja (*a*) "State Level Planning—The Rajasthan Case, "*Indian Journal of Public Administration*, Vol. XXII, No. 3, July-September 1976, (*b*) The District as a Planning Unit—Style and Locus, *Indian Journal of Public Administration, op. cit.*, note 4, (*c*) "District and Regional Planning—Some Aspects with Regard to India", *Journal of LBS National Academy Administration, op. cit.*, note 4, and (3) Rakesh Hooja and Harsh Sethi, "Planning for Industrial Development in Rajasthan", *Indian Journal of Public Administration*, Vol. XXI, No. 3, July-September 1974.
18. For the concept of administrative development, see Ramesh K. Arora (ed.), *Perspectives in Administrative Theory* (Associated, New Delhi, 1979) which contains the following three articles: (1) Rakesh Hooja, "Administrative Development—The Concept Re-explored", (2) Kumud Sogani, "Administrative Development—Some conceptual Premises", (3) Rakesh Hooja, "Administrative Development: The Debate Continued" all of which have drawn from Fred W. Riggs, "Administrative Development—An Elusive Concept" in John D. Montegommery and William J. Siffin (ed.), *Approaches to Development: Politics, Administration and Change*, McGraw Hill, New York, 1966.

9

Regions for Planning

V. NATH

The region is a conceptual tool for understanding the diversity in space and for organizing space for particular purposes. Every science has its regional scheme based on distribution of the phenomena in which it is interested. Thus in medical science there are regions showing distribution of cholera, malaria and other diseases. Frequently, regions are based on distribution of a group of related phenomena. Climatic regions are an example. The concept of regions based on multiple related phenomena is found to be particularly useful in sciences such as geography, economics and sociology. Geographers distinguish regions based on distribution of the physical phenomena—geological structure, topography, climate, hydrology, soils and natural vegetation—or regions based on distribution of these phenomena and human phenomena such as agricultural land-use, population density and the settlement pattern. Sociologists and cultural anthropologists distinguish cultural regions based on distribution of various cultural phenomena. All such regions are demarcated on the basis of internal homogeneity and external contrast; the areas included within them have certain common characteristics which set them off from areas outside. The economists also distinguish regions on the basis of homogeneity in economic characteristics. Industrial regions are an example. But the concept of economic regions based on the principle of inter-relationship is also used in economics. An economic area has been defined by Losch as the market area of a commodity, and an economic region as a system of such market areas.[1] Such an economic region may include areas with widely divergent economic characteristics. Typically, it will include an industrial producing centre and a consumption area which may be largely rural. The two are considered as forming part of an economic region because of their relationship.

Both these principles, homogeneity and inter-relationship, have their utility in demarcating regions for planning.

PLANNING REGIONS

Planning regions have to serve as the spatial units for formulation and implementation of development plans. They must, therefore, be demarcated, keeping in view the objectives of planned development and the nature of the principal development programmes. Secondly, since institutional and administrative arrangements for plan formulation and execution will have to be made with these regions as the units, they must be related to the existing politico-administrative structure of the country, its territorial divisions. Since most planning is done by Government (or by agencies established by Government), it is most convenient to adopt the territorial divisions or administrative regions as the planning regions. Planning and development agencies can be established for these regions simply by expanding the existing departments or adding new ones. Secondly, arrangements for association of the people's representatives with the planning process can also be made most conveniently with them as units, because legislatures, local bodies and other democratic institutions are already established for them. Other planning regions have undoubtedly to be adopted for particular purposes. But the need for them must be clearly established, because their acceptance involves supplementing or replacing the administrative regions.

Planning in India is the concurrent responsibility of the Central and the State Governments. It is being done with the States (and Union Territories) as the primary units. Below the State level the principal units of administration and planning are the district, the block and the village. Administrative and institutional arrangements exist at these units for formulation and execution of plans, and for association of popular leaders with planning. These administrative regions are in fact the principal planning regions of the country. However, they are not adequate for all planning purposes and have to be supplemented by other regions for some purposes of planning, and may even have to be replaced for other purposes. Thus, for development of water resources it is convenient to adopt a river valley or a river system as the region; in metropolitan planning it is necessary to plan with the metropolitan area of the city as the unit. Similarly, for planning of transport or development of power resources, regions may have to be specially delineated keeping in view the particular requirements of the planning task. Secondly, even when administrative units are adopted as the planning regions, it is useful for the planners to be aware of similarities, contrast or economic relationships between areas situated in different administrative units. Thus, the Himalayan areas of U.P., Punjab, Himachal Pradesh and Jammu and Kashmir have certain common physical features of topography, climate and soils and common patterns of resource use and economic activity. In all these hilly areas arable land is limited, specialized forms of agriculture (*e.g.*, horticulture), and grazing and exploitation of forest resources are important economic activities. Population is sparse, water supply and communications are difficult problems, and their is urgent need for programmes of conservation of soil and water. These common features, problems and needs have to be kept in view and arrangements for cooperation in plan formulation or implementation have to be devised between the States and Union Territories concerned. A regional scheme which expresses the common links between these areas is, therefore, useful for planners.

The planning tasks in India can be divided into the following four categories:

(*i*) agricultural and related development programmes—land reclamation, soil conservation, irrigation, animal husbandry, forestry and fisheries;
(*ii*) development of industries, power, transport and communications;
(*iii*) development of social services—education, medical care, social welfare etc; and
(*iv*) urban development.

The classification follows broadly the sectoral classification in the Five Year Plans. Urban development has been added. It is not a separate sector of development but it has been listed here because urbanization affects the economy in such a variety of ways and urban development is a task of such importance that it was felt that it should be listed separately in order to focus attention on it.

In agricultural and related development programmes, primary emphasis is on scientific and more intensive exploitation of the resources of land and water. This has to be done by changing present production techniques and by undertaking various resource development programmes. Since regional variations in the methods of resource use and the resource development economy—patterns of agricultural land use and cropping, development of livestock husbandry, forestry or fishing—are related primarily to the physical factors, regional schemes based on analysis of the physical factors and associated human factors of agricultural land use and rural settlement, furnish the basic mosaic for planning the development programmes. Such schemes bring out the contrasts within the country and within individual States which are most significant for planning purposes. Further, they bring out for each region (and its smaller divisions) the basic physical and human factors, and the potential and limitations of the physical environment. The scheme of "Regions for Resource Planning" developed by the Regional Planning Unit of the Indian Statistical Institute[2] and the scheme of Resource Development Regions and Divisions recently published by the Planning Commission[3] are both schemes of this type. The latter is described in Part II.

Such schemes are useful also for planning of social service programmes, especially in the rural areas, because planning of these programmes has to be related primarily to the rural settlement pattern. They are useful to a limited extent for planning of industrial, power, transport and associated development programmes. They furnish the basic facts on location of mineral and power resources, and agricultural raw-materials, and of distribution of population which have to be taken into account in planning of these programmes. Thus, the scheme of Resource Development Regions and Divisions published by the Planning Commission distinguishes the Eastern Plateaux and Hills Region. This region, consisting of the plateau areas of Bihar, Orissa, West Bengal, Eastern Madhya Pradesh and two districts of the Maharashtra, has been demarcated primarily on the basis of geological and topographic factors. But by distinguishing it the highly mineralized areas which contain most of the coal, iron ore, manganese and other mineral resources of the country, have been separated from the adjoining areas of the Genetic Plain or of the Deccan which are poor in minerals. Visualizing this mineral-rich area as one region is very useful in planning of industrial, power and transport programmes. However, it appears that regional schemes based on the principle of homogeneity are not adequate for planning of such programmes and that schemes based on the principle of inter-relationship have to be used. The latter are useful because they indicate how regions are related with one another and with the national economy and the potential or limitations for development which these relationships hold. Thus for any region the scheme of Resource Development Regions and Divisions would indicate only its agricultural, mineral, forest and other resources, but it would not indicate the potential or limitations for development which its location with reference to other regions creates. Consider the South Bihar Plain area (consisting of the districts of Shahabad, Patna, Gaya, Monghyr and Bhagalpur) as an example. It has a very large population in relation to its agricultural land, has few mineral resources and would appear to have a limited potential for industrial and urban development. But its location next to the coal and steel centres of Bihar and West Bengal and the principal transport routes of Northern India hold for it enormous possibilities of industrial and urban growth.

As an illustration of schemes based on the principle of inter-relationship, a scheme of metropolitan regions has been described in Part II. The scheme distinguishes four metropolitan regions, which are the hinterlands respectively of the metropolitan cities of Calcutta, Madras, Bombay and Delhi. The scheme is based on the concept of central places;[4] each metropolitan city is regarded as an apex central place, which is linked through a system of secondary and lower order central places to every part of its hinterland;

Accordingly, we consider in Part II three sets of regions:

(*i*) Administrative Regions,
(*ii*) Resource Development Regions, and
(*iii*) Metropolitan Regions.

ADMINISTRATIVE REGIONS

States (and Union Territories), districts, blocks, and villages constitute the different units in the structure of administrative regions. The planning process in India provides for formulation of plans with them as units and inter-relation of plans of different units. The plan of each State is drawn up within the framework of the goals, investment magnitudes and physical achievement targets of the national plan: but it reflects in its details—the financial and physical magnitudes of different sectors and the particular projects included in it—the development potential of the State and the needs and aspirations of its people. The plans of districts are related similarly to the plan of the State, and of smaller units to the plan of the district. Such inter-relationship between plans of different units is an essential aspect of the national planning process. It enables plans to reflect national goals and objectives on the one hand and local needs and aspirations on the other. Institutional arrangements have been established at various area levels for participation of the people's representatives in the planning process. The national and State legislators frame the policies for planning; the local leaders participate in detailed planning and implementation of programmes for their areas. The responsibilities of the local leaders in planning have increased, and much greater attention has begun to be given to local planning after the establishment of the Panchayati Raj Institutions. The district plan particularly is being given increasing attention, because it is felt that the area of the district is sufficiently large for formulation of an integrated development plan and officials and non-officials of sufficient calibre and experience are available for preparation of the plan. If the present trends continue the district will in time emerge as a distinct unit of planning in addition to the national and the State.

The administrative regions have some characteristics which enhance their claims to being accepted as planning regions. Most States of the Indian Union are quite large in size so that adequate planning organizations can be built up for them. Secondly, the areas of most States are co-terminus with the linguistic regions of the country and their people have a certain sense of linguistic-cultural unity. The importance of linguistic regions as basic planning regions can scarcely be over-emphasized in a large, multilingual country. The districts similarly are of sufficient size to be adopted as primary units of local planning. The population of most districts ranges between one and two million and their area ranges between two and five thousand square miles. Secondly, since the boundaries of most districts follow natural features such as rivers or hill ranges and have remained unchanged for long periods, and the district headquarters town is the principal administrative, commercial and educational centre of the area, there is among their people a well-developed feeling of "belonging to the district." There are of course districts which are quite unsuitable for local planning because they are too large or too small or contain areas of sharply contrasted physical and economic characteristics.[5] But the number of such districts is small.

Among the administrative units below the district level, the community development block is the most important for purposes of planning because the institutional and administrative structure of planning and development—the Panchayat Samiti and the community development organization—have been built up round it. A typical block consists of about 100 villages with a population of 50,000 to 100,000 but there are variations in different areas. Below the block level, the traditional unit of rural community life, the village, has also a certain importance in planning. The aspirations and needs of the rural people are articulated first through the village Panchayat and agricultural and rural development programmes must be formulated in the first instance with the village as the unit.

Supplement to Administrative Regions

(*i*) *Special Areas*: This structure of administrative regions is used mainly for planning of agricultural and related development programmes, social service programmes and others which are the responsibility of the State Governments. It is useful for planning of these programmes because it enables planners to relate programmes for successively smaller areas to local conditions and the needs and aspirations of the local people. But it has to be supplemented in various ways in order to meet planning needs for which it is found to be inadequate. One set of supplements consists of areas of special problems or promise for which special development programmes have to be undertaken and special administrative or institutional arrangements have to be established. Metropolitan areas of cities, industrial complexes, areas of river valley projects or other resource development projects, and backward areas are the most important among such special areas. In each case the boundaries have to be demarcated keeping in view the particular objects of planning and development. They have to be defined precisely in some cases but not in others. The boundaries of "metropolitan areas" have to be defined with precision because they have to be given the force of law. Control over urban land use which is an essential element in metropolitan planning cannot be enforced without legal sanctions. The boundaries of areas of irrigation and other resource development projects may also have to be defined precisely, because the areas which will receive irrigation or other benefits and those which will not receive such benefits have to be clearly distinguished. On the other hand, boundaries of backward areas need not be defined so precisely. The boundaries of special areas may change relatively quickly. The metropolitan area of a city may have to be enlarged from time to time as the city expands. The areas of irrigation projects may also be enlarged as the scope of the projects is enlarged. On the other hand, backward areas may be reduced progressively in size as backwardness is liquidated.

(*ii*) ***Zones, Macro-regions and Commissioners' Divisions***: Another set of supplements to administrative regions consists of groups of States and Districts and are useful for planning at Inter-State and Inter-District Levels. Inter-State action is required for water resource development, power generation and distribution, and various other development programmes. There is considerable experience of Inter-State co-operation for water resource development in India; the river valley projects undertaken during the last 15 years are outstanding recent examples of such co-operation. But as each case requires agreement among the States concerned, adequate institutional arrangements are essential for securing Inter-State co-operation. The need for Inter-State action in power generation and distribution has also begun to be recognised increasingly. The power systems of most adjoining States are already inter-linked. Formation of regional power grids has been under consideration for some time: the grids are visualised as the first step in the establishment (eventually) of a national power grid.

Since the re-organization of the States in 1956, an institutional arrangement for inter-State action has existed in the Zonal Councils. These Councils have been constituted for the five Zones—Northern, Central, Eastern, Southern and Western—into which the country is divided. Each Zone consists of two or more States and adjoining Union Territories. The agency of the Zonal Councils could be used for planning and co-ordinated execution of programmes of development of Inter-State interest more effectively than has been done so far.

Zones also provide a useful conceptual framework for macro-regional divisions of the country: most macro-regional divisions are variations on the Zonal scheme.[6] Macro-regions are useful for planning of various activities of the Central Government and for regional economic and social analysis. They can be very useful in planning flows of basic commodities—coal, iron and steel, cement, petroleum products, chemical fertilizers, foodgrains and agricultural raw materials—and deciding locations of industrial units keeping the flow patterns in view. This concept has been best developed in U.S.S.R., which has been divided into a number of "major economic regions" each based on one or more major industrial complexes. However, the related Soviet concept of self-sufficiency at major economic region level, very attractive in a country with long distances, sparse population and relatively under-developed transport, has distinct limitations in India. As the bulk of the coal and iron ore deposits of India are located in Eastern India, this region must remain the premier iron and steel producing region of the country and large flows of coal, steel and heavy engineering goods from the region to other parts of the country must remain an essential features of the Indian economy. Ignoring these facts and attempting to achieve self-sufficiency at macro-regional level cold lead to a distorted and wasteful pattern of resource development. Macro-regional schemes are useful for regional economic and social analysis because they make possible presentation of data on regional differences within a large country in terms of a limited number of units. In U.S.A., the Census Divisions are used extensively for this purpose, and the practice of using macro-regions is growing in India. The National Sample Survey, the Energy Survey and various studies of the National Council of Applied Economic Research present data on regional differences within India primarily by macro-regions.

In most of the larger States of India there has existed for a long time an intermediate unit between the State and the Districts—the Commissioner's Division. These Divisions, consisting of 5 or 6 districts were formed for co-ordination of work in the districts; but many of them express also the most significant differences in physical and economic conditions within the State. In any case, these Divisions furnish as the Zones do at the macro-regional level, the starting point for dividing large States into a limited number of relatively homogeneous units. Distinguishing such units is useful in planning for a large State because it provides to the State and the local planners a frame of reference to comprehending the diversity within the State and for modifying the development programmes accordingly. Such modification is particularly necessary in agricultural and related programmes which have to be adapted to the physical conditions and agricultural and settlement patterns of each area.

With these two sets of supplements, the structure of administrative regions consists of: nation, macro-region or zone, state, division, district, block and village, and the special areas. The latter cannot be integrated into the administrative structure, because their boundaries would frequently cut across the boundaries of States and districts. But since planning arrangements for them can be made without serious disturbance to the administrative structure, they can also be considered along with the administrative regions.

RESOURCE DEVELOPMENT REGIONS

The scheme of Resource Development Regions and Divisions of India published by the Planning Commission is based on analysis of data of topography, geological formations, soils, rainfall, agricultural land use, cropping pattern, population density and occurrence of mineral resources. The data have been analysed for each district of the country. The district has been adopted as the minimum unit for classification partly because the data for most of these variables were not available for smaller units and partly in order to make the scheme more useful for planning. It is considered that "the district is of such overwhelming importance as a unit for execution of most development programmes that a classification in which districts are not divided has a certain in usefulness which is lost as soon as districts are divided."[7]

The scheme recognizes five primary or major natural regions of the country: the Himalayas, the Northern Plain, the Peninsular Plateaux and Hills, the East Coast Plain, and the West Coast Plain. Each of these is divided into one or more regions to make a total of 14 regions on the mainland of India. The fifteenth region is formed by the Islands in the Bay of Bengal and the Arabian Sea. The regions are divided further into sub-regions, divisions and sub-divisions. But the important units below the regions are the divisions; sub-regions and sub-divisions are units of secondary importance and have been distinguished in a very few cases. Only one region, the Eastern Himalayan, has been divided into sub-regions and only five divisions have been divided into sub-divisions. The scheme distinguishes 61 divisions, each of which is located entirely within the territory of a State. The divisions are formed by inter-section of boundaries of the regions and the States or by further division of the area of a region located within a State. Each division is a unit, homogeneous in physical and socio-economic characteristics, and located entirely within the territory of one State which can be adopted as a planning unit by the State Government. The objects of the scheme are:

"(*i*) to provide a framework for understanding the variety of physical conditions and resource development potentials in different parts of the country to those concerned with planning at the Centre and in the States, so that these differences are given due consideration in planning of programmes, and adjustments in programme content and pattern are made to meet these, wherever necessary; and

(*ii*) to furnish to those concerned with planning at the State level, a scheme of division of their States into internally

> homogeneous units, each of which can be used as a unit for planning of most of the programmes included in State Plans."[8]

The reference to State planning will be readily understood because agricultural and related development programmes for which the scheme is particularly useful are the responsibility primarily of the State Government. Since the resource development division consists of a group of districts, it can be easily integrated into the structure of State planning. It can serve as an intermediate unit between the State and the districts and is in fact a better unit than the Commissioner's because it is demarcated scientifically. Its principal usefulness is in relating development programmes more closely to the different physical and socio-economic conditions of different parts of a State. *Such relation is particularly important in large States such as U.P., Maharashtra, and Madhya Pradesh within which there is such diversity of physical and socio-economic conditions.* The content of the plan of each sector can be decided first at the resource development division level and district plans can then be made within the framework of these decisions. The scheme also enables planners to keep in view the similarities between areas located in adjacent States. The example of the Eastern Plateaux and Hills Region and of the Himalayan Region of U.P., Punjab, Himachal Pradesh and Jammu and Kashmir, given above, illustrate this point.

METROPOLITAN REGIONS

In this scheme the country is divided into four metropolitan regions—the hinterlands respectively of the metropolitan cities of Kolkata, Mumbai, Chinnai and Delhi. Each hinterland is a macro-region consisting of two or more States together with Union Territories or parts of States. It can be divided further into sub-regions, divisions and smaller units going down to the service area of the small town (or large village) with population between 5,000 and 10,000 which performs various commercial and other service functions for a group of villages. Towns of different sizes located in a metropolitan region are considered to be central places of different orders; the metropolitan city is considered to be the apex central place of the region.

The areas included within a metropolitan region are dissimilar in physical features, land use and cropping pattern, population density and various other characteristics. The metropolitan region of Delhi includes the Himalayan areas of Jammu and Kashmir and Himachal Pradesh, the Punjab plain as well as the desert of Western Rajasthan. The region of Calcutta includes areas as dissimilar as NEFA and North Bihar. But all parts of a metropolitan region are bound together by the bonds of functional relations with the metropolitan city. The relations are primarily commercial—distribution of goods is the principal element in them,—but they are also cultural and administrative. Three of the metropolitan cities are ports but the fourth, Delhi, is an inland city. The external trade functions which the port cities perform for their metropolitan regions are shared in case of the Delhi region between Calcutta and Bombay. But the concept of the metropolitan region does not involve as a necessary condition that the metropolitan city be a part or that it be the only port in the region. It only involves that the metropolitan city be so important as a commercial, administrative and social service centre that it can be recognized as the apex centre of the region. Each of the four cities has this position in its metropolitan region. The cities are connected with every part of the hinterland through a succession of smaller towns—sub-regional centres, district towns, mandi centres, etc. These are Central places of different orders, each of which is connected upwards with higher order Central places and downwards with lower order places; it is also connected with its own particular hinterland (service area) for the specific services that it performs for it. In this way, a whole system of functional relationships—economic, socio-cultural, administrative—focusses eventually on the sub-regional and the metropolitan cities, and the influences emanating from these cities travel to every part of the hinterland.

Formulating such a scheme of metropolitan regions has many limitations at present. First, because of virtual lack of data on economic relationships between the metropolitan cities and their hinterlands, the regions cannot be demarcated precisely. Studies on demarcation of the hinterland have been carried out most extensively for Kolkata[9] and the boundaries of the Kolkata region can be drawn somewhat more precisely than those of the other regions. The regional transport surveys now being conducted under the auspices of the Planning Commission are expected to make available considerable data which will make possible more precise demarcation of the other three hinterlands. Similarly, studies on the economic relationships between cities and towns of different sizes within a metropolitan region and between them and their service areas, needed for dividing the metropolitan regions into sub-regions, divisions and smaller units, are virtually lacking. In Appendix I, central places of six classes have been listed, which implies that it should be possible to have a size hierarchy of six units, going down from the metropolitan region to the service area of the very small town or large village which functions as rural service centre. But this classification is only illustrative and will need to be verified by studies in the different metropolitan regions. It is most likely that central places of all the six categories are not fully developed in every region. However, the hierarchical order provides the framework for seeing the cities and towns of different sizes as linked parts of a spatial system.

As important as the paucity of data is the fact that the city-region relationship is not as well-developed in India as it is in industrially advanced countries. Since the bulk of the population is rural, depends upon subsistence agriculture and has limited extra-village economic relationships, the influence of the metropolitan city, or of any urban area for that matter, is quite weak. But this influence is increasing as means of communication improve and modern social services and consumer goods are used by the rural people to an increasing extent. One visible result of this increase, is use by large commercial firms of the four metropolitan cities as focal points for distribution of products within the regions. Various agencies of government, and such institutions as the Life Insurance Corporation are also using these cities as regional headquarters for their activities. The smaller cities are similarly beginning to be used increasingly as focal points for distribution of products or radiation of various activities, within their respective influence areas.

The metropolitan regions may be roughly indicated as follows:

1. The Kolkata Metropolitan Region—Assam, Nagaland and the Union Territories in Northeast India; West Bengal, Bihar, Eastern U.P., and Eastern Madhya Pradesh, except the extreme Southern portion.

2. The Madras Metropolitan Region—Madras, Kerala, most of Mysore and most of Andhra Pradesh.
3. The Bombay Metropolitan Region—Maharashtra, Gujarat, Southern Madhya Pradesh.
4. The Delhi Metropolitan Region—Punjab, Jammu and Kashmir, Himachal Pradesh, most of Rajasthan, Western U.P. and Northern Madhya Pradesh.

Transition Zones or Corridors

It is useful to distinguish transition zones or corridors between the metropolitan region. These are areas in which the influence of two metropolitan cities overlaps. *i.e.*, the advantages of obtaining services from the two cities are nearly competitive and the local people have a choice of obtaining services from one or the other city. The choices are exercised in favour of different cities at different times or for different commodities. Central U.P. is such a transitional zone between the metropolitan regions of Delhi and Kolkata. The transition zones are roughly indicated below, they can also be indicated more precisely when more detailed data become available.

1. Between the Kolkata and the Chennai Regions—extreme South Eastern Madhya Pradesh and Northeastern Andhra Pradesh (the hinterland of Visakhapatnam).
2. Between the Chennai and the Mumbai Regions—the Northern fringe of Mysore.
3. Between the Mumbai and the Delhi Regions—Southern Rajasthan and Central Madhya Pradesh.
4. Between the Delhi and the Kolkata Regions—Central U.P.

The transition zones will be seen on an all-India map as arc-shaped belts of varying widths. Their northern apex is in Central U.P. in the vicinity of Allahabad. From this point they go southwards dividing in Central Madhya Pradesh into three arcs going North-West, South-West and South-East respectively.

The metropolitan regions are units of the same size order as the macro-regions. In some cases, they are yery close to the zones or other commonly used macro-regions. The Chennai Metropolitan

Region is co-terminous with the South India Region of many macro-regional schemes. The Mumbai Metropolitan Region differs only slightly from the Western India Region of macro-regional schemes—it includes Southern Madhya Pradesh. The metropolitan regions based as they are on the economic fact of exchange of goods and services are even more useful than the macro-regions for planning, production and distribution of basic commodities. They are useful also for planning of power, transport and similar programmes. In fact, they appear to be the most useful macro-units for working out the regional implications of the long-term perspective of development. The national projections of population, its distribution between urban and rural areas and among various economic activities, of supply and demand of basic commodities and of requirements of power and transport can most conveniently be broken down in terms of the metropolitan regions. Programmes for attaining the targets of development can then be formulated with each metropolitan region as the unit. It appears also that Inter-State relationships for purposes of resource development are also visualized most fruitfully in terms of metropolitan regions.

But the metropolitan regions have their greatest utility in urban planning which will have to move in the not distant future from planning for cities to planning of entire hinterlands as units. The need for adopting in case of the large cities, a sufficiently large "metropolitan area" as the unit of detailed land use planning, and a still larger "peripheral region" as the unit of less detailed, directional planning has, already been recognized. The "metropolitan area" concept, first used in the Delhi Plan, is now being used in the plans of all major cities of India. The Delhi Plan also visualized planning for its peripheral region which is now being called the National Capital Region. This is an area of about 400 square miles located in U.P. and Punjab. In case of Calcutta, the CMPO has demarcated outside the Calcutta metropolitan district a Southern Plain Region, as the unit for less detailed, directional planning. The Maharashtra planners are already thinking in terms of planning with the Bombay-Poona Region as the Unit. In Gujarat, the entire strip between Ahmedabad and Surat, which is experiencing rapid urban-industrial growth, may be adopted as a planning unit. The process has to be carried further and entire hinterlands of metropolitan cities have to be viewed as planning regions. For each such region, the likely growth of the urban population can be forecast within the national perspective of economic development. This total can then be distributed in towns of different sizes located in different parts of the region. The location and size of some towns will, no doubt, be determined by such factors as distribution of natural resources and topographic conditions. Thus, the steel and heavy engineering centres of the Kolkata metropolitan region will be located mainly near the coal fields or iron ore deposits. But location and size of most of the towns in a metropolitan region can be planned in accordance with accepted policies of dispersal of economic activity and balanced regional development. Growth of local, district and multi-district centres can be planned in the perspective of the expected growth in the economy of their service areas. In fact, each such town can be built up as a focal point of modernization of agriculture and of the rural economy, which provides a constellation of services, ranging from distribution of supplies required for modern agriculture (chemical fertilizers, steel, petroleum products, power-driven implements) to facilities of modern education, medical care and recreation. The relations between these towns and their service areas can be improved through improvement of means of transport and communications. The more suitable among them can be developed as local growth points by establishment of various agro-industries and other industries. Some towns can be planned deliberately as growth points to stimulate the economy of stagnant regions or to serve as counter-magnets which will relieve the pressure on large cities. As one city or area approaches saturation point, growth can be transferred to other cities or areas within the metropolitan region.

Urban planning of this kind, with metropolitan hinterlands as units, is an essential counterpart of perspective economic planning. The metropolitan regions furnish the most useful conceptual framework for such planning, because the different cities and towns within each region can be viewed as inter-linked and mutually inter-acting parts of a spatial system.

REFERENCES

1. August Losch, *The Nature of Economic Regions,* and J. Friedmann, and W. Alonso: *Regional Development and*

Planning: A Reader, Cambridge, The M.I.T. Press, Mass, 1964, p. 115.

2. Unpublished.
3. Government of India, *Resource Development Regions and Divisions of India*, New Delhi, Planning Commission, 1964.
4. For a discussion of the hierarchical order of central places, see W. Isard, *Methods of Regional Analysis*, Cambridge, M.I.T. Press, 1960, pp. 222-27.
5. Some districts of Bihar and Chennai with population of three to four million are recognized as being too large for efficient local planning. The Chennai districts have been bifurcated for purposes of planning, and a similar bifurcation of the Bihar districts will be useful. On the other hand many of the districts of Rajasthan, Madhya Pradesh and Himachal Pradesh are very small.
6. One such scheme is that used by the Energy Survey Committee (Government of India: Report of the Energy Survey of India Committee, New Delhi, 1965, p. 85) which divides the country into the following six energy regions:
   (*i*) Northern: Punjab, Himachal Pradesh, Delhi, Rajasthan and Jammu and Kashmir.
   (*ii*) Central: U.P. and Madhya Pradesh.
   (*iii*) Eastern: Bihar, West Bengal and Orissa.
   (*iv*) Assam: Assam, Tripura and Manipur.
   (*v*) Southern: Andhra Pradesh, Mysore, Chennai and Kerala.
   (*vi*) Western: Maharashtra and Gujarat.

The only unsatisfactory feature of the scheme is inclusion of U.P. and Madhya Pradesh in one region. There are marked physical and socio-economic differences between the two States which are marked by their inclusion in one region. Each State is large enough to constitute a region by itself.

7. Planning Commission, *Resource Development Regions and Division of India, op. cit.*, p. 3.
8. Planning Commission, *Resource Development Regions and Division of India, op. cit.*, p. 2.
9. See for instance, Lastie Grean: *The Economic Hinterland of Calcutta*, to be published by Asia Publishing House, Mumbai.

Appendix I

HIERARCHY OF CENTRAL PLACES IN A METROPOLITAN REGION

1. Metropolitan city
2. Sub-regional centre—the principal town and service centre of the sub-region.
3. Multi-district centre—principal town and service centre of a group of districts. Some of these towns are also headquarters of Commissioners' Divisions.
4. District centre—the principal town and service centre for the whole or a major part of the district. Most of these towns are also district headquarters.
5. Mandi centre—town with an established permanent market (not weakly *hat*) serving an area approximating a community development block or a taluk. It may also be the headquarters of the block or taluk.
6. Rural service centre—small town or large village functioning as a service centre for a group of villages.

10

Area Development: Planning at District and Block Levels

V. NATH

CONCEPTS

A basic concept in area development, as in all regional development, is that the plans for the area are conditioned by its physical conditions, natural resources and social and economic situation. These indicate the development potential, the needs and the problems of the area: the development plan must develop the potential, meet the needs and solve the problems. Accordingly, systematic assessment of resources, needs and problems is the first step in the planning process. The assessment is done by compilation and analysis of existing information, supplemented by fresh surveys, to the extent necessary. The needs are articulated most effectively by the representatives of the people—members of Panchayati Raj Institutions, municipalities and legislatures.

Area Development and the National Plan

Area development is part of the national planning process. The plans for an area are conditioned by the general framework of the national plan, its policies and programmes, and its resource constraints. These prescribe the framework for "area planning", its overall goals as well as its limitations. The area plan is related also to the plans for larger spatial units of which the area forms part and of the smaller spatial units into which it is divided. The plan for a district has to be related on the one hand to the plans of the state and the regional division in which it is located, and on the other to plans of the blocks (and other smaller units) which are included within it. This linkage, upwards and downwards, is an essential part of planning for an area.

The development plans for districts and blocks, which came under the influence of an expanding metropolis or of large industrial or resource development projects, must reflect adequately the influence of these major developments. Providing in the local plans adequate complementary inputs, which would enable the local area to obtain full benefits from the resource development project or to withstand the disturbing influence of metropolitan development (unduly large areas in the peripheral regions of cities often get diverted to non-agricultural uses) is one method of reflecting this influence.

Two Approaches to Local Area Planning: "Area Development" and "Programmes"

Here it would be useful to distinguish between the "area development" approach and what may be called "programmes": approach to planning. The latter implies that certain development activities decided at the sate or national level are carried out more or less uniformly throughout the area of the state or the country. The plan for a local area, built up entirely through this approach is an aggregation of such activities—primary and secondary schools, health centres, roads, water supply schemes, etc. The two approaches—"area development" and "programmes"—are not contradictory or mutually exclusive: they are, to an extent, complementary. The "area development" plan has to be formulated within the framework of the objectives and priorities of the national plan, and will have a large component of the national or state programmes mentioned above. On the other hand, even when the "programmes" approach is followed, decision-making in relation to particular programmes in an area has to be related to its local conditions and needs. Thus, the number of primary schools to be opened in an area and the specific location of the schools, can be decided only on consideration of local factors. The influence of local factors is much greater in planning of more advanced or specialized services and resource development activities. Elementary service facilities such as primary schools, can be created more or less uniformly in all areas; but the same cannot be done in case of advanced service facilities such as secondary schools, colleges or polytechnics. Location of the latter has to be decided on careful consideration of various local factors, because faulty locational decisions will lead to inefficient service to the people and waste of resources. Resource development activities require even greater attention to local factors.

But the "area development" and the "programmes" approach are two different approaches to planning, and emphasis on one or the other leads often to different planning decisions. The "programmes" approach flows from constitution of departments at state or national level for particular development programmes—Education, Health, Agriculture. Exclusive reliance on it often results in inadequate consideration of local needs and problems, because of the inherent tendency of departments to decide the pattern of a programme at headquarters and to follow it in all areas. The result often is that attention is given to less necessary activities in preference to those needed more urgently in the local area; sometimes, unnecessary facilities are created. On the other hand, undue concern with area development would lead to inadequate attention being given to national (and state) objectives and priorities. One could generalize, perhaps, to say that the "programmes" approach is more suitable in planning of social services—especially elementary services such as primary schools, health centres and approach roads. These are needed everywhere and can be planned at the state (or even national) level on basis of criteria and patterns which can be defined with precision, *e.g.*, one primary school for 100 boys of school going age; a metalled road within one or two miles of every village. The "area development" approach on the other hand has distinct advantages in planning of resource development programmes. It is also frequently more suitable than the "programmes" approach in planning of more advanced services.

Area development includes both resource development and human development. Expansion of social services, building up the infrastructure of development and institutional reform are the principal instruments of the latter. The relative emphasis on resource development and human development activities in an area, at any point of time, is indicated by its stage of development—status of exploitation of resources and the potential for further development, status of development of social services, etc. However, it is well to point out that development of social services and the infrastructure is an essential pre-requisite of resource development, and until these are developed sufficiently, the progress of resource development activities will also remain slow. Thus, a large programme of resource development—mining of coal and iron ore, setting up power stations, steel plants and other industries—appears to be the obvious priority in the resource rich area called the Coal Steel Belt of Eastern India. But the area is backward. It is hilly and forested, has poor communications and few towns and has a large proportion of tribal people. This backwardness of the area hampers resource development activities in various ways. Development of social services and the infra- structure—improvement of communications, opening of schools, hospitals, training centres for craftsman, modernization of the towns—will not only accelerate progress of resource development activities, but will also enable the local people to participate in these activities more actively and to benefit from them. They will be able to obtain employment in new industries and attain higher levels of income and consumption. Similarly, institutional reforms and changes in social attitudes, *e.g.*, in the attitude relating to work, are pre-requisites for development of certain areas. The backwardness of areas like Eastern U.P. is attributed in part to the tradition of *Zamindari* and prevalence of growth-inhibitive attitudes (*e.g.*, people of high castes should not touch the plough).

Integrated Development

Integration of different development activities undertaken within an area is a fundamental concept in area development. It has been accepted in case of rural development programmes for a long time and was reiterated and reinforced when a unified agency for rural development was created in the Community Development

Organization. The structure of the C.D. Organization with a team of subject-matter specialists working under a Block Development Officer, emphasized co-ordination between developments in different fields—agriculture, animal husbandry, minor irrigation, soil conservation, co-operative social education, etc. Constitution of Block and District Development Committees and designating the Collector as the leader of the team of development officers further emphasized coordinated development and creation of Panchayati Raj Institutions has given it a statutory institutional framework.

A primary requisite in co-ordinated development is securing appropriate relationships in magnitude, space and time between different development activities. Thus, the quantum of operative credit and supplies of chemical fertilizers, improved, seeds, etc., in a C.D. Block should be related closely to the agricultural extension efforts of the block staff. In other words, if use of chemical fertilizers is being advocated by the staff and is being encouraged by making available supplies on credit given through the co-operatives, it should be ensured that the supplies and credit match the demand created by the efforts of the extension staff. Acceptance of this basic principle underlies the practice of formulating family production plans in the Package Programme districts, and regulating supplies and credit in accordance with these plans.

A second aspect of integrated development concerns the relationships between major resource development projects and local development activities. This relationship may be explained by the examples of power generation and irrigation projects. The villages located near a power project can derive benefit from it only if a programme of rural electrification accompanies the project. Power taken to the villages will, in the present stage of our rural economy, be used for irrigation, cottage and small scale industries, etc., only if adequate loans are given to farmers, artisans or small industrialists for installation of electric motors and purchase of power driven machines. Therefore, in order to carry the benefits of the power project to the villages it is necessary to secure appropriate relationships between programmes of power generation, rural electrification and financial assistance. Similarly, the waters of an irrigation project can be effectively utilized by farmers only if suitable technical assistance is given to them for changing their cropping pattern, from dry drops to irrigated crops, and financial assistance is given for measures like levelling, reclamation and preparation of land. Such assistance should be adequate in *magnitude* and should be available at the appropriate *time* and *place*.

In cases where the interrelationship between the large projects and complementary local development has been appreciated and the latter have been provided adequately, the result has been rapid resource development and appreciable rise in economic and social levels of the people (*e.g.*, the Bhakra Canal area of the Punjab). But where this relationship has not been appreciated, and complementary inputs have either not been provided or have been provided inadequately or late, the potential created by the resource development projects has been utilized very slowly or inadequately. This experience emphasizes the need for working out in detail the complementary inputs in case of each major project and ensuring that these are provided adequately, in time and at the right place. In case of irrigation and power projects, sufficient experience has been gained in recent years for working out *norms* of investment on the projects and complementary local development inputs. These norms should be worked out for a few selected projects and should be available for guidance for new projects.

The major industrial and other resource development projects have been called "nuclei of development" in the Third Plan.[1] This concept of the nucleus emphasizes the potential of these projects for attracting various development to their areas, and initiating a process of area development. Appendix I lists the developmental inputs related to a major irrigation project and a steel plant. These have been divided into three major groups:

(*i*) associated,
(*ii*) complementary, and
(*iii*) derived.

The associated inputs are essential for the functioning of the project itself. The relation between them and the project is so direct and clear that they are generally provided as part of the project itself. But the complementary and the derived inputs, which are not so directly related, deserve more attention for area development, because it is the adequacy of these inputs and the speed with which they are created in the area, that determines the pace of its development. The complementary inputs are necessary for realization of the development potential of the project. The derived inputs have a similar role, but they have been classified separately, because they "derive" from or follow the functioning of the project.

Primary Growth Factors

The major projects could also be called primary growth factors, *i.e.*, primary development activities to which secondary and tertiary activities are attracted. The term could also be used for certain negative factors, presence of which retards development of an area. Prevalence of malaria, bad communications and lower literacy are examples of negative growth factors. These too have to be regarded as "primary", because their removal needs first attention in any scheme of development of an area. The importance of removing them is often under-estimated. Thus, demands for development of backward areas usually take the form of demands for locating large projects in them. It is not sufficiently appreciated that removal of the negative factors is equally important, though less spectacular. Indeed, as mentioned above, the progress of the large projects will themselves be seriously retarded, if the negative factors are not removed.

Regional Growth

Another useful concept in area development is that of "regional growth". The economies of any area—blocks, districts or larger units—will grow with economic growth in the country. In most cases, this growth will mean change from exclusive dependence on primary industries to diversification of the economy. But in this process, the need for investment will increase progressively. The concept of progressive acceleration of the development process, and of the need for progressively larger investments is well-recognized in planning at the national and state-levels. The progressive increase in outlays and development activities in successive Five Year Plans is the best evidence of this. But at the level of the small area—the block and the district—the notion that a period of intensive development can be followed by one of lower investment (and development activity), because the area reaches "self-sufficiency" and is less in need of outside investment, seems to recur in Indian planning. The incompatibility of this concept with the dynamics of development was demonstrated by experience of the first community projects and blocks[2] in which an expenditure of about Rs. 22 lakhs per block for three years (or four years if the subsequent extension of time is taken into account) was followed by a post-intensive phase expenditure of about Rs. 1 lakh per year. But the idea seems to persist, as is evident from reference to it in intensive development projects of various kinds (agriculture, small industries, integrated development of districts) which are proposed from time to time. The idea has a certain attraction perhaps—it can be used as an argument to initiate intensive development in a limited number of areas. But there is a danger in adhering to it, because in any project undertaken with this idea there is bound to be a slide-back in development and frustration among the people when the period of intensive development is followed by the normal (slack) period.

It is true that after a period of intensive development, the character of inputs needed in an area changes—from elementary services to more advanced services, from service activities to resource development activities etc. It is true also that the people's capacity to pay for development activities increases and they are able to undertake themselves many activities (*e.g.*, drinking water wells) for which they would have required outside assistance earlier. But the savings in investment resulting from this change are more than compensated by the need for larger investments, *e.g.*, in more advanced services, and resource development activities, with the result *that the total quantum of investment needed in the area is much larger.* The people may not need assistance for irrigation or drinking water wells; but they will want electric motors on wells and piped water supply schemes, which are far more expensive. Therefore, whenever any area is taken up for intensive development, it should be clearly recognized that it is being put on a road on which it will need progressively larger total investment as time passes.

II
AREA DEVELOPMENT AT DISTRICT AND BLOCK LEVELS

The need for drawing up plans with districts and other local areas as units has been appreciated from the beginning of planned development. The Five Year Plan referred to district (and other) plans and the role of local institutions in the planning process. But a concerned effort to formulate plans at district and lower levels as made only at the time of formulation of the Second Five Year Plans. It was symbolized by the phrase "planning from below." As part of this effort, plans with districts and blocks as units were drawn up in a number of States. The Second Plan document defined the scope and content of the local plan (Appendix IIA) and the manner of its preparation in considerable detail. Districts and blocks have since been recognized as important planning units, formulation of plans for them has been recognized as an integral part of the national planning process and an important function of Panchayati Raj Institutions. Plans for districts and blocks were formulated as part of the Third Five year Plan and similar work has been in progress in most States in connection with formulation of the Fourth Plan. It is of interest to note that the scope of the district plan as defined in the Planning Commission's Memorandum on the Fourth Plan is very similar to the definition contained in the Second Plan.

However, experience with drawing up district plans at the time of the Second Plan and in subsequent years highlights some of the difficulties and problems of such planning (and points to the needs for safeguards), which may be summarized below:

(*i*) The tendency towards formulation of plans without adequate regard for resources which can be expected to become available—the tendency of plans to become catalogues of local needs and aspirations. This tendency was responsible, in part, for some of the planning effort made at the time of preparation of the Second Plan not yielding the expected results. But as a result of the Second Plan experience, an approximate indication of resources is now given in advance by the State Governments to the local institutions and officers.

(*ii*) The tendency to emphasize immediate need fulfillment in preference to longer terms resources development, to emphasize consumption-oriented activities in preference to production-oriented activities.

(*iii*) Emergence of competing claimants for social service facilities, works, etc., among which the planning agency must decide. Size-inflation of plans results often from the tendency to please as many rival claimants as possible.

(*iv*) The need for accurate and adequate factual data—the need for conducting surveys of resources of local social and economic conditions and technical possibilities.

(*v*) The need for posting sufficient technical staffs, both for surveys and for plan formulation. The very real difficulty of providing such technical staff constitutes a major constraint in local planning.

Area Development and Programme Planning—Experience of Community Development Programme

The need for local planning has been realized from the beginning of the community development programme and the scope and content of local planning has also been defined fairly clearly. But, within the area of local planning, the present practice is that priorities for different programmes and schemes, and the pattern of each scheme—content, staff, finance, institutional arrangements, etc., are worked out in great detail at the State (or even national) levels and decision-making at local levels is concerned largely with selecting locations and beneficiaries. The Panchayati Raj Institutions, like their predecessor officials of the community development blocks or other departments, often function primarily as allocating or distributing agencies, deciding where a primary school or a primary health centre should be located and who should get a *taccavi* loan, after the number of schools and health centres, to be opened in each block, the details of staff, equipment and buildings for these and the amount of *taccavi* loans to be sanctioned in a block, had been decided at the State level. (The typical situation in meetings of the Panchayati Samitis is somewhat as follows: The B.D.O. or another Extension Officer reads out a circular from the State Government which informs all Panchayat Samitis in the State that a particular scheme is to be implemented and gives the financial pattern and other details of the scheme. The meeting thereupon proceeds to decide which particular villages, persons or groups should benefit from the scheme. There is seldom any attempt to see whether the scheme is not suitable for the area of the Panchayat Samiti, whether another scheme would be more suitable or even to attempt to modify the pattern of the scheme in any way. Nor would such attempts be very feasible under the present procedures of sanction and implementation of development programmes.)

This practice of deciding patterns of development activity in detail at the State level and leaving the local institutions only the distributive functions has been the subject of considerable argument. Those opposed to the practice have argued that it does not allow plans to be formulated by local people in accordance with their needs and aspirations or the natural resources and development potential of their areas, with the result that less needed activities are often taken up in preference to those which are needed more and would have given better results—at times money is wasted on schemes which are not needed—and local people are not sufficiently enthusiastic about development programmes. This, they argue, results in development programmes not having the desired effect in terms of participation of people, and retarded economic development of the area. The protagonists of the practice have defended it on grounds of administrative efficiency, securing minimum level of development in all areas and ensuring that national and state priorities are reflected in local plans. Allocation of funds between different heads of development and on individual schemes within each development head is regarded as the chief instrument of securing development according to priorities. Working out detailed patterns of each scheme is considered essential for administrative efficiency and avoidance of waste, because it is argued that effective supervision and assessment of performance would be impossible in the absence of these.

It is also pointed out by many that so long as funds for development activities are provided by the State (or Central) Governments and the staff of Panchayati Raj Institutions form part of State cadres, the tendency towards detailed planning of programme at State (and even Central) level will continue. They go on to argue that the Panchayati Raj Institutions can have an effective role in planning for their areas only if they have their own staff and raise their own resources. The argument has some force. There is no doubt that when funds are given by the State Government there is a tendency for it to indicate not merely the schemes on which these may be spent but also in considerable detail the manner in which the schemes may be executed. On the side of Panchayati Raj Institutions also, there is a tendency to regard the schemes as those of the State Government, and to execute them according to the instructions of the latter. The immediate history of Panchayati Raj Institutions—their having been constituted in succession to the C.D. blocks and having inherited the programmes and funds of the blocks and other development departments—strengthens these tendencies. But financing by State Governments and technical staff forming part of State cadres is likely to be continued and the exercise of initiative in local planning by Panchayati Raj institutions has to be achieved within this situation. The alternative of Panchayati Raj institutions having their own staff and raising their own resources will, in the present stage of rural development and growth of these institutions, only result in greatly restricting their role in development besides reducing staff efficiency. It will reduce these institutions to the position of former district boards.

The tendency towards planning of programmes at State or Central levels has been encouraged by the fact that in much of the rural development activity of the last 13 years, the object has been to provide elementary services and facilities—primary schools, primary health centres, drinking water well and approach roads, co-operative credit societies, a basic agency for agricultural extension—which lends itself very well to planning through "programmes". The second reason for adopting the "programme" approach was that until local consciousness of development needs grew, it was necessary to provide certain leadership from above, and to take up basic activities which were clearly the most urgent needs of most areas.

This approach did create imbalances and difficulties in the community development programme. But since many of these were felt by the State Governments themselves, there was a tendency to resolve them through appropriate action between the State Governments and the Central Ministry of Community Development. Thus, when it was found by some State Governments that many of the activities included in the first community projects were not suitable for their areas, the Central Ministry allowed the States very considerable freedom in deciding the content of the programme within each major field of development activity. But the process was not carried over, to district or block levels to any appreciable extent, and once the pattern of activity in any field had been decided at the State level, it was applied without major modification to all blocks of the State.

The Need for Shift in Emphasis

But, as a result mainly of the development that has taken place during the last 13 years, the situation is changing. Firstly, as the need for elementary facilities has been met, emphasis is shifting to providing more advanced facilities. Planning of these requires much greater attention to local conditions, and it is not possible to apply a uniform pattern to all blocks. Thus, it is not advisable to decide that each block shall have so many secondary schools, marketing societies or centres for training of craftsmen. Block A may need more secondary schools and marketing societies than Block B because it contains a number of small towns in which secondary schools are desired by the people and which serve as *mandi* centres for the villages in their vicinity. Block B on the other hand may be more suitable for location of a training centre for craftsmen or a polytechnic because a larger factory located within it could provide employment to the trainees. The need for attention to local factors is even greater in case of resource development activities. Even a comparatively simple activity, *e.g.*, a processing factory (cotton gin or sugar mill) has to be planned primarily on consideration of specific local factors such as availability of raw materials, nearness to market, and advantage of transport. Thirdly, experience with development activities during the last 13 years has created among the local people much greater awareness of the need for development and of the specific development activities needed in their areas. They are more anxious to participate in the planning process and are more vocal in expression of their needs and aspirations. Finally, the programme pattern approach cannot provide adequately for inter-sectoral relations or for special planning needs of metropolitan, river valley project or industrial regions. The number of such projects and the areas coming under their influence is growing with economic growth in the country with the result that the need for area development is being felt in an increasing number of districts and blocks.

District as the Primary Unit of Local Planning

The emphasis on resource development activities and provision of more advanced services along with the other factors mentioned above, makes the district a more important unit of planning than the community development block. Let us take the examples of education and co-operation again. The community development block was quite a suitable unit for planning a network of primary schools, because the object was to provide every village, (or in case of very small villages or hamlets, a group of two or more neighbouring units) with a primary school. But it is not an equally suitable unit for planning location of middle schools and may have positive disadvantages when adopted as the unit for planning of secondary schools. Similarly, while location of credit co-operatives could be planned with the block as the unit, location of marketing and processing societies has to be planned with a larger area as the unit, because of the need for attention to specific location factors mentioned above.

The need for making the district the major unit of local planning is also felt for other reasons. Effective local planning will require a considerable measure of decentralization of decision-making from the State level to local levels. Such decentralization is more feasible at the district level than at the level of the block. There are several reasons for this. First, the district has the full complement of District Level Officers who can provide the specialist assistance needed for drawing up local plans and making fruitful modifications in schemes drawn up at the State level. On the non-official side, the Zila Parishad has the top-level leadership of the district. Second, for reasons of administrative feasibility, especially maintaining effective communication between the State and local levels, the district is more suitable than the block as a unit of local planning. The State Development Departments or the

State Governments find it more feasible to deal with a limited number of Zila Parishads and District Level Officers than with a large number of Panchayat Samitis and Extension Officers. Third, since intra-district variations (in physical or socio-economic conditions are generally not very large, the need for making further modifications in programmes to suit the requirements of particular blocks is comparatively small, after the pattern has been decided at the district level.

Here it is necessary to draw a clear distinction between the units of planning and the unit of implementation of programmes. The fact that the district is accepted as the unit of planning of a particular programme does not mean that it should necessarily be the unit for its implementation also. In some cases, the combination will be useful; but over a larger field of development activity covered by the district plan, execution could just as well be done through the Panchayat Samitis. The district is a more suitable unit than the block for planning the content of the minor irrigation progrmme, *i.e.*, deciding the emphasis that minor irrigation should receive in the total agricultural production effort in the district, and the specific schemes which should be taken up, but implementation of a large part of the programme is best done by the Panchayat Samitis. The decision regarding the unit of planning and the unit of implementation should be taken separately for each development programme keeping in view its nature, the technical staff and other resources required for it, and the structure of Panchayati Raj Institutions in the State.

Appropriate Inter-action Between Town and Villages

Let us consider an average district. Its headquarters is located in a medium-sized town which performs various services for all or most of the villages and small towns located within it. Frequently, the town is also the major commercial centre of the district. The sub-divisional headquarters towns, important mandi towns, and other medium-sized towns have similar roles for parts of the district. Within each block, the block headquarters town has a similar role in relation to villages of the block area. In addition, there are in most blocks one or more small towns (or large villages) which perform similar functions for groups of 25-30 villages.

One effect of the development of the last 13 years has been

that the inter-action between these towns and the villages served by them has increased, and the towns have a much more important role in the economy and social life of the villages. The village people come to the towns more frequently and obtain many more of their requirements from them than they did in the past. The very activities of Panchayat Samitis—distribution of *taccavi* loans, distribution of permits for supply of chemical fertilizers, cement or corrugated iron sheets, deciding appeals from decisions of panchayats, and various elections—have added do the frequency of the town visits. Many village leaders and affluent cultivators visit such towns almost daily. Most of the towns have expanded considerably in recent years, on account of growth of commerce, resulting from larger agricultural production and higher incomes in the surrounding villages, and of their service functions. This expansion will continue as the role of the towns as service centres for the surrounding villages becomes more important, because as agriculture gets modernized and rural electrification and rural industrialization make progress, these towns will have an increasingly important role as centres for distribution of new materials and of servicing and repair of power driven implements and machines. This, for the simple reason that facilities for distribution, of new materials and repairs and servicing of machines cannot be created at more than a few central places.

Yet, very little attention has been given so far to examining the inter-relationship between these towns and their surrounding villages and ensuring that development of the two is complementary and mutually beneficial. Indeed there are many instances of defective planning resulting from a failure to appreciate this relationship. The location of facilities like primary health centres and secondary schools has generally been decided on considerations like availability of local contribution, with the result that in many cases the facilities are located not in the place which is the natural centre of the area to be served by it, but in the place which came forward to pay the required contribution. In many blocks, the block headquarters town itself is not well-located for serving the needs of the block area.

The first community projects did contain the nucleus of the idea of securing appropriate inter-action between towns and villages. The programme of these projects included development of mandi centres, improvement of communications between them and the villages and using the centres for providing an increasing range of services and dissemination of new ideas to the villages. But the idea was gradually dropped, because other problems were considered more urgent. Moreover, the C.D. and N.E.S. Blocks which followed the first community projects had such small budgets that these more intensive development activities, could not be accommodated within them. However, the time has now come then this relationship should be given a adequate attention. The place of the district and block headquarters towns and of the smaller centres within each block, in the development of their service areas should be clearly recognized, and location of various service facilities should be so decided as to enable these centres to perform their service role efficiently. Further, the municipalities of the small towns and Panchayati Raj Institutions should be brought into relations of mutual inter-action.

The latter can be done only at the district level: the block is too small a unit for this purpose. The recent recommendation of the Sadiq Ali Report for providing for association of municipalities with the Zila Parishad in Rajasthan is evidence of recognition of this need.[3] This association will become especially important when integrated area development is accepted as the object of local planning and development of both towns and villages is viewed as part of it.

A Case of Local Planning: The Wardha Plan[4]

The Plan was drawn up jointly by the Gokhale Institute, Poona, the Regional Planning Institute, Wardha and the staff of the Wardha Zila Parishad. It illustrates some of the principles mentioned below:

(*a*) It is a district plan. The district was selected as the unit of planning for two reasons. First, the district institution, the Zila Parishad is the most important Panchayati Raj Institution in Maharashtra. Second, the district is considered a more appropriate unit than the blocks for drawing up a plan of this kind. Plans for blocks and smaller areas fit into the framework of the district plan.

(*b*) An indication of resources likely to become available for execution of the plan was given by the State Government at the outset.

(*c*) The Plan is based on analysis of existing data, which were supplemented by surveys of socio-economic conditions and technical surveys for location of minor irrigation works, etc.

(*d*) The Plan has been formulated by technical officers of the district and the special staff loaned by the institutes. The technical nature of the planning task has been fully realized in its formulation.

(*e*) The Plan has been formulated with the coordinated efforts of the State Government, the Panchayati Raj Institutions and the specialized institutes.

(*f*) The Plan puts primary emphasis on resource development, Development of certain services (transport, welfare of backward classes etc.) has been emphasized on account of special circumstances of the district.

(*g*) The Plan stresses inter-sectoral relationships, though these have not been systematically worked out. Further, it recognized that if a larger industrial or other resource development project comes to be located in the district, a major readjustments will be necessary in the plan.

(*h*) The Plan includes a section on rural-urban relationships and development of towns as service centres. Significantly, the centres selected are *mandi* centres and not block headquarters, thus emphasizing the economic rather than the administrative aspects of the relationships.

Efforts similar to the Wardha Plan can be made only in a few selected districts, where special arrangements can be made for institutional assistance. But these plans have considerable methodological value. They bring out the basic principles and the techniques of local area planning; the nature of work involved in it, and the place of local area plans in the National Plan. Appreciation of these will lead to more systematic and fruitful planning efforts in other areas.

REFERENCES

1. India, *Third Five Year Plan*, New Delhi, Planning Commission, 1961, p. 149.
2. Reference here is to the investment under the budget of the C.D.

Blocks and to the concept which inspired the pashing of this budgetary pattern. It should be made clear, however, that the total quantum of investment and tempo of development activity (including both programmes included within the Community Development budget and others forming part of the development plans of the State) has been accelerated in nearly every area because of general acceleration of development activity under the Five Year Plans.

3. Government of Rajasthan, *Report of the Study Team on Panchayati Raj*, Jaipur, 1964, pp. 37-38.
4. Wardha District Plan Frame (Unpublished).

Appendix I
Major Projects and Related Inputs

A. MAJOR IRRIGATION PROJECT

(1) Associated Inputs

(*i*) Transport (road, rail) facilities needed for movement of equipment, supplies and personnel needed for the project, communication facilities.

(*ii*) Housing, water supply, social services (education of children, medical care) facilities for the project staff; creation of a township, if necessary.

(*iii*) Soil conservation measures, in the catchment area.

(2) Complementary Inputs

(*i*) Land development and agricultural improvement: reclamation, clearance and levelling of land which is to receive irrigation; reorganization of agriculture, especially switching over from dry to irrigated farming; adoption of improved agricultural practices, *e.g.*, use of improved seed, chemical fertilizers etc.;
supplementary minor irrigation—digging of wells, installation of lift irrigation devices etc.; drainage and other steps to prevent water logging in the irrigated area.

(*ii*) Improvement of transport and marketing facilities.

Measures of category (*i*) require creation of services of technical assistance, supplies, etc., and also provisions for loans to cultivators for enabling them to take up land development or agricultural improvement measures.

(3) Derived Inputs

As the above measures take effect and agricultural production increases, the area will need agricultural processing industries, agro-industries (*e.g.*, manufacture of improved agricultural implements) and consumer goods industries. These may be called derived inputs, which derive from or follow the earlier developments.

B. STEEL PLANT

(1) Associated Inputs

(*i*) Facilities for mining of coal, iron-ore, limestone and construction materials.
(*ii*) Transport, rail and road, for carrying raw materials and intermediate and finished products.
(*iii*) Generation of power.
(*iv*) Supply of water to the plant and to the township.
(*v*) Urban development—construction of township to house industrial workers and those working in trades and services; organization of various essential services in the township.

(2) Complementary Inputs

(*i*) Rehabilitation of persons dispossessed of their lands.
(*ii*) Orderly absorption of immigrants and taking steps for ensuring smooth relations between them and the original residents of the area.
(*iii*) Training of craftsmen and other personnel for the plant.
(*iv*) Social education among tribal people with a view to ensure that they can derive adequate benefits from new economic opportunities within their area.
(*v*) Reorganization of local agriculture to meet the consumption needs of the larger population, especially for high value perishable products such as milk, vegetables, fruit, meat and poultry products.

(3) ***Derived Inputs***

Industries, which depend upon raw materials supplied by the steel plant or on use of other facilities like power and transport created for it.

(*i*) Heavy engineering industries, *e.g.*, machine building, manufacture of transport equipment, fabrication of structurals, etc.
(*ii*) Heavy chemical industries, *e.g.*, manufacture of chemical fertilizers.
(*iii*) Manufacture of other construction materials.
(*iv*) Light engineering, light chemicals and various consumer goods industries attracted by the raw materials and other facilities available in the area.

Appendix II
Scope and Content of the District Plan as Defined in the Second and the Fourth Five Year Plans

A. SECOND FIVE YEAR PLAN

"20. It was recognized that both at the district and at the State level three kinds of programmes sponsored on behalf of public authorities would be included in the plan, namely:

(*a*) programmes initiated at the level in question, *e.g.*, taluka district and State,
(*b*) programmes initiated at lower levels and integrated with those in *(a)* and
(*c*) programmes initiated at levels above and integrated with *(a)*, for instance, schemes sponsored by the Central Government but executed through States or schemes

sponsored by the State Government and implemented through machinery available, in the district.

23. The main constituents of district plan are:

(1) the community development and national extension programme,
(2) social welfare extension projects,
(3) agricultural production programme and allied activities in the field of rural development such as animal husbandry, soil conservation, etc.
(4) development of cooperatives,
(5) village panchayats,
(6) village and small industries,
(7) schemes for utilizing effectively resources developed through State projects for irrigation, electricity, communications, industrial development and expansion of training facilities,
(8) housing and urban development,
(9) the programme of small savings,
(10) aiding construction projects through labour cooperatives and shramdan,
(11) programmes for the welfare of backward classes,
(12) programmes in rural and urban areas relating to social services, especially expansion of education at primary and secondary levels, health units, health education, sanitation, malarial com-family planning, etc.
(13) utilizing and assisting voluntary organizations engaged in constructive social work,
(14) land reform,
(15) prohibition work, and
(16) dissemination of information about programmes of national, state, regional and local development."

Planning Commission : Second Five Year Plan, 1956, pages 156 and 158.

B. FOURTH FIVE YEAR PLAN

"A district development plan should comprehend various activities envisaged in the State Five Year Plan for execution at the district level without respect to the nature of the sponsoring authority or the location of the budget provisions. Some activities undertaken in a district are provided for in the plans of the Zila Parishad and the Panchayat Samitis, others in the plans of Departments at the State level. These latter fall technically outside the field of Panchayati Raj Institutions. The following are the principal sectors in which the local initiative and participation have to be carried as far as possible and can be developed around programmes embodied in the Five Year Plan:

(*i*) Agriculture (in its wider sense including animal husbandry, dairying, fisheries, poultry, horticulture, forestry, minor irrigation, etc.),
(*ii*) Co-operatives,
(*iii*) Village and small industries in processing industries,
(*iv*) Elementary and social education,
(*v*) Rural water supply and sanitation,
(*vi*) Rural health and medical services and family planning,
(*vii*) District and rural roads, including village approach roads (excluding National and State Highways),
(*viii*) Work programme's for the fuller utilization of rural manpower,
(*ix*) Development of focal points of growth like market centres, service centres, etc.,
(*x*) Social welfare, including welfare of weaker section,
(*xi*) Voluntary organization.

Planning Commission: Memorandum on the Fourth Plan, New Delhi, 1964, pp. 80-81.

11

Administering the Planning System

SHRIRAM MAHESHWARI

India adopted planning in the fifties as the vehicle of its development though its interest in it dates back to early forties when the Indian National Congress set up the National Planning Committee to prepare comprehensive plans of reconstruction for undivided India. Interspersed with 'holidays' and annual plans, India has completed five five-year plans with varying degrees of success; while the sixth one is presently on the agenda, it is engaged in the preparation of blueprint of the Seventh Five Year Plan. But this alone does not make a discussion on planning in India a subject of topical significance. Over the years, planning has lost a good deal of its credibility and glamour it had enjoyed in the sixties, which calls for a measure of introspection on the part of the society. The annual rate of growth of the economy since the beginning of planning has been quite low which compares very poorly with the growth rates achieved by other developing countries. Putting it in terms of per capita income, the rate of growth in India has been no higher than 1.5 per cent, which would take no less than fifty years for the country to double the standard of living of its people.[1] That more could—and should—be done through the mechanism of planning is the dominant belief underlying the present article.

One may do well to recall here the dominant traits of planning as it has evolved in India. First, planning in India is highly centralized, and this centralism acquires arresting nature when considered in the background of the federal system of government under the Constitution. Planning, to be sure, has an inherent centralizing slant, but it is possible—and desirable—to devise counter-balancing mechanism and encourage styles to encourage emergence of plurality of decision-making centres. This, however, is not the case with Indian planning. The centralist thrust of planning has also received powerful impetus from historical and environmental factors, such as the hang-over of the unitary arrangements of governance till the enforcement of the present Constitution, single party dominance, centralization of financial resources, etc. Once a tradition of centralist planning was built up, it began to feed upon itself with the passage of time.

The second feature of planning is its bureaucratic nature. This characteristic is to an extent implicit in the preceding one but has become a prominent feature not to be missed. The planning processes do not seek to involve citizen participation in any organized way. When slackness in execution is noted, the remedy is discovered in still greater bureaucratization.

Besides, it should look axiomatic that a five year plan builds upon its predecessors, making the latter as its base. Each plan registers gains—and some inadequacies—both intended and unintended as well as immediate and remote. The succeeding one should take full cognizance of all these changes no less than their implications. One may, for instance, argue that macro-level planning was necessary in the early stages of economic development when the infrastructure has to be created and a host of other fundamental decisions had to be taken. The phase is over, and now the time has perhaps come to plan at the unit level so that schemes of development correspond more closely with the needs and aspirations of the local people. This however, has not been done. With almost monotonous regularity, each plan is content to run into the old grooves.

ADMINISTRATIVE ASPECTS OF THE PLAN

Administrative aspects of the Five Year Plan do not generally receive serious attention of the country's planners. Generally, their concerns for implementation mechanism, if any, are more of a postscript or a tailpiece than a product of integrated thinking. It is not without significance that the chief executives at the National

Development Council sessions plead for greater autonomy, fiscal and otherwise, and make suggestions in various areas, but seldom is a word uttered to explicitly demand toning up of the administrative system or to stress administrative limitations.[2] Yet no plan can expect to accomplish more than its administration permits it to do; it is too much on its part to move much beyond its public administration. Indeed, administration is the single most critical factor intervening between planning and implementation though planning itself, strictly speaking, is a function of administration.

The implementation processes acquire a powerful meaning in a developing country for it is at the stage of implementation that the local interest groups become aggressively vocal and assertive, distorting the programmes and cornering the benefits, whatever be the explicit objectives or goals. The Indian experience amply proves this hypothesis. All told, administering the plan acquires top level priority: this is the message of all the plans. V.K.R.V. Rao is right when he attributes the failure of planning to "its implementation, its lack of cohesion with social factors and the impediments imposed by political, social, administrative and cultural forces..."[3] The Government of India's Economic Survey for 1984 also admits albeit shyly: "The degree of discipline in plan formulation and implementation needs to be greatly improved."[4]

PROFILE OF CHANGE

It is thus imperative for the country to evolve ad administrative system which can cope up with the challenge of the plan. The crying need of planning is simultaneously to formulate a comprehensive national administrative plan so that the five year plan gets administratively supported. The 'correction slip' approach, which is generally followed when confronted with embarrassing situation, would not be of much availing. This requires leadership role on the part of the political elite of the land. Without constant proddings and stimulations by the political chief executive and other ministers, public administration in the country is apt to run in its accustomed way. Public administration can be expected to remain efficient and positively oriented only when it remains under continuous political control, guidance and surveillance. Political concern, one may again emphasize, is prerequisite of administrative reform, and without administrative reform no plan can be put into operation in the way originally visualized.

The National Development Council, the summit institution of the chief executives of the Indian Union, has gradually become a body without much brief which is confirmed by its infrequent meetings and occasional non-serious nature of discussion in its sessions. It is not without significance that the NDC has met only thirty-seven times since its inception in 1950. This weakens the processes of consensus politics and prevents plans from reflecting the ground level realities of a vast and diversified country like India. In theory, the NDC is the sovereign body, and the Planning Commission is made subordinate to it. But in practice, it has got largely reduced to the level of a decorative body. The NDC must be made stronger, politically, organizationally and operationally; and efforts in this direction must not be delayed. Presently, the centre-state relations are marked by numerous strains and the NDC is an appropriate body to promote cooperation between the two levels of government. It must be borne in mind that unfriendly relations between the Centre and the States create a climate which is inimical to both planning and its executives, and bridges, therefore, need to be built between the two levels of governance. Nor should the Planning Commission remain what it has been over the years It should be made a more vigorous body, and the inconsistent relationship between it and the constitutionally established finance Commission be removed.

Antiquated administrative structures and leisurely procedures of work are incompatible with the accomplishment of tasks visualized under the plan.

Inefficiency, delay, motivated harassment, corruption, wastage, misuse of resources, etc., must be censured wherever these are noticed and professionalism in administration must be promoted at all levels and in all sectors. Administrative delays are notorious in India. The Prime Minister recently asked the Central Government secretaries to insist upon quicker action and cut down delays in administration and she quoted the private comments of the Japanese and US entrepreneurs that what is done in a day in other countries takes no less than a month in India.[5] Delays harass the people, bread corruption, cause cost escalation, to name a few consequences. By causing cost over-runs, they bring plans under disrepute. There should be 'single window clearance' of industrial proposals, and citizen dealings should also be without harassment and delay. Delays in project implementation by now a common feature of Indian planning. This is bad in itself as it inflicts adverse effects on the project economies but it is bad also because of the chain effect it is apt to generate. This happens on account of poor project design, incomplete preparation of project report and inadequate appraisal, and the surprise is that such things happen in a planned economy in which planning has been in progress for over three decades. Training in project formulation and implementation is of critical importance to avoid delays as huge funds from the limited resources have been locked up in these.

The state level public administration is necessarily to be called upon to bear the brunt of the new tasks and, therefore, it will have to be considerably strengthened, more in terms of quality than quantity, so that it becomes an apt instrument for undertaking programmes of development. A series of measures are imperative; the states are well advised to scan the reports of about twenty administrative reforms committees, set up by them from time to time since 1947, and to see that the urgent reforms are swiftly carried out. The well-known tenure system, which operates rather erratically at present, needs to be enforced more systematically. Not only should a civil servant coming to the Central Government on a tenure revert to the state (or service) of his posting after completion of his spell of duty, the tenure system should also be applied in an orderly way within a state itself, ensuring regular exchange of personnel between the field and the headquarters. Meaningful training programmes should be organized for state level personnel in various areas to improve their functional proficiency.

As early as in 1971, the Planning Commission had asked the State Governments to set up planning boards—broadly on its own pattern—to attend to the task of integrated planning of their respective states. These bodies have since been set up in a few states but have hardly been effective. Machinery for evaluation is weak and in many states it is even non-existent. There is thus no regular and reliable mechanism for feedback to flow to planners, and in such a circumstance mid-term corrective action is not possible. It is necessary that planning bodies be set up in each state with status and function similar to those of the Central Planning Commission and their responsibilities should extend to plan formulation, annual plans, project monitoring, evaluation, mid-term appraisal, etc.

Similarly, reform of local governments—rural as well as urban should not remain shelved, as has generally happened in most states so far. Local government will necessarily have to be involved more meaningfully, more closely and more widely in the efforts at development. It would be good if the states go through the various reports, about twenty in number, having bearing on this subject and quickly implement the necessary reforms. Indeed local government should be recognized as the third level of the Indian federation.

Planning necessarily leads to recruitment of a large number of experts and specialists in various sectors and levels of administration. But, in India, the technical personnel generally suffer from low morale, the reasons being excessive control from above, manning of top level policy-making positions even in technical sectors by generalist administrators, lack of promotional opportunities, etc. According to a recent news report, "...more than the promotional aspect, what is really disturbing is the fact that the technical officers in the Planning Commission find themselves handicapped in their very functioning. It is stated that there is 'some hesitancy' on the part of the IAS officers from the Planning Commission as well as other ministries and departments to attend meetings chaired by technical officers. Sometimes, secretaries and additional secretaries from other ministries are invited to hold the meetings in the Planning Commission."[6] Such attitudes hamper functioning, and must be eschewed. A certain ascendancy in the status and role of the specialists is inevitably built in the very logic of development, and the imbalance must be corrected. Stress may also be laid on the need for experts and specialist acquiring administrative experience and training to enable them to move into positions of administrative responsibilities in various areas and levels of government. At the same time, tasks of integration and coordination grow increasingly weighty under a planned economy and the place of the generalist administrators also becomes much more important. Correctly speaking, the relationship between the specialists and the generalists is complementary, not competitive provide both play their respective roles in an upright way. Besides, the generalist administrators must also specialize in one or the other sector of administration so that they may make an intelligent contribution to the work in hand.

India's weakest link in administering of the development plan is the ground level machinery, and reference here is particularly directed to district administration headed by the District Collector. Whether District Collector should be associated with developmental administration or not is a question which has been debated since the days of the Bengal Administration Enquiry Committee (1945).[7] Both Gujarat and Maharashtra have, however, hived off developmental functions from regulatory ones and have set up an entirely new functionary—chief executive officer/district development officer—to look after the former set of functions. But, other states have taken the view that developmental tasks would get more effectively performed by a close association of the traditionally honoured District Collector, and accordingly have made him the head of development. Howsoever, highly an office is traditionally viewed by the citizens, an excess load on it is apt to bring it under heavy stress and strip off its supposedly magical potency; and precisely this has happened to the office of the District Collector.

Besides, the member of the IAS appointed to this point is too inexperienced an officer having barely put in four or five years of service to command the cooperation and respect of other district level functionaries who possess much greater experience and are older in age. What is even worse, he is subjected to frequent transfers, his average stay being less than eighteen months. With all such parameters within which he has necessarily to function, he is hardly in a position to provide meaningful leadership to development administration. The larger truth, today, is that he is not in a position to administer either the traditional regulatory affairs or even the newly acquired developmental ones with an acceptable level of efficiency. Strengthening of the field administration is an unpostponable item on the agenda of national policy-makers, and postings at this level should be made compellingly attractive. It is implied that some of the gloss needs to be taken off the secretariat postings.

PEOPLE'S PARTICIPATION

Administration of plan of India's scale and magnitude cannot be possible without active and widespread citizen participation. In July 1984, the Prime Minister told the National Development Council: "I look to the people's involvement in the plan as a means for speedier and more efficient implementation. For me the relationship between the plan and the people is an organic one." She further added: "The decentralization of the planning process to the district and the block levels will ensure the fullest participation of the people in the formulation and implementation of programmes. There is no other way of making our anti-poverty programmes a living reality."[8] Yet the fact is that people's participation in the development plans is more conspicuous by its absence rather than presence. Panchayati Raj is not active in most states, and even in states like Maharashtra and Gujarat, where it is in reasonably good health, no effort has of late been made to strengthen it further, by endowing it with additional functions and resources. Citizen participation, a prerequisite of effective implementation, calls for decentralization both of planning and administration decision-making. Planning must be pushed downward remembering fully well that the fundamental belief underlying the local level planning is that the lower unit's priorities may not be the same as those of the higher level. To put it concretely, the State Government's priority may be agriculture but a particular district—or block—may have forestry as its acute current need. In this sense, there is little decentralization of planning in India despite the continued urgency to do so. The district and the block should become the new lower units of planning. As V.K.R.V. Rao observed: "The administrative unit for local planning should be at the block level with necessary provision for finance, technical expertise and administrative coordination, with the block level officer instituting a two-way dialogue with an elected body like the block-level panchayat for guidance in formulating the block plan, reporting to it on progress in implementation and seeking its cooperation and participation in dealing with the difficulties faced in implementation. The next higher unit in the hierarchy of planning units should be the district development officer (whose status and authority for both spending and coordination should be similar to that of the District Collector) an the Zila Parishad which would be an elected body, representative of the district as a whole in addition to special representation for the block level panchayats in the district. The relations between the DDO and the Zila Parishad should be similar to those between the BLO (block level officer) and the block panchayat."[9] The next higher authority for planning should be a composite unit comprising the state planning board, the state cabinet, the state legislature, and the state development commissioner. Interesting in this context is also the recommendation recently made by the Economic Advisory Council to the Prime Minister for the setting up of a planning authority at the divisional level.[10]

It must be remembered that when people participate, they organize themselves and even think for themselves. While participating in implementation of programmes, designed for their benefit, social consciousness emerges, releasing energy and imparting dynamism to the programmes. This, surely, is a time-consuming process, but any human development programme requires investment of time.

ADDITIONAL THOUGHTS

A sound administrative strategy for planning should take into full account the previous experiences of plan implementation and also make optimal use of knowledge made available by modern management as well as the experience of other developing and developed societies which faced more or less similar developmental problems. Besides, there should be a continued search for strengthening of the capabilities, and various mechanisms should be devised to this end.

The top level planners should also expose themselves more and more to the field, especially planners to rural realities by spending a reasonable portion of their time in villages. This would not only make planning less esoteric and more meaningful but also ensure better implementation. This would happen if the planners would have occasions of seeing planning and implementation from the other end and thus getting a clearer vision of how the plans are interpreted, operationalised and distorted to suit the local power structure. The proposed ruralisation of the top level planners is particularly necessary for the success of the rural development programmes.

The implementation process also suffers from a certain multiplicity of objectives which each five year plan holds before itself. It would perhaps be a great advantage for the smoothness in implementation if an excessive dispersal of attention is avoided at the time of development of plan objectives. A noted economist has, for instance, warned: "The larger the number of objectives the easier it would be to justify alternative courses of action as fulfilling one object or another..."[11] It is true that concentration on just one objective may not be feasible in a democracy where diverse interests project their demand on the polity, and furthermore, plurality of objectives may keep various groups of people integrated within the limits of a common institutional framework. Yet, the lesser the number of objectives, the better it is for the line functionaries.

There are some other ideas worth consideration. The implementation failures recurring since the fifties, perhaps call for a small tight plan, which may perhaps be supplemented by an 'indicative' plan. The administrative energy, presently scattered all over, would thus be released from the 'indicative' sector, and become available for the performance of the essential part, resulting in its smarter implementation. Besides, the 'indicative' sector, freed from administrative shackles, would be enabled to show unhampered initiative and drive in its liberated area. At any rate, as Sachin Chaudhuri once commented: "Much unnecessary rigidity has entered the process (planning). A great deal of deadwood needs to be hacked away."

This is not to imply that planning has been a futile exercise and that it should be given up. India's achievements flowing from the planning process are many-sided and well-marked, and it would be utterly churlish to deny the gains of planning: planning is essential because it helps to channelise the national thinking in certain well-marked directions and to draw up a set of norms regardless of the fact that the unexpected might occur. But planning in India is basically incomplete: it is based on models constructed in purely economic terms, thus, seeking to project an absolutely apolitical image. This makes Indian planning rather theoretical and unimplementable—at least in full.

Mention in the end must also be made of the need for creating a climate at the national level which is positively supportive of economic development and planning. An important component of it is the existence of a structure of national morality and what is more, practice of it by the governing elite. This is apt to restore credibility to planning and administration and in the process generate much-needed goodwill for such efforts. Life is not worth living if it is not motivated by higher norms and values of conduct.

REFERENCES

1. I.G. Patel's address at the Calcutta Chamber of Commerce on August 24, 1984. Patel is the former Governor of the Reserve Bank of India.
2. There was hardly any discussion of administration as a variable in planning in the National Development Council when it met in July 1984 to discuss the Approach to the Seventh Five Year Plan.
3. V.K.R.V. Rao's First V.T. Krishnamachari Memorial Lecture on March 20,1984, *The Financial Express*, April 2, 1984.
4. Quoted in *The Financial Express*, March 26, 1984.
5. *The Economic Times*, June 27, 1984.
6. *The Financial Express*, April 9, 1984.
7. Report of the Bengal Administration Enquiry Committee, Alipur, Superintendent, Government Printing Press, 1945, para 65.
8. Prime Minister Indira Gandhi's speech at the National Development Council in July 1984. See. *The Economic Times*, July 13, 1984.
9. V.K.R.V. Rao's First V.T. Krishnamachari Memorial Lecture delivered on March 20, 1984, *The Financial Express*, April 3, 1984.
10. Also see S.R. Maheshwari, *State Governments in India*, New Delhi, Macmillan, 1979, pp. 86-94.
11. D.T. Lakdawala, *The Economic Times*, April 28, 1984.

12

Planning and Administrative Development

P.S. BHATNAGAR

Since the end of World War II, development planning has assumed a significant role in the process of economic development of a large majority of both the developed and the developing countries. Although planning at the national level is being practiced in a majority of nations, it is hardly 60 years old having been introduced in Russia in the late twenties, and is less than three decades old in most of the countries of the Third World. In India, a citadel of planning, the credo took roots quite early largely due to the initiative of Prime Minister Jawaharlal Nehru. He cogently perceived that *laissez-faire* in economic policies would least suit a poor and exploited country like India in its path toward economic modernization and there was no alternative but to resort to a system of comprehensive development planning controlled and guided by a central organization.

IMPORTANCE OF PLANNING

National planning has become an integral part of development strategy of nations in all the continents and has become a symbol of sovereignty and modernity. Prior to 1945, Soviet Union was the only country engaged in systematic planning having launched its First Year Plan in 1929. The Bolsheviks considered planning to be the only vehicle to achieve the goals of Marxism. Success of central planning experiment in Russia has been a major factor in its being adopted as an instrument of achieving societal goals in a majority of developing countries, including India. Moreover, the experience of World War II, when even free enterprise economies resorted to physical planning to ensure better utilization of scarce materials and other commodities, also demonstrated that "even when the people of a country were moved by a common aim under emergency conditions, ambitious plan could be carried out".[1]

The general belief prevalent now in developing countries is that if faster rates of growth are to be achieved and effects of a rising population to be countered so that per capita may arise, there is no alternative but to plan the economies in a more systematic and controlled manner. Planning is regarded as an open sesame by countries of the Third World which will facilitate their emergence from backwardness and help them become an economically strong and viable nation. According to a keen observer of planning, the worldwide acceptance of planning as a means of achieving national developmental objectives has made academic the doctrinal debate about whether a country should plan. For most countries, the questions now is how to plan.[2]

This comprehensive planning exercise has met with complete success only in few countries while in a vast majority it has ranged from being partially successful to almost total failure. Reasons for partial success of planning have been many including inadequate data base, poor formulation and implementation of plans, ambitious targets, wrong priorities, faulty assumptions of planners, and though most important yet least emphasized, administrative obstacles on account of inefficient, and outmoded administration. In fact, any of these problems arise as a consequence of poorly managed and ill-organized administrative apparatus in these countries.

ADMINISTRATIVE SYSTEM AND PLAN IMPLEMENTATION

Most of the Third World countries inherited administrative systems which were designed by their colonial rulers. Even those who had remained independent had systems which were established long ago with different aims. The tasks entrusted to administration were mainly to maintain law and order, protection from foreign aggression, collection of taxes and some public utility services. After the end of the Second War and in the fifties and the sixties when the government of these countries realized the need to develop at a faster rate, plans were hurriedly drawn to modernize the economies and the existing administration was entrusted with these new tasks. The policy-makers were soon faced with a dilemma: How to restructure the public administration to suit the imperatives of rapid economic development and the process of modernization? More specifically, could the present system of administration act as an instrument of social change? The issue became more topical as a large majority of these countries adopted development planning for taking their societies on a path of change and progress.

Development planning was thus adopted in the hope that the existing administrative machinery would be able to cope up successfully with various demands that would be made on it. In fact, history of development planning in many of these countries aptly reveals faith in this belief. However, the later events have clearly demonstrated that one of the major obstacles coming in the way of formulation and implementation of developmental programmes has been none other than the administrative system itself. The experience of many of these countries suggests that the state of a country's public administration sets the tone and limits of development policy and planning. Administrative inadequacy is not something peculiar to developing countries alone; it is also to be found in many of the developed countries but it assumed critical importance in case of the former as administration seems to be the only well-organized viable medium to achieve developmental goals. Moreover, inefficient administration not only impedes developments, it may even lead to a fall in the growth rate.

Developing countries, in fact, need a better and efficient administrative system as in addition to the existing tasks of maintenance of law and order, collection of revenue, etc., challenging tasks of development and planning have also to be performed. Waterston, therefore, observed:

> The primary task in most ex-colonial territories is to reorient government machinery to meet the demands of accelerated development. The complexities of this task are considerable. But the task is even more complicated in most counties which have been politically independent for a long time.

> Administrative structures must not only be modernized to meet the needs of development planning; they must also be made to function with tolerable efficiency in providing the usual government services, collecting taxes and preserving law and order.[3]

The paradox of the situation is that these developing nations, which need well-organized administrative systems more than advanced nations, are saddled with archaic, inefficient, and outmoded systems. Not only have these systems come in way of many of the developmental schemes initiated to improve the lost of impoverished masses but have become a burden on their already weak and fragile economic system.

A careful study of expenditures incurred on maintaining their administrative systems would reveal that these have risen manifold as compared to developmental expenditures and proving more or less counter productive as regards their role in taking the nation on a path of development is concerned. This is a matter of serious concern, but hardly any worthwhile attempts have been or are being made to improve the functioning of the administrative machinery qualitatively so that it could serve as a vehicle of change and progress.

The administration of development programmes efficiently and economically is one of the main concerns of policy-makers in the Third World countries. Administration of development in developing countries "has always had some serious drawbacks, both during and after colonial rule. Despite serous attempts, after independence, to restructure the system of development administration and to increase its effectiveness and impact, there still exists a number of factors, primarily a legacy of the colonial past, which impede the process."[4] Therefore, each of these countries is trying according to its needs, resources, and political and social environment—to adopt suitable policies and measures to make implementation of these programmes more effective.

Public administration in these countries is afflicted with a host of problems, of which the most important one are: lack of suitable manpower, outdated personnel policies, dilatory procedures, centralized bureaucratic structure, archaic accounting and financial controls, lack of coordination among various ministries and agencies, poor administrative organization, maladministration, lack of support to improve administrative system, multiplicity of authorities and agencies, inefficient public sector, corruption, inefficiency, red-tapism and *paperasserie*. This list is only suggestive and not exhaustive. In fact, a score of other problems affect their administrative systems, some of which being more prominent in one than in the other, mainly due to their specific historical, cultural and social context.

ADMINISTRATION AND DEVELOPMENTAL TASKS

Many scholars, in order to focus on the important role of administration in the development process, have emphasized categorizing administration for development as development administration', distinct from general purpose or regulatory administration. As Riggs has noted:

> ...development administration refers to the administration of development programmes, to the methods used by large scale organizations, notably governments, to implement policies and plans designed to meet their developmental objectives.[5]

The purpose of differentiating development administration was to focus on the new and crucial role of public administration as an instrument of social change. The overall transformation of the society was to be brought about mainly though implementation of comprehensive development plans by it. It was, therefore, emphasized that in order to ensure that development administration may be able to perform its role effectively, it was considered necessary to strengthen the administrative capabilities of government. It was argued that if the new goals of development are to be achieved more quickly, with efficiency and economy, old patterns and practices of administration will have to be replaced by more dynamic, result-oriented procedures. Copying of Western administrative traditions may help only to a certain extent, but main effort will have to come indigenously. As Thompson has observed:

> Administrative practices and principles of the West have derived from preoccupation with control and, therefore, have little of value for development administration in

> under-developed countries where the need is for an adaptive administration, one that can be derived from the researches and theories of the behavioural sciences, and these should become the administrative objectives of development administrators. Illustrative of such objectives are the following: an innovative atmosphere; the operationalizing and sharing of goals; the combining of planning (thinking) and acting (doing); the minimization of parochialism; and diffusion of influence; and increasing toleration of inter-dependence; and the avoidance of bureaupathology.[6]

Majority of countries, which have embarked upon planning, have seriously recognized the urgent need to change their administrative apparatus. Experience of these countries suggests that far-reaching changes and improvements are needed in administration if the goals of economic and social development are to be accomplished. A conference of Asian Planners organized by ECAFE emphasized:

> deficiencies in the administrative machinery constituted a major obstacle to the effective implementation of development plans. The reform of the administrative structure, its strengthening and reorganization...had to be carried out urgently if the administration as a whole of each country was to be fully geared to the enormous obligations which planned development placed upon it.[7]

In India, like some other countries of the Third World, attempts have consistently been made to improve upon the capabilities of administrative structures, rules, and procedures right from the time independence was achieved. A number of committees and commissions from time to time, both at the Central and the state levels, have gone into the working of governmental machinery to reorient it towards the new tasks of development and planning.[8] In fact, improving and strengthening the capability of administrative machinery has become sine qua non of the success of development effort of a nation.

The techniques and means of effective changes in public administration have differed from country to country depending upon the level and sophistication of both the administrative system and the development planning employed to achieve national goals. However, administrative department has emerged as one of the crucial variables that determine the success or otherwise of both the formulation and implementation of development plans and, in fact, the whole of planning strategy.

ADMINISTRATIVE DEVELOPMENT AND ECONOMIC DEVELOPMENT

Administrative development may connotate from a minute change to a fundamental change in the public administration of a country. It may include changes in the existing administrative machinery and procedure to total replacement by a new system. But whatever be the extent of change, administrative development is taken to mean the improvements which make the administrative system more efficient, more effective, more streamlined, and innovative,[9] John D. Montgomery emphasizes that administrative development indicates "a pattern of increasing effectiveness in the utilization of available means to achieve prescribed goals."[10]

It also involves changes in both the structural and behavioural patterns of the bureaucracy. As a leading administrator of India has suggested, administrative development is concerned with:

> both qualitative and quantitative changes in bureaucratic policies, programmes, procedures, and methods of work, organizational structures and staffing patterns, number and quality of development personnel of different types and patterns of relations with clients of administration.[11]

Administrative development could also be viewed as "the growing capacity of an administrative system to take decisions in order to meet the ever increasing demands coming from environment and with the objective of achieving large political and socio-economic goals."[12] Leonard Binder includes in attributes of administrative development, '"increases in size, in specialization and division of tasks, and in the professionalization of its personnel".[13]

From another angle, administrative development is considered as part of the broader process of political development.[14] Thus according to Braibanti, "bureaucratic systems of developing States must be viewed in the context of such issues of political modernization".[15] F.W. Riggs, who has done pioneering work in the area of development administration, also takes a similar viewpoints:

> the increasing complexity and size of bureaucracy should not, by itself by equated with administrative development. Rather, administrative development occurs only if we find a bureaucracy becoming increasingly responsible for the implementation of policies formulated by institutions outside the bureaucracy. In this sense, administrative development is counterpart of political development, a corollary to the institutionalization of rule-making institutions capable of imposing accountability on public officials.[16]

Administrative development, thus, is part of the process of political and economic development and consists of increasing and strengthening capacity and capability of the administrative system to meet the flow of demands coming from the environment with the objective of achieving larger social, political, and economic goals. As has been already emphasized, development planning is the means through which poor countries are trying to accelerate the rate of economic growth, and, therefore, it has close relationship with administrative development.

As important aspect of this relationship is concerned with the question as to whether administrative development should precede, follow, or accompany the process of economic development. There are many administrators and planners who:

> take the position that administrative improvement is a pre-condition to sustain development. But another view is that good administration is a consequence of development, especially development of an industrial base, which then provides the impetus needed to improve patterns of administration. There is finally, the position that administrative reform is neither the cause, nor the effect but a concomitant or development.[17]

There are differences of opinion among scholars and practitioners of planning regarding approach to be followed. Albert

O. Hirschman has sought to "demonstrate that a society can begin to develop by neutralizing or even by making beneficial use of such well-entrenched obstacles to change as bad administration".[18] It would certainly be quite unrealistic to first initiate measures for improvements in public administration and only after such measures have been completed, resort to development planning. This approach pre-supposes that the existing administrative machinery is incapable of accomplishing goals of planning and development. This premise that nothing of value exists in administration is untenable even though the nation might have remained under colonial rule for quite some time.

Moreover, improvements in administration are closely related with the nature and type of economic development that is envisaged. Administrative development cannot be thought of independently nor it can be brought about without keeping in view the goals which are sought to be accomplished. Though the process of administrative development narrowly viewed is internal to administration but to make it more realistic it will have to be related with the external operations or objectives of administration, *i.e.*, economic development and planning. Administrative development cannot be brought about without linking it with the nature of external environment. The question of time limit also crops up, that is up to what period of time the planners should wait for administration to change and then initiate measures for planning and development.

Similarly, the argument that good administration is a consequence of economic development, and the nation can wait until such time before changes in administration are initiated is not convincing though there is some truth in the proposition. Experience of some countries indicates that administrative performance does improve along with improvements in other sectors of the economy. But such changes in administration are not substantial and may take place even if development planning is not adopted.

The approach suggested by Prof. Hirschman is realistic and practical. Both administrative and economic development have to begin simultaneously. It would be in the interest of any nation to initiate measures for reforms in administration along with formulation of plans for development. Of course, the decision regarding desired changes in administration has to be related to the nature and the extent of planning exercise. Planners would do well, if they could incorporate a sort of monitoring system in the planning process itself, which would indicate continuously what measures will be needed in future in administration to help in better formulation and smooth implementation of plans. Whatever be the strategy of introducing reforms in administration, it should be clear to policy-makers that it is a slow and gradual process and undue haste in pushing desired reforms should be avoided.

NEED FOR REFORMING ADMINISTRATIVE MACHINERY

In their anxiety to achieve higher rates of economic growth, development planning was accepted by almost all of the developing countries either at the time of their independence or immediately thereafter. Ambitious plans and schemes for development were prepared either with the help of foreign experts or indigenously and were launched with great fanfare. It was impressed upon the masses that these efforts would lead to positive improvements in their living standards and take the country on to a path of rapid growth and prosperity. But as later events have shown, this belief proved to be erroneous as not only the goals of planning were not achieved but in case of many countries the whole planning process got bogged down due to a multiplicity of factors, the most important of which turned out to be the administrative apparatus.

Third World countries have belatedly recognized the need to reform their administrative machinery to bring it in true with the requirements of planning and development. Experts, both foreign and local, have suggested appropriate solutions to reduce delays, wastefulness, inefficiency, improving rules and procedures governing administration, but the basic problem faced has been with their non-implementation. As Waterston pointed out:

> It has proved easy to 'solve' administrative problems by redrawing organization charts, showing unequivocal chains of command and logically developed personnel, and indicating who makes decisions on whose advice and gives orders for execution to whom... Experts from different countries have produced differing formulas for correcting specific administrative deficiencies, each based on a particular national experience, all of which appeared to be equally

workable. The practice formula adopted has shown itself to be less important than achieving the desired result. But the desired result has generally been elusive.[19]

Western solutions for improving structures, methods of functioning and effectiveness of administration to meet the requirements of development have met with little success. There is often a big gap between measures adopted to strengthen public administration and their subsequent implementation. The reasons for this gap according to Waterston are:

> increased size of administrative machinery once a country embarks on development planning, scarcity of trained and experienced personnel, lack of political stability and maturity, pressure from vested interests, the force of deeply rooted traditions, as well as underlying cultural, social and psychological values, have each been mentioned as accounting in varying degrees, for the tenacity of old administrative institutions and methods.[20]

Between the old patterns of behaviour, based on traditional values and beliefs, and the modern administrative practices, borrowed from abroad in most of the developing countries. The inbuilt resistance to change in governmental bureaucracy has also come in the way of efficient functioning of administration. Administrators and policy-makers have miserably failed to reorient existing administrative systems to fulfil the requirements of new economic and social order. Not only has this conflict between traditional and modern administrative practices brought the process of development to a standstill in many countries, it has even led to negative growth. At a more specific level, the attitudes of administrators toward work, performance and public, have remained more or less static. The organizational culture which conditions the behaviour and the attitudes of administrators has remained wedded to traditional values, beliefs and customs.

Some of the blame for failure of planning in many developing countries also rests to a large measure with the planners also. They have failed to take into account the capability of the administrative system to carry out development plans. Experience of many developing countries shows lack of realism on the part of planning agencies to realistically assess and incorporate in their development strategy the drawbacks and limitations of administration. Most national development plans have been formulated on the basis of what planners considered feasible or desirable within the available resources. The plans have concerned more with the economic possibilities or needs and much less with the capacity of administration to carry them out. As Waterston has observed:

> Unless a plan takes adequate account of a country's administrative and managerial capacity, and its will to develop, as well as its economic potential, the plan is not really so much a plan as it is a hortatory instrument of propaganda. It can hardly be surprising then that most plan targets are never achieved...They usually are set so unrealistically high-not in terms of potential or need, but in terms of administrative capacity and will to develop—that they never have much chance of being fulfilled.[21]

Difficulties in improving administrative system are difficult no doubt and in many cases insurmountable, but planners often tend to ignore them while formulating planning strategy. Many planners are of the opinion that basic changes in administration must be made before the planning process can even begin. Sometimes plans are formulated which call for a reorganization of the basic structure practices of advanced countries. This certainly is a naïve approach to the problem because expecting such overall changes, as pointed out earlier, is neither feasible nor desirable because of the sheer impossibility of the task.[22]

A large number of developing countries which have adopted planning on a comprehensive scale have experienced that administrative development is a slow process beset with many difficulties which come off only gradually as development proceeds. It is a continuous process of adapting and adopting techniques and practices suited to country's administrative environment. Administrative development and planning are both continuous processes and must be carried on simultaneously. These efforts, however, have greater chances of success if adaptations and changes in public administration are compatible with established and traditional institutions, practices, and procedures.

A seemy side of the situation is the disagreement between administrators and planners regarding how, when and where the reforms in administration be initiated. The practitioners in each field tend to adopt parochial views about the importance of their own specialities and think that they are separate activities and often these trivial conflicts bring planning process to a standstill. Waterston has suggested that in many countries "planners and other officials are often unable or unwilling to give administrative reform the high priority it deserves."[23]

Even higher administrators tend to ignore shortcomings of the administrative system at the cost of poor implementation of plans. Planners as is the case, are located outside the administration and thus have little knowledge and experience of administration and its shortcomings. Even if they discover any shortcoming or bottleneck in the administrative machinery on their own, they cannot take any preventive or reformative measures. At best they can suggest to the government to remove these impediments to facilitate implementation of plans. However, they must endeavour to impress upon the policy makers the urgency of initiating such reforms/measures. If they find their efforts not bearing any fruit, they should appeal to top policy-making bodies like cabinet.

What is lacking in planning agencies of quite a few of the Third World countries is the precise knowledge of those areas in administration where reforms are essential to increase the pace of development effort. Planners would do well if simultaneously a strategy is evolved to identify administrative bottlenecks. Once the planners are able to locate and identify the kind of reforms that are needed in administrative structures and procedures their task of both is where majority of countries which have resorted to planning have failed. Plans for administrative development have lagged behind resulting in poor and haphazard implementation of schemes of development.

Not only has the administrative development to proceed parallel to economic development, in many instances it must move ahead of it if the planning experiment is not to prove a failure. Planning will have greater chances of success if planning agencies can develop such capability and capacity in their systems which can facilitate in anticipating administrative structures and processes that would be required in future consistent with the overall planning strategy of the country.

CONCLUSION

Administrative development is, thus necessary if development planning has to become a success in countries which have embarked on it to raise standards of living of their poor and impoverished people. Majority of the Third World countries have administrative systems which are outmoded and lack capacity to successfully implement the schemes of planning and development. Few countries can cope up with the type of administrative problems development planning brings in its wake. Fewer still can come up with the right type of solutions which would enable them to successfully tackle these problems and move ahead on the path of progress and prosperity. Only pragmatic way out is to initiate gradually and systematically, improvements in administrative machinery alongside plans for development. A realistic strategy for overall development of the nation should, without fail, incorporate in its planning strategy plans for administrative development.

REFERENCES

1. Albert Waterston, *Development Planning*, Baltimore, The John Hopkins University Press, 1979, p. 31.
2. *Ibid.*, p. 44.
3. *Ibid.*, p. 251.
4. Kempe R. Hope, "Some Problems of Administering Development in Developing Nations", *The Indian Journal of Public Administration*, January-March, 1983, Vol. XXIX, No. 1, p. 1.
5. F.W. Riggs, "Introduction" in *Frontiers of Development Administration*, Durham, Duke University Press, N.C., 1970, p. 6.
6. Victor A. Thompson, "Administrative Objectives for Development Administration", *Administrative Science Quarterly*, Vol. 9, June 1964, p. 6.
7. UN, ECAFE, "Economic Development and Planning in Asia and the Far East", *Economic Bulletin for Asia and the Far East*, December 1961, p. 80 as quoted in Waterston, *op. cit.*, p. 278.
8. The more important among these have been the reports of the Central Pay Commission (1947, 1959, 1973) and the several reports of the more famous Administrative Reforms Commission set up by the Government of India in 1966. Similarly, Paul Appleby (1953, 1956) and A.D. Gorwalla (1951) also submitted their recommendations to

improve the functioning of governmental machinery. Besides, at the state level too, a number of commissions and committees have been set up from time to time to suggest improvements in State administrative systems.

9. Rakesh Hooja, "Administrative Development: The Concept Re-explored", *Administrative Change,* Vol. 1, No. 1, 1973, pp. 78-91, and "Administrative Development: The Debate Continued" *Administrative Change,* Vol. 3, No. 1, 1975, pp. 80-86.
10. John D. Montgomery, "A Royal Invitation: Variation on Three Classic Themes" in *Approaches to Development: Politics, Administration and Change,* New York, McGraw-Hill, 1966, p. 230.
11. J.N. Khosla, "Development Administration: New Dimensions", *The Indian Journal of Public Administration,* Vol. XIII, 1967, pp. 20-21.
12. Kumud Sogani, "Administrative Development—Some Conceptual Premises", *Administrative Change,* Vol. 3, No. 1, 1975, pp. 109-13.
13. Leonard Binder, *Iran: Political Development in a Changing Society,* Berkely, University of California Press, 1962, p. 57.
14. Faisal S.A. Salem, *Development Administration,* New Delhi, Associated, 1977, p. 190.
15. Ralph Braibanti, "Administrative Reform in the Context of Political Growth", in F.W. Riggs, *Frontiers of Development Administration, op. cit.,* p. 241.
16. F.W. Riggs, "Administrative Development: An Elusive Concept", in John D. Montgomery and W. Siffin (eds), *Approaches to Development,* op. cit., pp. 253-54.
17. Waterston, *op. cit.,* p. 281.
18. *Ibid.,* pp. 281-82.
19. *Ibid.,* p. 280.
20. *Ibid.,* p. 281.
21. *Ibid.,* p. 344.
22. *Ibid.,* p. 282.

13

People's Participation in Planning

C. ASHOK VARDHAN

It is a sordid fact of reality that despite quite a few decades of economic planning and concerted efforts at revamping and reorganizing the administrative monolith, the notion of active participation and involvement of the people in the plan processes including plan formulation, implementation and monitoring has, by and large, remained a mere myth. This is in spite of the myriad pronouncements in the successive plan documents as well as in the policies and programmes put forth by the Central and State Governments from time to time, with regard to involving people in the plan processes.

Some Major Constraints

It would not, therefore, be entirely out of place to examine the factors, at the outset, responsible for rendering the notion of popular participation a bare Will o' the wisp. One major constraint that comes out to our notice is the overriding nuances of the political milieu itself—negative political interface between politics and administration that tends to engender a sense of mutual distruct between the politician and the bureaucrat. While bureaucracy, barring exceptions, tends to be autocratic, swayed by fond notions of intellectual excellence and a certain broadness of vision, the political element castigates it as being too 'wooden', mechanical and stereotyped to respond to the needs and aspirations of the common man, much less to the "vote bank" which demands special cares and cajolery. Barring exceptions, in a situation stated above a desperate class of bureaucrats bends over backwards to win political favours and employs all 'talent' and 'powers' at their command to further sectional interests, howsoever narrow. The initial reaction to this phenomenon, especially in the minds of the young entrants, is one of repulsion, disregard and distrust, rooted again in the belief or presumption that a politician is corrupt, selfish and desperate to the core. No wonder quite a few among this lot are so much obsessed with their pre-conceived beliefs, fostered again with the passage of time, that they treat politicians, in general, as an untouchable lot and often refuse to give a patient ear even to seemingly genuine pleadings and remonstrances. Such a state of cynicism and distrust essentially betokens an overall degeneration in values and standards, in the post-Independence era and is often said to associate itself, may be as a by-product, to democracy itself—and the concomitant electoral process, that thrives most often on money, force and personal favours rather than on values, principles and performance.

Yet another reason for the notion of popular participation in plan processes to remain merely on paper is that nowhere it has been designed and tailored to fit into the labyrinth of our administrative process itself. Instances of institutionalizing people's involvement in our administration, from the Secretariat to the grassroot level are, admittedly, few and far between. No training designing for the IAS and the state administrative service probationers takes it as an essential ingredient to remove some of the false notions and negative generalizations regarding political and administrative interface and no legislative enactment, concomitant rules or executive orders accords a place of manifest priority at a given stage to people's involvement in plan formulation, execution and monitoring in a specific manner.

Sycophants and Middlemen

As a result, direct popular participation at the grassroot level is substituted by an involvement of elected or nominated representatives, who have an eye more on narrow personal and political gains and are as much far removed from the beneficiary at the cutting edge as are the bureaucrats themselves. This, in turn, breeds and harbours a whole class of sycophants, brokers, middlemen and self-styled spokesmen, who exist as parasites in field establishments, and connive with, intimidate or blackmail field officials in the grab of 'representing' the man in the streets. We are aware, for instance, of Scheduled Caste and Scheduled Tribe rural elite, who in the name of representing and serving the down-trodden mass capitalize on their own superior awareness and accessibility to various levels of bureaucracy and also on the ignorance of their own kin, and in connivance with unscrupulous elements in the administration—whether in a block or in a tehsil or in a works department—indulge in the general plunder of the public exchequer.

In dealing with such stumbling blocks, psychological as well as institutional, one often wonders as to what extent will it be really possible to revamp the administration effectively, while political milieu remains the same or even worsens? To what extent, will we be able to break the unholy nexus between the unscrupulous elements in administration and politics? To what extent do we succeed in getting rid of the ever-lengthening shadow of 'pseudo-representatives', brokers and middlemen? Or is it that we have reached the limits of toxic proportions, and are already a deadwood and all talk of revamping and regeneration is going to be a mere eye-wash? To what extent can we really train and educate the hard-core black sheep who are already past masters in cornering public allotments and getting away with their omissions and commissions—with a long political hand readily available or purchaseable to boost them up?

Wrong Perception of Public Interest

We often blame missionaries and mercenaries for educating people the wrong way in the interior country-side, especially in tribal areas, where, incidentally, our own machinery has so far not been able to set up a school or a hospital or even the bare minimum social and hygienic facilities. Quite a few years back, I had to visit one such tribal village where the villagers had been putting up stiff resistance to a major irrigation scheme, the costs of which had escalated from two to eight crore over a period of time. No irrigation man dared to touch that village and quite a few of their survey staff had even been detained by the tribals in the past. My mission to the village as to persuade the villagers to accept the irrigation reservoir scheme in 'public interest'. I was placed under the shadow of bows and arrows to the tumult of deafening drums and a young lad of 15, a student in a local missionary school, asked me in fluent English, "How much of these eight crore you are going to usurp yourself?" I was stunned, but later on when they took me around the proposed site and explained the reasons for their resistance, I realized how senseless the whole idea had been as water channels were supposed to flow upwards against an adverse gradient! They cited yet another inter-district command project in which water never reached even mid-way, not to talk of touching the tail end. I was further told that in several such projects in the district, bare compensation had yet to be paid despite years of acquisition, not to talk of land for land, jobs for the land-losers and the whole theory of a 'package deal'. I was told how truck-loads of political henchmen had been brought from outside and given jobs in a neighbouring coal-mining unit, while those who had lost their hearths and homes were loitering about for a bare square meal. I saw with my own technically illiterate eye, with the eye of a villager on the spot, that the whole reservoir project was a project of siphoning out quite a few crores of rupees from the public exchequer at the cost of scores of tribal peasants who were being asked to part with their bread-earning parcel of land. The villagers demanded, instead, a large network of large diameter dugwells with the same money, with pumping sets issued on loans, a demand which neither entailed acquisition nor attendant botherations and which was yet capable enough to turn the barren lands into a lush green habitat. This might, perhaps, bring home the difference between interest articulation at the village level and an imposition of humpty-dumpty projects from the above.

Corruption

If we look at the cost-benefit ratios enshrined in the various minor, medium and major irrigation schemes, we find that a majority of them are spurious, home-made and inflated simply to get technical and administrative approval of the competent authorities. The buck to explain shortfalls in *Kharif* or *Rabi* coverage, is conveniently passed on to the successor. I vividly recall how, in course of a senior scale development posting in a certain district, I counselled the Divisional Commissioner not to accord administrative approval to a whole lot of minor irrigation schemes, unstudied, in a hurry, just on the eve of his transfer. He had faced only recently a spate of political vendetta and an approval to the schemes would certainly have given rise to criticism, howsoever wild and baseless. The Commissioner had been kind enough to heed my counsel and he thanked me heartily for the rather uncalled for intervention.

If a pillow is bought from open market at Nazarat price and the same by someone at a personal price, the difference in quality and price is marked. If I construct a room at my cost and ask an engineer to construct the same at government cost, the difference is again a marked one. If I buy a cow at my cost and ask a BDO/ Banker to buy the same at government cost, the difference again is marked. And one can go on adding to the list. The question is, who has to bear the brunt eventually for inflated official cost? It's the tax-payer, the common man, who has to bear, and whose involvement we now seek in our administrative processes.

I recall an episode again, from my development posting, in which the then Chief Minister was visibly moved and disappointed to be presented with a sick, rickety, dying cow by an old village woman, no sooner than he had descended the podium after distributing assets worth crores of rupees, much of which went through credit papers and pass books. The old, dying cow had been imposed upon the poor lady by the Banker and the BDO ignoring her complaining wail. However, her wail soon petered into silenced sobs at the top of overriding noise let loose by crowds of garlanders brokers, official and politicians, who were flabber gasted though at the sudden exposure, yet had several other goodie-goodie things to relate to camouflage the brazen scenario. What people's participation in planning do we want where assets are willy-nilly thrust upon a poor, old widow who is made to fall into a never-ending-debt trap and whose daily bread is rendered rarer still? This is not to talk about inter-department linkages, backward and forward, health cover, insurance relief and protection against forces of a hostile market. It's this lone, illiterate, resourceless widow who is to be brought into the administrative mainstream. The question is, can we ever do this? A facile answer in any case will be yes—for if she can come up before the Chief

Minister why can't she approach the district collector, given the necessary accessibility. So, it is not an entirely no-return situation. The million-dollar question is how to institutionalize random and stray exceptions of the common man coming up with an exposure. Are we really attuned and geared up to hear self-criticism?

We are all aware of certain percentage for checking and physical verification of assets given or created under IRDP, NREP, RLEGP and district plan schemes in a district, which is fixed from collector downwards. The fact remains that barring exceptions our collectors are 'too busy' today with revenue matters, when their development performance is reviewed. They are 'too busy' with development matters when their revenue side is reviewed. They are always too busy elsewhere, in VIP visits, visits to state capitals—called or uncalled—and finally with Law and Order, the ubiquitous, last resort umbrella which can take any amount of hail and rain.

One major complaint of the common man is that he has to grease the palms of clerks and officials in the Collectorate or in Mufassil offices to get a work done. In course of three and a quarter years of my current posting in a certain district settlement, I have been abreast with an unparalleled environment of bribery and foul play. Survey camps are manned among others by the classifically mischievous Amin of Mr. Collin's description. And yet cases of corruptions don't come to surface as it is a mutual give and take. Backdated, smoke-charred papers are cooked up to grab government lands. I am little contented in a way that I have at least reached the tip of the iceberg by digging out circumstantial evidence on record in umpteen number of cases where public lands were made over to a rural power elite, in flagrant violation of standing enactments, rules and executive instructions. And this I could bring about by spending 20 out of 30 nights in a month on halts and by carrying out on an average 10 formal, vitriolic inspections in month over the last three years.

A Remedy of Corruption

It is often said that corruption could be avoided if superior officers' shadows were looming large on the officers at the cutting edge. The tragedy of our times does not lie merely in the fact that our inspections have become of late a sheer formality, while compliance reports remain an all the more formality, with scribbling like "acting being taken" or "letter being sent", but it is also the fact that most of the time the superior officers, the Collectors, SPs, ADMs and SDOs keep only at the District or Sub-divisional Headquarters. The system of night halts has almost vanished. The idea behind a night halt, ever since the British days, has been to bring people of the area and the officer closer to one another. At the headquarters, the normal dark of a Collector demands a daily 3-hour toll at the minimum. Besides, there are any number of files, court-work, VIP visits, law order situations, etc. etc. A single day tour and night halt means an arrear of workload back at headquarters which doubles the pressure on time. Therefore, the collector moves out at the most to touch the Sub-divisional or Block office and finish by asking questions of a general sort. Seldom does he get into a jeep or a station wagon, going down the rugged rural roads, talking to people, verifying assets, holding camp-courts and returning home dust-bathed. As a result, most of our collectors and SPs have become HQ Collectors and HQ SPs, giving as large a rope as possible to the BDO and the Police Station Incharge to rule the roost. Little wonder, crimes are suppressed and the same cow is sold over and over again under IRDP.

If we look at the other end, the daily wage earning peasant or the labourer has to visit the District Headquarters only at the cost of his day's earning and even when he opts a sacrifice, there is no guarantee that he will meet the Collector as the latter might be 'too busy' elsewhere. Even if he is lucky enough to meet him, he is asked to tender a petition which is placed into the routine humdrum of the public grievances cell and breathes its last somewhere at a blind turn, escaping the notice of even the clerk who sent it forth.

At this juncture, I can cite the instance of a Divisional Commissioner, who used to go uphill, very frequently, to Pahariya villages, an area which seldom saw welfare, block, police, medical, agriculture or PHED men. There is no dearth of officers, who spend a fat term in a field situation and yet have not been able even 'to see' more than one to two per cent of the villages, in person.

I am further reminded, in the context of people's involvement, of yet another Divisional Commissioner in our State. It was an almost 'mela' scene being with him at his office or residence. He talked to the people directly. No brokers, no middlemen, no politicians. And he used to issue acknowledgement receipts and replies to each single petition that he received in person. He had his own personal chase-book for cases of importance. He talked over to DIG, Deputy Commissioner or SP on phone or in person, whenever a serious matter of civil or police outrage was brought to his notice by a villager. His capacity of prolonged patient hearing were enormous. When on tours, he was equally close to the peasantry and the toiling mass on the spot. His journey never ended in a Collectorate or a Block office. Once, with myself accompanying him, he touched an old-age pension camp on way and enquired about complaints on graft. Next he touched a village *hat* and enquired about sale-price of kerosene oil. The news must have flashed far and wide and acted as a deterrent. He studied pendency of mutations, the money mint, case by case and demanded explanations on time lag, etc. At his behest, I organized several training programmes for tribal villagers in survey methodology and he had himself been to one such camp in a remote village. Amplifiers and interpreters had been pressed to enable him to talk to the tribals in their own dialect. He collected petitions on the spot, made frantic enquiries and remained there until mid-night, hearing peasant after peasant and keeping bureaucrats (including the Deputy Commissioner and myself) on their toes.

It is fine to talk of people's participants, but are we geared to orient and mould our administrative apparatus, office procedure, time-management, and an obsession with paper-work, including reports and returns (needless to say that some of our breed 'specialize' in sending inflated figures, knowing well that that alone will count for the PCRs—letting go the tree for the wood, quality for quantity). Are we going to make sufficient night-halts or hold camp-courts? Are we prepared to carry out inspections regularly and pointedly while ensuring a personal monitoring on follow-up? Do we at all have to keep a personal track of the disposal of public grievances? After all, people's involvement hardly means that the poor old widow or the exploited Pahariya or the land-loser are going to join our rank and file. They will remain as they are and we will have to tackle their grievances, on the one hand, and to allow an interest articulation among them from within the obscure, hazy depths of their respective local situations to come out and cry for themselves, on the other.

Faculty Administrative Procedures

Our administrative procedure and rusted time-old conventions and standards are indeed the greatest stumbling blocks in our interface with the people. A settlement camp is organized, for instance, with the pious hope of obtaining an updated land record. But in the process, in connivance with local landed gentry, we put our legal seal of approval on tribal land alienations, alienations of the rights of the under *raiyats*, illicit transfers of government waste-lands and the like. We hardly bother to educate the villagers in bare minimum legal procedure, whenever it is. We feel puffed up in creating some sort of a 'halo' or 'mysticism' about our own knowledge of technicalities. We do not share. We do not open up. Consequently, compromised *ex-prate* decrees are passed to the detriment of the poor, illiterate, resourceless *raiyat* or his cases are dismissed for being time-barred or for lacking in evidence as juxtaposed to the tyranny of evidence cooked up by the landed gentry. We terrible lack in a sensitive vein and mechanically tilt judicial balance to favour the power elite. What use is this survey which puts the *raiyat* at a 'legalised' loss for several years, may be, perennially?

This is just to cite one illustration which can be supplemented by several others. There is no in-build system of a road-estimate, for instance, being circulated among some of the residents of the locality, who could have kept a people's vigilon the civil works. There is no system of circulating a Harijan housing or village school estimate, for instance, even among few villagers, who could have at least seen if the door planks were to be of mango or of sal wood. Any number of rural houses have been raised far away from the hearth and home of the beneficiaries as a result of which, they lie abandoned or serve as shelter for stray miscreants.

A modicum of revolutionizing impact had been expected of Balwadis, Anganwadis and Adult/Informal education centres, but that too has come to naught. It had been hoped that besides teaching in the three 'Rs', these systemic innovations will conscientise the masses and instil a modicum of awareness in government's on-going schemes in development and revenue administration, in labour legislation, including minimum wages, in redemption of bonded labour and the like. But tragically enough, while these Centres run on paper, the supervisors, drawn as they are from urban areas, are missing. They, in connivance with their officers and head clerks, can afford to spend month after month somewhere in a town, as if enjoying a 'paid leave'. It is the 'urban-based' village-level employee—whether he is Adult Education Supervisor or the Sub-centre Doctor or the VLW or the Panchayat Sewak or the Halka Karmachari—who has to be tamed and made to learn a lesson first by making him stay in the allotted areas if we are really sincere about forging linkages with people at large.

A viable way out for mitigating the so-called bureaucratic steel-frame, apathy and irresponsiveness as well as taking care of a sense of resignation of the common man, could have been conceived in terms of floating small cooperatives or of aiding voluntary organizations. Some concurrent evaluation studies are indeed on record, exposing our pitfalls and missing linkages. But while milk, IRDP and credit cooperatives remain pocket institutions of vested interests, much of the work carried out by voluntary agencies remains too theoretical and academic to ruffle and stir the bureaucratic frame, which is better suited—with far more accessibility to seats of power, information and action—to come out clean with a saving grace and alibis.

Conclusion

Admittedly, I began my article on a rather skeptical note but there is not much to be so in toto resigning ourselves to circumstances. Perhaps, it is the individual effort that counts in the long run.

To quote a proverb: "It is better to be Scorates dissatisfied than a fool satisfied. It is better to be a human being dissatisfied than a pig satisfied". In the given scenario of constraints and stumbling blocks, it is advisable not to become despondent by adopting a holistic-cynical view, but to make whatever small contribution an individual administrator within his own functional and territorial limits can make to the system and to the environment by adopting suitable corrective measures *vis-à-vis* local situations, including evolution of checklists, demystifying and simplifying work procedure and finding as much time as one could snatch to get into the midst of the people at their door-step. If we learn not to make a prestige point in an abrupt, manipulated transfer, and don't bend backwards to obtain personal favours, I think there still remains scope for cornering narrow political elements, brokers and self-styled representatives, who stand between ourselves and the general mass of silent, exploited beneficiaries and the working class. In the absence of any explicit bar, here also remains some virgin ground to tread in trying with initiatives and innovations in our respective field and vocations in a bid to institutionalize popular participation in plan processes.

While all is said, I must say, at the end, that there is absolutely no bar whatsoever laid down anywhere on an officer intending to interact with his beneficiaries whether in his office or in the thick of a village situation to the native refreshment of a cool unadulterated village breeze, on sundry occasions, in marked contrast to the monotony, pollution and tension so oppressively present at the headquarters. At best, it is to be a question of choice and according priorities before oneself.

14

Organization for Metropolitan Planning and Development

ABHIJIT DATTA

The study[1] undertaken jointly by the Indian Institute of Public Administration and the Indian Institute of Management, Calcutta, was focused on: (*i*) the institutional framework of the four metropolitan areas and the evolution of the metro-authorities; (*ii*) the role of the metro-authorities as a platform for interaction as a device for integration of metropolitan activities; (*iii*) the effectiveness of the metro-authorities in performing the tasks adopted; and (*iv*) the efforts for mobilization of resources for metropolitan development by the existing public organizations operating in these areas. It was presumed that metropolitan planning and development needed a support system in terms of organization, autonomy in decision-making and resource adequacy, so that the existing metro-authorities could function effectively. A series of working hypotheses were advanced around the four major areas of enquiry indicated above. The study covered the four metropolitan areas of the country, *viz*, Delhi, Calcutta, Madras and Bombay. Within these metropolitan areas, all public organizations responsible for physical development were studied so as to hazard some generalizations about the efficacy of the existing metro-authorities. A comprehensive check-list was prepared for collecting information on area delineation, the institutional milieu, evolution and role-effectiveness of the metro-authorities and the success of the public authorities in mobilizing resources for metropolitan development.

Problem Definition

Since the study was concerned with the working of the metro-authorities in India, the approaches of public administration and organization theory were brought to bear on the problems of environment of these authorities and their informal organizational issues. The administrative problems were, firstly, the question of area and administration in a metropolis to see whether the existing organizational system had the capacity to respond to the problem of public service delivery, and the specific contribution that a metro-authority could make to improve the arrangement. The second problem is inter-agency coordination within a given development area and the capacity of the metro-authority to under-take the task. The third problem relates to the methods of financing metropolitan development, including issues, such as inter-governmental fiscal relations and cost recovery of urban projects.

Problems specially related to organization theory were, firstly the degree of convergence or divergence between the formal tasks and actual working of the metro-authorities. Secondly, the degree of autonomy in decision-making by the metro-authorities in terms of the structure and boundaries of their decisions. Thirdly, the suitability of the existing organization-structure by the metro-authorities for making effective decisions.

AREA DELINEATION

Unlike the census delineation of the metro-cities, which followed a single set of criterion and undertaken at one point of time, the planners delineated the metro-areas at different points of time. However, two approaches were common: (*a*) all these delineations were made on the basis of daily interaction of people and goods between the metro-core and its periphery, and (*b*) the planning, rather than administrative considerations were predominant in these delineations. The consequences of these approaches have been somewhat varied, if not unintended; for instance, in Delhi, it was found that delineation beyond the boundaries of the union territory was not operational. The operational mandate of the metro-authority also nullified the planners' delineation in Delhi and Bombay, while the convenience of administration modified the planners' delineation in Calcutta and Madras. In view of this, one might seriously question the criticality of the planners' delineation for the effective functioning of the metro-authorities.

INSTITUTIONAL SETTING

The institutional setting of the four metro-areas was examined in terms of the local governmental structure and the role of the special authorities. On the local government front, it was noticed that each of the metro-area had certain unique characteristics—in Delhi, the local government question was mixed up with the political status of the territory's administration, in Calcutta the situation called for a realignment of local government boundaries, in Madras the existing pattern of local government seemed capable of accommodating differentiated interests of the rural and urban areas, while in Bombay the artificial boundary of the metro-area failed to provide a meaningful jurisdiction of metropolitan interests. In the three metro-areas of Calcutta, Madras and Bombay, it was necessary to shift the external locus of rural decision-making and relating it to the metropolitan jurisdiction; the regulatory organs of the states' field administration also needed to be similarly adjusted.

In all the four metro-areas, there were a number of special authorities constituted specifically to undertake a particular function or a set of closely related functions. The emergence of the metro-authorities marked departure from this approach through the creation of multi-purpose construction agencies. If one viewed construction as a process, then all the special authorities in the four metro-areas could be termed single-purpose, either by function or by process.

The jurisdiction and ownership of the special authorities within the four areas are indicated in Table 1.

One notes that the funding assurance from the Central and State Governments have been instrumental in the creation of the metro-authorities. The Central Government had been actively advocating the idea of a development authority through the financial incentive of plan assistance and the creation of the Madras and Bombay metro-authorities could be traced to these efforts. The financing responsibilities of the Central Government in respect of the metro-authorities in Delhi and Calcutta were also instrumental in their creation.

Table 1: Jursidiction and Ownership of Special Authorities

Functions	*Delhi*	*Calcutta*	*Madras*	*Bombay*
1. Water and sewerage	UT(L)	M(S)	S(S)	S(S)
2. Bus transport	UT(N)	M(S)	M(S)	L(L), S(S)
3. Suburban railway	UT(N)	M(N)	M(N)	M(N)
4. Tramways	—	L(S)	—	—
5. Port	—	M(N)	M(N)	M(N)
6. Post and telephones	UT(N)	M(N)	M(N)	M(N)
7. Electricity	UT(L,N)	M(S), S(S)	S(S)	L(L), S(S)
8. Gas	—	L(S)	—	—
9. Town planning	UT(N)	M(S)	M(S)	M(S)
10. Urban Acts	UT(N)	—	—	—
11. Area development	UT(N)	L(S), M(S)	M(S)	M(S), S(S)
12. Housing	UT(N)	L(S), S(S)	M(S)	M(S), S(S)
13. Slum improvement	UT(N)	L(S), M(S)	S(S)	S(S)
14. Industrial development	UT(UT)	S(S)	S(S)	S(S)

Note: L = Local; M = Metropolitan; UT = Union Territory; S = State; and N = National. Outside notation indicates jurisdiction, notation within brackets indicates ownership.

Attempts were made by the municipal political interests to secure elective representation in the top-level organization of the metro-authorities, with varying degrees of success. These efforts were less successful where the premier corporations were superseded; where, however, such interests could be mobilized, major concessions regarding the jurisdictions of the metro-authorities were obtained.

OPERATIONAL ASPECTS

Roles

From the varying starting points, the metro-authorities have come to more less the same position. In Delhi, the metro-authority has taken the role of a promotor; in Calcutta, the metro-authority started off as the supreme developer, but by now has been content with the role of a promoter; in Bombay, having tried the role of a promoter, the metro-authority has reverted back to its original stance of being a subordinate authority; in Madras, the metro-authority never questions its subordinate status. All this is a far cry from the professed intention of creation of the metro-authority as a model agency for metropolitan development. In terms of the primary tasks of these authorities, their dependency on the higher levels of government for actualization seems paramount—here also the relative position of the four metro-authorities vary somewhat, but all are basically agent of the higher level governments, with no command or authority to control other public organizations. This may be illustrated diagrammatically as a continuum of the primary tasks of these metro-authorities as follows:

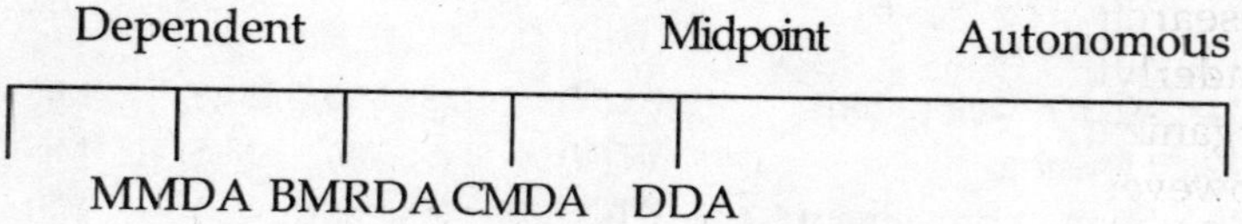

Effectiveness

The organizational effectiveness of the four metro-authorities vary. In Delhi, there is a clear demarcation of functions, as if the environment is discretely visible—and the organizational structure is flat. At the top-level, there are no mechanisms for conflict resolution. In Calcutta, the organization follows the general functional differentiation prevalent within the government; however, workable format for integration of different activities is typically lacking. In Madras, it is difficult to say how exactly the structural arrangements have worked out, because the metro-authority has never functioned autonomously—its major thrust being enforcement of development controls, which is an administrative, rather than a development task. In Bombay, the metro-authority basically serves as a forum where other organizations can come and confirm their own spheres of action and, consequently, has not been able to develop a clear identity of its own.

The four metro-authorities have staffing characteristics that are desirable from their task-structure. For instance, compared to the metro-authorities of Delhi and Calcutta, those of Madras and Bombay are 'top-heavy'. This is largely due to the execution role that the former authorities have taken up. The later organizations are generally engaged more in staff than in line functions.

Informal Structure

The organizational structure examined here is the formal one, and although the formal decision-making structure affects task formulation and implementation, there are other operative factors that influence such processes in decisive ways and the operative structure is usually different from the formal structure. The study did not yield enough data regarding the informal organizational structure of the four metro-authorities and, undoubtedly, further research would reveal the basic organizational assumptions underlying the authorities that are not peculiar to any given organization, but may be generally shared. An attempt was made, however, to delineate the informal structure of the metro-authority in Calcutta and the result is presented below:

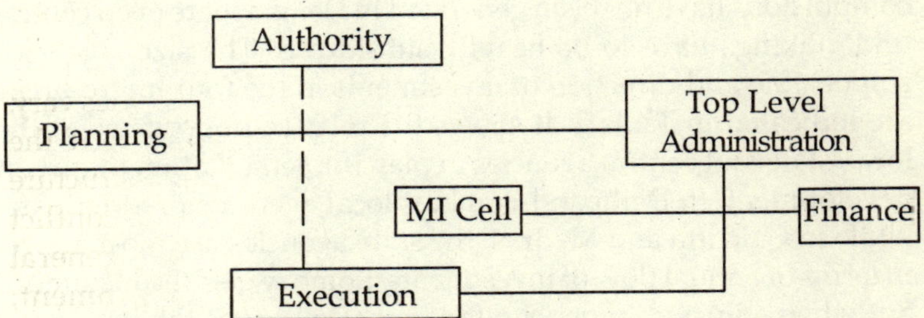

In the formal structure, the countervailing balance to planning is the top-level administration, coupled with the finance and the management information cell, representing the operational resources and the instruments for dealing with the major funding source. For all practical purposes, the separate identity of the finance cannot be usefully deployed as an instrument in its own right, but must always subserve administrative objectives. The executing departments are not involved in policy-making; rather their use is found only in carrying out orders. Thus, a lot of potentialities of the organization is being overlooked.

RESOURCE MOBILISATION

The variety of institutional arrangements for plan implementation in the four metro-areas, as also the differing stances of the metro-authorities, have influenced the manner in which resources are mobilized for development. In the case of Delhi, urban development efforts are not integrated with the national planning process of he country and metro-authority is one among the many implementation agencies without any means of effecting fiscal coordination. In Calcutta, the metro-authority was initially created to channel central assistance and state plan allocations for metropolitan development; later, it lost its redistributive role and emerged as the most important implementation agency for metropolitan development, but without any power to influence other agencies. But in Madras and in Bombay, the metro-authorities have marginal role in plan implementation, nor do they have any influence on resource mobilization.

Regarding cost recovery, efforts are being made in Calcutta, Madras and Bombay to adopt appropriate tax and price policies, largely due to the insistence of the lending agencies. Similar compulsions have not been generated in Delhi, where even central undertakings have to be heavily subsidized. The size, agencies responsible and direction of investments in the four metro-areas are indicated in Table 2. It shows the relative importance of the local, state and central agencies in plan implementation for urban development. In Delhi and Bombay, local agencies predominate, while in Calcutta and Madras, the state agencies are most active. In terms of annual flow of investments, Bombay gets the maximum but when adjusted in per capita terms, Delhi tops the list. In the case of Calcutta, the central agencies seem to be least active.

ORGANISATIONAL META ISSUES

In the field of institution-building for urban development, creation of the metro-authorities does raise the expectation of a break from the traditional mould of Indian administration, inherited from the past. However, a closer examination reveals a strengthening, rather than weakening, of the traditional administrative stranglehold. A few basic features which could be identified as a colonial legacy, were: (*a*) separation of development and maintenance responsibilities, (*b*) erosion of general government, (*c*) uniform model of organization, (*d*) depoliticization, (*e*) lack of autonomy, and (*f*) absence of public participation; one could identify these features as hangovers from past practices in urban administration.

Table 2: Investment for Metropolitan Development 1970-71 to 1974-75

Metro-area	*Amount (Rs. Million)*	*Percentage Share of Various Levels*					*Average Annual Amount (Rs. Million)*	*Per capita (Rs.)*
		MA	L	UT/S	SA	C		
Delhi	2658.45	24	36	11	—	29	532	131
Calcutta	3375.91*	13	23	36	22	6	844	102
Madras	2034.01	—	5	20	30	45	407	117
Bombay	4810.78	—	37	4	29	30	962	125

* For four years, 1970-71, 1973-74.

Note: MA = Metro-Authority; L = Local Authorities; UT/S = Union Territory/State Government; SA = State Authorities; C = Central Government.

The creation of metro-authorities, with all the mentioned tenets of traditional administrative practices being dominant, does not represent any substantial departure from the colonial administration, nor does it offer any clue to a durable system which conforms to the democratic ethos and subjected to the control of the general government.

REFERENCE

1. Abhijit Datta and Bappaditya Chakravarty, *Organizing Metropolitan Development*, IIPA, New Delhi, 1981.

15

District Plans, Monitoring and the Poor: An Administrator's View Point

M.A.S. RAJAN

Extraordinary changes have occurred and continue to occur in the external environment which bears on district planning. Extraordinary is a mild word here. But then, in describing the changes that the world has undergone, we seem to have run-out of sufficiently startling words! Fantastic, incredible or mind-boggling, even in their devalued state, seem to be inadequate words. Or else one can use imagery, such as that of Alvin Toffler and others. One can note that the last few decades, and a decade is but one-sixth of a 'life time', have witnessed changes which are far more profound than any that occurred in previous life time; or even centuries.

Post-Independence Changes

Our independent existence as a nation has been characterizes by stupendous changes, many of them of autonomous origin and many generated outside the country, changes in all fields and in many dimensions—size, complexity, sophistication—startling changes that have often deceived the planning mechanism. The pace of change itself has been far from constant. Changes that at first occurred rapidly have accelerated to occur by leaps and bounds. If the speed of change had remained as it was before Independence what we see all around us today would still be a couple of "life times" away into the future.

How have we, as a country, managed our passage through these frenetic decades? We have done our best to keep the changes under the control of Five Year Plans but to say that the country has travelled on an unswerving pre-planned path will be a self-congratulatory exaggeration. We seem to have muddled through in a national climate of planning. We seem to have reached our present state of affairs by a process of dynamic interaction between an active, ambitious multi-faceted population and a changing world, mediated by a boisterous democracy.

However, though we have jostled along rather than precious-marched, we have by no means moved slowly. Even a superficial view will show that phenomenal strides have been made in many spheres of economic life in comparison with the low base at which the country had to start after Independence. But this mode of progress has spelt disaster for the task of plan monitoring, which is the topic of concern here. Muddling and monitoring, just do not mix! What with changes bobbing up everywhere, mostly in unexpected ways, frequently and with increasing rapidity, even planning has faced acute problems. Planning is at its best when there is orderly, foreseeable progression. But planning, required in our context, was more akin to planning for the unknown and unexpected, the planning of the gambler or the adventurer. The cry is heard often that in this or that activity, there was no "proper planning" or that the planner had overlooked this or that aspect, economic, demographic or sociological. Such criticisms imply a view of planning which is of the ideal kind. The divergence between reality and plan expectations is a measure of the complex and rapid changes adverted to earlier. If planning itself has this kind of hurdle, the accompanying process of plan monitoring was even worse off. Retaining relevance became difficult. If plan monitoring had to avoid falling into disuse and irrelevance, it had to bob and twist rapidly, in unison with planning itself as well as with the changes in the external situation. It did just that. Planning and monitoring both turned and twisted with the maddening changes. They saved themselves from irrelevance but in the process they were far from being abreast of the changes.

This, of course, is an overall view from an all-inclusive perspective. The position as seen at the disaggregated level is naturally uneven. For example, if we take the different sectors of the economy or the different geographical regions and so on, the picture would include both success and failure of planning. The concrete measures taken under the planning process during the last 40 years have enabled the country to take significant strides. For example, the living standards of several segments of the population have substantially improved. But other segments, mainly those below the poverty line, have fared badly. Again, in the highly organized sectors, planned intervention by the government has yielded many successes. But these are the sectors which are inherently amenable to planning and where sophisticated management information systems and decision support systems can be applied to achieve sound monitoring even amidst a singularly fluid external situation. But when one goes down from the national level and the organized sectors to the local or sub-state level planning, monitoring get increasingly weak and porous. Rapid changes of the ambient conditions take a heavy toll there. The debility is particularly severe in the case of programmes beamed towards the weak and the poor. Are there any special reasons why planning at the district level and planning for the poor and weak should be worse affected by changes than planning at other levels? It seems worthwhile to look into this question.

DISTRICT PLANNING PERSPECTIVE

We need first to look at certain basic aspects of the perspective behind district planning, and the practices that have emerged over the years. How does it appear through the slanted view of the administrator? To begin with, we may ponder the meaning of the expression objective or goal for the district officer who is interested in the economic and social welfare and upliftment of the rural area. The expression would cover a broad spectrum of components. But in practice, more often than not, the officer is saved from exercising his or her mind or expressing any predilection about those components; he or she would be served with predetermined targets. Schemes and programmes tend to come not with open-ended directions for ensuring meaningful welfare or fundamental social good of one kind or the other, but for carrying out this or that specific programme with numerical or other targets and time-limits for execution. Typically the expression 'objective' has the narrow connotation of a target figure and a target date. Let me elaborate.

At the time of the First Five Year Plan the district administration was totally unaccustomed to planned activity extending into the rural area. This was so even in a kingdom like the old princely state of Mysore, even though planning was a familiar word to the bureaucracy there, for after all it was the homeland of Sir M. Visweswariah, the champion of the subject. Planning was only a word, it had no trace on the ground in the rural sector. Rural development meant nothing but exhortation and creative motivation. At the district level, in the early 50s making of plans meant assembling of proposals which consolidated the good old village-wise lists of major and minor wants. But this led to rather amorphous proposals which lacked the cohesion and purposeful optimization that characterizes a plan. Perhaps this was inevitable in that early era of planning.

CD Projects and Their Problems

The Community Development (CD) programme was a landmark in the evolution of regional planning. It was the first in a long series of programmes with the Development Block as the unit. A good lot of innovation and rational analysis went into the formulation of the schemes under it. Under the national CD programme, 55 pilot projects were launched all over India in October 1952. I was the Deputy Commissioner of a district at about that time and one of these pilot projects was located in that district.

The project was called upon to organize villagers' efforts in various sectors, like agriculture, cooperative organization, health, etc. My recollection of it is that of a top-town exercise which had to carry out commands from ivory-like towers under ready-made schemes which were unalterable. Yet one of the principles behind the project was said to be "aided self-help". The guidelines demanded that project officials should aim at seeking that every family in the project area had a plan of self-improvement; for that purpose maintain communication with people in the villages on a day-to-day basis; and so on. Considering the state of rural communication in those days and the unfamiliarity with this kind of ideology, this expectation was unrealistic, to say the least.

My recollection of those days is also that there were two factors which raised serious difficulties for the project. One was that the distilled wisdom embedded in the schemes tended to evaporate before it trickled down from New Delhi to the villagers. The field staff had not been indoctrinated in the new ideology, and there were not enough specialist staff at the project who had a good grasp of the technical content of the suggested procedures. The second hurdle was the built-in provision for contributions from the public. "People's participation" was the euphemism used to describe these contributions. It was partly a measure to minimize the outgo on target amenities but its other aim turned out to be a delusion, if it was not a pretence; to generate people's involvement in the plans rather than perpetrate imposed plans. Since the people had nothing to do with the formulation of schemes, people's participation became simply short-hand for resource contributions extracted from the public. Indeed, it became a misnomer, almost amounting to a joke. For a scheme or project (say drinking water well or à school or dispensary building) costing four rupees, one rupee had to be produced somehow in cash or kind by the public, beneficiaries and others. The staff that went about implementing the scheme had first to muster this contribution and they had a hard time doing so. It was openly said that the Deputy Commissioner was made the Head of the CD project so that the clout of the Revenue officials could yield the people's participation.

The project staff were pragmatic. If the community will not come forward to dovetail into the CD scheme, he will execute it somehow to fulfil targets or to please the bosses. He will collect contributions from a few rich folks (they are ever ready to please) and call the collection whatever the CD people want it to be called. All kinds of devices were adopted to satisfy the rule. Some of them bordered on subterfuge if not sheer mendacity. This aspect of the CD project was very distasteful and I remember that it served to diminish the enthusiasm and ideological fervor of the project officials. The basic lack of ethics took a heavy toll eventually.

Explosion in Rural Development

For some two decades thereafter, I was away from the State serving in ministries and public sector posts of the Central Government. These were decades which saw a virtual explosion in rural development activity. At the listening posts, such as the National

Academy of Administration at Mussoorie and the Ministry of Information and Broadcasting where I worked for few years each, one did get inklings of the transformation occurring in the districts. It is only when I returned to a Sate-level assignment that I could see its stupendous magnitude. The volume of governmental activity had become gigantic. The number of government officials deployed was astronomical. And they belonged to a much wider range of disciplines. The level of government spending had grown explosively. This flow of money was accompanied by another vast flow through the banks and private commerce—not to speak of the flows in the parallel economy. The communication scene had become transformed out of recognition. Transportation and telecommunication had become faster by several orders of magnitude. They, as well as other communication services, like the postal system and the mass media, had taken several quantum leaps in size. Plan-based activities had jumped sky-high and rural development had become a thing-in-itself. Interestingly enough, more than ever before among planners and bureaucrats, there was much discussion and activity on the topic of the poor and the downtrodden. Terms like the poverty-line and weaker sections were ringing in the ear everywhere. Whether the activity resulted in ground level betterment or not was different question. The system had installed the required apparatus. And what a tremendous apparatus it was!

Inept Target Setting and Monitoring

Here, again, was a period in which plan monitoring was hardly meaningful. For the district planner had to carry out his duties such as they were, at a time when rural transformation was going on at a furious pace, rendering plans as well as data obsolescent with equal speed.

This was an era in which the achievement of targets dominated the rural development scene. And, it is from this period that one derived the impression stated earlier, that the expression 'objective' had acquired a narrow bureaucratic connotation. The objective of rural development got 'concretised' and converted into target figures and target dates. Everybody concerned was engaged either in disaggregating targets and distributing portions to individual officers, or aggregating performance figures against targets and writing reviews thereon. Often times, the field officers were goaded by their superiors with punitive instruments tipped with target figures, and officers correspondingly ran races in narrow tracks marked by targets achievement numbers.

One could say that this was part of the process of muddling through. It is interesting to recall here statements in a report prepared by the Perspective Planning Division of the Government of Karnataka in October 1985. Target fixation for various sub-sectors in the State Plan, it says, is attempted in two dimensions, *viz.*, aggregate/impact target and micro-level target. The report goes on to describe how the draft plan divides the entire economy into 11 broad sectors of which rural development is one (and it emerged between the Sixth and Seventh Five Year Plans); and how at the sectoral level target fixation has been attempted at best in terms of income level and investment requirement. At the sub-sector level, some targets arise from general norms (GN) statements of the Planning Commission, and some are arrived at outside this framework.

Target fixation of the latter kind is primarily intended for effective monitoring and implementation and is primarily concerned with micro-level targets. At the end of the Report, a dozen disheartening shortcomings in target fixation have been listed and the Report regrets that with a fairly long list of shortcomings enumerated, one becomes really pessimistic about the feasibility of fixing meaningful, realistic and consistent targets for programmes at the sub-sectoral level, leave alone the sectoral and the economy levels. Several additional reasons contribute to this pessimism, like: "gaps between target and achievement observed; presence of several unknowns, specifically in the context of a mixed economy with the operation of an unorganized segment; the fact that outlay-target relationship at the micro-level cannot be established for the entire outlay; peculiar nature of the schemes—assets creation, financial assistance, supporting the establishment, promoting manpower skills, development of infrastructure, inputs development, etc., the benefits of which can be direct, indirect, remote or delayed data constraints; and resource constraints."

This is a very incisive statement of the central dilemma in the monitoring of micro-level welfare programmes. Another element of the perspective is the approach adopted towards the bureaucracy and its problems.

The planners utilize concepts, such as general norms and outlay-target relationships and so on. When it comes to monitoring, the targets are applied mechanically, ignoring not only the unknowns but also the operation of the unorganized and unaccounted sectors. Thus, typically the planners tend to regard implementation as a separate matter and, what is worse, they take it for granted. No attempt is made to relate the feedback that comes from monitoring to the travails of implementation. The more common approach is to consider planning as right and, if monitoring reveals poor or unacceptable results, to attribute them to faulty implementation. Rather than assuming that all plans are by definition implementable, it seems necessary to consider implementability as a separate factor and take it into account, at the planning stage itself. Monitoring procedures may be devised to give feedback on the validity or otherwise of the assumptions made as to the implementability factor. Such assumptions would relate to matters like behaviour pattern, logistics, infrastructure and timely provision of resources.

It is, thus, clear that neither planning nor monitoring can stand alone, and policy space has to be provided for implementation and this is where the role of the bureaucracy comes in. Yet it would appear that the bureaucracy and its needs and problems have been side-stepped in the planning process.

Massive Expansion of Bureaucracy

Earlier, we have noted that there was an explosive expansion of bureaucracy, technical and administrative. The blast took a toll. The enormous size of the administrative apparatus meant that a very large amount of administrative the energy had to be spent on keeping the apparatus going, even if its effectiveness was low. Technical and welfare departments spent so much effort looking at themselves that their ability to look outward to serve the public effectively and with the needed sympathy, became limited. Once-efficient organizations and institutions, known for their meticulousness and public concern, became superficial and sloppy; discipline became lax. These changes were noticed but poorly diagnosed. Whereas they were mainly the consequences of organizational obesity and structural flabbiness, they were dismissed as issues of coordination. Or they were swept along with the implacable generalist-specialist conflict, and shoved under the carpet. No doubt problems of coordination did exist, but they would have been less sever than they were, if each and every component of the bureaucracy had attended to its discipline, efficiency and integrity. But what existed all round was sloppiness, lack of concern, dishonesty, brought about by too rapid expansion. To quote a member of the Planning Commission: "Bureaucracy became a bottleneck to both growth and equity. Having originated as a response to a shortage economy it tended to recreate and reproduce deficit conditions. By its insensitivity at the implementation level, it kills initiative and breeds corruption. In these ways it sullied welfare operations which were in any case beset with complexity."

THORNY ISSUES IN DISTRICT PLANNING

Operating and monitoring welfare-oriented programme in the rural areas at micro-level are tasks which are full of thorny issues. A few of the issues which are of basic significance to district planning may be usefully enumerated here.

An important fact about the district level is that the district is simply an entity with purely administrative rationale, which often has come into being by custom and usage or sentiment rather than by eco-economic logic. In any technical sense of planning, its boundary makes no sense. This is a more important issue than, say, the distribution of planning responsibilities between different levels of hierarchy. Each district is part of a larger area, which itself is an area within another area. The dimensional shift is based upon specification of areas for purposes of administration. In a development framework we need hierarchical steps which take into account concentration/localization or dispersal of resources, contiguity and economic viability. The significance of contiguity changes with the type of regional economy, for example, metropolitan or hill-forest of glassland or liverstock economy. The divergence between territorial hierarchy (resource regions and rural settlements) and administrative hierarchy is an unresolved one. The ecological dimensions, which act across the sectors, territories and levels, further complicates the problem. The arbitrary nature of district boundaries becomes more evident in the transitional area, for example, the urban fringe, the upstream watershed, and the region between forest and arable land. When these transitional areas develop their resources and complementary relationships they call for special treatment specific to them. In these areas, the concept of district level integration tends to break-down except for local welfare measures and labour absorption. Recent advances of extraction processing and production technologies demand classification systems based on resource complexes rather than a single resource, which is the common practice now. In the integrated planning of development strategy, it is the multiple use that should be taken into account. Thus, an over-emphasis on specific location/area, local resources and potentials, local community needs and priorities coupled with local institutions with vast decision-making powers to develop the area, would need the corrective of a regional framework. And the whole system has to be dynamic to react to changes in the various settlements that go into the plan.

Thus, one has to view the district as an administrative convenience and no more. Planning has to be independent of its outline. However, there are deeper complications to district planning.

In the less developed societies, a development project or programme or scheme is, more often than not, an intervention to provide a new facility, an attempt to meet some basic needs or calling for a new class of social behaviour. What prevented the desired state from occurring, on its own in the first place, were existing institutional/market forces that were so powerful—so systemic—that they overcame the system. By the same token, those forces can successfully spoil the intervention by way of the project/programmes. This complicates the task of monitoring.

Further, developing societies have certain unique problems in ensuring desired outcomes from planned interventions. There are, of course, the normal cases where expected outcomes do not occur, and where non-expected (often undesirable) outcomes occur. In other kinds of cases, macro influences strongly bear on micro outcomes and there are the cases where monitoring procedures have to be enormously extended in order to capture factors, which lie beyond the individual scheme or programme. For example, a scheme may encourage emergence of some village-level production, but its benefits may be nullified by a macro-level policy, which systematically destroys the value of the product so generated. (Village pottery versus large scale ceramics is a prime example). Other complex issues arise from the time-span required for emergence of expected beneficial changes and the time-span adopted for monitoring. When a longer time-span is taken for evaluation purposes, second, third or higher order effects will become visible. In that case, the satisfaction derived from the project may get changed. For example, some communities may desire material benefits, such as consumer and luxury goods, whereas other communities may desire institutionalized benefits, which ensure a better overall quality of life though relatively austere. Only when higher-order effects are seen, can the monitor say whether the communities have got what they respectively desired. Predesigned monitoring will be unable to predict the verdict. Nor will short-range monitoring reveal the subsequent effects.

Thus, when we get down to the local area at the sub-district level, planning of programmes and their monitoring confront a multiplicity of difficult issues. They are rendered complex by the perceived need to impart a centrally conceived development impetus to all corners of a large variegated and multifaceted country. However, the worrisome fact remains that, mammoth efforts notwithstanding, the lives and the future of the poor and the weak have not improved nor their numbers reduced.

Recently (1989) a study made by a National Institute has given a graphic picture of this matter through a set of charts. The charts show the distribution of income per capita and depict the efforts that poverty removal essentially demands. The income distribution chart for 1975-76 understandably has the shape of a long sharp needle with a short conical base (see Fig. 1). In the decade 1975-85, the Five Year Plans liberalized policies in various ways towards industries in the public sector and private sector which gave the industries additional economic impetus to generate wage employment. The income-levels above which income-generation has taken place under these measures, however, are well above the poverty line, and even leave a substantial population above the poverty line untouched (see Fig. 1). Looking at the post-1985 period, one notices high-tech emphasis, black money proliferation and further reduction of restrictions on the private sector. This has, of course, altered income distribution. A recent estimate has been cited in the above mentioned study, which states that one crore of the population have incomes exceeding Rs. four lakh per annum. The area and target group schemes under the Five Year Plans (DPAP, MNP, NREP, RLEGP, TRYSEM, etc.), which have been implemented without reference to micro-locational and recipient characteristics, and monitored and evaluated in terms of sectoral targets (whereas they ought to be seen in terms of qualitative changes, involving extremely complex regularly redesigned schemes) have tended to take only small segments of the people residing just below the poverty line into the next level. All these forces have simply narrowed the neck of the cone and lengthened the needle. This scenario can be depicted somewhat as shown in Fig. 2.

According to the study, what is required is decentralized planning with a strong economic impetus, which operates at the very base of the poverty segment, and settlement-based implementation and performance monitoring. This would serve to push the poor segments through the poverty line and convert the base cone to a flask-like base, which sits above the poverty line, the neck reaching up to two or three times of the lowest income, but letting the needle go as far as it can. This picture would look somewhat like the one shown in Fig. 3.

We, thus, see that in order to make any impact on poverty at depths which lie well below the surface of the poverty level, action plans have to be driven with a visionary approach to push the poorest of the poor up from the very bottom, applying the pressure up from below the very base of poverty.

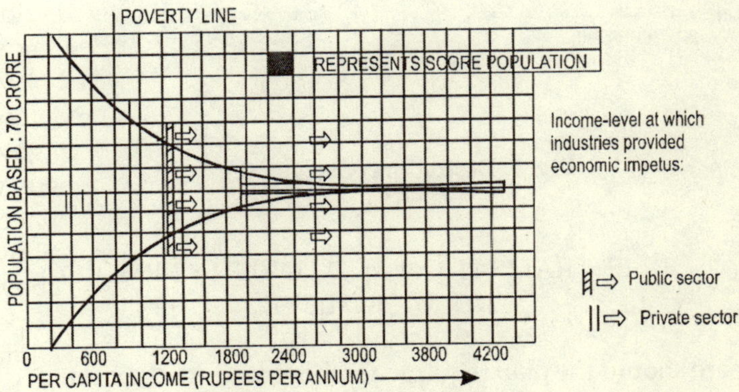

Fig. 1: Income Distribution 1975-76.

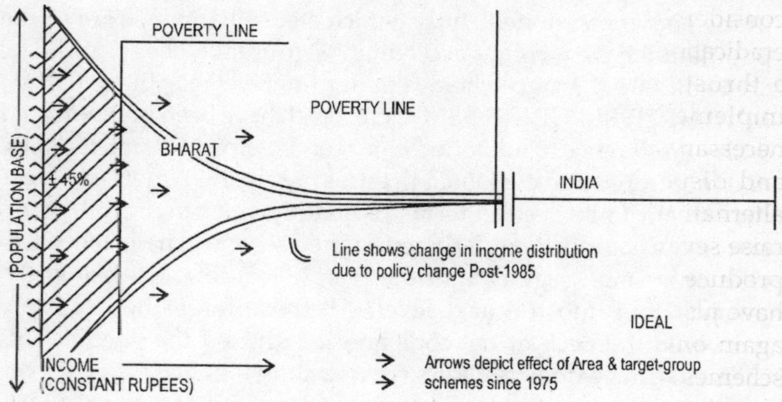

Fig. 2: Change in Income Distribution.

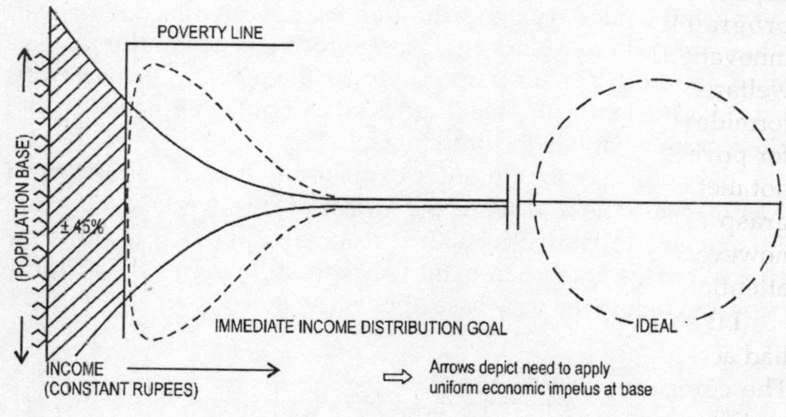

Fig. 3: Desired Income Distributions.

II
DECENTRALISATION AND POVERTY REMOVAL AT MICRO LEVEL

Where should the plan required for this grand strategy come from? They are, at present, devised in a centralized system. Since they have not delivered the goods, some other system has to be considered which would be a thrust of policy aimed at poverty eradication at the micro-level. Decentralization is canvassed as such a thrust; decentralization of both the power to plan and to implement. No body disputes that such decentralization is necessary. But there is much debate as to the kind of structures and dispensations to which power should be entrusted. The alternatives that are being considered in this context now-a-days raise several further issues for a resolution. Can these structures produce the kind of pressure from below-the-base which, as we have just seen is so essential? Or will the decentralization effort again only skim the surface of the poverty level as the earlier schemes seem to have done? It seems worthwhile to look at these questions in some detail. They are of much relevance to the administrative aspect of district planning.

The planning process had before it, right from the start, the objective of poverty removal. Over the years, a large number of programmes, schemes and projects, displaying enormous innovation and rationality, have been evolved for promoting rural welfare. Thanks to project-evaluation exercises, there is also a formidable body of knowledge about their usefulness or otherwise for poverty-alleviation. But the desire to reach out the poor has not met with success. Poverty-removal has evaded the planners' grasp and resisted their prescriptions. The current decade, however, has witnessed a tremendous upsurge of governmental attention to the problem of poverty alleviation.

Likewise right from the beginning, the planners of the country had accepted in principle the concept of decentralized planning. The community development programme was, for example, motivated by the desire for decentralized area development. Over the years, committee after learned committee has been asked to report on block-level planning, panchayat raj planning or district planning. Issues have been examined threadbare. In the process, concepts and techniques appropriate to the decentralized system have been developed, both for functional and spatial planning. Every kind of technique-cartographic, scaling, graphical, and mathematical—has been explored. Techniques have been sharpened through pilot studies and wide discussion. But their actual utilization does not seem to have been equally widespread. However, there is latterly an upsurge of debates over the principles and practices of decentralized planning. They were subdued in the beginning. Now-a-days they are widespread and vigorous.

Political Thrust Towards Decentralization

To my mind, part of the explanation for the new-found interest in these long-standing topics is the 'success' achieved in the case of the non-poor segments of the population. Another part of the explanation is, of course, that the political leadership has developed anxieties about the continued prevalence of extremes of poverty in the midst of prosperity. While there may be a basic element of compassion towards the weak and the poor behind all this concern, there is also an element of double talk and more than a dash of political opportunism. It is cynical but true that poverty and the plight of weaker sections have become chips in a frantic game of political one-up-manship. Governments of different political shades make pronouncements as if they are competing for the good-will of the down-trodden, but in fact they do not mean what they say. There is also realization that the poor, despite their poverty, have received political education through successive elections, since Independence, and now constitute a self-conscious vote bank. In the earlier era, this vote bank could be taken for granted as it was influenced by personalities like the Father of the Nation or a darling Prime Minister or a powerful slogan or symbol. Now they seem to require concrete and tangible benefits for themselves. And politics has opportunistically turned attention their way.

Recently a new twist has been given to the political thrust towards decentralization. Some States have decentralized on their own and they see decentralization to the district-level as a means for the district to protect itself against the political predators from the Centre, who operate in the garb of planning. In the remaining States, it is the Centre that has given the thrust in favour of decentralization and the move is advertised as an effort to protect the district from the political predators of the State-level. Some thinkers discount the altruism of both the Centre and the State. They consider decentralization to the district and sub-district as political venality which betrays the poor and weak of the villages to favour the local-level exploiters and powerbrokers.

However, although interest—political and other—in poverty removal and decentralized planning may be plentiful, and it has also led to legislative measures, there are lacunae in the policy thrust. One of them belongs to the political plane. Decentralization of power, to be effective, must not merely be founded on executive commands within existing elected bodies. That kind of devolution is ephemeral, it tends to be erratic and can be misused. If central authorities truly intend to delegate powers to a certain level; new political entities need to be created at that level, which are directly elected by the voters. Periodical elections, which will help to rotate the power elite need to be enforced. However, this area of policy is outside the scope of this article. Another lacuna widely noticed is that there is as yet insufficient recognition of the need to let the poor and the weak decide what they want and how their lot can be ameliorated. At present, their participation is sought but they are asked to participate in modes of the planner's choosing, through organizational instruments, which treat them as no more than "receiving mechanisms" rather than as people with traditional wisdom, values and skills. This gap must go.

Karnataka Model of District Planning

In this context, let me take a brief look at the recent advent (April 1, 1987) in Karnataka of the Zila Parishads and Mandal Panchayats under a brand new legislation, as an example of a strong attempt at decentralization of development activity to the district-level. The new Act is said to have generated a new phase of district planning. Procedures for formulation of district plans were first introduced in Karnataka during 1978-79. Earlier, the attempt to take the planning mechanism to the district did nothing more than disaggregate the State-level plan outlays in some *ad hoc* fashion. In 1978-79, the concept of demarcating sectors and schemes between the state and the district levels was made on the basis of criteria linked to the prevailing levels of development. The districts were allowed to formulate plans within their allocation but their plans had to get the approval of the government; and in the process they typically got totally distorted.

Under the new act, this process was radically transformed. For the first time an elected district body, the Zila Parishad (ZP), acquired the authority to plan and execute all developmental activities relevant to the district. Organizational arrangements were made for this purpose, such as the transfer of staff from the development departments to the control for the District Zila Parishad, provision of a planning unit headed by a Chief Planning Officer and so on. The plan outlay available to the State for utilization at the district level was distributed among the districts on the basis of a formula akin to the Gadgil Formula of the Central Planning Commission which provided weightage for various economic and social factors in order to "achieve regional balances." Sanctioning, re-appropriating and other financial powers have also been duly delegated to the Zila Parishads and even to the Mandal Panchayats (sub-taluk level) from the state level.

One major change relates to the manner in which the district level copes with the near hopeless task of achieving coordination between strong and independent technical departments in order to focus activities on the people's requirements. Earlier, all kinds of strategies were evolved. Committee and councils were tried. Various chairmanships were tried; a senior civil servant like Divisional Commissioner, or the Minister in-charge of the district and so on. These proved to be cantankerous exercises in the task of bashing unwilling heads together to carry out a concerted plan. What tended to succeed was the political clout of the individuals concerned, bureaucrats and non-officials. In the changed set-up, this tasks of coordination is placed squarely on the ZPs. The modality of grinding unwilling technical view points together to a common plan of action still remains. But now the voice of the district level will be more powerful and this is expected to elicit a better response to the local needs and aspirations. Where previously the Head of a specialized department, like Rural Water Supply or Agriculture, would not condescend even to attend a development council meeting and would send a junior functionary merely to mouth his decisions without yielding any ground to contrary views, now the department has no escape from the adjustments of district level coordination.

Apart from this kind of administrative gain, if one asks whether the dispensation in Karnataka has resolved the basic dilemma of planning and monitoring, one has to answer in the negative. The new system certainly increases the planning space allocated to a district-level authority, which includes a strong component of elected individuals. In the transitional stage, this space is limited by the fact that money under the plan placed at the disposal of the Zila Parishads comes in packets, which are explicitly labelled as intended for certain types of projects and programmes which have spilt over from the previous period. In a recent (1989) article, the Secretary to Government for Rural Development and Zila Parishads mentioned that the percentage of totally uncommitted funds given to the ZPs in 1988-89 come to about 14 per cent. But this percentage will alter to the advantage of the ZP, as the spill-over and committed works get exhausted over the next few years. However, even then the untied allocations given to the Zila Parishads are not expected to go very much beyond 30 per cent of the total plan outlay of the States. So the district-level bodies in Karnataka are masters of much less than all they survey, but even that is a lot of planning space.

On the question of the size of the ultimate unit for planning, the new dispensation has opted for a unit which consists of 10-15 villages and covers about 10,000 population at the lowest level of the hierarchy, the Mandal. But this unit is not armed with anything like a team of experts. Its office consists of just two non-specialists, who may, however, get trained in planning procedures. The hope might be that the district level which has been beefed up with a whole planning outfit (a Chief Planning Officer and six other specialists, including an economist) will service the local unit also and the latter's planning will be more effective than before. (What, however, is more likely to come down from the ZP to the Mandal are readymade plans rather than planning know-how!) But as we shall see presently, the seeming non-availability of the Mandal's planning staff may not be a drawback after all. It might conceivably lead to action plan which are more satisfying to the local people!

Integrating District and State Plans

In any case, according to the authorities (in mid-1989), the issue of the integration between the district plans and the state and national plans remained unresolved in Karnataka. How to effect a compromise between the two is "an interesting issue worthy of further debates". As for monitoring, the quandaries have increased and not diminished. "The biggest management problem", "fairly difficult if not impossible", "monitoring of activities at the Taluk level is very difficult, it will be more so at the Mandal and village levels and to provide relief to needy villages of neglect will be doubly more difficult." These are the expressions used in a review. We cannot fail to notice how they resonate with the view, cited earlier of the Perspective Planning Division. So the new system, a system aimed at decentralization has provided no direct answer to the plan monitoring dilemma at the decentralized level.

The essential problem here has been formulated in many ways. Simply stated, in a country as big and complex as India, a national plan is essential to provide a coordinated effort of utilizing resources under a broad concept of equity, social justice and regional balance. Good local-level planning, dovetailed into national level planning, will give depth and wholeness to the national plan. Good national-level planning, which takes the trouble of accommodating local-level features and needs, can give power and resources to the local-level plan. Neither mere aggregation of discrete local plans of various departments and states nor mere disaggregation of a national plan downwards through different hierarchies will suffice.

MERGING LOCAL PLANS WITH NATIONAL PLAN

Going deeper, it would appear that basically national planning and local level planning are like oil and water. They do not mix! When mixed together, a boundary layer separates them. If the central planning mechanism has assumed, as it seems to have done, that its action plans can cross this layer, it would be in for disappointment, as it seems to have experienced. Nor have the local authorities, in the converse case, been able to penetrate the layer to reach to ask some questions; how much do we know about the boundary layer? Is this a region where the two kinds of plan undergo an integration or is it an impervious barrier? If porous, what are the pores and how do they work? Where does the layer reside? Evidently, it is somewhere above the poverty line. Is the barrier at the same relative height above the poverty line in all districts and regions? To my mind the poor and the weak and their problems, contrary to appearances, will remain un-resolved unless these questions are faced squarely.

Viability of Local Plan Unit

By way of elaboration, let us consider only one out of the issues raised in discussions over decentralization of the planning process. It concerns what is termed as the viability of the unit that formulates the local plan at the sub-district-level. To enhance the participative (and hence democratic) aspect of local planning, the unit has to be as small as possible. But valuable resources are being made available to such a unit, and so anxieties arise about what that unit will do with those resources. What it actually does may have unwanted effects on the planner's plans for the unit territory. After all, brilliantly devised goodies would have been ingrained in the plans for the benefit of the grassroots people. Having invested resources on them, one would be keen to ensure that the goodies are delivered in their pristine state to the root dwellers. Otherwise they would lose their sublime superiority. In the macro planning context, it has been well put that "if decentralization is equated with equity and centralization with efficiency, there are limits to both and returns diminish beyond the limits." This means that (just as too much centralization leads to diminishing equity) too much decentralization leads to diminishing efficiency. It is this reasoning which brings the concept of viability into the picture. The plans, say the planners, have to be entrusted to local units with a modicum of efficiency. For this, they must be able to engage the requisite technical staff with the needed expertise. The management concept of scale economy is applied here. The local unit will be able to afford the staff only if it is larger than a particular size. Seen in this light, the concept of viability is directly linked to the content of the technical expertise for which the staff has to be engaged. If we examine this content closely, we see that it comprises techniques and knowledge-inputs which are but feeble replicas of those prevalent at high levels. Could it, thus, be said that when one treats a local-level unit as non-viable, one is in fact saying that the unit has passed beyond the oil-water barrier!

Relating Poverty Eradication Programmes to the Poorest

The oil-water layer resides well-below the district level. But viewed from the bird's eye located at a high perch in the summit of national planning, district planning is the micro-level. This causes problems in the case of programmes which ought to get below the layer. For want of fine-grain details, district planning will make the same dispensation for all packages of programmes, although some are intended for all segments of the populace and some are intended to serve the poor and the weak. Welfare-oriented programmes of the latter kind would suffer from this mis-joinder. The former kind of packages, which are the more numerous of the two, are as we have noticed earlier, aided by a vast armamentorium of techniques and action-schemes as well as procedure for monitoring. Doubtless, the programmes need improvement. Greater efficiency, motivation and such like organizational tonics have to be administered. Monitoring techniques have to be refined. Monitoring should be weaned away from broad average values and, at the district level, given measuring tools which are less coarsely calibrated than at present. Public participation through elected representatives in the decision-making bodies would be helpful as in the case of the ZPs and Mandals of Karnataka as that would lead to better spatial distribution of the schemes (even if they suffer from being modular pre-set structures) and provide improved surveillance from the view-point of the beneficiaries.

But the latter—the kind of programme that deal with poverty alleviation and upliftment of the weaker sections—is a different kettle of fish altogether. It is influenced by the oil-water barrier. On the lee-ward side of the barrier, that is, where the programmes are mainly devoted to poverty alleviation, certain vital requirements have to be met. The poorest of the poor are not very visible; they are risk averse because they are vulnerable to disaster; their social problems require extensive study and sensitivity to the local field situation. These factors mandate that the executive agency for the programmes should observe certain cardinal principles. Decisions affecting the poor should be taken by the poor themselves; with leadership based on consent rather than mandate; in an informal structure with the activities reflecting clients' priorities. Authority should be earned rather than conferred, and outside control should be minimum; the size should be such that each member knows all others and the group has a personal stake and commitment in the successful outcome of the activity decided upon; and there should be common interests, identity and homogeneity in the group. Such an agency would be much more than an organization. It would be a social system, interacting with the poor sympathetically and purposefully. Its activities involve changes which cannot be coerced or delivered and so they must be such that they are accessible, accepted, utilized and sustained by the users. The stress would be on being effective rather than merely efficient. The role would be that of a facilitator, which would be ready to make itself redundant rather than seek expansion. Organizationally, the stress would be not on functionaries delivering service or technology but on task-teams for problem-solving. The executives would be friendly observers, who would be able to spot problems which could arise from other programmes in the field, pursued by other localities or other agencies, and give advice about overcoming those problems. Further, a fund of information about useful schemes and action programmes is available with the government as a result of years of experience. The executives would translate the useful ones among them into the local idiom and convey them to the local community for them to pick and choose. And so on. A tall order all this, but not impossible to carry out if there is a will.

Need for Open-Ended Funding for Micro-Level Programmes

The financial, technical and organizational resources of the district plan agency should (following the excellent prescription of Mukul Sanwal) support rather than direct these micro-level efforts. The apparatus entrusted with this tasks should itself be comprised of trained teams with shard goals, wherein the distinction between line and staff and parallel operating units as well as between implementers and clients, will be effaced. Each local area is physically and socially distinctive and the organizations should, therefore, have a fluid structure in which coordination and control are by mutual adjustment, through informal communication and interaction; and power is constantly shifting. Looseness between levels of organization is essential for productive adaptation. A drastic departure this though—from the rigid field bureaucracies that prevail in the departments that operate Rural Development now—yet the change is essential for the intended goal.

One notable corollary of what is stated above is that micro-level poverty alleviation programmes should be given open-ended funding. That is, the local-level executives should be handed bags of gold without labels to be used as they, and the target people's representatives in mutual consultation, deem fit. The present method is to give bags which contain labelled packets, and to breathe hard down the executive's necks to make sure that the money is spent as labelled. This should stop.

What would then result is decentralization based on lump-sum budgets, inter-sectoral choice availability and divergence of planning activity across plan units. This arrangement would be addressed to an operational system, which is so independent of government—that all economic activity is in the hands of non-government agents comprising the poor and weak. The arrangement would imply self-monitoring by these agents. The motto would be that virtue is its own reward and that the "invisible hand" of group-interest acts as the coordinator. This leaves the question of what happens in the case of failure, especially if there is no centralized corrective or intervention. Clearly, failure will occur in some of the local groups (equivalent to 'bankruptcy' in the Adam Smith context) and this ought not to be a cause of astonishment. Poverty alleviation within that group would cease and expectation would be that punishment will be swift retaliation from the clientele, emergence of reform group, fresh beginnings and so on.

Need for Unfettered Decentralisation

In this context, some serious and concerned observers call attention to the generally iniquitous social structures said to prevail within the villages where the poor and the weak eke out their livelihood. Is it wise, they ask, to give unfettered operational powers to the local micro-level in these circumstances? The answer is two-fold. Bringing the poor and the weak into a participative mode of decision-making is one way of combating the iniquity of the prevalent structures. Secondly, the poor and the weak have been the object of numerous welfare measures which so far do not seem to have produced a meaningful impact. And yet these measures have been devised at some level high above the poverty line in the hope that in those higher elevations there is a layer of just, secular, egalitarian and equitable forces which can provide the micro-level with the 'right' or 'desirable' advisory inputs. Past experience seems to show that such a benign and wise layer does not exist.

Indeed the kind of unfettered trust-driven decentralization described above is what poverty-alleviation needs. It needs courage and deep perception and it needs vast compassion. For generous, not paltry resources have to be funnelled below the oil-water barrier. And the arrangement will have serious consequences for monitoring from above.

We can readily see that the information streams generated under a dispersed self-monitored system, with non-standardized activities, would be vastly different in character from what we now specify as the prime requirement of a field-level management system. Beyond this, we can only speculate on how information will move. There is no current practice which can provide concrete data. If local level 'Planning' is made genuinely and intensely dependent on participative decision-making by the people to be helped, the style and character of that activity will be very different from the familiar pattern. So much so that one may doubt if the terms planning and monitoring, as used conventionally, would be applicable at all.

For one thing, the plans (or more aptly, action programmes) would be based on extensive local knowledge about resources, people, micro-climate, terrain, etc. The needs and aspirations taken into account would be true to life and realistic. We can visualize further that the programme would be pragmatic and comprise activities which employ feasible locally available techniques and skills and would not hesitate to take recourse to traditional technologies and crafts. Dependence on age-tested techniques and native wisdom used to be frowned upon at one time, but no longer. In fact, there is these days a lot of breast-beating over the gradual extinction of traditional knowledge and hankering after traditional skills. Population pockets which even today, despite the brandishments of planners and technologists, are rooted in that wisdom which have been applauded as people with efficient means of survival! Where modern technologies or processes are utilized, they would be adapted to suit the village-level economy and the local availability of labour, material and competence. The result would be a veritable mossaic of programmes falling into no set pattern, not amenable to standardization or to measurement, and capable of evaluation by coarsely calibrated yardsticks.

As a consequence, the need for written reports, for purposes of monitoring, would be reduced drastically. Reporting of progress and checking of results would be largely by word of mouth and visual inspection. In the dispersed system, reports to higher authorities would not be essential. From the viewpoint of these authorities, the local areas would become virtually like the black holes of the cosmos from where no information comes out. This would mean that planners entrusting funds to the local-level would not be able to monitor results in the classical paper-based mode. New ways, which will cope with oral reporting, would have to be devised. Information systems, which do not move from bottom up, have to be envisaged. Information, so accumulated, would have to be collated and classified so that overseeing planners (assuming they are truly devoted to decentralized activity) could evolve some form of an information exchange system between local areas. At least the success stories of one area can become known in other areas.

But central authorities' first desire, usually, is to standardize. They would want action programme in repetitive patterns; and information easy to aggregate; under parameters of their devising; so as to be able to set yields against expectations. If the system of locally decentralized planning militated against these requirements, they would rather give up decentralization than their own desires! The "black hole" of information would be anathema.

This has to change. It would need a radical change, somewhat on the lines indicated. The present, as we have seen before, is an era of enormous changes. Given the will, plan monitoring can change and harmonise with the environment of change and make a clean turn-about at the sub-district micro level of the poor.

16

Evaluating Planning Machinery at Sub-National Levels: An Integrated Framework

Y. VENUGOPAL REDDY

There are a number of considerations that go into the setting up of planning machinery at sub-national levels in India (*i.e.*, state and sub-state levels). These relate to economic, political and administrative aspects within the existing constitutional frame. The article aims to present, in a nutshell, an integrated framework for evaluating the alternatives in terms of:

1. Factors that should determine setting up of planning machinery with special reference to sub-national level in India;
2. Composition and functioning of apex body at the state level;
3. Organization of planning department at the state level;
4. Characteristics of the planning body at the sub-state level; and
5. Administrative machinery for planning at sub-state level.

The factors determining the planning machinery at state and sub-state levels can be summarized in terms of the following eleven rules governing setting up planning machinery:

1. The planning machinery should be in a position to provide necessary rationality or technical input to the process of

decision-making on developmental issues in general and plan-investments in particular. This would mean creating institutional capabilities for analyzing the socio-economic factors, identifying the objectives, indicating strategies and schemes through which the objectives can be achieved, ensuring the implementation of the schemes and having a constant feedback about the effectiveness so that planning capabilities are enhanced.

2. The planning machinery should also ensure interaction with political leadership since, in the ultimate analysis, the interventionist policies (duly influenced by rationality) are decided upon through political processes only. To put it differently, the political leadership has to indicate (formally or informally) value-judgements from time to time, and final approval to the plan has to be accorded by political executive.
3. Close link between finance and planning departments is also essential both at the professional and at political level. Planning provides only a framework of needs and priorities but actual operationalisation of the plans will be attained essentially through budgetary mechanisms of the government.
4. Planning, as a function will mean continuous interaction with various developmental agencies. The interaction may involve location of counterpart functionaries in other agencies. The interaction could additionally be with professional experts, such as specialists from autonomus research institutions or universities.
5. Machinery for planning should ensure that expertise is identifiable within it to perform distinct functions within a timeframe, viz., perspective plans, medium-term plans, and annual plans. Similarly, distinct elements of activity could be visualized, viz., plan formulation, manpower planning, implementation, monitoring and review and (ex-post) evaluation. Implementation, however, has to be essentially through the departments or agencies concerned.
6. Yet another factor relates to the fact that state is a unit in the Federal set-up of India. It would imply that the machinery should be in a position to interact appropriately with the national level body, viz., Planning Commission.

It would also imply that the machinery in the state reflects the overall framework of planning process indicated by the Planning Commission and the framework of machinery that the Planning Commission itself encourages the states to adopt.

7. The governmental set-up, viz., the existence of a cabinet, a legislature, secretariat, autonomous bodies and field level agencies, etc., will have to be taken into account.
8. Existence of regional forces (such as Telangana, Rayalaseema and Coastal Andhra in Andhra Pradesh, Marathwada in Maharashtra, etc.) and the strength of these forces may not be ignored.
9. Elected bodies created for sub-state levels, such as Zila Parishads and municipalities, should also be recognized, and their role vis-à-vis planning machinery specified. Similarly, the emergence of semi-autonomous bodies like District Rural Development Agency (DRDA) at the district level and local offices of autonomous public enterprises should be recognized.
10. The emerging policy orientations in the substance of the plan are also to be taken into account in understanding the planning machinery. For instance, the emphasis on 20-Point Programme declared by the Government of India and implemented in the state and important element of the ideology of the state (such as Pragathipadham in Andhra Pradesh) will have to be reflected in the machinery.
11. Finally, and most importantly, the nature of planning machinery should take account of the extent of decision-making and implementing powers that are available to the level or institution with reference to which plan-function is performed.

APEX PLANNING BODY AT STATE LEVEL

In this background, the issues that arise in respect of composition of Apex Planning Body at the state level may be summarized as follows:

1. The Administrative Reforms Commission of India as well as Planning Commission have indicated that there should

be apex body of planning at the state-level in addition to Planning Department and somewhat similar to the Planning Commission in New Delhi. However, many states have not considered it necessary of useful to constitute such a body. In quite a few states, where it has been constituted, it is not very active. It is sometimes argues that the nature of plan activity at the state level does not warrant detailed economic analysis relating to allocative mechanisms of investments as of now. The real thrust, it is argued, has to be in terms of proper project preparation, improvements in technologies and appropriate framework for location. These are best undertaken as decentralized exercises within the implementing departments. In this light, it is argued that apex planning body serves no purpose. At best, the existence of an autonomous body could strengthen hands of planning department in providing technical and rational inputs to the process of decision-making at the state-level.

2. If a separate body is created, the question would then arise as to whether it should be on a statutory basis or should it be similar to Planning Commission which has been created through an executive order. The statutory basis by itself does not confer any advantage in terms of effectiveness as evidenced by a comparison between zonal councils provided for in the Constitution and Planning Commission created by an executive order. A planning body is essentially an advisory body and the extent of its importance would depend on the faith and trust which the political leadership puts in the planning process as well as in the apex planning body that is created.

3. The size of the body and the mix of official and non-official: experts is also a matter requiring attention. It is generally agreed that the chief minister should be the chairman as planning is concerned with overall policies. Where there is a separate minister for planning, he is the chairman or deputy chairman (if chief minister were to be chairman) of the apex body. It is also common to advocate that there should be deputy chairman, who should be the kingpin of the planning board. The Planning Commission has recommended a whole-time non-official to be the deputy

chairman or the working chairman. It was also indicated that the deputy chairman should enjoy the rank of a Cabinet minister of the State. The Administrative Reforms Commission also favoured a similar set-up. In some states, they have a non-official, full-time deputy chairman sometimes from public life and mostly from political set-up (that is planning minister or equivalent). The problem really is one of getting the services of a professional person who could command the respect of functionaries, like the minister and secretaries to government. In respect of membership also there is a genuine problem of enlisting members who are distinguished enough to command the respect of the rest of the establishment on a full-time basis (perhaps this problem exists even at the Union level). If one were to depend on part-time members, the exposure of such members to the complexities to governmental set-up may be too limited. Hence they may be handicapped. Broadly speaking, apex body could theoretically consist of four categories of members, viz., non-official whole-timers, non-official part-timers, official whole-timer and official part-timers. In reality, most of the boards of the states have a mix of different types of members depending on local circumstances.

4. Yet another issue relates to the allocation of subjects to the members. Considering the nature of work, it is felt that the allocation of subjects to individual members would be useful but such allocation may be practical only if the members are available on a full-time basis.
5. The nature of relationship between the ministers and the board is also important. In any state government, the ministers can take active part in the details of administration. Hence, it may be necessary to take the ministers into confidence at least whenever the relevant subjects are discussed in the apex planning body. The secretaries to government will, of course, have to assist the apex body.
6. Depending on the composition and functions, the frequency of meetings can be prescribed. It may also be necessary to have two types of meetings, viz., technical sessions and full-fledged sessions with the apex body

(somewhat similar to the practice in the Planning Commission at New Delhi where the Commission meeting is distinct from full Commission meetings since in the latter the Prime Minister and the select ministerial colleagues participate.)

Composition of Apex Body

In regard to the functioning of the apex body, there are a number of issues related to the composition, which are as follows:

1. The need for separate secretariat or exclusive technical support for the apex body should be considered. In the Planning Commission of India, the Commission's secretariat operates as a Ministry of Planning also. In most of the State Governments, there is a Department of Planning as distinct from the apex body. Incidentally it may be noted that planning, as a function, virtually started with the Constitution of the National Planning Commission while in many states the apex bodies like boards have been instituted well after the establishment of the planning department. In the Planning Commission, the staff is recruited by the Commission and the responsibility to build the organization vests with the Commission. Such a system is seldom prevalent in respect of various State Governments though there is nothing to prohibit creation of such a set-up.
2. It is also sometimes advocated that there should be a separate budget to be operated by the apex body not only to run its own affairs but also to be able to fund technical studies. The alternative is to provide necessary budgetary allocation to the planning department. In such a case, formal approval of the government is needed for the apex body to incur expenditure.
3. The nature of relationship between the board and other departments of the secretariat and the heads of departments has also to be considered. The Planning Commission interacts with the ministries directly since it functions as a Department of Planning in India. In most State Governments, the Apex Body interacts with the

secretariat departments essentially through planning department. Except for obtaining information, contact between the apex bodies and the heads of departments is generally minimum.

4. The related issue concerns the extent to which the Apex Body could go into substantive issues of allocation and selection of projects as against concentrating on analytical inputs and methodological issues. It has been noted by the Planning Commission that apex bodies in many states have confined their activity to one of merely considering the plan as formulated by the Department of Planning, which vets proposals of the developmental departments.
5. Yet another issue concerns the relationship of the apex body to the Planning Commission at the national level. The Planning Commission would invariably be discussing various elements of the plan with the state chief ministers or their planning departments. While there is nothing to bar a state level apex planning body to represent the views of the State Government, no procedures have been evolved for holding technical sessions between the Union and the state level apex planning bodies in advance of discussions at the level of political executive.
6. The apex planning body at the state level should also determine the nature of its relationships with the planning agencies at the sub-state level mainly at the district level. No direct link seems to exist between the apex body at the state level and the planning departments at the district level. However, in some states, the machinery and methodologies of district planning are the subject matters of advise by the Apex Body.

ORGANISATION OF PLANNING DEPARTMENT AT STATE LEVEL

The planning function is generally performed at the state level by the Planning Department. In some cases, planning department is part of finance department. While number of other functions may be added, the core functions of the Planning Department relate to five-year plan, annual plans, monitoring and review, evaluation and sub-state planning. The department of economics and statistics is the only field agency to support planning department while in few cases, separate cadre in the planning department is maintained.

Issues Relating to Separate Planning Cadre

These are as follows:

1. On the question whether there should be a separate planning cadre in the Planning Department, dispersed over the state with districts and/or field agencies, the report of Planning Commission's Working Group on District Planning (1984) advocates a single planning cadre for the state encompassing block, district and state levels.
2. Similarly, a question might arise as to whether planning officers should be located in different departments. In view of the importance of project formulation and appraisal, there has been a demand that the project appraisal capabilities should be strengthened either by having a project appraisal division in the Planning Department or by having specialists in project appraisal in the individual secretariat departments or locating cells with the heads of departments.
3. In regard to professionalism in the state planning department, there has been a demand to obtain outside expertise preferably by contracting experts on a tenure basis or employing them as part-time consultants. Neither approach has been found feasible in many states partly because people having technical qualifications and expertise are not willing to join the department and partly because supporting systems have been evolved outside the departments to provide professional expertise (such as various institutes of economics and social sciences funded by the State Governments).
4. It operational terms, formulation of Five Year Plan generally requires substantial technical input. The Apex Body, where exists, is able to contribute to this process. Outside expertise is utilized through mechanisms of working groups or assigning studies. However, in operational terms, it is the Annual Plan that is of

significance. Most often, the annual plan exercise, though within the five year plan framework, is undertaken by the Planning Department. This exercise is essentially in terms of making sectoral allocations and obtaining schemes from different departments. The role of Planning Department in monitoring, particularly physical aspects, is generally emphasized. The Planning Department has still to depend basically on the progress reports from the heads of departments, both on financial and physical aspects. A multitude of returns and monitoring reports are sought by the ministries of Government of India by the Planning Department and even by agencies providing external assistance. Standard and uniform systems of generating and maintaining developmental statistics (*i.e.*, hospitals extensions, etc.) are yet to be evolved (though we have such systems for national accounts). In respect of ex-post evaluation, there is a distinct preference for evaluation to be undertaken by an independent agency and definitely by an agency other than implementing agency. Occasionally, outside agencies are employed for making quick evaluation. In recent times, a number of Centrally-sponsored schemes, such as IRDP, are insisting on building evaluation function into the programme itself. The role of Planning Department and its evaluation wing in the context of such emphasis on decentralized evaluation mechanisms has to be determined.

APEX PLANNING AT SUB-STATE LEVEL

The most common sub-state levels in India are the village, the block, the district and in some of the states a division (consisting of a group of districts). As far as village is concerned, while there has been emphasis from time to time on formulation and implementation of village plans; there has been no serious discussion on planning set-up at the village level. At the block level, interest was shown in the process of block-level planning, particularly when Prof. Dantwala had gone into it in great detail in 1977 at the instance of Government of India. Maximum interest, however, is found in regard to the planning at district level. Planning at the divisional level is advocated in respect of some of the larger states and, in any case, is not considered relevant to most states. In this background, the following discussion on the Apex Body concentrates on the divisional and districts levels.

The Economic Advisory Council to the Prime Minister in its report on Decentralisation of Development Planning (1984) (henceforth called Council Report) advocates a level similar to the division, viz., a level involving cluster of say four districts on an average. In this connection, the Council Report has stressed some danger in placing district at the apex of decentralized planning on the ground that district could be too small a unit for planning to have some of the infrastructural facilities required for decentralized development. In this connection, the Economic Council's Report advocates elaborate apex machinery called 'Policy Planning Council' consisting of some representatives from the state cabinet, state legislature concerned zila parishads and the panchayat samitis. The Counsil Report advocates direct assignment of funds to the divisional development authorities. Planning set-up at the divisional level was, however, disfavoured by the Report of the Working Group on District Planning (1984) of the Planning Commission (henceforth called Working Group). The Report recalls the experience of Maharashtra also. The major argument is that an intermediate tier at the divisional level would only delay the matters. In this background, it may be enough to pose issues relating to apex body at the district level on the assumption that an intermediate tier at the divisional level is not warranted.

In examining the apex planning body at the district level, it is necessary to recognize certain important relevant features.

Firstly, there is no constitutional provision in order to ensure uniformity in the political as well as administrative set-up at the district level. It should be readily conceded that there are a large number of common factors in terms of administrative machinery among the districts.

Secondly, the nature of political bodies that are created (that is local self-government) are changed from time to time even in the same state.

Thirdly, there are a number of autonomus bodies involved in the planning and developmental activities at the district-level. While Zila Parishads (where they exists in some form or the other) represent the locally elected political body, a number of other district level agencies, such as DRDA/DPAP/ITDA (*i.e.*, District

Rural Development Agency, Drought Prone Areas Programme, Integrated Tribal Development Agency) have been created. The apex planning body should be able to deal with all these autonomus agencies without any co-ordinating centralized power-source (such as a Cabinet in the State or the Centre).

Fourthly, unlike Union Government or the State, where the planning function has developed as part of the governmental system, there is no such compulsion so far at the district level in as much as there is no district government in the real sense of the word.

In this background, some of the important issues that crop up in the constitution and working of apex planning body at the district level can be summarized as follows:

1. Whether a locally elected body, such as Zila Parishad, should really be he political executive to determine the frame of the plan. Theoretically and on the analogy of the Centre and the states, this should be so. The working group concedes that ultimately district planning will have to be taken over by the Panchayati Raj Institutions and other local government institutions. However, in the scheme suggested by the Working Group, a different set-up is advocated.
2. If it is conceded that the Apex Body does not get subsumed in the local self-government, it follows that the constitution of any apex body will have to be determined by the State Government. In such an event, it can be on a statutory basis (sometimes as part of legislative provision relating to local self-government as in the case of Andhra Pradesh) or through an administrative order (as in the case of Maharashtra and Gujarat). In the latter case, the planning body cannot but be a totally advisory body.
3. The related issue in respect of such apex planning body would be involvement of a minister at state level in his capacity as a minister. The state minister, if he is to be associated with the district level planning body, would normally be the chairman of the district body. The propriety of a state-level minister, in-charge of a specific portfolio, presiding over a district-level planning body can be questioned.

4. The involvement of all MLAs is often advocated. In some cases, select MLAs (*i.e.*, Members of the Legislative Assembly at the state level) are nominated by the state government. Where legally constituted local-bodies exist, their representation should normally override that of MLA's. The real issue here is whether people elected by the people to be in-charge of legislative affairs of the state be actively associated with planning at local level.
5. Yet another issue relates to the membership of the presidents of panchayat samitis (*i.e.*, elected heads of block level body) where, again, the pattern could be mixed, viz., involvement of all select few chosen by the State Government, and none else (as in the case of Andhra Pradesh). To make district planning comprehensive, the chairmen of municipalities have also been involved. Here, again, the pattern can be none except select few or all.
6. Often it is suggested that interests of weaker sections—like SCs, STs, women, etc.—be represented (on a nomination or co-option basis) in the apex planning body. It may be noted that this idea or issue is raised only with reference to sub-state planning and not at State or Union-level. Similarly, association of interest groups, such as farmers, is advocated. These ideas are relevant only if apex planning body is meant to enable participation rather than (or in addition) being a technical body.
7. As regards officials, the role of Collector seems to be a matter of concern. The association of Collector with such a body is generally recognized though the importance to be accorded varies. Here, again, the working group on district planning favours providing a crucial role to the Collector. The logic appears to be three folds: first, Collector as representative of state should be involved; second, Collector is the main coordinating official at the district-level; third, the traditional image helps. A number of other officials representing autonomous bodies or departments are also associated. Association of officials as members appears to be a deviation from the common practice at the state level.
8. Another major issue relates to the association of experts other than permanent civil services in the government.

Unlike the State or Union level, a reluctant or part-time association is practised/advocated. In other words, among the large membership of the body, occasionally there are some educationists, economists, etc. In this connection, an interesting suggestion made by the working group is that there should be an expert body in addition to the apex body which will scrutinize the proposals before being placed for consideration at the Apex Body.

9. Sometimes having a smaller body, like executive committee is advocated to carry out the transactions.
10. Distinct units/functionaries to perform identifiable functions as annual plans or evaluation are seldom noticed. The emphasis appears to be on combining planning and programming functions. For instance, DRDA or ITDA do attempt to develop such expertise.

ADMINISTRATIVE MACHINERY FOR PLANNING AT SUB-STATE LEVEL

In regard to the administrative machinery for planning at the district level, the general thrust is towards locating Chief Planning Officers (CPO), whose status will invariably be below that of the District Collector. It is not clear as to whether CPO will be answerable to the local self-government, the collector or the Planning Department at the state level. Here, again, the Working Groups preference is for a separate planning cadre from the state level and the CPO is expected to be part of this state level cadre. In regard to planning machinery to assist the CPO, there are three possibilities (1) Expertise could be drawn from disciplines like economics, statistics, cartography, sociology, geography, engineering, banking, etc., and located in the office of CPO; (2) Expertise could also be drawn from special areas, like agriculture, animal husbandry, horticulture, etc., and kept in the office of CPO; (3) The planning capabilities of district level officials in departments/bodies could be identified and strengthened.

So far, no separate machinery at the block level has been positioned. However, the Working Group advocates appointment of planning officer of the rank of chief executive of the block to be assisted by two research assistance. Here, again, it is not very clear as to how the planning officer should function with reference to the district level body as well as other elected and bureaucratic institutions at the block level.

It is, thus, evident that in the absence of appropriate political bodies and relevant budgetary procedures for sub-state planning, it is difficult to even identify framework for analyzing the apex planning body or machinery for planning at sub-state levels.

In fact, the various issues discussed above would indicate that there is confusion about the role of sub-state planning body/machinery in terms of popular participation in project-identification, location and implementation vis-à-vis the process of planning as one which introduces rationality.

On a more general plane, the distinction between plan and non-plan and confining the activities of planning machinery to plan gives rise to incrementalism. In other words, substantial developmental activity (even within the budgetary mechanisms) occurs outside the technical definition of plan and the consideration of such non-plan developmental activity tends to be outside the planning process in the country.

REFERENCES

Anand Sarup, "District Planning for Integrated Development", *Journal of the Lal Bahadur Shastri National Academy of Administration*, Mussoorie, Vol. XX, No. 1, 1973.

D.M. Nanjundappa, "Decentralised Planning-Problems of Administration and Coordination", *National Seminar on Decentralised Planning and Implementation*, Bangalore (mimeo), 1984.

K.V. Sundaram and R.P. Misra, *Micro-Level Planning and Development Processes*, Vol. 1, Mysore, Institute of Development Studies, University of Mysore, 1976.

Nirmal Mukharji, "Choice of Implementing Agencies", *National Seminar on Decentralized Planning and Implementation*, Bangalore (mimeo), 1984.

Planning Commission, Government of India, Delhi:

The Planning Process, 1963.

Guidelines for the Formulation of District Plans, 1969.

Report of the Working Group on Conceptual Framework for Multi-level Planning and Spatial Analysis (Mimeo), 1972.

Draft Fifth Five Year Plan, Volumes I and II, 1974.

Seminar on Block-Level Planning for Full Employment, Summary of Proceedings, 1977.

Draft Five Year Plan, 1978-83, 1978.

Report of the Working Group on District Planning, (mimeo), 1984.

Economic Advisory Council Report on Decentralisation of Development Planning and Implementation System in the States (mimeo), 1984.

Report of the Working Group on Block Level Planning (mimeo), 1984.

Proceedings of the Second Seminar on Multi-level Planning (1984), Part I, Hyderabad, Administrative Staff College of India, 1984.

Report of the Committee on Panchayati Raj Institutions Department of Rural Development, Ministry of Agriculture and Irrigation, Government of India, 1978.

Report of the Three-day Seminar on Decentralised Planning and Implementation, Bangalore, Institute for Social and Economic Change, 1984.

S. Chakravarty, *The Planning Process in India—An Appraisal and a Framework*, (mimeo), New Delhi, Planning Commission, 1972.

S.K. Rau, "Administrative Aspect of Decentralised Planning—Lessons From Past Experience", *National Seminar on Decentralised Planning and Implementation*, Bangalore (mimeo), 1984.

Second Seminar on Multi-level Planning, Hyderabad, Administrative Staff College of India, 1984.

V.D. Divekar, *Planning Process in Indian Polity*, Bombay, Popular Prakashan, 1978.

Y. Venkatesawara Rao, "Machinery for Planning—A Case Study of Andhra Pradesh" (mimeo), 1984.

Y. Venugopal Reddy, "Issues for Multi-Level Planning", *Indo-French Symposium on Multi-Level Planning*, New Delhi, Centre for Development Research, March 1984.

Y. Venugopal Reddy, *Decentralised Planning—Rhetoric and Articulation*, Bangalore, Institute of Social and Economic Change (mimeo), 1984.

Y. Venugopal Reddy, *Multi-Level Planning in India*, New Delhi, Vikas Publishing House, New Delhi, 1979.

17

Evolution and Practice of Decentralized Planning in India

B.M. JOSHI

After independence, development through planning and state initiative was the aim of the policy makers. With the establishment of the Planning Commission at the national level and launching of the First Five Year Plan in 1951, the planning process started in the country. Under the constitutional arrangement, all the subjects were divided into three categories—Central, State and Concurrent. The Central Government was entrusted with the task of evolving a national plan, to work out a coordinated policy for implementation of the same, and to watch and assess the progress of major development schemes in different parts of the country. The states were to plan for and implement the subjects in the State list. But some of the subjects, like social and economic activities, were to be dealt with both by the Centre as well as the State Governments.

Thus, in the beginning, a two level planning was initiated at the national and state levels. The planners and policy makers did, however, realize the limitations of this system for a country as high in size and diversity as India. They felt that multi-level planning was needed if the fruits of development were to reach the grassroot level also, because there was always a possibility of loosing sight of problems, requirements and potentials of the areas much below the state level while planning from the headquarters.

This dichotomy of establishment a mechanism which was

inadequate and hoping at the same time, that a lot more needed to be done has been the characteristic feature of development on the theme of decentralized planning in the country. This article attempts to review the efforts made at the national level in this direction as also the current status of its practice at the operational level. In this process, some basic issues have been posed which need serious consideration by the planners and policy makers at the highest level.

EVOLUTION OF THE THEORY AND PRACTICE OF DECENTRALISED PLANNING IN THE POST-INDEPENDENCE PERIOD

The idea of decentralization of the planning process below the State level has featured consistently in all the five year plans. Of course, the emphasis has varied. The First Five Year Plan, for instance, talked about breaking the national and state plans into local units based on district, town and villages.[1] It did not, however, elaborate the manner in which this idea of decentralization would be put into operation, how the activities were to be dis-aggregated and how coordination was to be achieved.

The Community Development Programme was the first experiment in this regard. The Community Development Blocks were established and an infrastructure was created at the block level for integration of the administrative and development functions. The block level staff was entrusted with the responsibility of initiating allround development of the villages. This experiment at block level was closest to the idea of micro level planning but it certainly lacked the popular involvement.

During the Second Five Year Plan, two important steps were introduced. On the one hand, there was talk of village plans and District Development Councils. On the other hand, there was the idea of the popular participation through the process of democratic decentralization. It was clearly stated that district would be the pivot of the structure of democratic planning. In emphasizing planning at the district level and below, the objective was to carry the district and state plans as close to the people as possible, to make these plans as means of solving the pressing problems of each local area and through local community participation and cooperative self-help, to augment the total effort and provide greater scope for local initiative and leadership.[2]

In the process, an attempt was also made to identify the activities which were to be performed at the district level with peoples' participation and community action. The main constituents of such a district plan were identified as:

1. Community development and national extension programme;
2. Social welfare extension project;
3. Agricultural production programmes and allied activities in the field of rural development;
4. Cooperation and village Panchayats;
5. Local development work;
6. Programme relating to social services, specially extension of education at primary and secondary levels, health units, malaria control, family planning etc.;
7. Schemes to secure more effective utilization of resources developed through:
   (*a*) large schemes, such as irrigation, electricity, road transport, communications, industrial enterprise, etc.;
   (*b*) new training institutions; and
   (*c*) new services, *e.g.*, assessing village and small industries, and backward classes.
8. Programme of small savings; and
9. Prohibition work.

These were set up in many states. The idea of creating such Councils was quite good but it did not succeed because it was conceived in isolation. I did not fit in any framework of multi-level planning in which its relationship with other levels were precisely defined and integrated. Hence, they merely remained advisory bodies.

The village development plans were also formulated but they became a charter of demands only because they were prepared according to the felt needs of villages without any relationship with the available resources. Hence, they could not be incorporated in district and state plans and remained a paper exercise only.

Then came the Balwantrai Mehta Committee Report[3] on community development and plan projects. In the course of its review of plan projects, it recommended decentralization of administration and democratization of power. Under the scheme of "democratic decentralization", it suggested a democratic body in each development block for all the development activities at that level. It suggested a three-tier integrated organic structure with Panchayats at the base, Zila Parishads at the apex and Panchayat Samities or Kshetra Samities in between.

After acceptance of these recommendations by the National Development Council, the state legislatures passed legislation to create these bodies in their state. Different states created different types of structures keeping in view the existing structure as well as the requirements of the state. These legislations provided for development of districts as their main duty and simultaneously these bodies were given enough powers not only to raise resources but also to requisition the machinery at the district and lower levels to implement Panchayati Raj Institutions (PRIs) development plans.

Initially these Panchayati Raj Institutions worked with enthusiasm and the period 1959-64 can be called the period of ascendancy in the history of PRIs. However, the experience during the period thereafter belied the hopes on this front. Except in Maharashtra and Gujarat, where there are regular elected bodies, in most of other states either these have been superseded or are working only for the name sake. The institutions lost their dynamism because of unusually long durations of supersession on one pretext or the other.

During the period of supersession of these PRIs, there has been considerable erosion in their powers and activities. Their financial position also became very weak. Many functions were taken away from their domain and new agencies created to implement those very programmes for which the PRIs were created.

The idea of decentralization was again reiterated in the Third Five Year Plan and it was proposed that the states should formulate their annual plans at least in the following activities on the basis of district and block level plans.[4]

1. Agriculture, including minor irrigation, soil conservation, village forests, animal husbandry, dairying, etc.;

2. Development of cooperatives;
3. Village industries;
4. Elementary education, specially provision of school buildings for local communities;
5. Rural water supply and programme of minimum rural amenities, including construction of approach roads linking each village to the nearest road or rail;
6. Works programmes for fuller utilization of manpower resources in rural areas.

It was also envisaged that the block plan would include all social and economic activities undertaken within the block which call for: (*a*) planning initiated locally at the block and village levels, and (*b*) coordination with plans of various departments which are implemented within the block. But this idea could not be operationalized because of lack of adequate planning machinery at either district or block-level.

The Administrative Reform Commission[5] also examined the question of planning at the district level. It came out with its reports which strongly advocated decentralization of planning activity. It emphasized that the core of District Planning should be related to those sectors of development where local variations in the pattern and process of development are likely to pay dividends in terms of rate of growth. It advocated integrated approach towards development of the urban and rural areas in the district and pleaded for giving the district planning authorities a much clear understanding of the resources that would be available to them for development purposes and for reducing the rigidity regarding outlay for different sectors in deciding upon the financial assistance to the district.

The importance of district and local planning was again highlighted during the Fourth Five Year Plan period and it was thought that with successive annual plans, district planning in the states should become more general and detailed and a coordinated programme in various directions should be evolved. It was also said that state plans will be successful only if they are formulated in relation to physical features, resources and institutional organizations in each area. Thus, reduction of regional disparities as one of the objectives of district planning was added during this period.

It was at this time a set of detailed guidelines for preparation of district plans were issued by the Planning Commission.[6] These guidelines, in fact, were first of their kind in elaborating the concept of district planning as well as detailed methodologies for its preparation. These guidelines also visualized preparation of a perspective plan along with medium term and annual plans.

It was also realized that the concept and methodology of district planning cannot be operationalised unless there was a strong planning machinery not only at the state level but also at the district levels. Hence, it underlined the need for strengthening it suitably. Accordingly, a scheme for strengthening the planning machinery at the state as well as the district levels was launched by the Planning Commission and if offered to share half of the expenditure in this respect. Because of this incentive, some states did strengthen their planning apparatus, not only at the state level but also at the district level. Some states did prepare district plans according to these guidelines but these could not be incorporated in respective annual plans.

On the basis of Planning Commission's guidelines, the State of Maharashtra started preparation of district plans in 1972. It not only identified the schemes for district planning but also set apart plan funds for it and also created separate planning boards known as District Development and Planning Councils at the district level. Gujarat initiated district planning in 1979. Karnataka was the third state which also started with district level planning around this time. All these states evolved their own procedures of devolution of plan funds to the districts as well as formulation.

During the same period, three significant development took place. First, the banks were nationalized and given responsibilities in the massive programme of rural development. This responsibility for area development through banking resources was entrusted to 'lead bank' which was expected to survey the area and identify the opportunities for development and prepare 'district credit plans'. The idea was to relate these district credit plans with district development plans. This dovetailing, however, could not be done though these credit plans continue to be prepared even today.

Second, a new concept of integrated area development came up during his period and a large number of research studies were undertaken in different parts of the world and India could not remain unaffected by this new development. According to this new concept, growth centres (which were small towns or large villages which had the potential of becoming a nucleus for the future economic, social and political development of the surrounding areas) were to be established. After identification of these centres, Action Plans were prepared for their development. Pilot experimentation of this type was undertaken in many states of the Indian Union.

Third, many area specific and beneficiary oriented programmes (like CADA, DDA, HADA, TDA, DPAP, SFDA, MFAL, etc.) were introduced. These area specific programmes were implemented by special agencies created for this purpose. These were, by and large, centrally sponsored programmes on a sharing basis and operated at the district or area level independent of each other. But they were not part of the total development plan of the district. In fact, total development plan of the district should have "been prepared in the first place and these special programmes should have been derived from such an overall plan of the district. It was only when such approach is adopted that integrated development would take place. But such an approach was found lacking.

Then came a change of Government at the national level in 1977. The new government realized that the Five Year Plans did not make much impact on the poor as well as backward regions. Successful implementation of anti-poverty programmes and backward regions required systematic identification of really poor and formulation of appropriate programmes for them. This required door to door and village to village survey. This kind of survey and formulation of programmes for them could not be done at the district level. Hence, block was identified as the appropriate level having adequate size for planning and implementation.

A Working Group under the Chairmanship of M.L. Dantwala[7] was appointed to draw up guidelines for block-level planning. The Working Group noted that the remoteness of the planning agencies from the areas of implementation and vastness of geographical coverage hamper matching of sectoral financial allocations with location specific needs as well as potential for regulating the distribution of the gains of development. Hence, it was advocated that the block level planning will accelerate the process of decentralization in the hope that a more systematic planning effort with a smaller coverage will not only help to speed up the development process but also improve it qualitatively in the sense of making it more responsive to the needs of weaker sections of society.[8] In the opinion of Working Group, block level planning was not to be viewed as an isolated exercise but as a link in the hierarchy of level from a cluster of villages below the block level to the district, regional and state levels.

The Planning Commission issued detailed guidelines on the basis of this Working Group's report to all he States in the hope that the States will start the process of formulation of block plans which will, in turn, form part of the district plans and finally the State Plans. Some States did prepare block plans through private consulting agencies/universities/research institutions though the Working Group wanted that the plans be formulated as a joint effort of block and district level machinery with the assistance of available local experts.

Although the block level planning was contemplated as a multi-purpose planning device for the overall development of the block, but in practice, it became an integrated rural development planning. The IRDP, in turn, came to be defined as plan for lifting the poorest families in the block above the poverty line by providing credit and other inputs to start viable economic activities. But these plans were not dovetailed with other existing economic activities of the block.

During the same period, another committee, headed by Asoka Mehta[9], was appointed to enquire into the working of the Panchayati Raj Institutions and to suggest measures to strengthen them so as to enable the decentralized system of planning and development to be effective. The Committee felt that development work in future needs intricate designing and greater coordination which it would be unwise to attempt at the State level.[10] It also suggested that district planning unit consisting of a professionally qualified team should be placed within Zila Parishad under direct supervision of Chief Executive Officer of the Zila Parishad. The Committee further stated that the PRIs at district and other levels were not merely a forum for obtaining the views of the popular representatives but in due course should be capable of planning the most suitable schemes that they consider will be appropriate for their areas.

The Sixth Five Year Plan again highlighted the importance of block level planning for eradication of poverty through provision of gainful employment opportunities to the poorest of the poor. Thus, block level planning became only a single-point programme of employment generation and it in no way reflected the integrated area development plan.

In the year 1983, the Prime Minister's Economic Advisory Council (EAC) concluded that there were clear limits to planning at the district level and a district could be too small a unit for planning some of the infrastructure facilities. It, therefore, suggested a cluster of four districts on an average as a level of decentralized planning. This tier could be termed as Divisional Development Authority (DDA) which would have a Policy Planning Council and also a Progarmme Executive Council. The planning and budgetary procedures would also need to be suitably amended to strengthen the divisional agencies. The EAC also suggested earmarking of plan funds to these DDAs. Thus, the EAC suggested a process which was against the trend that had been advocated in the past. However, the later developments showed that the recommendations of the EAC were neither incorporated in the Approach Paper nor the main document of the Seventh Five Year Plan. In fact, both these documents reiterated the earlier practice of decentralized planning a the district level.

The Planning Commission again set up a Working Group on district planning under the Chairmanship of C.H. Hanumantha Rao.[11] The Working Group submitted its report in 1984. It made detailed recommendations on all the aspects of district planning and hoped that the Report would stimulate district planning activity in the states enabling them to adopt the 'stages approach' to district planning and to prepare specific guidelines/manuals for district planning. After having done so, the States may take up comprehensive district planning during the Seventh Plan period. The Working Group further indicated that the district is seen as a sub-system of multi-level planning. The totality of all planning activities at the level of this sub-system would vest with a single district planning body which would determine the priorities and allocate funds accordingly among various development sectors.[12]

During the Sixth Plan period, Andhra Pradesh and Uttar Pradesh also started district planning. They evolved their own procedure of devoluting of plan funds to the districts and also set up committees with people's representative at the district level to formulate as well as monitor implementation of district plans.

Other States also started thinking about introduction of the process in their States according to the guidelines suggested by the Working Group in 1984.

The Seventh Plan document (1985-90) re-affirmed its faith in the process of decentralization and resolved to follow the process on the lines suggested by the Rao Committee. The Planning Commission proposed to play a promotional and guiding role in order to impart momentum to the district planning process.[13]

In 1985, the Planning Commission appointed a committee under the Chairmanship of G.V.K. Rao to review existing administrative arrangements for rural development and to suggest appropriate structural mechanism (CAARD 1985).[14] The CAARD report emphasized the need to activate PRIs.

Apart from reiterating the concept of properly prepared district plans, the Commission has suggested the concept of district budgeting. According to the report, one of the reasons why decentralized planning has not got off the ground is that the arrangements of preparation of budgets have not been suitably modified to incorporate the suggested district-wise preparation of budgets.[15]

On the question of revival of the PRIs, it would be appropriate to make a reference to the Sarkaria Commission which had been appointed to examine and review the working of the existing arrangements between the Union and States in regard to powers, functions and responsibilities in all spheres. In its report, the Commission has reiterated the importance of a system of participation by people's representatives in the process of planning and supporting administrative machinery provided at local level. This would also ensure accountability on the part of these institutions for the utilization of vast development finance which is now flowing into the rural areas.[16] The Commission recommended effective participation by elected bodies and also creation of a body like Finance Commission at the state level to enable State Government to take an objective view of resources to be devolved or transferred to the districts.

Very recently, this subject was discussed in the District Magistrates' Conferences at Gorakhpur, Jaipur, Bhopal, etc., which was addressed by the Prime Minister. Four model District Plans were also presented in these conferences. The basic thrust was that the value of district plan is derived from the fact that it reflects the real needs of people and is close enough to them to adequately reflect their aspirations. The PRIs are bodies which could articulate the needs and aspirations of the people. It was also suggested that a clearly laid down system of devolution of funds from the State Government to the districts should be laid down. In the process, the conference suggested setting up of State Finance Commission so that funds could be allocated the districts on the basis of well-defined criteria and that the levels of development in various districts could be taken into account while laying down the principles of resource allocation.

CURRENT STATUS

In the backdrop of historical evolution of the concept at the methodological as well as operational levels, the current status of decentralized planning may now be summarized:

1. Though the need of the decentralization has been successively stressed in the Five Year Plans, only a few States of the Indian Union have actually tried to operationalize it. Maharashtra, Gujarat, Karnataka, Jammu and Kashmir, Uttar Pradesh, Andhra Pradesh, West Bengal and Madhya Pradesh belong to this category. Now Bihar has also joined this group. Even in these States, the process has gone to one level below, *i.e.*, the district level only.
2. After publication of the Balwantrai Mehta Committee Report, most of the States introduced Panchayati Raj Institutions. However, after the initial enthusiasm had died down, these institutions lost their importance as well as their basic functions because of long bouts of supersession and apathy of the State leadership towards them. Wherever they exist, they do not exercise any control over district plan funds.
3. Instead of entrusting the job of district planning to the duly constituted Zila Parishads, new planning bodies have been created at the district level for the decentralized planning work. In most of the states, these Panchayati Raj Bodies have not been associated in any manner with the formulation and monitoring of the district plans. In some others, the Zila Parishads have become subordinates to

the district planning bodies. In still others, the Zila Parishads have become implementing agencies. The only exception is Karnataka where a comprehensive legislation "Karnataka Zila Parishads, Taluka Panchayat Samitis, Mandal Panchayat and Nyaya Panchayats Act, 1983" has been passed which has entrusted the Zila Parishads with all the functions of district planning.

4. During the years, many new autonomous and semi-autonomous bodies have mushroomed at the district level. Some of these (*i.e.*, DRDA/DPAP/TDA) have been established on the directives of Central Government. They have their district level functionaries and they work independently of each other and are not part of the district planning bodies.
5. A demarcation of activities between the State and the district has been done on the basis of twin norms of location and coverage of benefit. But this classification is also not very accurate and scientific and many of the activities which ought to have been done by the districts have been retained at the State level.
6. The decentralized district plans are prepared at the district level strictly according to the guidelines and norms fixed at the State headquarters. This results in disaggregation of State Plan into district plans and not district plan coming up with proposals based on local needs and requirements. The devolution of plan funds, though based on population, area and level of development, does not give any elbow room to the district authorities to prepare 'new' schemes. The funds given to districts and priority fixed are hardly sufficient to carry on the continuing schemes and their contingent expansion. In a few States, 'incentive money' or 'untied funds' are allotted for preparing purely new schemes at the district level.
7. So far as the administrative and financial delegation is concerned, not much headway has been made. There is great resistance from the bureaucracy at the top level to shed their powers. The old system of centralized accounting and budgeting system is still being followed. The rules, regulations and budgetary procedures have not been suitably modified to suit the requirements of the new process.

8. In almost all the States, the technical planning machinery at the district level is extremely inadequate both quantitatively and qualitatively. The idea of preparing an integrated district development plan with clear-cut forward and backward linkages is a far cry. The district plans prepared now with the one-man technical planning cell is simply a collection of sectoral plans prepared by different departmental heads at the district level.

The general position with regard to district planning has been aptly summarized by the Working Group on District Planning:[17]

> District planning in most of the States follows a similar pattern with minor variations. It seems to be a case of diverse structure a common characteristics. Usually after the State budget is voted in the Assembly, the different Heads of Departments are required to make a district-wise break-up of the outlays provided in the plan budget. This is then communicated to the district either by sectoral Departments or Planning Department of the State. After communication is received, the district attempts to incorporate a write up for the district-wise outlay and a document called, 'District Plan' emerges in this manner which is purely an aggregation of departmental outlays.

Thus, it is seen that there is a glaring contrast between the ideal concept of decentralized planning and the operational reality obtaining at the district-level.

EMERGENT ISSUES

Given this background, it is proposed to pose a number of issues for detailed consideration. In posting these issues, it is fully realized that the question of decentralized planning should no be restricted to one of planning techniques but extended to the whole process of socio-political changes. Further, it has to be viewed with reference to institutional structures.

Willingness to Decentralize

One of the basic issues which emerge out of the above discussion is whether there has been a genuine desire and will to decentralize even in the limited field of planning and development. This, to a great extent, is the basic prerequisite for the success of decentralization and if it is there, the other pre-requisites, like delegation, technical planning machinery, etc., automatically follow.

The concept of decentralization is more than a technique of administration, it is a philosophy which has a close relationship with the sharing of power and granting autonomy to various levels. Hence, it requires strong political will and commitment to the philosophy to push through the concept and to shift the locus of decision-making and implementation closer to the people.

The political party in power at the Centre and its leadership always advocated, in no uncertain terms, the need for decentralization of the whole process of planning from top level to the lower levels. All the Five Year Plans and other official documents have been testimony to this faith of the political leadership.

In a multi-level planning set-up, though there is some degree of consistency and inter-dependency to some extent yet each level has, within a broad sphere, freedom to plan and implement the programmes. Secondly, there is also a clear-cut demarcation of functions between the Centre and States. The Centre has 97 subjects whereas the State List contains 66 and the Centre can prevail even in the subjects in the Concurrent List which are 47 in number. Social and economic planning is in the Concurrent List but most of the developmental and welfare activities with which planning is concerned are in the State sector. But the more than three decades of planning have tended to push the system to greater centralization.

Though the States have full freedom to prepare their own plans keeping in view the national priorities and objectives, but they have little freedom and elbow room in this sphere because of heavy dependence of States on Centre for resources for development. This dependence has further increased because of the demands of development. The Centre's share in the form of central plan assistance is a substantial portion of the total plan outlay of the States.

This heavy dependence on Centre and the dominant role of the Planning Commission—a non-constitutional and non-statutory organization—has greatly increased the Central control over the States. The Planning Commission imposes two types of disciplines. One, financial, in the sense of conforming to ceilings of State and Central resources settled in consultation with the Centre and substantive in that broad features, like targets, priorities, types of schemes, etc., have to fit in with the thinking at the national level. Further, the Central plan assistance is subject to the approval of the plan by the Planning Commission which has to ensure that the guidelines are observed, that the national plan targets will be fulfilled, and that proper provision has been made for core plan items. A shortfall in the approved plan may invite penalty of a proportionate cut in Central Plan assistance.

Though, in theory, it fits in well with the concept of multi-level planning, but in practice, it meant more of Central control. States are also required to have schemes of special complexity or size individually approved by the Centre. In addition, Centre generally disapproved any deviation from the agreed plan.

The increase in the number of Centrally sponsored schemes is yet another example of trend towards centralization. The National Development Council had, in 1979, decided that centrally sponsored schemes should be limited in total value to one-sixth or one seventh of the quantum of Central assistance to the States, but the actual position is quite otherwise. Both the number and quantum of Central assistance through these schemes has increased enormously. In 1980-81, this assistance was 47.3 per cent of normal Central assistance which increased to 73.74 per cent in 1984-85. The most notable part of these Centrally sponsored schemes is that these relate to the subjects which fall approximately within the purview of States.

The general criticism of these types of schemes was that they are drawn too rigidly leaving little scope for flexibility at the operational level and too much control by the Central ministries. Further, these schemes are normally sponsored during the course of implementation of plan, resulting in undue financial hardships to the States as they have to provide a matching contribution in many of the schemes.

The system of this type of central assistance introduces considerable confusion, delay and uncertainty in the process of planning and cripples the initiative of the States. Even when the Centre desires to introduce any new scheme on a countrywide basis, it could be correct, appropriate and wise to advise the States only on the broad outlines of the scheme and allow them to work it out with such modifications as many be required by local circumstances. Otherwise it is difficult for any State Government to resist financial bait that the Centrally sponsored schemes offer.

In this limited sphere of planning, the States, therefore, come to conflict with the Centre and this conflict becomes more sharper when the political leadership at the State level is ideologically different than the political leadership at the Centre. In these States, the Centre uses the institution of Planning Commission and the clearance of projects of importance as a mechanism of control over these States.

The same tendency of centralization is visible in more stronger terms at the State level because there is no constitutional safeguards provided for the sub-state level as have been provided to the States under the Constitution. Local Government is included in the States list and it is for the States to pass legislation defining their scope and authority.

Though Panchayati Raj Institutions have been established under the banner of democratic decentralization, but most of the time they have remained superseded and the bureaucracy have run these institutions as regular government departments. The same is the case with urban local bodies.

During the period of supersession, many of the activities have been taken out and regular departments have been entrusted with that job because it is much easier to control the departments than to control a democratic institution. Asoka Mehta Committee has identified the lukewarm attitude of the political elite at higher levels towards strengthening these local institutions as one of the crucial reasons which undermined the role of these bodies.

Wherever, these PRIs existed, they were not given the responsibility of district planning though the Act specifically provided for it. Instead parallel executive bodies have been created. Further, in many places, the elected representatives of PRIs were not included in their committees and only members of Parliament and State Legislatures were included.

This tendency of superseding the democratic institutions and controlling them through officials is not confined to rural and urban local bodies, it is seen in all the areas where there is a provision of duly elected body, be it cooperative institutions at all levels from State downwards, cane unions and councils and mandi samities. This has resulted in officialization of all democratic institutions at the local levels.

But even in the sphere of planning, no genuine decentralization has taken place. Though most of the States have planning departments and few have State Planning Boards also but the records show that these planning boards have very little role to play in the formulation of State Plans. Even the Plan document is not formally approved by these boards before submission to the Central Planning Commission.

The State headquarters exercise same type of control and scrutiny with regard to district plans as is being done by the Central Planning Commission with state plans. Districts are strictly bound by the State guidelines and norms and they cannot deviate an inch from them with the result that district planning has become more of planning for the districts by the departments at the State level then by or of the districts. They became a programming exercise only. Further, this scheme has not been fully backed up by administrative and financial decentralization with the result that for a petty purchase or minor re-appropriation of funds, the people have to run to the State headquarters for sanctions. A lot of time and money is wasted in these small matters.

Thus, the states have also not fared better than the Centre in the matter of genuine decentralization of planning process. The tendency of centralization is more prominent at the State level because of the complete dependence of districts in the matter of plan funds on the State and no constitutional recognition to that level.

Its' a fact that we have talked of decentralization for the last 35 years without giving it a genuine trial and also that we are not prepared to entrust it to the popularly elected representatives of the district. But why this is so? In order to find an answer to the basic question, we will have to look into the larger question of social and political climate prevailing at the particular time. Some of the basic reasons for this types to tendency in a democratic set-up can be summarized below:

1. While development needs a direction towards decentralization, the political compulsions many at time pull towards centralization. Political parties in power

which are uncertain of their position tend to resist and resent any attempt at setting up local organizations (other than their own) outside their control.

2. Political leaders at the level of members of parliament or legislators or belonging to middle-level party hierarchy, to not tolerate, let alone encourage, independent a grass-root political leaders as they are seen as a threat to their power base. In a multi-party country like India, these problems are further compounded by the possibility of different political parties controlling local institutions. In this context, the tendency to thwart moves towards the genuine devolution of power to local levels may become inevitable.
3. The Central and State leaderships look with suspicion at the emergence of any strong decentralized institutional political leadership and hence evolve ways and means of controlling the power and authorities at the decentralized levels.
4. Adequate political forces have yet to emerge strongly pushing for decentralization below the state level and such interest as has been shown by particular parties has been limited to the extent that they were themselves in a position to take advantage of it. Even among political parties in dominant positions and broadly committed to decentralization in principle, there has been fear of their leadership being undercut from below by elements belonging to other parties or even their own. Such fears have grown in recent years as the coalition basis of political power and its resulting fragility have become more evident and correspondingly the tendencies towards centralization have also grown.

Institutional Structure Below State Level

Decentralized planning presupposes active and effective involvement of people's representatives. Therefore, the question arises as to what should be the institutional structure below the state level. Whether it should be statutorily constituted body like Zila Parishad or an executive planning body like the DPDCs or DPBs. The consensus of opinion is in favour of duly elected body like Zila Parishads. To ensure this pattern and people's participation, some have even suggested a constitutional amendment. In order to have regular elections and sessions, the Sarkaria Commission has suggested a legislation analogous to Articles 172 and 174 of the Constitution.

Functions of Institutional Structure

What are the functions that have to be allotted to these institutions? A planner has always to take a more comprehensive and total view of development. Fragmented approach often leads to wrong decisions. The practice followed hitherto of going from scheme to scheme to decide as to which of these should belong to 'state sector' or 'district sector' has led to a situation where within a 'sector' or 'sub-sector' schemes are divided between 'state' and 'district' sectors thereby assigning the function for a sector or sub-sector to two parallel institutions whose perceptions may not necessarily be the same. This dual control and direction of planning may be counter-productive. It is for consideration, therefore, if instead of continuing with the present practice of treating individual schemes as units for decision whether the same should belong to 'state' or 'district' sectors of a plan, and if the same may appear to be covering too large and diverse an area than sub-sectors, within individual sectors, having schemes of a similar character with more or less the same object, can be identified for classification between 'state' and 'district' sector.

Identification of sub-sectors and their classification accordingly will be a more rational approach and apart from ensuring the advantage of unity of direction for a sub-sector as a whole, it will also stop frequent and erratic shuffling of schemes from one sector to anther. Even if some shuffling of sub-sectors is intended to be done, it would not be confined to one or two schemes, but a bunch of several schemes of a sub-sector, and because of the very numbers involved and their implications, the decisions in this regard may have to be taken after a very careful consideration. Depending upon the view taken on this issue, sub-sectors which are amenable to planning and control at the district level and should belong to 'district sector' can be easily identified and a mechanism worked out to reduce possibilities of arbitrary and frequent changes in the classification once finalized after full consideration. The classification in this case will not only carry greater sanctity but also demarcate, in a more meaningful way, areas or zones of responsibility for "planning and implementation" at district and state levels.

Financial Resources

After identification of functions, it is necessary to ensure that financial resources are available to the district discharge the allotted functions. It has to be automatic devolution of finances and also powers to raise resources.

The experience in the past has shown that certain plan funds were earmarked on an ad hoc basis for distribution to the districts and a formula based on population and backwardness has been adopted by various states. There is no resource generation at the local level for funding of the district plans. This has resulted in inadequate flow of funds at the sub-state level. In regard to resource devolution, the Karnataka Act has made a provision for setting up a State Finance Commission. The Sarkaria Commission has also suggested a similar arrangement to enable the State Government to take an objective view of resources to be devolved or transferred to the districts. A similar recommendation has also been made by the Conference of the District Magistrates.

Commensurate Change in Other Sub-Systems

Planning, implementation and administration are not separate and unrelated sub-systems. The success of a model approved for one of them will largely depend upon whether, among other things, consequential changes have been made in models of other sub-systems also to make them harmonious and compatible with each other. In case, this harmony and compatability is not established, the purpose for which the new model has been approved may not be achieved. At the end of it, it may even be wrongly concluded that the model has failed. In the present case, changes, made in the sub-system of 'Planning' were no accompanied by changes, as required, in the sub-systems of administration and implementation. These sub-systems remained, more or less, unchanged with the result that the modified model of planning is not working smoothly. These changes are specially required in the field of administrative, technical and financial power as well as extensive delegation of budgeting and re-appropriation procedures. The existing procedures and practices do not fulfill the requirements of the schemes. Unless these procedures are changed to meet the needs of decentralization, the hurdles in the smooth functioning of the decentralized planning would remain. One of the reasons why decentralized planning did not get off the ground was that the budgetary and re-appropriation procedures had not been suitably modified.

A plan becomes an instrument of action only when financial provisions stipulated in it find a place in the budge and provisions, thus made, are also available for actual use. There has to be a mechanism, therefore, to ensure that a District Plan, once finalized, is faithfully reflected in the budget and financial provisions made therein are made available to actual users without further loss of time. This objective can be achieved by:

1. Requiring a district budget to be framed on the basis of 'district plan' finalized in the prescribed manner;
2. Incorporating district budgets into state budget in a suitable manner so that consolidated provisions as well as provisions representing totals of district budgets are shown in it separately;
3. Authorities empowered to operate on provisions made in district budgets are also mentioned clearly at appropriate places;
4. District budgets thus framed and incorporated in the State budget will be authenticated jointly "by Planning and Finance Departments" immediately after the passage of the State budget and the authenticated copy made available to the district and its extracts to concerned Departments will be deemed to convey Government sanction authorizing officers/authorities concerned to draw on funds indicated therein and to take other necessary steps for use of such funds in accordance with orders issued from time to time by appropriate authorities; and
5. There shall be a senior officer of Finance and Account Service in every district answerable to District Magistrate, who shall be responsible, among other things, to watch the progress of expenditure to ensure that expenditure does not exceed budgeted provisions, to submit periodical

returns of expenditure and to vet all proposals for re-appropriation of funds in accordance with the orders issued by the Government from time to time.

Qualified Manpower for District Planning Machinery

Like any other delegation of authority or powers, decentralized planning is also a delegation of authority or powers by State Government to districts in the field of planning. In other words, the implication is that the authority or powers will be better exercised in the interests of people after the same are delegated to districts. But at the same time, it amounts to vesting districts with additional 'responsibilities'. And once a decision on these responsibilities has been taken, it becomes necessary to identify and provide support required to be given to districts in terms of qualified manpower and other resources to enable them and others concerned to discharge these responsibilities efficiently. In case this support is denied, it will recoil adversely on the performance of delegated functions. This calls for a multi-disciplinary technical planning cell at the district level.

REFERENCES

1. Government of India, *First Five Year Plan,* New Delhi, Planning Commission, p. 145.
2. Government of India, *Second Five Year Plan,* New Delhi, Planning Commission, p. 58.
3. Government of India, *Report of the Committee on Plan Projects,* New Delhi, 1957.
4. Government of India, *Third Five Year Plan,* New Delhi, 1961, Planning Commission, p. 334.
5. Government of India, Administrative Reforms Commission, Study Team on the Machinery for Planning, *Final Report,* 1967.
6. Government of India, *Guidelines for the Formulation of District Plans,* New Delhi, Planning Commission, September 1969.
7. Government of India, *Report of the Working Group on Block Level Planning,* Planning Commission, New Delhi, 1978.
8. *Ibid.,* p. 2, Para 2.3.
9. Government, of India, Ministry of Agriculture and Irrigation (Department of Rural Development), *Report of the Committee on Panchayati Raj Institutions,* New Delhi, 1978.

10. *Ibid.*, p. 31.
11. Government of India, *Report of the Working Group on District Planning*, New Delhi, Planning Commission, 1984.
12. *Ibid.*, p. 23.
13. Government of India, *Seventh Five Year Plan*, New Delhi, Planning Commission, 1985, p. 415.
14. Government of India, Ministry of Rural Development, *Report of the Committee to Review Existing Administrative Arrangement for Rural Development*, 1985.
15. *Ibid.*, p. 33.
16. *The Report of the Sarkaria Commission*, para 11.8.04.
17. *Ibid.*, p. 32.

18

Public Administration and Plan Implementation

NITISH R. DE

"Founding itself upon love, humility and faith, dialogue becomes a horizontal relationship of which mutual trust between the participants is the logical consequence…true dialogue cannot exist unless it involves critical thinking...thinking which perceives reality as process and transformation…thinking which does not separate itself from action, but consistently immerses itself in temporality without fear of the risks involved." —Paulo Freire[1]

"India's forte is one of crisis management. Instincts of its leadership are to cope, rather than innovate, and to work within an existing frame work not only on institutions but of ideas as well."
—Myron Weiner[2]

This paper will be in two parts. The first part will be an assessment of the current status of Public Administration in relation to Plan implementation, raising some of the obvious issues. The second part will deal with certain parameters of action so that concomitant changes in Public Administration can be brought about with a view to increasing the capability of Plan implementation.

On the whole, a systems approach will be maintained so that diagnostic data, policy planning and policy implementation are perceived as an ongoing process and not as discrete elements merely calling for an integrative machinery. A point will be taken that coordination is often perceived as a supreme need arising out of a mechanical conception of the inter-relationships of various complex forces. As an alternative, a premise will be maintained that integration of various complex socio-economic and political variables is not only a matter of technology of administration but also a matter of management of attitude, values and authentic behaviour. A whole ocean of techniques will not be adequate, it is believed, to ensure the full implementation of the Fifth Plan programmes just as the waters of the Arabian Sea could not have effaced the sense of guilt from the heart of Lady Macbeth consequent upon the murder of the King. An essential point of the paper will be that commitment to the Plan objectives a process, subtler and deeper than the knowledge of techniques and procedures.

I
THE CURRENT REALITY

There are four issues to which reference will be made:

(1) The Draft Fifth Plan has nine chapters in Part I and fifteen in Part II. None of these chapters refers to the public administration machinery either in the Centre of the States. One does not get an insight as to how the working role of the Department of Personnel and Administrative Reforms will be revitalized or reoriented in the light of the requirements of the Plan objectives. Nor does one know as to how the working tradition of the Cabinet Secretariat will be restructured with a view to bringing about a convergence between its working and the Plan objectives. Similarly, one searches in vain in the Plan document for an emerging role, if any, for the Chief Secretary of a State Government.

One may indeed refer to, in rebuttal, the work done by the Administrative Reforms Commission and the gradual process that has been initiated to bring about reforms in the administrative machinery. One may also mention what some of the State Governments have been doing by way of setting up Administrative Reforms Committees.

The essential point, however, is that the fountain head of the complex gamut of the administrative machinery has been kept outside the purview of the Plan document. The implication is that while machinery other than the civil administration will need to be looked at for the purpose of success of the Plan, it will itself remain untouched in terms of stock-taking, reflection, and consequent change. While changes is the core theme of the planning process, public administration by implication can remain immutable. It seems that this incongruence may become a stumbling block in Plan implementation.

The consequence is obvious. The elites of the public administration are thus rendered free to look at other agencies and find out what their flaws and failures are. They have no compulsion to look at their own houses. Delays in implementing various projects are well-known complains. Attempts are being made to streamline he decision-making process in such a way that the delays can be avoided. But no worthwhile attempt is being made to short-circuit the delaying processes in various ministries of the government. While some attempts are being made in some of the economic ministries such as, Heavy Industry, the old conventions and culture doggedly persist in the non-economic ministries, particularly the social ministries. There is no conscious effort at monitoring the delays in some of these ministries even though the officials here are expected to ensure that the various field organizations responsible to the ministries do operate effectively. This is an obvious contradiction.

How expensive the inabilities of the ministries in scrutinizing their own operations can be, is cited here:

> "...When a decision was taken to set up the Madras Refinery Project, it was also decided that Madras Port would need to be enlarged to accommodate 70,000 dwt. crude oil tankers. This tanker size was taken into account without working out the economics of the Madras Refinery. With the Refinery under the administration of one ministry and the Madras Port Trust under another...expert and effective coordination of the two parts of the project became necessary. As it turned out, the ministry of ... was unable to ensure that the port expansion proceeded so as to synchronise with the completion of the Madras Refinery...The Refinery was commissioned in June

1969 and the expansion of the port was still incomplete in December 1972. The consequential loss to the Refinery, obliged to run at reduced throughput and pay higher freight rates on account of the use of smaller size tankers, is about Rs. 17 crore up to March 1972..." (quoted from an unpublished report.)

Yet another consequence, is a more serious one. Paul Appleby, on the basis of his studies of the administrative culture in India, has repeatedly mentioned about the role of the audit culture. His diagnosis as well as warnings seem to have fallen on deaf ears. No doubt, some marginal changes have been made but the basic flaw has remained. We may quote from Appleby's report.[3]

"The functions of the Comptroller and Auditor-General in India are in large measure an inheritance from the colonial rule...the Comptroller and Auditor-General is today a primary cause of a widespread and paralysing unwillingness to decide and act.

"This repressive and negative influence is in considerable part indirect, impinging on the bureaucracy by way of Parliament because of the exaggerated and unselective attention given by Parliament to the petty exceptions and the inflated *pretensions built around the pedestrian function of audit*...What special competence for appraising objectives and appraising administrative performance in general has the Comptroller and Auditor-General? What is Cabinet for, what is the Prime Minister for, what is Parliament for, what are the individual ministers for, what is the secretariat for and what is bureaucracy for?...Too many of his reports are mere substitutions of hindsight for the kind of judgement possible and necessary and proper at the time of action. Too many merely raise questions that are really questions of differences in judgement.

"...The Comptroller and Auditor-General's function is not really a very important one. Auditors do not know and cannot be expected to know, very much about good administration...What auditors know is auditing—which is not administrative; it is necessary but highly pedestrian functions, with a narrow perspective and very limited usefulness....Audit reports take Parliamentary attention on little things. This demeans he Parliament." [3]

The implications of the unwillingness to link up the compulsions of the planning process with the requisite changes in public administration can indeed become a serious problem as highlighted recently by Jha analyzing the data that are available. Jha makes the following points:

> "The least understood today is the relationship between the growth in unproductive expenditure and mounting unemployment. Politicians and officials react to any suggestions that employment in the bureaucracy should be curtailed by raising the bogey of unemployment. What they fail to realize is that the creation of one sinecure in the bureaucracy or for hat matter, anywhere else in the economy deprives at least ten people of productive employment over a period of roughly three decades....
>
> "It is a sobering thought that if the Central and State governments had created three million less jobs in the bureaucracy, their annual savings today would have been sufficient to generate thirty million extra jobs over thirty years, or a million extra jobs every year."[4]

All in all, one major weakness in the Plan document is the neglect of attention to the urgent and long overdue administrative innovations in the very citadel of development administration—central and state government machinery including the role of the audit functionaries.

(2) The second issue of current relevance is the problem of values and attitudes of the public administrators. It would be fair to include the higher as well as the lower echelons of the government administration in this category, irrespective of whether they are generalists or technocrats including educationists.

That the Harijans, despite what Mahatma Gandhi sought to do to alleviate their misery—psychological as well as physical—have not been able to improve their lot in an appreciable measure during the Four Plans is well-known. Psychological humiliation apart, physical pain and torture to which the Harijans have been subjected are fairly well known. The case of Keezhavenmani's death by burning is well-known. Similarly, the status of the Harijans in U.P. has been documented by Juyal.[5] Despite the fact that Uttar Pradesh has 21.23 per cent of its population belonging to the Harijan caste, their conditions are no better here compared to other states. One reason for continuation of the depressed conditions of the Harijans is obviously the attitude of the ruling elite. The subtlety of this attitude is obvious from a report published in a Hindi Daily from Banaras. The report reads as follows:

> "Dhobi (Jaunpur)—June 28. Caste tensions are increasing in the rural areas following the stoppage of work by the Harijans for other castes. Harijans have boycotted cutting of navel strings and disposing off dead cattle. They have even raised a demand for increase in the wages of ploughing and other kinds of agricultural work. The Harijan leaders are raising a storm of casteism by misguiding the Harijans in the villages which may lead to dangerous consequences."

Similarly, a survey of Primary Health Centres (PHC) in the states of Andhra Pradesh, Bihar, Gujarat, Kerala, Maharashtra, Tamil Nadu, Karnatak, Rajasthan, Uttar Pradesh and West Bengal brings about this conclusion from the researcher:

> "On the whole, the dispensary projects a very unflattering image. Discrimination against the poor and the oppressed, poor quality of medicines (only red water), lack of medicines, overcrowd and long wait, nepotism, bribery, and indifferent and often rude behaviour of the staff are some of the charges that have been levelled against most of the dispensaries. Complaints about medicines and overcrowding and long wait are made even against the best of the PHC's studied."[6]

The essential point emanating from these and many other experiences is that the administrative elite is essentially bound by what Joshi has called "social parasitism."[7] Social parasitism is an attitudinal problem based on an economic premise. The economic premise is that the surplus that is created out of non-productive, circulatory functions is more significant than the basic productive function itself. In another context, the implication of the culture of social parasitism has been described.[8]

(*a*) Non-productive phenomena, such as gold and precious stone smuggling and hoarding, hoarding of essential food-grain items, conspicuous consumption, individualised services, sweat-labour based secondary comforts, etc., do receive a premium. Social values in the garb of "an act of wisdom" as in the case of hoarding and "a shining example of success in life" as in the case of conspicuous consumption acquire legitimacy in our behavioural norms. Such forms of parasitism will have the "Gresham Law" effect on the productive culture. The "sanskritisation" effect of parasitism thus takes hold;

(*b*) Black money and corruption will remain a major force in the determination of relevant behaviour, including key level decision-making role, thereby weakening such processes of decision-making as involve productive parameters;

(*c*) Members of the community involved in production activities will carry on with their responsibilities in the tradition of parasitism manifested in the forms of *competitive economism and complementary economism.* In other words, the internalised values of parasitism will gain entry and then ascendancy in the production culture. In this sense, no fundamental distinction will be maintained between social goods and services and those for private gains;

(*d*) There will develop a yawning chasm between the public posture and the private faith, between the stated objective and the reality, between the creed and the dead generating a climate of mass inauthenticity and abortion of political morality;

(*e*) The reaction against the consequent erosion of national self-esteem and promiscuity in national identity will develop into mass alienation in the young generation—either in the form of retreatist sub-culture, or angry backlash, or anguished martyrdom, or docile conformism, or perhaps a combination of some of these, thereby fostering he values of "lumpenism";

(*f*) As an apparent reaction to the economic stagnancy and the hypocrisy of existence that is inherent in the culture of social parasitism, obvious patriotic responses will generate in the cause of production orientation. These indignant votaries of non-parasitic culture will seek the commanding heights of decision-making roles for themselves so that the vantage ground of parasitism can be maintained; and

(*g*) The "hard core" of productive culture will get fixated, as a reaction against parasitism, at task-orientation levels with cynical concern for human values and esteem for fellow human beings. Some of them may seek retreat in compensatory activities, such as "re-search" and non-collaborative work, and join the "braindrain" club. Performance orientation may become a caricature of economic progress with an empty moral and ethical shell.

It is, in his context, that one will view the three paragraphs on public participation and commitment in the chapter on Plan Implementation in the Draft Plan. Reference to the public is to various representative institutions, local bodies and academic institutions. Participation of the people in the planning process in the form of more direct and vigorous involvement is missing. It is not as if adequate instruments of vigorous and meaningful participation of the people are not available. Those who are familiar with Paulo Freire's work in Brazil are aware of the immense potential that exists in a polyarchical participation of the people and their leaders, both playing the role of actors in a change process.[9]

A number of studies on Indian Administration have come to the conclusion that it essentially represents a culture of elitism. Pai Panandiker[10] maintains that while there is some behavioural flexibility in the bureaucracies at the field level, such as in agriculture, bureaucracies in the office involving regulatory and directional functions are essentially structurally more rigid and behaviourally less flexible. It is precisely at this level that the key decisions are made and the parameters of action are determined.

Ali Ashraf, in his study of rural development in U.P., has come to the following conclusion:

"There is little doubt that bureaucratic organizations develop a tendency towards centralization and rigidity and demand

> conformity from their members. The feedback process does not function well and this is especially true in the Indian context where normal bureaucratic tendencies are further reinforced by cultural values of hierarchy and superior-subordinate social relationships. Thus, the bureaucracy has little capacity to improve itself by learning from its errors. There is indeed no effective way for the bureaucrat to learn of his errors, and even if such knowledge of internal weakness was available, there would be hardly any will to modify its organization or behaviour."[11]

Subramaniam comes to the following conclusion at the end of his study of he Civil Services in India:

> "It is clear that all these services are drawn in common from the urban salaried and professional middle class of India to the tune of 80 per cent or over."[12]

A significant aspect of social parasitic culture can very well be a type of bureaucratic operation which has been labelled by Presthus as "welfare bureaucracy"[13] as practiced in Turkey. The welfare premises centre around certain benefits, privileges and augmentation of some tradition-bound orientations which foster and sustain the culture of non-achievement and non-production. The seniority principle, loyalties on the basis of caste, region and language, concern for superficial measures of effort as opposed to performance and an elastic concept of time, are some of the characteristics of the administrative milieu that is suffered, if not supported, by the administrative elite.

It thus appears that the administrative elite in India is on the whole of an urban middle class background, given to the culture of social parasitism in accordance with which non-productive culture is the *sine qua non of* elegance and performance. This attitude appears to be another major stumbling block in the Plan Implementation process, particularly, in respect of the production objectives as well as the social programmes of change.

(3) The Draft Fifth Plan can be credited with certain improvements. The chapter on Plan Implementation is comprehensive and in some respects its has gone into operational details which were missing in the earlier Plan documents. There

is requisite emphasis on monitoring and evaluation organization and utilization of certain management techniques, such as project evaluation, critical path method and other quantitative management techniques of proved utility.

In particular, implementation of agricultural programmes refers to the structure of the decision-making machinery in the ministry in some detail which is lacking in respect of other programmes and ministries. The administrative structure incorporates the role of the technical heads in the decision-making process not as staff specialists as is very often the case, but as substantive decision-makers. The role of the technical department in the states and those of the subject-matter specialists in the area development programmes have received particular attention. That the traditional organizational design will be inadequate in dealing with the area development programmes has been recognized.

To quote from the Draft document:

> "It is proposed that in the area development schemes of the nature of command area development and drought-prone area schemes and any such similar schemes which may be worked out in the tribal or backward areas, an area development authority is constituted by the government which has got administrative and financial powers duly seconded to it by the government and which controls the staff of all the disciplines which are important for the field programmes."

Although not wholly, this statement partly recognizes the need for an integrated agency, utilizing some of the insights of a matrix organization.

These innovative ideas, however incomplete, are totally missing in the section on Railways. While one finds certain statistical information in the smaller section on Railways (in the Plan Implementation chapter), one looks in vain for the administrative innovations and personnel policies which are long overdue in the basic transport system of the country.

As already mentioned, Monitoring and Evaluation Organization (MEO) has received welcome attention in the implementation programme. A nucleus of MEO has been created in the Planning Commission with professional competence and a desire to succeed. This group, though small, has already started working on pre-requisites of monitoring rather than preparing itself for audit type evaluation long after the event has occurred. It seems that this is a positive augury, however limited, for the Fifth Plan.

(4) There seems to persist the basic dichotomy between the planning process and the implementation process, even though there is the universal recognition that implementation seems to be proverbially the weak link in the Indian planning process. It appears that there is a sense of resignation to the inevitability of the duality of the planning process and the implementation process of the variety that has been in existence in India for many decades. It is necessary to appreciate that the Plan objectives are required to be examined in terms of the stated objectives, *real* objectives and *legitimate* objectives.[14] The stated objectives, incidentally, are always the desirable ones and a statement of these issues is probably the easiest. The real objectives are those which are sought to be implemented by those who are concerned with the process. The legitimacy of an objective—whether stated or real—depends upon the social relevance of the objective. It seems that in India there has been a closer concordance between the real objective and its illegitimacy and, in he process, is distance from the stated objective. While an organized trading community, to provide an example, may become most articulate in its statement of the social responsibilities of business, the "get-rich-quick activities" are matched only by the illegitimate machinations that are undertaken, taking advantage of the growing demand for a variety of essential commodities.

Similarly, the social parasitism of the administrative elite has been able to maintain a distinction between the stated objectives of the Indian Constitution and the successive Plan objectives on the one hand and the execution of these objectives on the other. Whether it is the implementation of the various tax laws or the provisions of Land Reforms Legislation or the execution of the social welfare measures for the tribals or the depressed classes, one inevitably confronts the ever-widening schism between the profession and the practice. One also cannot deny the over-active compromises of the political wing of the Indian elite that accentuates the hiatus between the stated objectives and the real objectives.

It seems that the planning process is usually concerned with the stated objectives and an elaboration of the same including *inter se* priorities of these objectives. The criteria for measurement to ensure the fulfillment of the stated objectives are wholly or predominantly ignored as an integral part of the planning process. The implementation process, on the other hand, is usually concerned with the real objectives. Real objectives are those which are actually implemented utilizing the administrative authority. While, to give an example, augmentation of production is consistently set as a desirable objective, the various administrative decisions like the linkage of the annual bonus payment to profits and many other similar decisions go against the grain of the productive culture. Many a leisure-time comfort that is provided to the managerial elite in an industrial system may indeed be an integral part of welfare bureaucracy, but not necessarily a contribution to production ethos. The chasm between the stated objectives and the real objectives is thus the chasm between the planning process and the implementation process.

This summary survey is an assessment of some of the problems involved in Plan Implementation in the context of the reality of Public Administration.

II
SOME ELEMENTS OF ACTION PARAMETERS

Should we accept the diagnostic premises made in the earlier section, it will become somewhat obvious that certain infirmities in the administrative culture would need to be attended to with a view to effectively implementing the Plan objectives. Three such infirmities are listed below:

(*a*) The elitist bias towards non-productive culture and a propensity towards "welfare bureaucracy" cannot sustain the Plan implementation programme.

(*b*) The values of elitism are enshrined in a supercilious attitude towards, if not an outright prejudice against the down-trodden, particularly the ethnic poor, which makes the administrative machinery distinctly insensitive to public needs and even hostile of public criticism. The voice that is often raised about anonymous petitions against members of administrative elites and the touchiness that is displayed against public criticism voiced in the national and state legislatures are indicative of the lack of concern for fellow human beings' sentiments. Their sentiments and frustrations are ignored along with the factual part of allegations which could very well be exaggerated and inaccurate.

(*c*) The elitist bias towards profit motive, particularly relevant to private trade and industry, is yet another aspect of the dominating culture that has stood between the societal objectives of the Plan and their translation into action. Bauer and Fenn have referred to the American phenomenon in these words, while discussing corporate social audit:

"With the industrial revolution came the concept that competition should serve as the regulator and determinant of proper business conduct; if you survived and prospered, you were, by definition, doing 'the right thing', and 'in the right way'. The appeal of this view was and is compelling; it lives on today in the often expressed conviction that 'the cash register is the final arbiter of our performance. If the customer does not like what we are doing, we find it out soon enough'. 'Safety does not sell', said the pre-Nader automobile manufacturer. 'We are giving the public what it wants', says the broadcasting executive."[15]

On the positive plane, what needs to be done is to establish a culture of performance and achievement, as distinct from the culture of acquisition. It is apparent that if our records of Plan implementation are poor, it is an admission of our poor performance-orientation. This orientation is required to be established and strengthened by a series of positive steps as a reinforcement to the corps of public administrators and not by action of punitive measures and negatively-oriented control devices as is the case with audit culture.

The Action Plan will be devoted to the resolution of these issues:

(1) The various ministries in Delhi and their counterparts in the states will be required to critically examine their rules and

procedures and systems of work. While addressing the 28th Annual Convention of Oil Technologists' Association of India two months before his death, S. Mohan Kumaramangalam had this to say about decisions-making in the Government:

> "Suppose Rourkela wants to have a new coke oven battery...The Rourkela gentleman will discuss with his own G.S., A.G.S., Coke Oven Superintendent and so on...a feasibility report will be commissioned by the CEDB...the best minds will work on it...Finally, after it has been cooked properly, it will be brought before the Board of Hindustan Steel and then it will be sent up to the Government:
>
> "The Government naturally means the Secretary. The Secretary will mark it to the Joint Secretary; the Joint Secretary will mark it to the Deputy Secretary...to the Section Head...the Section Head is the foundation of everything. Without him, Government cannot function. The Section Head looks at this big document...and prepares a self-contained note...he does not know one end of a blast furnace from another or a coke oven...(but) at the end of it all, he has to make a recommendation.
>
> "Then again it rises to the surface...In between, probably the Joint Secretary may add four or five lines giving reasons why it should go to the technical wing...From there when it reaches the Secretary, he chits it saying let it go to the technical wing...what do you expect this young engineer (in the technical wing), a very good quality young man, to do?...In order to justify the fact that he is there...he asks for clarifications...and the Secretary reads it. He is not a technologist and naturally he cannot say that the clarifications are not necessary. So he puts it ultimately to the Minister.
>
> "This is the way the Government will operate...It is not the wrongness of the individuals; it is the wrongness inherent in the system...In Government, the magic word is *sanctions*...The basic difference between administration on the one hand in terms of civil service administration, and administration on the other in terms of industry is that...(one) is rule-oriented and (the other) is result-oriented...What counts ultimately is what results you get..."[16]

Needless to point out that a body of the type of the Administrative Reforms Commission will, doubtless, be able to amass enormous data on the strength of which it can recommend certain steps. Whereas such commissions are hallowed by the tradition of British Parliamentary democratic system innovated in an era of comparative unchangeability, the present state of Indian reality is a different picture altogether. It will indeed be necessary to bring about vigour, determination and unorthodoxy of approach to critically submit the work culture of the decision-making apparatus to a scrutiny. What will be relevant are short reports for action unlike the reports emanating from prolonged deliberations. The essential purpose of such drastic reorganization of work culture will be to generate a culture of self-renewal in the various ministries in Delhi. John Gardner laid down five rules which might become the cornerstone of the self-renewing process:

> "The first rule is that the organization must have an effective programme for the recruitment and development of talent."
>
> "The second rule for the organization capable of continuous renewal is that it must be a hospitable environment for the individual."
>
> "The third rule is that organisation must have built-in provisions for self-criticism."
>
> "The fourth rule is that there must be fluidity in the internal structure."
>
> "The fifth rule is that the organisation must have some means of combating the process by which men become prisoners of their procedures."

Given the weight of tradition that sustains the anti-work or non-work culture in the halls of decision-making in the metropolises, it may be desirable that either the Prime Minister takes upon herself the responsibility of administrative innovation or she puts someone in-charge of it who is known for his tasks orientation and the ability to *preact* even in a hostile climate. To fight organizational "dry-rot" is the essence of requisite action in making public administration responsive to the demands of the planning process. The ultimate repository of government—the ministries—which operate on the written words in files will need to be exposed to reform in terms of tasks, targets, quality of decisions, timeliness and the ability to help the field organizations.

(2) The controversy involving the generalists and the specialists will need to be resolved. The Prime Minister, while inaugurating the Indian Institute of Management of Bangalore in October 1973 has made this statement:

> "Our experience is that the generalists and the specialists both tend to be somewhat bureaucratic when they come into the system. The specialists are not more arduous than the generalists when suggesting new approaches to administration, new ways of getting things done and new methods of economy....Both are subjected to human feelings, feuds, hatred, jealousies and narrow-mindedness and these are not diminished in new institutions headed by specialists...the important issue is to evolve a system by which we are able to get the best out of our personnel and to ensure that the entire administration can...be levelled so that it comes in direct touch with people...with a sense of service and understanding. We do not want more officers but a competent and creative human being."

The culture of competence and humanness is certainly an essential requisite. Such a culture calls for a redefinition of the concept of efficiency. In a work-sky culture, a public servant wedded to the techniques of efficiency may receive high encomium. But working with complex human systems, his effectiveness may be blunted by his over-simplistic assumptions about human beings. He may adopt a posture of arrogance and/or wisdom and this will undermine the commitment of his subordinates and the people, without whose willing cooperation no project can be effectively implemented. Such votaries of efficiency are usually given to a "black-box" concept of human nature and human motivation.

In order to operationalise Mr. Gandhi's concept of competence and humanness, one will need to begin with a new concept of administrative values. An administration leader will need to internalise the values of "adaptability" and "flexbility"[18] which will enable him to change roles whenever that is needed and to cope with unpredictable situations when these will confront him.

The administrative reward system will need to be geared to the task of identifying competent administration leaders who possess in requisite measure the values of adaptability and flexibility. Performance-oriented appraisal system, to give one example, will be able to put the nail to the coffin of bureaucracy-technocracy debate.

(3) Performance orientation will call for a major revision of the roles of the government audit department, the finance ministry as well as the finance departments of the State Governments. While post-audit of actions and decisions is necessary for public services and public sector industries, the essentiality of such a function does not lie in creating a climate of inaction or hesitant, low-key action on the part of public functionary. On the contrary, the audit objective should be to foster a sustained performance culture and not to stultify it by fear psychosis. Today, the audit department derives its status from its constitutional sanction to "tick-off" any authority other than the Parliament. Its immunity extends to the privilege that no one scrutinizes its contribution to the culture of delays and despondency, and in particular, the obstacle it sets to initiative, drive and innovativeness in public administration. It will be necessary to substitute the culture of "sanctions" by a culture of "performance". This prescription does not imply that failures should be slurred over nor does it mean that the Central Bureau of Investigation be abolished. What it means is that the audit department should develop a composite of performance criteria to audit various governmental activities so that culture of results gets stabilized. On the strength of its accumulated experience, the audit department should be encouraged to initiate suggestions as to the extent of the obsolescence of various rules and procedures so that appropriate corrective measures can be taken without fuss or delay.

Similarly, the finance ministry should be able to exercise scrutiny and fuller review of various proposals and projects before it and its associated bodies can accord their sanction but, thereafter, the executive agency should not be required to refer a particular item of expenditure for a second-time approval. It is one thing to lay down functional norms for incurring expenditure and it is quite another to operate on the premise that the finance ministry represents the government's conscience and the accumulated wisdom of public propriety.

When it is suggested that measures of administrative innovation be adopted, it is implied that action be initiated to effect a major modification of the "mental set" that is prevalent today in the resource allocating activities and the agencies that perform the guardian role of procedures rather than the inspecting role of results.

(4) Debureaucratisation of the administrative culture will call for planned recycling of the public administrators between field assignments and office work. One of the positive lessons of the Chinese cultural revolution (1966-69) is that the party officials and administrative functionaries pegged to office work in the cities not only divorce themselves from the problems of the common mass but also foster the culture of bureaucratic functioning. The Chinese have sought to restore the balance by ensuring prolonged field assignments for the white collar bureaucrats, irrespective of their rank and status. The weight of tradition in India that public administrators after having attained certain rank would invariably be posted to headquarters assignments, would call for hard scrutiny. If the implementation process is our weak spot in the planning operation, then prestigious public servants would need to be involved in field operations irrespective of their status.

The recycling process will further help the administrators to appreciate as much the integration of theory and practice as the convergence of the planning process and the implementation process. Placed in such a role, they will realize that action without reflection is an inefficient form of utilizing resources and that thinking without reality orientation is a verbal gymnastic leading to no desirable ends.

(5) It will be desirable to develop a "dialogical" relationship between the administrators and the people. The elitist bias for planning by the elite for the people will need to be substituted by healthy concern for people's sentiments and the potential of their contributions. Mao Tse-tung made the following statement in an interview:

> "You know I have proclaimed for a long time: we must teach the masses clearly what we have received from them confusedly."[19]

The leadership role, therefore, is not one of leading or of being led but of being able to establish an active transactional relationship between the self and the others.

Freire[20] has shown that the words of the teachers emotionally integrated with the work experience of the taught can, not only initiate a meaningful programme of mutual education, but also a programme of great force for social change. This has happened in a dramatic way among the poor peasants of north-east Brazil. It seems that such an orientation will be necessary to operationalise the concept of commitment of the masses to the objectives of the Plan. The common masses will get involved so long as the Plan objectives are translated in terms of their work experience and work interests.

It is suggested that such an active transaction will need to be established by providing a mechanisms for outflow from the relevant people to the administrators and inflow of the equally meaningful feedback from the administrators to the relevant people. Once again, the experiences of cultural revolution in China indicate that the social turmoil was launched there in a number of ways, one of which was the provision of feedback to the authority figures by the young generation in the form of posters. The battle was fought, as it were, in the form of feedback rather than with the use of the instruments of offence. This is a lesson that is required to be integrated in the administrator-people dynamics for the purpose of the Fifth Plan.

It may even be necessary to develop what is known as "feed-forward loop" so that an advance system can be developed to organize to and fro movement of meaningful information which can assist the parties to develop action programmes for tomorrow.

It is possible that many public servants will look upon such a programme of involvement of the people as a time-consuming process. Experiences of Freire and many a leader of people, including Mahatma Gandhi, have indicated time and again that it

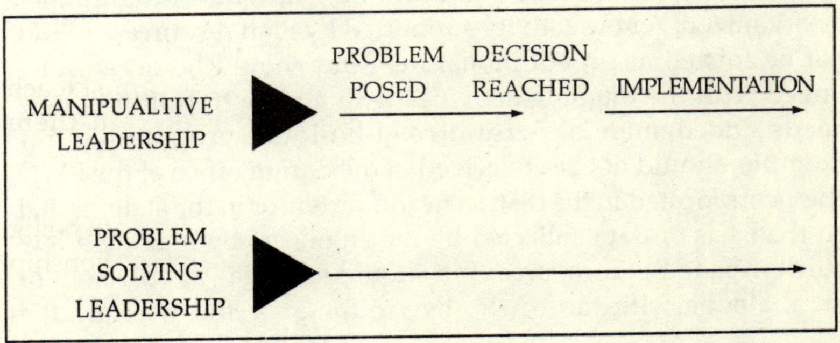

was not so. Commitment is not a mechanical process. It has to be earned not on the basis of manipulation but on the strength of a genuine desire to involve and get involved. The diagram below will show that a manipulative process will involve a time consuming implementation programme while popular participation will smoothen out the Plan implementation process.[21]

(6) In the matter of mobilizing popular support as a resource to the Plan implementation programme, a newer variety of organizational design will need to be conceived. Conventional wisdom invariably leads to the institutions of representative organs such as punchayats. While such forums should be more progressively utilized for the right cause, their limitations should also be recognized. These bodies, more often than not, do represent the elitist culture in the rural areas. The leadership of the representative organizations usually stands for such values and priorities which do not necessarily foster the production culture at grassroot levels.

So, the need will be to search for meaningful alternatives, not necessarily to weaken the representative institutions, but to establish deeper roots for Plan objectives by seeking wider linkages among the people. A number of core activities in the Plan do justify such a mobilization plan: national programmes for minimum needs, land reforms measures, area development programmes, democratization of work-place in the basic sectors of industries and essential services and so on.

The first requirement for a new organizational design will be to replace comparative passivity by activity on the part of grassroot members. If activity is the basis for participation, then, the production systems in operation, whether we consider the minimum needs programme or the democratization of work-place in the factory, should be the core around which new programmes be organized. A new activity supported by Plan resources should not be foisted as an additional item but should be organically linked with the ongoing activities with a view to fulfilling new needs and demands. A rural road-building programme, for example, should not be conceived in the design office of the PWD engineers located in the district headquarters or in the state capital on the basis of data collected by the engineers by making a few quick trips to the rural areas but should essentially evolve out of the dialogue with those who live in the area and who are the potential beneficiaries and such a dialogue would essentially provide the linkage between the on-going economic activities and the need for rural road-building programme. Time and again, the lessons from other developing countries have shown that people's participation by simply sharing information with them does not necessarily commit them to the tasks. On the other hand, should they perceive the new project in terms of their needs and their on-going experiences, such a project does evoke spontaneous and constructive responses.[22]

Even in the matter of implementation, the workmen involved in the project should, as far as possible, be from the local areas and their commitment should not be perceived simply in terms of inducements for contribution made but should be conceived in terms of semi-autonomous group-working on the basis of spelling out the parameters of the task and challenges and developing norms of group-working including monitoring and control mechanisms. A work culture, in other words, is to be established by such organizational designs as would facilitate participation culture.

We have already referred to some of the stereotypes that the elites hold about the common masses. These stereotypes refer to what they perceive as the weak elements in the tradition and culture of the masses. At the same time, if one examine carefully the behavioural dimensions of the norms of our tradition and culture, one may find that they do not differ so very dramatically between the elite group on the one hand and the common masses on the other. Many of the divisive elements built on the practices of caste, language, religion and region are as much a part of the culture of the elite as the common masses.

The significant element, however, is that this culture relativity is often seen as symbols of weakness for task performance, adversely affecting the goals and the pace of economic development. It is possible that the same elements of culture can be converted into an advantage as was done by the Japanese. From an elitist slant, many of the social and familial practices in Japan should not have been allowed to interfere with work organisation. But the Japanese have shown that these values and practices could be utilized in organizing work structure as well as the work-group norms to get the best out of the technology and material resources.

Similarly, a dramatic example has been provided by the design of the rural hospital system in Nigeria on the principle that a patient with the tribal background would not accept the status of an indoor patient in a hospital even if he is seriously ill, unless the members of his family are allowed to be near him during the critical days. Keeping this element of cultural relativity in view, the rural hospital system was designed by incorporating this tribal value, making such a system to be socially acceptable in Nigerian culture. This is essentially then a matter of appreciation as to whether one should build organisation structure on the basis of cultural relativity or one should seek to make changes in cultural norms in order to conform these to the elitist conception of the desirable design. It is suggested that we have to revise our train of thinking and replace it by a new interpretation of cultural relativity and its worthwhileness.

(7) There will be certain identifiable primary activities on which the programmes of Plan implementation will depend heavily. Such identifiable primary activities will need to be organized on somewhat non-traditional lines because of the high stake involved in their being able to provide inputs for the dependent activities. To provide an illustration, with the situation that is created on the energy front, coal has become the most vital energy source on which will depend power generation and the factory production system spread all over the country. The movement of coal will involve the railway transport system as well as the handling facilities in some of the ports. This will also involve the effective field-level operation of the State Governments in eastern India and obviously the industrial relations climate, in addition to supply of technical skills, provision of equipment and spares, R & D activities in mine development and responsive role of the Mine Safety Organisation. The coordination mechanism involving so many complex system is admittedly weak today. Keeping in view the importance of coal in the national economy and the ambitious programme of coal raising and transportation during the Fifth Plan, it will be necessary to establish a super-ordinate agency with requisite competence and authority to cut across the boundaries of various involved systems, like ministries in New Delhi, railway system, coking and non-coking coal production organizations, state governments and so on. It is suggested that similar other key activities of primary importance should be identified and super-ordinate agencies be created so as to facilitate the problem of systemic coordination. The existing

administrative machinery backed by the current administrative ethos and the weight of past experience will be unable to deliver the goods thereby jeopardizing the performance of the downstream operations. It will, indeed, be desirable for these super-ordinate agencies to be manned by highly competent persons with the ability to work with people under stress conditions and that they remain accountable to the Central Cabinet or to a committee of the Cabinet. Such is the importance of these tasks in ensuring other tasks to be accomplished.

(8) Lastly, for the elites to provide a new pattern of leadership to others in the planning process as well as the implementation process, it will be essential that such key personnel do cultivate values of self-awareness, self-introspection and pronounced proneness to psychological success. Self-oriented behaviour, practicing the virtues of self-gain, and short time-perspective would indeed fail to enable effective leadership role to be performed as has been the case over past two decades and a half. Mere technical competence or a more than average record of past performance is no guarantee that there would be a match between the profession and practice. In systems language, congruence between the stated objective and the real objective would be possible when the leadership is willing to exercise the qualities of sensitivity, adaptability and flexibility. Edgar Snow has quoted Mao Tse-tung in the following words:

> "If you want the masses to understand you and want to become one with them, you must be determined to undergo a long and even painful process of remolding. I began as a student and acquired at school the habits of a student; in the presence of a crowd of students who could neither fetch nor carry for themselves I used to feel it undignified to do any manual labour such as shouldering my own luggage. At that time, it seemed to me that the intellectuals were the only clean persons in the world and peasants seemed rather dirty beside them."
>
> "Having become a revolutionary, I found myself in the same ranks as the workers, peasants and soldiers of the revolutionary army, and gradually I became familiar with them and they with me, too. It was then and only then that a fundamental change occurred in the bourgeois and petty-

> bourgeois feelings implemented in me by bourgeois schools. I came to feel that it was those unremodelled intellectuals who were unclean while the workers and peasants are after all the cleanest persons even though their hands are soiled and their feet smeared with cow-dung. This is what is meant by having one's feelings transformed, changed from those of one class to those of another."[23]

Mao is not alone in this reflective skill. Mahatma Gandhi has done it, time and again. While one need not reach that commanding height of leadership to acquire the skills of reflection and self-exploration, in a country like India where there are intricate currents and cross-currents of social forces and the temptation towards soft options is rather high, impinging on the administrative leadership as well as the masses of people with whom the leaders are required to work, singular determination along with the ability to change and improve is a necessary prerequisite for those who seek to lead and motivate others. On the basis of the comparative undistorted perception of self-role relationship, these leaders will be able to examine their own behaviour and values in relation to their assigned responsibility. It is only a leader with a continuous growing edge who will be able to empathise with the people as also to provide modelling motivation to others. The dialogical relationship that is necessary for establishing the culture of result-orientation thus calls for not only a sense of humility in the leader but also an itch for learning from others and the environment. Authority conceived in terms of status and formal power is a major hurdle between the planning process and the implementation process and between the people and their ability to contribute. The administrative leader will need to overcome this barrier in his own person before he can claim effective popular participation. The operational significance of the new role of the public administrator is whether he will receive institutional encouragement to develop and sustain authentic behaviour under the stewardship of political leadership. In a socialist state, during the period of transition, an administrator is bound by the umbilical cord relationship with the party leadership. It cannot be substantially otherwise between a public administrator and the people's representative who acts as his beacon in a parliamentary form of democracy as ours.

REFERENCES

1. Paulo Freire, *Pedagogy of the Oppressed,* 1970, Herder and Herder, New York.
2. M.V. Kamath, "India Has Not Done Badly At All: MIT Professor's Analysis", *The Times of India,* December 10, New Delhi.
3. Paul Appleby, *Re-examination of India's Administration Systems,* 1965, Government of India Press, New Delhi.
4. Prem Shankar Jha, "Too Many Unproductive Jobs: Core of the Economic Crisis", *The Times of India,* December 10, 1973, New Delhi.
5. Juyal, "Twilight World of Harijans in U.P.," *New Wave,* December 30, 1972, New Delhi.
6. D. Banerji, "Healthy Behaviour of Rural Populations: Impact of Rural Health Services," *Economic and Political Weekly,* December 22, 1973, Bombay.
7. P.C. Joshi, "The Cultural Dimension of Economic Development: Past Experience and Present Dilemmas", Draft Paper, 1972, Institute of Economic Growth, Delhi.
8. Nitish R. De, "Social Context of Organization Development: Man-Work Environment Nexus", Draft Paper, 1973, Indian Institute of Management, Calcutta.
9. Maria, Mies, "Paulo Freire's Method of Education, Conscientionisation in Latin America", *Economic and Political Weekly,* September 29, 1973, Bombay.
10. V.A. Pai Panandiker, "Bureaucracy in India: An Empirical Study", IJPA, Vol. XVII, No. 2 (April-June), 1971, New Delhi.
11. Ali Ashraf, "Bureaucracy Leadership and Rural Development in Uttar Pradesh," *Indian J. of Politics,* Vol. V, No. 2, 1971.
12. V. Subramaniam, *Social Background of India's Administrators,* Publications Division, Ministry of Information & Broadcasting, 1971, New Delhi.
13. R.V. Presthus, "Weberian vs. Welfare Bureaucracy in Traditional Society", *Administrative Science Quarterly,* June, 1961.
14. C. West Churchman, *The Systems Approach,* 1968, Dale Publishing, New York.
15. Bauer and Fenn, *The Corporate Social Audit,* Russel Sage Foundation, 1972, New York.
16. M. Kumaramangalam, "Confessions of a Minister", *Science Today,* April, 1974, Bombay.
17. J.W. Gardner, "How to Preven to Organisational Dry-Rot?" *Harper's,* October, 1965.
18. P.E. Mott, *The Characteristics of Effective Organisations,* Harper & Row, 1972, New York.

19. Andre Malraux, *Anit-Memoirs,* Hamish Hamilton, 1968, London.
20. Paulo Freire, *op. cit.*
21. Gordon L. Lippitt, "What Do We Know About Leadership", *National Education Association Journal,* December 1955, Washington.
22. T.E. Cook, *et. al., Participatory Democracy,* 1971, Canfield Press, San Francisco; Fred E. Emery, *et al., Hope Within Walls,* 1973, Centre for Continuing Education, Australian National University, Canberra, R. M. Kanter (ed.), *Communes,* 1973, Harper and Row, New York; and Jan Myrdal, *et. al., China: The Revolution Continued,* 1971, Chatto and Windus, London.
23. Edgar Snow, *Red China Today,* 1970, Random House, New York.

19

District Planning Process: A Case Study in Karnataka

L. SHRIDHARAN

While reference to district planning exists since the Second Plan, the Planning Commission suggested states to initiate it under the Fourth Plan and issued a detailed guidelines for the purpose.[1] In accordance with this, Karnataka initiated district planning with the commencement of Fifth Five Year Plan in 1974-75. This paper attempts to review the experience of nearly a decade in this regard through a case study of a sample district in the state. The paper looks into the planning process in general and in the district and makes some observations on them. This is followed by a section on related financial aspects in district planning. A discussion was also held with key district officials on the problems faced by them on plan formulation and implementation. Finally some suggestions are made. With focus on the process, the choice of the district itself was not of much significance.

The Process[2]

Under the Fifth Plan a District and Regional Planning Division was set-up in the Planning Department at the State level and district planning officers appointed in each district. A short training programme was organized to acquaint the District Planning Officers with the issues in the methodology of district planning. Subsequently, they prepared a draft Integrated District

Development Plan of perspective nature spanning 1974 to 1984 for their respective districts.

At the organizational level there is a District Planning Committee in each district comprising of Project Director, District Rural Development Society; General Manager, District Industries Centre; District Development Assistant; District Publicity Officer; District Statistical Officer and District Planning Officer (Member-Secretary), headed by the Deputy Commissioner. This body is responsible for the initiation of the first draft on district plan which is then placed before the District Development Council for approval (with or without modifications). The Council consists of all MPs, MLAs, MLCs of the district, the TDB Presidents and all officers of the district with the Deputy Commissioner as the Chairman. With this basic introduction, we shall discuss the process.

In the early stages, the process mainly consisted of communicating the state-level sectoral financial allocations to the State Heads of Departments, who in turn communicated the district allocations to their counterpart in the districts. While there was no assessment of the relative needs at the state level, the district heads prepared schemes in departmental isolation. Thus, district plan essentially turned out to be an aggregation of departmental schemes. With a view to integrate sectoral and spatial aspects of planning in view of local resource endowment and needs, District Sector Schemes were delineated in early 1978 based on whether a scheme benefits a district and its people, and whether it can be planned and implemented at the district and lower levels without any adverse implications for integration of district plan with the state plan. For the 1978-79 Annual Plan, 75 per cent of the District Sector outlay at the state level was allocated among district on an objective basis, keeping the other 25 per cent as a cushion to make up deficiencies in the distribution of plan benefits or to accelerate some priority programmes in selected districts. The lumpsum outlay thus conveyed was to be apportioned over the departments by the District Planning Committee in consultation with their heads. The draft plan evolved by them was to be first approved by the District Development Council and then by the Government both with or without modifications. For implementation, the State Departmental heads released funds out of the approved outlay at the request of their district level counterparts. This process continued till 1981-82. A team for quarterly review of progress of implementation was constituted in 1980-81 consisting of district departmental heads and the District Planning Officer, headed by the Deputy Commissioner.

In 1982-83, the sectoral outlay at the district-level was indicated from the state-level in effect withdrawing the freedom of the district in deciding the departmental allocations, as the plans received from the districts tended to include state sector, central sector and non-plan schemes also.

Generally the planning process began at the district level around February for the coming year and it was well within the year by the time the district received the plan finally approved by the Government. A distinct departure from this pattern emerged under 1983-84 plan. The process was initiated by July 1982 with the draft plan approved by the DDC and sent to Government by September 1982. The plan finally approved by the Government was received by the first week of April 1983 by the district. This schedule still continues. During this year, minor headwise allocations for each sector at the district level were indicated by the State level, thus curtailing the freedom at the sectoral level also in the district. This measure was wth a view to bridge the gap between what is proposed by the district and what is approved by the State. As a compensatory measure, a discretionary outlay of Rs. 750 lakh (to be divided over the districts based on an objective criterion) was introduced to encourage initiation of schemes[3] of local importance by the DDC on its own.

A new dimension was introduced in April 1983 by asking the districts to provide scheme-wise monthly break-up of physical and financial targets for the approved district plan and the districts were to adhere to it strictly. In case of any unspent amount in a quarter, it could be revived only by convincing the Development Commissioner of the state. The monthly progress of physical and financial achievements was also to be filed in a similar proforma to the state by the 20th of the following month. Monthly state level reviews were to take place by the 30th of the month.

A similar approach continued for 1984-85 also. The 1985-86 plan saw a departure of the minor head-wise allocation pattern.

The districts were suggested to formulate plan for different sectors assuming a 10 per cent increase over the approved outlay of 1984-85 for the respective sectors. The schemewise allocation was left to the departmental heads. The plan formulation was to be on the monthly multi-level review proforma. Monthly reviews were also to be filed on the same proforma.

Some Observations

We shall make here some general observations on the process as also observations from the experience in the sample district:

1. It is to the credit of Karnataka that the plan process for the subsequent year now regularly begins by August of the current year and the various steps are carried out as per schedule. The plan duly approved by the Government reaches the district by the first week of April.
2. The requirement of plan formulation on the monthly Multi-level Review (MMR) proforma and the need to send a monthly review on the same proforma has brought a significant improvement on the implementation side, particularly, since a lapsed fund can be revived only by approaching the Development Commissioner of the state. As one officer jokularly said, "Now people will have to work round the year and not from January to March".
3. A copy of the approved plan on the MMR proforma is directly sent to the district treasury by the Government. The treasury allows withdrawl of funds against this to the concerned district officers without any further sanctions or approvals. This is another good administrative achievement saving unnecessary paper work and time.
4. The gap between what is proposed by the district and what is approved at the state level should not be bridged through administrative prescriptions, like Minor Headwise allocations or even sectoral allocations, curtailing the freedom of the districts in deciding their priorities. The situation needs to be rectified through better communication between the two levels and suitable development of skills among the district staff through appropriate training which seems to have ended as a one

time effort in the mid-seventies. With not a single district official, including the District Planning Officer of the sample district, aware of the Integrated District Development Plan, 1974-84, the Annual Plans were naturally not formulated against this framework.

5. The role of District Planning Officer appears to be mainly providing secretarial assistance to the Deputy Commissioner in the form of coordinated administrative work relating to planning and review of implementation handed over to him from time to time. With regard to District Annual Plan, he is responsible for getting various sectoral plans from the departmental heads, compile them together and present it to the Deputy Commissioner, with little say in the plan formulation or implementation. His office does not even have a few technical books. For the success of district planning, it is important that his key role in the process is recognized and his office suitably strengthened, including provision of training to him and his staff. Recognizing the vital role, the Working Group on District Planning recently suggested a status next only to the Deputy Commissioner for him.[4]
6. Generally a mechanical approach was found on the part of many key officials at the district level towards their work. Most of them did not have a clear perception of planning approaches and changes in them in their fields over time and called for the files when any information of even general nature was sought. Their limited views and compartmentalized nature of work seems to be responsible for this. It is necessary to arrange suitable training programme with a view to broaden their outlook, develop their skills and motivate them suitably.
7. Decentralization of planning and full public participation in development is emphasized for a long time and has been affirmed under the Seventh Five Year Plan also. In practice, however, district planning seems to be an aggregation of departmental schemes from a shelf of schemes identified and approved under district sector for each department. A plan should identify strategies and priorities for the district in view of its resource potential (both natural and human), ensure redressal of intra-district

imbalances through suitable spatial and locational policies, evolve approaches in view of the magnitude of poverty and ensure synchronization of development programmes, keeping the national and state priorities and approaches at the back of our mind. The present approach to planning seems to be only an administrative devolution. Public participation takes place only through the role of a few elected representatives in the District Development Council. More direct and innovative modes of public participation could and should be explored as attempted in Gujarat.[5]

Financial Aspects Relating to District Planning

In general, planning at the district level takes place at three 'parallel' levels. These are the District Plan, the Zila Parishad Plan and the District Credit Plan. In Karnataka, currently there is no Zila Parishad Plan as Zila Parishads do not exist. Normally the District and the Zila Parishad Plans are prepared annually for the financial year whereas the District Credit Plan is prepared for 2 or 3 years spanning over the calendar years and apportioned annually. With this general introduction, we shall study the financial aspects in our sample district.

Sectoral information on District (Annual) Plan relating to Outlay Approved by the District Development Council (OADDC), Outlay Approved by the Government in Planning Department (OAPD), Budget Released by the Head of the Department (BRHD) and the Expenditure Incurred (EI) over the period 1978-79 to 1983-84 were obtained from the District Planning Office which were obtained from the individual departments by this office earlier. The DPO did express doubts about a total reliability of these data. Attempts to obtain these data from individual departments failed with all of them not providing the information and the concerned clerks interpreting the information sought in their own ways. Consequently, we have analyzed the data supplied by the DPO in the hope of gaining some general understanding. Information on residuary sector consisting of all special programmes initiated by the State and the Centre were obtained from the District Rural Development Society. To save space, these data are not reproduced here.[6] The broad conclusions reached are:

1. The OAPD for the District Sector Schemes has gone up by nearly three times between 1978-79 and 1983-84 and so has the Expenditure Incurred (EI). Even if discounted for inflation, it does signify an increased availability of funds at the district level though the share of district sector schemes may not have gone up significantly.
2. The OAPD generally tends to be between 70 and 80 per cent of the OADDC for the district sector as a whole. This, however, does not imply a uniform slashing of OADDC by the Planning Department over the sectors with sometimes even a rise in the OAPD as compared to OADDC and sometimes the items completely dropped. Such drastic changes at the state level of OADDC are justified on the grounds of bringing the District Plans in tune with the national and state priorities. While to an extent, the DDC may propose a higher outlay in anticipation of a slash from the state level, the significant fluctuation in the percentage of OAPD against OADDC from 100 over the sectors (roughly in the range of 50 to 130 though sometimes it is as high as 190) points essentially to a poor communication of the national and state priorities to the districts and an absence of a realistic indication of the financial availability to the districts. These run counter to the very concepts of district planning being evolved against local potentials and resources. These problems should be tackled through better communications and understanding between the State and the Districts, and through suitable training of the district level staff.
3. Since OADDC may be considered notional in asfar as the final outlay is OAPD, a comparison of BRHD against OAPD was attempted. While BRHD was often significantly less than the OAPD ranging between 75 and 90 per cent (though it was 102 per cent in 1978-79) for the District Sector Schemes as a whole, it fluctuated widely over the sectors. In a number of sectors, including key sectors like agriculture, soil and water conservation, horticulture, minor irrigation, etc., often the BRHD was far below the OAPD. Given OAPD, the reasons for low BRHD are not clear. On the other hand, in a number of

departments, the BRHD exceeds OAPD (ranging between 130 and 300 per cent). When enquired, the departmental heads said that some additional approval must have come during the year, though they could not provide any details as most of them had taken over the positions only recently. Thus, there appears to be a mismatch between planning (as approved by the Planning Department) and its actual implementation as reflected through financial provisions. Thus, a serious attention needs to be paid to the financial matching of planning and of implementation at different levels.

4. When all district sector schemes are taken together, the EI is lower than BRHD, though close to 100 per cent. However, considerable under-expenditure (sometimes as low as 40 per cent) and sometimes over expenditure against BRHD are observed over the individual sectors. No clear reasons were offered on enquiry.
5. Financially speaking, planning can be said to be realized through the expenditure incurred. In this sense, the realization for district sector schemes as a whole fluctuate between 49.0 per cent (1982-83) and 92.5 per cent (1983-84) of OAPD, it being only around 68.8 per cent for the period 1978-84 taken as a whole. Considerable over-expenditures and under-expenditures against OAPD are observed at the level of individual sectors. While the reasons for these are not clear, they can be only symptomatic of some serious deficiencies in both our planning and implementation systems.
6. Observations very similar to the above ones hold good for the residuary sector also.
7. A number of state sector schemes are also implemented by the districts. It would be reasonable to assume that observations similar to the above ones hold good for them also. Thus, the situation warrants an immediate attention.

A Discussion with Senior District Officials

A discussion was held with senior district officials of the sample district on the problems of District Planning. The following observations emerged:

1. It was pointed out that district plan in a broader sense must encompass the state sector schemes being implanted at the district level which form a sizable chunk. This reality should be taken into account while planning for the district. This implies that the state sector plan should be ready and communicated to the districts before the District Plan can be prepared. As this may not be feasible in practice, the district plan should at least take cognizance of the on-going schemes of the state sector in the district.
2. The officials pointed out the 'policing' nature of our administrative system than it being production and purpose-oriented. Thus, while the system comes down strongly on a negative aspect, it hardly provides for an appreciation of good work, individual initiative, etc. This in effect questions the crux of our administrative system and needs being looked into urgently.
3. The problem of inter-departmental/inter-official coordination was noted to be mainly a problem of human ego. Thus, it needs a very tactful handling of his counterparts in other departments and the subordinates by the concerned official whether it is at the level of Deputy Commissioner or the District Departmental Heads. Solution can emerge only through an appreciation of their mutual roles. Suitable training in inter-personal and organisation behaviour may be useful in this regard. This view was endorsed by the senior district officials.
4. According to the Deputy Commissioner, the prevalence of stronger departmental loyalty as opposed to horizontal loyalty does not pose any difficulty in coordinating the various district level activities. However, officials handling matters on behalf of the Deputy Commissioner do express this difficulty. An effective solution to this problem is a reorganization of the district administration in tune with the area planning concepts advocated for district planning. This point has been elaborated elsewhere.[7]
5. On the issue of frequent transfer of key district officials, the authorities felt that though it disrupts developmental activities, vested interests may develop if they are posted at one place, for more than 3 years. This view seems to emanate from the 'policing role' of administration. To

believe that most of the officials staying beyond 3 years will develop a vested interest in the area seems to be an exaggeration. The five year duration suggested by the recent working group on District Planning seems appropriate.[8]

6. The Deputy Commissioner of the sample district considered the current role of District Planning Officer adequate. He also did not feel the need for a district level monitoring body (either independent or under the DPO) when asked. However, the DPO presently seems to mainly provide secretarial assistance in planning related matters to the Deputy Commissioner. As suggested by the working group on District Planning, this position needs to be headed by an officer whose status is next only to that of the Deputy Commissioner. Such an officer should undergo training in broad national/regional issue and priorities, area planning techniques, organization behaviour, etc., on the one hand and should have leadership qualities and capacity to handle human engineering problems (particularly in the context of bringing about inter-departmental coordination) on the other.
7. As for unconventional approaches, *i.e.*, not submitting to standard norms prescribed), it was pointed out that such departures are not questioned from the state level, provided the concerned Deputy Commissioner has okayed them. However, the advantage of this flexibility has been taken only on a few occasions. This flexibility, if properly utilized, can bring a sea change in district planning.
8. Senior district officials were not aware of the details of Lakhina experiment[9] of reforms in Ahmednagar Collectorate administration. It is important that the details of this experiment are widely circulated to all the districts in the country for suitable emulation. The district officials were also not aware of the working group report on district planning which was out then for more than a year. This report too should be circulated in all the districts.
9. It is often pointed out that political and administrative superiors are basically opposed to decentralization as it means delegating more power to lower order units, which

are otherwise held by them in their respective spheres. In this regard, we can only say that a genuine political commitment in favour of decentralization and district planning is a must.

Suggestions

The close link between multi-level planning and decentralization itself arises out of our constitutional faith in democratic decentralization which provides the basic framework for decentralization in planning. Our suggestions given below follow from this tenet and our earlier observations:

1. A substantial portion of the available funds at the district level get committed to on-going and spill-over schemes. This necessitates us to take a long-term view of district planning against the national-state priorities; and local needs and potentials. Thus long/medium term district plans should be prepared from which annual plans can be apportioned and passed by the state assembly. Such an approach will develop an overall understanding of the district economy and help in monitoring the progress, apart from throwing up the peculiar setting (economic/ social/physical) of the district. To accommodate such peculiarities and exploit the potentials of the district better, it may be necessary to deviate from national and state priorities at this level, ensuring an overall balance at the state level. Such an exercise can be undertaken only against a long/medium term plan.
2. While schemes are assessed in terms of financial and physical targets achieved, no attempts are made to assess their economic and/or social impacts on the district economy. In view of its importance, such a role should be assigned to a monitoring and evaluation cell under the District Planning Officer.
3. The role of District Planning Officer and his team needs to be identified clearly, and accordingly supported and upgraded. The state should be able to establish a better rapport with the district so that resorting to administrative prescriptions can be avoided. It is essential that the District

Planning Officer, his team and others (at least the various district departmental heads) connected with planning and implementation are trained to have a broad outlook on the economy; technical skills of project planning, management, monitoring and evaluation; area planning concepts and skills; leadership and motivational and organizational behaviour skills to overcome the human ego problems at different levels, etc.

4. The District Plans are prepared for the financial year and the District Credit Plans are prepared for the calendar year. While there are reasons for both being as they are, attempts should be made to break-up the District Credit Plan into quarterly modules which enable its alignment with the branch performance budget on the one hand and facilitate integration with the District Plan on the other. The fact that District Plans are prepared in time with monthly break-ups in Karnataka should be very helpful in preparing the District Credit Plan and its quarterly modules.
5. In general, it is felt that there is scope for improving/ rationalizing/simplifying the administrative procedures for liaisoning between a state and its districts, within a district among different departments, the general administrative procedures, etc., in addition to the scope for the improvement in record/filing systems. As noted by Prof. Nanjundappa,[10] Planning Secretary of Karnataka, in district development, planning, programmes should be integrated first horizontally and then inter-district, vertical sectoral integration should be achieved. He also suggested a change in the accounting system in tune with the spirits of decentralization. It may be advisable to appoint a committee in each state to evolve simplified and efficient administrative procedures to facilitate decentralization. Such a body should keep in view the recommendations of the Committee on Administrative Arrangements for Rural Development and Poverty Alleviation Programmes released recently.[11]
6. Public participation is essential for the success of decentralization and development. It has been pointed out that Panchayati Raj bodies have often acted as hand-

maidens of vested interests. Such misuses should be off set by including representatives of the dispossessed in these institutions and through the right to recall a member if he does not serve the interest of the people. People's Participation can be sought in other ways also. Recently Gujarat introduced an incentive outlay for the districts against which a matching contribution of 50 per cent or 25 per cent depending on the backwardness of the area had to be raised locally. The approach proved very successful with the people's contribution coming to 96 per cent of the targeted amount in 1982-83. Innovative schemes like rural fire-fighting arrangements, purchase of laparoscopic machines for tubectomy operations, para-medical vans, pipeline and stand-posts for water-supply, electrification of street lights in Harijan colonies, etc., emerged on local initiative.[12] Such examples should be emulated.

7. The approach in our planning at all levels has been highly resources oriented, resource in the financial sense. Attempts to explore non-conventional resources, particularly at the district and lower levels should be made. Thus, the vast manpower resource, better management and utilization of water, use/adoption of local resources/methods in activities of government or otherwise will go a long way in making our efforts of decentralization a success. Finally, one can only emphasize the need for a change in attitude through a genuine commitment and will in favour of decentralization, at the political and administrative levels accompanied by delegation of authority to appropriate levels. As noted by late Shri D.P. Dhar,[13] former Union Minister for Planning, power "is something that comes from new ways of doing things in new combinations and in new institutions" and "not something that one is holding on to." This vital fact needs to be recognized.

In conclusion, inasfar as our planning and administrative systems are broadly similar over the state, we believe a number of these findings will hold good for other states also and the suggestions useful to them.

REFERENCES

1. Planning Commission, *Guidelines for the Formulation of District Plans*, New Delhi, 1969.
2. This section is based on various state government circulars on planning process issued from time to time and personal discussions with district officials.
3. Schemes involving subsidy or additional posts were not to be taken up. At least 30 per cent of the outlay was to be spent on programmes benefiting the weaker sections.
4. Planning Commission, *Report of the Working Group on District Planning*, Vol. 1, New Delhi, May 1984.
5. Sanat Mehta, "Planning in Gujarat", *The Economic Times*, October 30 and 31, 1985.
6. See for details L. Shridharan, *District Planning Process in Karnataka*, Study sponsored by the Planning Commission, Government of India, ASCI, March, 1986.
7. L. Shridharan, "Decentralization and District Planning", *The Economic Times*, August 9, 1986.
8. Planning Commission, *op. cit.*, May, 1984.
9. Anil Kumar Lakhina, "Reforms in the Collectorate of Ahmednagar (Maharashtra): A Report", *The Indian Journal of Public Administration*, Vol. XXX, No. 2, April-June, 1984.
10. D.M. Nanjundappa, "Decentralized Planning—Problems, of Administration and Coordination", a paper presented at the National Seminar on *Decentralized Planning and Implementation* held at the Institute for Social and Economic Change, Bangalore, November 19 to December 1, 1984.
11. Department of Rural Development, *Report of the Committee to Review the Existing Administrative Arrangements for Rural Development* and Poverty *Alleviation Programmes*, Ministry of Agriculture, December 1985.
12. Sanat Mehta, *op cit.*
13. Planning Commission, *District Planning*, New Delhi, 1973 (a talk by late Shri D.P. Dhar).

20

Multi-Level Planning and Local Government Structure

DEVA RAJ

In the formulation of the Fifth Five Year Plan, multi-level planning has been looked upon as the arch-stone for regional development strategies. Similar hopes of correcting regional imbalances were entertained through district planning and area planning in the earlier Five Year Plans without success. Unless appropriate steps are taken to provide the necessary administrative and technical infrastructure and certain anomalies in the present planning processes—particularly at the local levels—are corrected, all the excellent work being done in Planning Commission may fail to yield any results.

Multi-level planning, to be a reality, stipulates certain basic factors, such as:

1. identification of levels of planning with territorial, spatial and administrative jurisdictions;
2. a hierarchy of levels inter-related to a hierarchy of functions, in matters of planning and implementation;
3. a system of inter-level or inter-governmental relationships—technical, financial and administrative—including arrangements for reviewing and determining policies, programmes and priorities as well as providing an integrated framework for local, state and national plans;
4. viability of the local and the regional planning and executive units, agencies or levels of government for effective functioning and availability at each level

appropriate expertise for project formulation with necessary guidance and support from higher echelons; and

5. a basic commitment to an all out local planning and development efforts with its attendant responsibilities of mobilization of local resources and exploitation of local potential with such outside support as may be necessary to induce self-generating growth.

Planning Machinery

Before analyzing the administrative problems in multi-level planning, it will be desirable to have a quick look at the performance of the planning functions, particularly at the local levels. India has been a pioneer in national planning in the third world and the Planning Commission, with all its limitations, has been an outstanding institution, with a high degree of expertise. Its dominant character, however, combined with detailed schematic approaches had a stifling effect on the initiative of the States, which were themselves hardly equipped for any long-range exercise in planning. The pre-occupation of the Planning Commission with detailed sectoral planning also left some vital gaps in the planning mechanism at the Centre. There were at least three areas essential for multi-level planning, which did not receive adequate support.

1. In spite of recent solicitations, spatial planning has not yet found a berth in the Planning Commission and there has hardly been any expert group engaged in integrated rural-urban planning to link up socio-economic development with physical and natural resource planning. The continued omission of urban areas and urbanization processes from the plans is an admitted fact that it is a measure of this unconcern that even the National Malaria Eradication Programme did not recognize the existence of urban areas and it is urban malaria today that threatens to undo the tremendous achievements of this internationally prestigious programme.
2. There are problems of planning and development involving inter-state regions for harnessing resources, developing communications and building up the

necessary infrastructure in larger national interests. There is need of a special organization for the purpose in the Planning Commission.

3. A neglected field has been the development of administrative infrastructure to match the tasks of planning and implementation. The administrative organization has been taken for granted and no attempt was made to build up and try out administrative models to meet the new challenges.

The State plans reflected less of policy planning than programme budgeting combined with strong pleas of backwardness with their eyes on maximizing their share in central assistance. It was not till 1963 that the States considered setting up of Planning Boards following a recommendation by the Planning Commission. However, these *ad hoc* bodies did not meet the requirement of an expert high level planning agency that could provide an integrated planning framework and necessary guidance and supervision to the field organizations in the districts. It was as late as May, 1972 that the Planning Commission addressed a letter to the State Governments indicating broad lines of organization of an apex planning agency with separate units for Perspective Planning, Regional/District Planning, Project Formulation, Plan Coordination and Monitoring, Plan Information and Evaluation. The additional expenditure involved in strengthening the planning apparatus was proposed to be shared between the Centre and the States.

Local Planning Scene

It is, however, planning at the sub-state levels that is fundamental and crucial to the concept of multi-level planning. As one scans all the sectors a local level, one comes across a variety of isolated *ad hoc* planning effort by various agencies with different objectives. Some of these plans, their scope and perspectives are discussed below:

District Plans have been the foremost instruments of local planning, which are reflected, however, inadequately in State and National Plans. It was 20 years ago, on the eve of the formulation of the Second Five Year Plan, that village, lock and district plans were required to be prepared. Ever since, attempts have been made to make them more realistic but even at the time of the preparation of the Fourth Plan proposals most district plans were mere collection of felt needs of the people and demands for financial provisions in the State Plans for allocation to the districts. Many States did make an attempt to prepare analytical plans but it was a long way towards planning based on assessment of resource potential and development of local infrastructure that could sustain higher rates of growth. During 1968-69, the Planning Commission undertook an exercise for Karnal and Amritsar and developed guidelines for the preparation of district plans which were circulated to the State Governments, but it is realized that the necessary expertise for such integrated planning is hardly available at the district level.

Even these plans, as all their forerunners, can in no way be considered to be complete or the following reasons:

(1) The district plans have been purely rural plans and totally ignore the existence of urban areas, and their growth processes;
(2) These have been mostly sectoral programme plans without spatial dimensions, practically oblivious of physical planning. These hardly reflect an awareness of the existence of local planning authorities under town planning enactments in a number of States.

It would be utterly unrealistic to have any regional development plan without taking into account the interaction between these elements and the rural sectoral activities.

District planning, in fact, failed even to take note of urbanising processes within the panchayat raj areas leading to haphazard growth and land speculation, particularly in the periphery of municipal jurisdictions or at other growth points. Even the Rural Industrial Estates were laid out without any integrated rural-urban spatial planning and no wonder they came to grief. Even the recent thinking in respect of development of growth centres and rural service towns is a case of isolated micro-level planning. Growth points, growth centres and growth poles represent an interrelated hierarchy, requiring integrated land-use and communication planning.

Towards City and Metropolitan Planning a provision for the 'preparation of detailed Master Plans for urban and regional development' was made in the Third Five Year Plan under the growing strains of urbanization. A hundred per cent central assistance was given through the Town and Country Planning Organization of the Government of India, for planning of metropolitan cities, State capitals, port towns and industrial centres. About 72 cities and towns were covered during this plan period and it was proposed under the Fourth Plan to cover all cities and towns with a population of 50,000 and above, although the programme was transferred to the State sector. In sharp contrast to district plans, these urban area plans are largely physical, land-use and communication plans for cities together with a minimum of the peripheral areas being backed by town planning laws in some of the States. A number of plans for major cities embrace somewhat wider metropolitan area within the district, such as Master Plans for Bangalore, Hyderabad, Cochin, Ahmedabad, Poona, Nagpur, Kanpur, etc. The recent plan for metropolitan Bombay, the plan for the Calcutta metropolitan district covering about 36 municipal areas along with some rural districts and the Master Plan of Delhi have, however, the character of regional plans crossing district limits. In the case of Delhi, the National Capital Region presents the problems of an inter-state urban complex. Another type of a plan prepared under the scheme covering a mixed rural-urban area has been the Asansol Regional Plan, including the Durgapur industrial area, which was developed as a counter-magnet to Calcutta. Sometimes, these plans are drawn up by temporary statutory boards, while mostly the exercise is carried out by the State Town Planning Directorates without much involvement of the local municipal authorities.

It would be pertinent to remark here that these physical plans do not bear any relationship with economic plans and in spite of the intention of the Third Plan to bring at least cities of 1,00,000 or over into the national planning process, it has not been possible to integrate these physical plans with the District or State Plans. Another serious handicap from which all urban plans have suffered is that with minor exceptions, they are not backed by an overall administrative machinery for implementation or legal powers of enforcement. The Calcutta Metropolitan Development Authority (CMDA), set up only towards the end of 1970, is but a halting attempt to provide a coordinating mechanism. In Bombay, the City and Industrial Development Organization (CIDCO) is an *ad hoc* device to undertake the Twin City Project within the framework of the larger metropolitan regional plan. Delhi is an exception in many ways insofar as the entire Union Territory is within the Master Plan area making for some integration between the urban and rural plans but plagued by a multiplicity of authorities. Nor could any satisfactory arrangements be evolved for dealing with problems of development in the parts of the National Capital Region that lie in the adjoining States.

There are also programme plans of a number of Central and State agencies which are being executed in a city or its peripheral areas or elsewhere often without reference to the city master plans, if any. These may include State Housing Boards, Electricity Boards, Industrial Development Corporations, and various departments dealing with water-supply and drainage, communications, trade and commerce, agriculture and industry and social services. This has created far reaching problems of coordination, duplication and often wastage of resources, too often decried and too well-known to be enumerated here.

Fragmentation of District Administration

This brief survey presents a confused picture of multiplicity of plans with varying objectives, often overlapping or working at cross-purposes with no organization for a coordinated approach to the problems of the district—to say nothing of integrated planning and development. Multi-level planning at the crucial level of the district calls for an overall planning and development authority. Instead, we have the administration in the district hopelessly bifurcated and fragmented with decision-making and accountability scattered between various local statutory and administrative agencies, subject to checks and controls exercised horizontally and vertically. In the early years of the century, local district administration was unified under the Collector and District Magistrate with lines of control running through the provincial governments to the centre—leaving, nevertheless, wide authority and decision-making in local matters to the District Officer. The vast changes that have since come about on the political and developmental fronts have culminated in a pattern shown in Chart I.

It is clear from the organization chart that district administration, instead of being looked upon as local government as a whole, is a queer admixture of State Departments and their field institutions and a host of not so important statutory local bodies as concessions to democracy and local-self government, which can be terminated at the will of the bureaucracy or the political bosses at the State-level. Alternatively, some important local developmental tasks are entrusted to not-so-democratic, special purpose agencies—starting a vicious circle of weak truncated and inefficient local government. What authority, under the circumstances, can undertake integrated local level planning and how? And what departments and ministries at the State and Central-level are to provide the necessary guidance and support? In most States, at least the urban sector of local government is split into two or three departments, dealing separately with municipal administration, town planning and housing and water supply and drainage. Even at the Centre, it was only in February 1973 that all these aspects of urban local government were brought under one Ministry—that of Works and Housing. Rural local Government has been under a separate ministry at the Centre since 1958-59.

The picture would be somewhat different in Maharashtra, where Zila Parishads have come to constitute a level of Government bringing under its canopy all the development departments at the district-level or, where the District Collector has been relieved of developmental responsibilities, and a separate senior officer has been entrusted with these responsibilities. To that extent, there has been a distinct improvement in the capacity, and effective functioning of local district governments. Nevertheless, the compartmentalization between rural and urban governments in the district continues and whatever plans are drawn up are rural sector plans without any spatial perspective. This is district government minus the urban areas.

Administrative Infrastructure for Planning

Under the circumstances, multi-level planning is a far cry. It must only continue to be planning from above in spite of all protestations to the countrary. The organization of local and regional planning and development agencies at the sub-state level is a pre-condition of any approach to multi-level planning. This will require

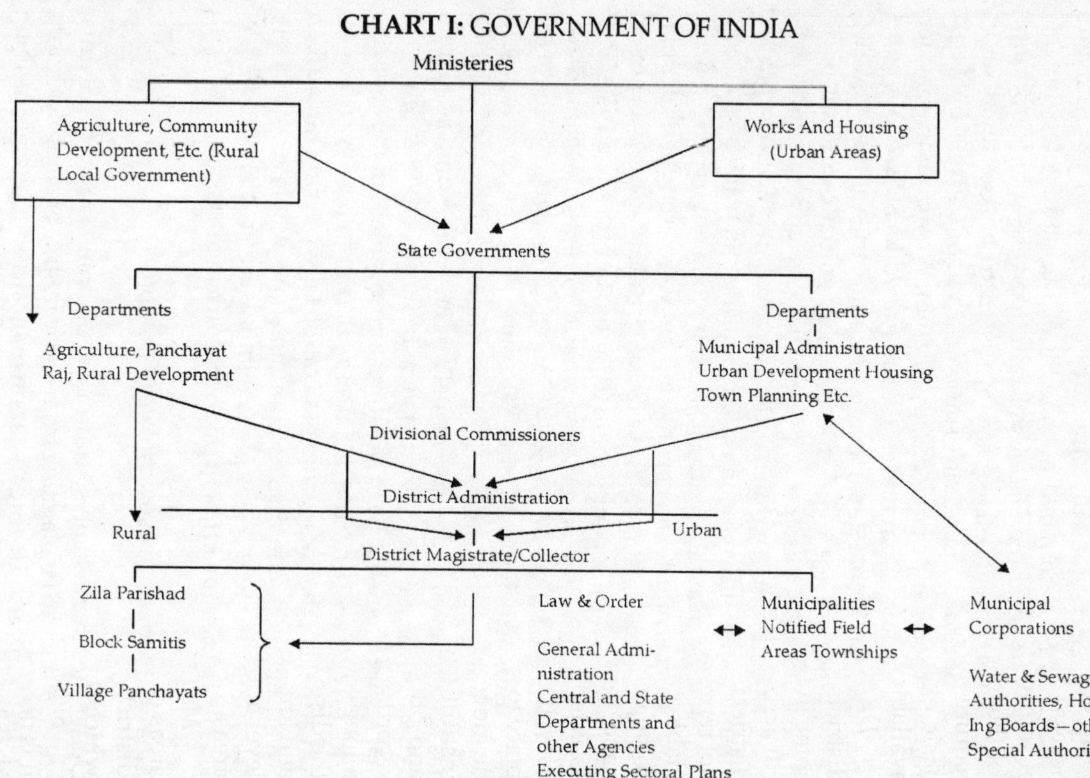
CHART I: GOVERNMENT OF INDIA
Ministeries
Agriculture, Community Development, Etc. (Rural Local Government)
Works And Housing (Urban Areas)
State Governments
Departments
Agriculture, Panchayat Raj, Rural Development
Departments
Municipal Administration Urban Development Housing Town Planning Etc.
Divisional Commissioners
District Administration
Rural
Urban
District Magistrate/Collector
Zila Parishad
Block Samitis
Village Panchayats
Law & Order
General Administration
Central and State Departments and other Agencies Executing Sectoral Plans
Municipalities Notified Field Areas Townships
Municipal Corporations
Water & Sewage Authorities, Hous-Ing Boards—other Special Authorities

identification of viable areas under unified administrations which could ensure effective organization of productive and social activities and appropriate institutional frames with due regard to socio-economic and geographical factors. They must have the necessary capabilities for data collection, processing and analysis of information to work out probable alternatives and priorities for the most effective utilization of scarce resources. That they will require higher level support and guidance is conceded, but some basic expertise must be provided by proper redistribution of available talent.

District as Local Planning Unit: The existing boundaries of districts and the wide variation in their area and population have come in for considerable criticism. Sometimes district boundaries cut across physico-agronomic regions; it is an expert's view that a district is not the most appropriate planning region as it often does not represent homogeneity or possess the attributes of an internally viable entity. That the area and jurisdiction of districts will bear some considerable adjustments cannot be denied. On the other hand, the district has, because of its strong administrative identity, asserted itself as the basic unit for economic and sectoral planning as well as plan implementation. Moreover, if the district is to yield place to scientifically demarcated regions or sub-regions, it would be necessary to reorganize the entire administrative and institutional structure and it will raise a number of political issues and other problems of territorial orientation and adjustment of records. While the adjustment of district boundaries may remain a long-term objective, the odds are overwhelmingly in favour of the district being adopted as the basic unit of local-level planning and implementation. This will, of course, require an overall district level authority for integrated planning for both rural and urban areas.

Metropolitan Regions: There will still be some highly urbanized areas of inter-district dimensions or covering the major part of a district. This will need demarcation of Metropolitan Regions of which there may be about a dozen in the country.

Sub-State Regions: While district reorganization can be deferred, it is necessary to identify and demarcate regional areas at the sub-state level. In most cases, a combination of districts would make a region, and would also help to overcome the inadequacies of district as a unit of planning. The Commissioner's Divisions as well as the Superintending Engineer circles have been there with us, although without the necessary administrative frame that could enable them to play a broader role in planning and development. It should not be difficult at all to work out a regrouping of districts with common characteristics and area problems and set-up a planning and development machinery at that level and even clothe it with certain authority and power.

It may be mentioned in this connection that most countries have undertaken a regrouping of their traditional local areas. In France, for instance, about 89 departments (more or less corresponding to our territorial districts) have been regrouped for purposes of planning in 21 regions with one of the Prefects (the administrative head of the department), functioning as the regional Prefect having a special supporting technical team, as well as the deliberative body known as the Commission de Development Economique Regione (CODER). It is true that the administrative structure of these 'regions' is still evolving, but it is significant that even in France, where the departments as local units of administration have survived many a revolution, it has been found necessary to give them a regional perspective to meet the challenges of growth and development, due to the widening range of governmental activity and the change in the scale of operations due to technological advancements. Similarly, the Local Government Act of 1972 in U.K. divides the entire country into 6 predominantly urban metropolitan countries with second tier authorities and 38 countries with lower level rural and urban units of appropriate size.

There is no reason why we should not approach the question of identifying district groupings and set them up as regional units for planning tasks and for coordinating and guiding programme implementation at the district or city levels. The *Perspective Plan of Gujarat* 1974-84 (Vol. III) suggests six possible regions. It may be that in the smaller states, with a few districts, the state level organization may be in a position to function as both the state and regional-level organization because of sheer size. But most of the major states will find it convenient to undertake this exercise of identifying groups of districts which are: (*a*) administratively feasible and manageable, (*b*) economically viable, and (*c*) have a hierarchy of settlements and technical and financial institutions, necessary for a self-generating effort.

Needless to say that such a regional set-up will require strong support from the States and the Centre, which should have separate expert Regional and Multi-level Planning and Development Cells to demarcate the regions and to lend technical and administrative support to the field organizations. In this regard, the following diagrammatic model is put forward as a basis for debate and detailed analysis (Chart II).

Chart II

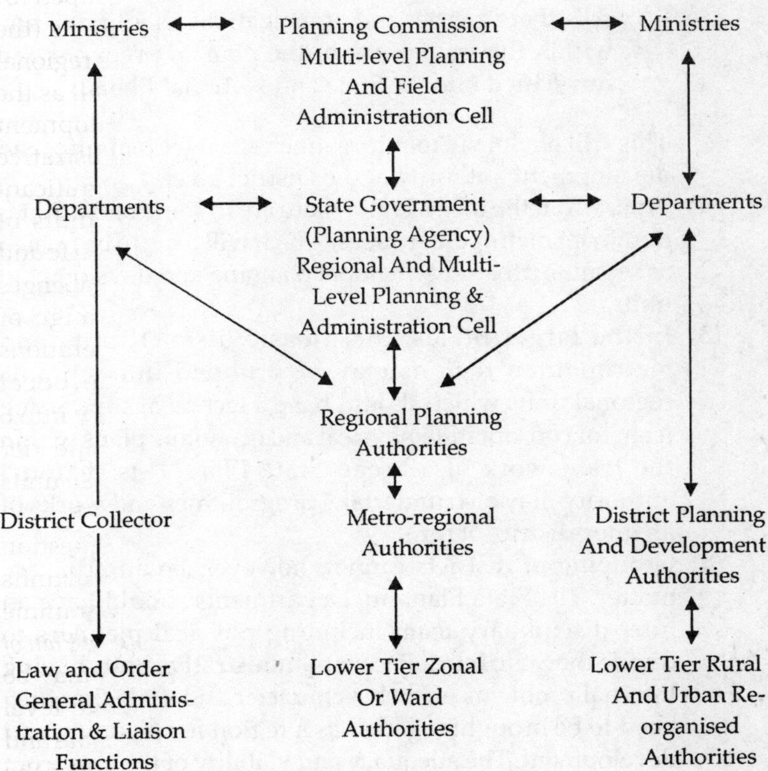

Conclusion

The discussion can be briefly summed up as follows:

(1) The existing district units should, apart from any possible boundary adjustments, be oriented in the following respects:

(*a*) They should become apex units for both rural and urban authorities and their plans should cover both rural and urban areas;

(*b*) The plans should be based on a physical spatial plan, interlinking the rural and urban areas for a balanced development of infrastructure in relation to identified growth points and the hierarchy of rural and urban settlements in the district; and

(*c*) All other agencies and organizations should function within the framework of the plan so prepared and dovetailed into the State and National Plans.

This will obviously require a much stronger planning and development authority at the District level.

(2) Apart from the district unit, there are in some of the States dominant metropolitan areas, which will have to be treated as separate urban sub-regional planning and development units.

(3) In the larger States, these basic district units and metropolitan regions may be grouped into suitable regional units which should have a technical supporting team for coordinating physical and economic plans within the framework of a broad State Plan. This regional authority may also undertake programmes and works of an inter-district nature.

(4) Grouping of districts cannot, however, be an arbitrary matter. The State Planning Departments should have an inter-disciplinary team including physical planners to divide the State into adjacent administrative units having internal problems of such a character and scale that they need to be brought together as a region for planning and development. The adequacy and viability of the area from the point of developmental administration will also have to be taken into account. The State Plans can then be based on regional plans and the programmes of the respective State Departments will need channeling through the Regional, District and Metropolitan authorities except in

the larger spheres of technical and financial support and studies and research.

(5) At the Centre, the Planning Commission's Multi-level Planning Cell must not only attune itself to lend support for developing appropriate techniques but should concern itself with the planning of inter-State regions and national infrastructure, particularly in matters of Water Management and Communications, in the context of resource regions cutting across State boundaries and ensure necessary allocations of funds for such purposes on a priority basis.

In the end, it must be emphasized that we have too long been pre-occupied with administrative reforms at the top. It is, however, the reorganization and strengthening of local government and field administration that is looked upon around the world as providing the necessary balance between centralization and the compelling need of decentralization of power to lower echelons of Government. The superstructure of the State and Central Government can only be raised on sound foundations of local and regional authorities encouraged and equipped to shoulder the field responsibilities. The field administration has received little attention and is being steadily denuded of capable managerial and technical talent. Realistic planning and effective implementation depends on sound and viable local government structure which at once needs smaller and larger units reconciling democratic aspirations with a strong executive to carry out programmes and policies.

21

District Planning in Maharashtra

N.R. INAMDAR

District planning is a species of regional planning in a broad sense of the latter term. In this broad sense, regional planning covers in its objectives national planning seeking to achieve balanced regional integration, investment in particular geographical areas to boost up their retarded growth and regionalized economic planning. In its application, the concept of regional planning includes metropolitan development, comprehensive growth of resource complexes and rural reconstruction programmes. District planning could be conceived as an offshoot of regional planning in its objectives of regionalized economic planning and programmatic aspect of rural reconstruction.

Apart from the areal, economic, social and political implications of unbalanced regional development, the organization of economic space affects the pace and structure of economic growth. So, it has been by now unanimously accepted that developing societies in the transition of industrial development take to the process of regional planning, which is expected to play the role of an instrument to hasten the transition as well as of a palliative to soothe its injurious effect. The western literature on regional planning[1] generally overlooks the equally urgent need for regional planning to step up the pace of comprehensive rural development so as to set in motion quicker industrial growth. In the west, a naturalistic frame is assumed for the operations of regional planning. In the context of planned development in developing counties, like India, regional planning has to start on the assumption of the planning objectives and strategy at the national level in applying itself to the specific spatial features of the national plan in a particular region.[2]

Regional planning in the west is different from urban planning in both its theoretical concerns as well as practical tasks. The theoretical concerns of regional planning revolve round the economics of location and the central places concept developed respectively by Alfred Weber in the first decade of this century and Christaller in the thirties, both in Germany. The theory of urban planning, on the other hand, is rooted in the science of ecology, land economics and the aesthetics of form. The practical tasks of the regional planner involve resource allocation and augmentation, while those of the urban planner are concerned with physical land use and design. In the perspective of Indian planned development, an awareness of the need of reducing the gap between regional and urban planning, both in conceptual and practical aspects, has grown recently. District planning in this country, as a variant of regional planning, has to use the mechanism and techniques of urban planning, among those of other categories of planning, such as project planning and programme planning. In taking over the objectives of regional planning—*viz.*, achievement of balanced regional integration, areal investment and regionalized economic planning—district planning has to take note of planning of urban areas. Further, within and across the districts, metropolitan development is really an amalgam of city planning and planning for preservation of the rural landscape as well as of social facilities within the rural fringe.[3] The towns, along with large villages, within the districts form hierarchies of nodal points or control centres for location of infrastructure and social facilities to activate multisided development in the rural hinterland or 'density-field'[4] In fact, within the districts in the country, the lines of distinction between towns and villages and also among towns are blurring.

The main task of the regional planner are to state the ordering of control centres within the area, to identify the functions to be performed by each centre, and to study interregional effects to the expansion of economies. The overstress in these tasks on the physical aspect of the inputs and their functions puts aside the role of human inputs, the most significant factor in the viability of the process of district planning. The visualization of the district economy as an integrated unit with internal consistencies and balances is taken care of by the concept of homogeneity of the planned region, the district in this case. But the role of the human inputs has not received due attention in the scheme of the 'spatial' planner. The concept of 'planning from below', an inherent element of the district planning process, seeks to correct this deficiency in the scheme of the regional planner. The practical implications and limitations of the concept of 'planning from below, are analyzed in the following section.

II

Planning from below has been invariably associated by the Indian planners with district planning. Within the overall framework of the national plan objectives, financial resources and format of plan schemes, district planning has been given a high place in the consideration of the planners. This has been the position right from the First Plan. In a letter dated 11 October, 1950, the Planning Commission emphasized the vital role of the local authorities in any scheme of planned development. The Commission, however, did not overlook the essential requirement of the eventual coordination of the local authorities' plans with the State plans.[5] But the idea of district and village planning emerged clearly in 1954, during the process of formulation of the Second Plan. The Planning Commission then asked the States "to arrange for the preparation of such plans, especially in respect of agriculture, production, rural industries and cooperation".[6] Continuing the thread, the Fourth Plan expected strengthening of the planning apparatus at the State and the district level. It laid a particular stress on more active popular participation in plan formulation though the panchayati raj organizations at the district level.[7] In the framing of the Fifth Plan, the State of Maharashtra, following the organizational guidance of the Planning Commission, decided to adopt the district as the unit and to formulate the perspective plans for each district with the twin objectives of giving opportunity to all the districts to attain full development in keeping with their resources and of removing the imbalances in development as between districts and areas within the same districts to the extent possible.[8]

District planning and planning from below have been parts of the accepted strategy of the planners. Even then, until the Third Plan, a proper organizational machinery in the districts had not been created to facilitate the actualization of these components of the plan strategy. During 1959-62, the necessary organizational framework became available in the Zila Parishads in some of the States. But the Panchayati Raj Bodies were, by and large, helpless and mute observers of dictates from above until the needed personnel, financial and other suitable conditions were provided. This reorganization and strengthening of the district machinery was tied up with the restructuring and strengthening of the State Planning process and mechanism. The realization of this double process was facilitated by the changed political temper during 1967 and after.

The formulation of the First Plan did not afford sufficient time for consulting district and local organizations. It was a hastily drawn patchwork of the departmental and state plans.[9] Framing of the Second Plan, however, gave more than adequate leeway for the fermentation of the plan proposals at different levels, including the district, block and village units. But the creation of the consultative machinery at the district, the block and the village levels did not ensure even a reasonable extent of discussion of the developmental proposals by the popular representatives, both elected and non-elected.[10] The state of affairs in Maharasthra (then a part of the Bombay State) was not different from the conditions in other states. The account of plan formulation process in an 'A' grade community development block in Maharasthra during December 1956 to September 1957—as observed by the present author[11]—indicates inadequate popular participation even during the phased plan-framing process for the Second Plan. The Block budget formulation in this 'A' grade block was looked upon as an administrative matter with which people had very little to do. The development proposals, especially in irrigation and communications, broached in the rural development registers, filled in by the revenue personnel in consultation with the villagers (perhaps the only basic village data available to the block planners) required to be processed before they were finalized. No direct popular participation was in evidence during the stage of block budget formulation. The district Congress Committee had conveyed some proposals which were taken into consideration. Neither the village panchayats nor the Vikas Mandals (development committees), where they existed, discussed proposals of their own for inclusion in the budget or those contained in the budget prepared by the block officials. The discussion by the whole body of villagers was out of the question. Nor was much discussion held in the block advisory committee meeting convened for the purpose. Later, the State Legislature Estimates Committee report noted an observation that during the Second Plan, various district development boards in the State were not aware of the schemes allotted to them.[12] The Plan Evaluation Organization (PEO) of the Planning Commission reported that only in 44 per cent of its sample of 161 villages in the whole country was any attempt made to prepare local plans, and even in these, the village bodies did not seem to have played an active role.[13]

The main factor in the paltry realization of the recognized objectives of district planning and planning from below was the States' inability to know the firm size of the States' Plans until the whole process of consultations at the Central and State levels was over. Lack of reliable, and in some aspects, of any statistics and absence of an adequate complement of expertise were other factors for the sorry state of affairs. An overdrawn account of the villagers' disinclination and incapacity for an effective participation in plan formulation in some of the literature on the subject does not give a proper perspective regarding the role of the village people and their representatives in the planning process.

A near consensus by the latter half of the Second Plan period was expressed on the need for involvement of the popularly elected organizations of rural masses in the planning process.

III

On the background regarding the plan formulation and implementation related above, the Planning Commission as well as the State Governments decided to utilize the Panchyati Raj Bodies, wherever these existed, as consultative organs in framing the district plans within the Third Plan. The most obvious advantage in the process was the possibility of closely relating the plan schemes to the physical conditions and the popular preferences as articulated through their genuine representatives in the local elective organs. The process would also help more effective mobilization of resources for the plan and a more vivid appreciation of the national objectives and policies among the local people. It might also lead to a better coordination and synchronization in the implementation of plan programmes and schemes.

The decision of planning from below through the Panchayati Raj Organizations did not automatically solve all the problems in the way. To enable them to work effectively as planning authorities, the panchayati raj organs needed to be equipped with the requisite financial resources, delegations of development functions and expert personnel—both administrative and specialist. The expertise to prepare integrated development plans for the districts had to be posted with the Panchayati Raj Bodies. The plan formulation for integrated development of districts required more extensive and deeper information on fresh aspects of social and economic development. The Government of Maharashtra claimed to possess a fairly satisfactory statistical organization going down to the taluka level by the end of the Second Plan period. But, even then, it made it a point to list the important gaps in the statistical information.[14]

The states had also to take decision on the basic unit of district planning and the hierarchy of sub-units with their relative ordering. The village was obviously too small a unit for overall district planning. The village was the unit for provision of civic facilities, like roads, water, and community centre. Organization for agricultural production and extension in various aspects, like health education and cooperation, had to be provided for in the villages. The village was also a unit for collection of data bearing on agriculture, land revenue, demography and human settlement. The community development block or taluka/tehsil assumed importance because it was the nucleus of rural development finance and activity since 1952. Where the block coincided with taluka/tehsil it also afforded another source for data preserved in the taluka/tehsil records, such as those on land revenue and proprietorship, certain demographic aspects, like birth and death, marriage, etc. The block was also the next closer administrative unit to the village people. Perhaps, the only asset of the district as the overall roof unit of uniform regional planning throughout the State was its long career as the unit of coordinated administration for various departments of the State Government. Recognisedly, it was not a rational unit for spatial as well as locational planning.[15] Natural regions, like drought areas or coastal areas or ghats (e.g. 'malnad'), or resource region, like mining areas or harbours, were accepted by the geographer as most suitable units for regional planning. The district was not a homogeneous region in this sense. But no other higher unit above the block/tehsil was readily available which did not contain diverse sub-regions or which did not cut across a natural region. The States of Rajasthan and Andhra Pradesh, which had introduced panchayati raj earlier than Maharashtra, also experienced the inadequacy of the block as the overall unit of district planning.[16] The analysis would tend to confirm the soundness of the widely accepted concept of the district as the unit of overall regional planning within the States and the block/tehsil and the village as the sub-units of lesser orders for varying purposes of decreasing dimensions within the directing and supervisory ambit of the district.

The Zila Parishads, in Maharashtra, are better equipped for the function of district planning than those in Rajasthan or Andhra Pradesh or even Gujarat. Apart from the provisions in the State Zila Parishads and Panchayat Samitis Act, 1961 (Maharashtra Act V of 1962) enabling both the zila parishads and the panchayat samitis (which are mostly executing regional committees of the parishads) to formulate long-term and annual plans, the Zila Parishads are endowed with sizable financial and pesonnel resources. It is an obligatory function of the Zila Parishads to promote planned development of the districts by utilizing, to the maximum possible extent, local resources and for that to prepare annual and long-term plans giving regard to the plan prepared by the panchayat samitis [Section 100(4)]. Similar plans are to be framed by the panchayat samitis as preparatory to the Zila Parisahds' plans as well as for the utilization of the Block grants [Section 108(1)(a)(i) AND (ii).[17] The village panchayats also have to prepare plans for development of the villages and of agricultural and non-agricultural sectors under Items 59 and 60 of the Village List. The zila parishads in Maharashtra are given grants by the State Government for various ends, like land-revenue grant, plan grants, purposive grants, incentive grants, establishment grant, and deficit grant. The Zila Parishads have also to levy a cess on the land revenue. While the income from the plan grants, purposive grants, establishment grant and deficit grant is earmarked for specific purposes, proceeds of the matching incentive grant on the basis of levied land revenue cess and of the cess can be utilized by the Zila Parishads towards their own schemes and works. No doubt, this financial provision has been found inadequate to cope up with the expectations of every zila parishad to adopt schemes and works of its own choice apart from the transferred plan schemes.[18] The administrative and specialist personnel of the former district level offices of the state departments are pooled in the Zila Parishads. The overall result of both these financial and personnel provisions has been a better capacity of the zila parishads in Maharashtra to formulate and implement development plans. To actualize this capacity, a planning branch, with a planning officer at its head, has been created in each zila parishad. The main functions of the planning officer are:

(1) distribution of various grants, including block grants;
(2) preparation of plan budget;
(3) review of progress of and expenditure on plan schemes;
(4) watching observance of terms and conditions on which plan schemes are entrusted to zila parishads; and
(5) collection and process of data relating to plan schemes.[19]

Items (2) and (5) are strictly within the purview of the plan-formulation function.

The unhesitating conclusion of the Evaluation Committee on Panchayati Raj of the State Government was that they did not find any particular evidence to show that there was any conscious and systematic planning in the local sector,[20] *i.e.*, by the Zila Parishads and the panchayat samitis. It was earlier observed that even advanced village panchayats did not prepare five year plans of village development,[21] despite the high knowledge content and keen social awareness of the village and the panchyat leaders.

The neglect of the planning function by the Zila Parishads and the panchayat samitis is indicated by several trends. Meaningful physical planning in terms of targets-setting is rarely done. In the plan allocations by the State Government to the Zila Parishads and by the parishads to the panchayat samitis specific norms, such as population or regional backwardness, have not been laid down; this has benefited a few deft zila parishads and areal pockets within the parishads. Further, the State Government has not attempted any categorization of schemes and resources for different sectors on the basis of certain priorities. The limited resources of the parishads themselves did not afford enough freedom for planning.

The grant of free resources, such as a larger land revenue grant and establishment grant, latterly has no doubt improved the financial and consequently planning position of the parishads. The process of preparing the drafts on the Fifth Plan by the Zila Parishads, dealt with in the last section of this article, would show the extent to which the above shortcomings in the plan-formulation by the zila parishads have been got over.

The Planning Officer was also found ineffective in fulfilling the task of plan formulation by the Evaluation Committee. It was observed by the Committee that they were not even aware of the existence of the above cited job chart.[22] While the Heble Commission favoured discontinuation of the post of planning officer,[23] the Evaluation Committee rightly recommended the continuation of the post and the planning branch under him in view of the strengthening of his role and development of his functions.

A case study of a Zila Parishad in Maharashtra mentioned absence of financial and resource planning in the draft report of the Fourth Plan of the district framed in October, 1964. While the draft plan did much work in detailing the broad picture of development of the district, the pattern of schemes suggested conformed to the earlier prototype of the plan schemes.[24]

IV

In the face of the start fact of the blurring out of the role of district planning, the Wardha District Development Plan, formulated in Maharashtra during 1961-62,[25] stood out both as an indicator as well as a hope. The Wardha Plan was an indicator of the tasks involved in district planning as well as the limitations on and requirements of full-fledged district planning. The Wardha Plan kindled the hope of district planning becoming a reality with the marshalling of the resources of the Planning Commission, the goodwill of the State Government and the expertise of an experienced and dedicated research institute—the Gokhale Institute of Poona.

The objectives of the Wardha Plan were three-fold: to draw up a consistent, integrated and concrete plan of development of the district; to plan from below; and to indicate development schemes for the uplift of the downtrodden ('Antyodaya').

A survey of the physico-geographical and socio-economic conditions of the district would indicate the specific needs and the possibilities of development. The departmental schemes, accepted till then as the basis of the State and the district plans, led to the adoption of the schematic patterns laid down by the Planning Commission. The schematic patterns did not take into account the varying situation from one district to another and even within the districts. They were also wasteful because they did not heed the existing staff in different departments capable of further utilization and the possibilities of coordination and integration. A survey of the basic physico-geographical and socio-economic data, thus, was a desideratum for the framing of a realistic and integrated development plan, within the terms of a long-term development perspective.

A detailed survey of 54 selected villages from 21 groups of villages within six broad regions of the district revealed a fairly typical picture of the actual situation and the specific needs of the district. The surveyed selected villages covered six per cent of the occupied villages and ten per cent of the total rural population of the district.

The survey, preparatory to the framing of the Wardha Plan, pointed out several 'significant and locally important problems' never conceived as being related to the development of the resources of the district. These problems pertained mainly to land utilization, soil conservation, irrigated farming and water supply, dry farming, animal husbandry and dairying, pasture development, and fodder and fuel supply.[26]

The extensive waste and pasture lands which were practically unutilized and acreage of marginal cultivation pointed up the need of land-use survey of the district. In spite of the sizable extent of waste and pasture lands and 30 per cent of the cropped area being under jowar, the district suffered from an acute shortage of fodder. A peculiar problem revealed by the survey concerned a type of water-logged area called 'Panbasan' lands. Another was that of conservation and drainage in the region of black soil and heavy rain. The problem of water-logged lands called for detailed research and experimentation, while conservation and drainage required the use of contour ploughing, strip-cropping, deep ploughing, nallah plugging and control of gullies. The survey also pointed up the fact that about 66 per cent of the total wells were not in use, the average land irrigated per well being below two acre. There were a few of the factual problems presented by the basic survey.

The process of 'planning from below' consisted of three stages; discussion of the district plan; consideration of the block plans; and finalization of the district plan. The Zila Parishads were not constituted under the new act during the first stage, but they participated in the discussions during the second and the third stages. The participants in the discussions of the plan during the first two stages included, besides the officials and the non-officials involved, outside experts, social workers and progressive farmers as well as non-agricultural producers. This made the discussions more broad-based and representative. The third and the last stage covered discussions in the Zila Parishad and its constituent committees.

The deliberations in these meetings not merely highlighted unknown aspects of the known problems but also threw up novel suggestions to tackle the problems. The need of a hydrological survey to assess the underground water, as also of a survey of surface water resources was stressed in the discussions at the meeting during the first stage. A fresh suggestion to deal with the shortcomings of the forest department in the management of the grazing land was put forth at the same meeting; it hinted at transferring the work to the animal husbandry department. A cattle breeders' association at the district level would, among other things, look after fodder distribution and bull-breeding.

The discussions at the Block level proposed locations for the schools, dispensaries, drinking water wells, milk collection centres, and roads. A suggestion, disturbing a widely prevalent belief, was thrown up in the course of these discussions. The suggestion was to the effect that rearing of goats and sheep should be discouraged and separate grazing land should be reserved for them. Another suggestion deserving consideration was regarding the need of conducting experiments to increase milk production on various breeds of cows and buffaloes. Organizational problems of small cultivators and the landless labour, and utilization of water resources of a river basin were also discussed, among other matters, in these meetings.

Apart from substantive suggestions on the contents of the district plan, these deliberations also briefed the planners on the adequacy of the procedures of the planning process, as also on the methods of implementation, such as cooperatives, for solving the problems of the landless labour. The meetings also provided forums to the planners and development authorities to explain the objectives as well as the frame of the national plan.

It was remarkable to find that the Wardha Zila Parishad increased the already expanded plan size from Rs. 462 lakhs to 890 lakhs, much larger than that of any other zila parishad in Maharashtra. This was due to the attempt by the Zila Parishad to accommodate "all conflicting claims by different panchayat samitis."[27] Certain priorities were also changed, an almost equal emphasis being placed on operations in different fields.

The Wardha Plan comprised programmes bearing on three aspects: the physico-geographic aspect or the creation of the framework of socio-economic overheads; the conservation and development of resources; and the increase in production and efficiency. The three aspects are too familiar to need elaboration. The creation of the framework of socio-economic overheads brought in the concept of *mandi* (market) centres. The concept of *mandi* centres is similar to the concept of rural growth centres conceived later by the national planners. The concept is wider than the location of market and covers both actual and potential nuclei for the creation of socio-economic overheads, for the benefit of the rural people as well as to act as catalysers for extensive and intensive development. The 37 *mandi* centres (13 existing and 24 new) in the district were selected in a descending order of importance on the criteria of availability of an established market, centre of administrative services, nucleus for serving a minimum size of population within a specific radius, transport and communication facilities and existence of health and education facilities. The problem of employment of the landless attracted the special attention of the Wardha planners. As prospects of increase of employment for this section of the rural community were limited, it had to be based mainly on the socio-economic overheads and the conservation plan.[28]

The Wardha Plan itself indicated a longer duration for the basic survey to feed the district plan with more meaningful and necessary data, such as on material availabilities and balances. The frame of the Wardha Plan was not as much integrated as it should have been. The Wardha Plan also revealed the need of a larger number of supplementary surveys with deeper coverage. The importance of continuing the work through evaluation during the plan-execution stage was also established. The most important factor in the evolution of a rational district plan was the setting of an order of priorities by the Zila Parishads. The original Wardha Plan was expanded to almost double the size by the Zila Parishad. The compulsive adjustment of the district plan size within a normal outlay, bound to be smaller in view of the special central assistance given to the Wardha District, would underline the importance of setting of an order of priorities. From the organizational point of view also, pointers on several urgent sectors emerged out of the thinking on the Wardha Plan. The need for the departmental officials to scrutinize the plan schemes in the light of the given situation in the district was more pressing than ever before. More strenuous efforts in organization and coordination at the district level were highlighted by the Wardha Plan for the efficient execution of the Plan. A series of working plans were also necessary to streamline the plan-execution.

The entire programme outlined in the Wardha Plan was sanctioned later by the State Government to be implemented over a seven-year period.[29] Although the State Government recognized the Wardha Plan as being helpful in formulating the district plans, actually the experiment in district planning was extended only to two more districts, Kolaba and Osmanabad. The next result was that a valuable lesson of the Wardha Plan was lost sight of and the district plans in Maharashtra within the Fourth Plan were prepared without any planned collection of initial information in the frame suggested by the Wardha Plan.[30] With the vesting of a proper plan apparatus and knowledge of plan techniques, the zila parishads in Maharashtra much better equipped for planning than those in any other State, would have performed it well.

V

By the end of the Third Plan period, the situation in regard to district planning in the country,[31] so also in the State of Maharashtra was not hopeful. The difficult economic situation in 1966-67, the changed political environment during 1967 and the compulsions of planning strategy made for a substantial turn in the thinking about the State and District Planning. This turn in thinking was clearly reflected in the various reports of Administrative Reforms Commission and its Study Teams during 1967-1970. The Study Team on District Administration (February, 1967,)[32] that on Centre-State Relationship (September, 1967),[33] the Commission's Report on Machinery for Planning (March, 1968)[34] and the Commission's Report on State Administration[35]—all these were unanimous on the need for making state and district planning a genuine exercise, strengthening the state and district machinery for planning and delegating the district planning function to panchayati raj bodies in districts. Prospect of decentralizing the formulation of the contents of a large segment of plan schemes to the States also brought in districts and democratic representative bodies in the districts for consideration as participants in the same process.[36] The Commission's Report on State Administration has also stressed overall involvement of the Divisional Commissioner in large States, *inter alia,* in regional planning for urban and rural areas with special reference to environmental purity,[37] without disturbing the primary responsibility of the district planning set-up. The revised Fourth Plan[38] recorded the consensus regarding the role of the State and the district Plans.

The PEO report on District Development Staff in Maharashtra pointed out, among other things, disproportionate per capita development expenditure in different selected district.[39] The defect called for rationalization of the district plans and plan outlays on the basis of well-defined objectives and criteria. A basis for a revised practice relating to district planning in Maharashtra was laid down in the beginning of the framing of district perspective plans during 1970, i.e., the early year of revised Fourth Plan.[40]

VI

In keeping with the changed planning strategy, for the Fifth Plan, the State of Maharashtra decided, *inter alia,* to adopt the district as the unit.[41] Earlier, the Government had prepared indices of development for districts and tehsils and also village-wise index cards.[42] The decision favouring the district as the planning unit was prompted by twin objectives. The first objective was to give opportunity to all the districts to attain full development having regard to their potential, available manpower and other resources. The second objective was to remove steadily the imbalances in development as between districts and areas within the same districts to the extent possible.

With the formulation and implementation of the plans, various bodies in the districts were connected. These were government departments, local bodies—*viz.* Zila Parishads and its constituent organs and municipalities—financial institutions—like district cooperative bank, district land development bank, nationalized and commercial banks—the public enterprises and the corporate sector. The coordination was so far effected through the *ad-hoc* District Planning Advisory Committee and, in the main the District Collector. The District Collector has been undoubtedly an effective coordinator for non-developmental administrative matters. But in developmental administration in Maharashtra, he has not been in the Centre of the picture since the setting up of zila parishads in 1962. This anomaly has now been removed by the State Government by constituting district planning boards and entrusting secretarial responsibility for the boards to the chief executive officers of the Zila Parishads. Earlier, the State Government had strengthened the Zila Parishads by vesting larger financial resources in them and transferring to them most of the remaining development schemes with the State Departments. This step was taken on the recommendations of the Evaluation Committee on Panchayati Raj.

The changed district planning process has given a greater freedom to districts in adopting individual schemes within the broad patterns of major and minor heads. Secondly, districts have been intimated a firm minimum limit of the size of district plans. This size, which does not include zila parishad's own resources, is to be double the size of district plans during the Fourth Plan. The size is, however, to be discounted to an extent in view of the outlay of some of the State-level schemes, such as irrigation schemes, being included in district plans. The purposiveness of district plans has now certainly been pinpointed by compulsive translation in plan formulation by these district planning boards of definite criteria laid down by the State Government in keeping with the proposals of the Planning Commission and its own priorities. Barring these criteria laid down by the State Government, district planning boards are free to frame their own schemes within both the State's and their own outlay. The definite criteria referred to the national programme for minimum needs covered by the

Approach Paper and the Draft Fifth Plan, of the Planning Commission, the State's own 15-point programme and the special requirements of the critical areas.

The national minimum needs programme covered seven aspects of education, drinking water supply, public health, rural electrification, rural roads, house sites for rural landless, and slum improvement and clearance. In education, the minimum programme is to attain 100 per cent enrolment in the age-group of 6-11, 60 per cent enrolment in the age group of 11-14 and to ensure that there is a primary school within 1.5 kms and a middle school within 5 kms from each village. In respect of drinking water supply, the Approach Paper of the Planning Commission has not laid down any specific norm, but the State Government has decided that by the close of the Fifth Plan all villages should be provided with this minimum need that has eluded the grasp of the government through all the Four Plans. In public health, the minimum programme laid down is one primary health centre supported by 8-10 sub-centres for 80,000 persons. Further, at least 40 per cent of villages in each tehsil are to be electrified by close of the Fifth Plan. All-weather roads are to be laid to link every village with population of 1500 and above and in hilly or coastal areas to link a cluster of villages. House sites of 100 sq. yards are to be furnished to rural landless persons. Besides, in urban areas in the districts, a programme of slum-improvement and slum clearance is to be adopted. The 15-point programme of the State Government is supplementary to the minimum needs programme of the Planning Commission; it stresses improvement in the condition of the underdeveloped sections of the community. The schemes under the 15-point programme include the following guarantee of employment in manual work to all adults needing work, local employment works, self-employment of the educated unemployed, uplift of adivasis, provision of hostel facilities for economically backward classes and special welfare schemes for denotified tribes and navabouddhas. The district plans have also to include special programmes for the critical areas, drought pone areas, hilly and adivasi areas, coastal and industrially backward areas.

The district plans formulated for the Fifth Plan in the state have provided for national minimum needs programme. They have tried to deal with the 15-point programme of the State Government, but not to the desired extent. The district plans seek to accommodate standard schemes to tackle the problems of the critical areas affected by chronic drought or industrial backwardness or natural handicaps of hilly location. But the provisions for these areas in sectors, like communications, animal husbandry, and soil conservation, have been withdrawn from other areas in the district. The district plans also indicate a special attraction of irrigated areas, even irrigated by wells, for additional cooperative sugar factories. The State Government is also willing to sponsor and assist the new cooperative sugar factories as sources of excise and other revenue. But alternative channels of economic development and utilization of irrigation facilities ought to have been experimented in some areas. About 50 per cent of the district plan outlays has been devoted to irrigation, which is a desirable priority in a chronically drought-affected state like Maharashtra. The District Plans expect outlay on irrigation above 55 per cent of the total outlay to be available through loans from the Sixth Plan. This needs rationalization at the state-level.

Formulation of draft district plans commenced hardly one month before the constitution of district planning boards. This haste has naturally favoured adoption of departmental schemes leaving practically no time for fresh local surveys to suggest and to test the viability of new types of schemes. The composition of district planning boards does not indicate much expertise in various aspects of planning and administration. The larger district planning consultative councils, consisting of legislators and officials, have also not included any such expertise. The appointment of a state minister as chairman of the district planning board would provide for a link with the thinking of the State Government, but how for it would be conducive to free thinking of development proposals is a moot question. The Draft District Plans do not seem to have been placed before the Zila Parishad probably the posting of the plans with the State Government by the end of August, 1973 has left no margin for this step. The availability of a planning and a statistical officer with an administrative branch to support should enable the Zila Parishads to be equipped with local surveys to suggest experimentation and improvements in the types and contents of plan schemes suited to local situations.

This kind of district planning process has certainly made for a change in favour of autonomous thinking on plans by Zila

Parishads. Availability of a longer time and better expertise would enable the new district planning apparatus to put the process to a still more fruitful purpose. The District Plans have not integrated within them the plans of other public authorities in the districts, including nationalized banks, the cooperative sector and the municipal bodies despite the declared object to that effect.

REFERENCES

1. J. Friedmann and W. Alonso, *Regional Development and Planning: A Reader*, Cambridge (Massachusetts), M.I.T. Pess, 164 (fourth printing 1969) is a good introduction to the subject and gives a comprehensive bibliography; and W.Isard, and J.H. Cumbeland (ed.), *Regional Economic Planning Techniques of Analysis* (Paris, 1960); *Surveys of Economic Theory*, Vol. II (ed.) by American Economic Association and Royal Economic Society (New York, 1965) are among several other books on the subject. Bhat, *Regional Planning* (Calcutta, Stat. Pub. Soc., 1972); M.D. Sathe, *Regional Planning* (Poona Saraswat, 1972); S. Wanmali, *Regional Planning* (Hyd, NICD, 1970) are some of the scarce Indian literature on the subject.
2. D.R. Gadgil, *District Development Planning* (Poona, Gokhale Institute of Politics and Economics, 1967).
3. *Vide* Government of Maharashtra, *Report on Metropolitan Regional Planning in Bombay and Poona* (Bombay, 1967), N.R. Inamdar "Metropolitan Planning in Maharashtra", *The Indian Journal of Public Administration* (July-Sept., 1968), pp. 670-681, Calcutta Metropolitan Planning Organization, *Reports on Rural Local Governments* (Calcutta).
4. L.K. Sen, *Integrated Area Planning* (Cycl.) (New Delhi, Training Division, Department of Personnel, Cabinet Secretariat, Government of India, Sep., 1972).

   The Ford Foundation and the Council for Social Development, *Preliminary Projects* (New Delhi, May 1969).
5. A.H. Hanson, *The Process of Planning: A Study of India's Five-Year Plans 1950-1964* (London, Oxford, 1966), p. 399.
6. Government of India, Administrative Reforms Commission, *Report on Machinery for Planning* (Delhi, The Manager of Publications, March, 1968), pp.47-48.
7. *Fourth Five Year Plan, 1969-74 Summary* (New Delhi, Publications Division, Ministry of Information and Broadcasting, Government of India, January 1971), p.12.
8. *Vide* Government of Maharashtra, Government Resolution GAD/ No.PD/SPM/1072-P-1, dated 20.10.1972.

9. Hanson, *op cit.*, p. 399.
10. Gadgil, *op cit.*, p. 11; Hanson, *op cit.*, pp. 400-402.
11. N.R. Inamdar, *Report of the Survey of the Administration of the Community Development Block Haveli* (Poona, University of Poona, 1962), pp. 20-21; 28-29; 35-44.
12. Maharashtra Legislature Secretariat, *Report of the Estimates Committee, 1961 Thirty-Third Report "Planning Section (pertaining to the Finance Department)"*, (Bombay, 1961), p.10.
13. Programme Evaluation Organization, Planning Commission, *Sixth Evaluation Report* (New Delhi, June, 1959).
14. Government of Maharasthra, Finance Department (Planning), *Third Five-Year Plan Maharashtra State* (Bombay, November 1961), p.145.
15. L.S. Bhat, *Regional Planning* (Calcutta, Statistical Publication Society, 1972), p.103.
16. G. Jacob (ed.): *Readings on Panchayati Raj* (Hyderabad, National Institute of Community Development, 1967). pp.145-166.
17. Government of Maharashtra, *The Maharasthra Zila Parishad and Panchayat Samiti Mandal*, Vol. I (Bombay, Government Printing and Stationery, 1965), pp. 89,94.
18. *Report of the Administrative Reorganization Committee* appointed by the Government of Maharashtra (Bombay, 1968), pp. 142-147; 153-154.
19. *Reorganization of Maharashtra Administration Report by Shri M.N. Heble*, Vol. I (Bombay, Government Central Press, 1971) p.133.
20. Government of Maharashtra, Rural Development Department, *Report of the Evaluation Committee on Panchayati Raj* (Bombay, 1971), p. 84.
21. N.R. Inamdar, *Functioning of Village Panchayats* (Bombay, Popular, 1970), pp.75-76; 317-355.
22. *Report of the Evaluation Committee on Panchayati Raj*, pp. 37-38.
23. *Reorganization of Maharashtra Administration Report*, p. 136.
24. V.G. Nandedkar, *Zila Parishads as Local Government and Development Bodies* (Unpublished Ph.D. Thesis of the University of Poona, July 1972), p. 252.
25. *Wardha District Development Plan Important Features* (Cycl.) (Poona, Gokhale Institute, 1963), pp.1-15.
26. *Wardha District Development Plan Important Features* (Cycl.) (Poona, Gokhale Institute, 1963), pp.4-5.
27. *Wardha District Development Plan Important Features* (Cycl.) (Poona, Gokhale Institute, 1963), p. 11.
28. D.R. Gadgil, *Wardha Plan—A Commentary* (Cycl.) Poona, Gokhale Institute, 1965), p. 4.
29. Government of Maharashtra, Finance Department (Planning), *Annual Plan 1966-67 Part I—Outline* (Bombay, 1966), p. 13.

30. D.R. Gadgil, *Supplementary Note to the Notes on the Present Position of Wardha Plan* (Cycl.) (Poona, Gokhale Institute, 1965), p. 2.
31. A survey of the formulation of Block Plans in two blocks in a district in Uttar Pradesh presented dismal findings. The basis of target-fixation mostly by higher officials was unscientific and inconsistent. Non-officials in general and the panchayat secretary and the lekhpal among officials were not well-disposed towards plan formulation (R.B.Dass and D.P. singh, *Formulation and Execution of Block Plans—A Case Study*) (Lucknow, The Institute of Public Administration, Lucknow University, 1968, pp. 69-70). A majority of the respondents of survey in the same State on the topic for earlier years were not familiar with the national as well as the village plans [P.N. Masaldan, *Planning and the People: A Study of Public Participation in Planning in Uttar Pradesh* (Bombay, Asia, 1964), pp. 23-29].

    The situation about the awareness of the community development programme in Maharashta was relatively consoling during about the same period as Das-Singh's study [P.A.Bhagwatwar, *C.D.Programme—A Psycho-Social Study* (Nagpur, Anand Prakashan, 1972) p.69].
32. ARC, *Report of the Study Team District Administration* (Delhi, 1967), pp. 115-116.
33. ARC, *Report of the Study Team Centre-State Relationship*, Vol.I (Delhi, 1967), pp. 134-135. On an examination of the Third Plan of three states selected at random, the Study Team found that in the agricultural programmes 80-90 per cent schemes suggested in the 'central (government) group' reports were adopted while health and education plans were almost totally built upon the centre's thinking.
34. ARC, *Report Machinery for Planning* (Delhi, 1968), Ch. V, pp.46-48.
35. ARC, *Report on State Administration* (Delhi, 1970), pp.64-65, 69-70.
36. H.K. Paranjape, *The Reorganized Planning Committee* (New Delhi, IIPA, Sept. 1970) mentions absence of an independent planning machinery in the States, but does not dwell on district planning. His *Centre-State Relations in Planning* (IIPA, Sept. 1970) (Original article in IJPA, Vol. XVI, No. 1, Jan-Mar, 1970) refers to the States' failure to develop a proper machinery for effective district planning (p.13).
37. ARC, *Report on State Administration*, Recommendation 34, pp. 64-65.
38. *Fourth Five Year Plan 1969-74 Summary* (New Delhi, Publications Division, Ministry of Information and Broadcasting, Government of India, Jan. 1971), p.12. The document also refers to the inclusion in the revised Fourth Plan a centrally sponsored pilot study in growth centres with a view to integrating the centres into the frame of the district to help planning from below (p.64).

39. PEO, Planning Commission (Government of India), *Study of Development Staff at the Districts and Lower Levels* (New Delhi, Nov. 1968), p.201. The study also deals with the under utilization of the development schemes by individual schemes and lack of coordination between the district development authority and other authorities like the District Collector, Irrigation Department (pp. 202-203).
40. T.V. Parvate, "District Perspective Plans", *Lok Rajya,* February 16, 1970 (Fortnightly in Marathi) (Bombay, Government of Maharashtra, Director of Publicity), pp. 7-9. *Also see* D.G. Tungare: "Some Features of District Planning", *Lok Rajya,* February 16, 1969.
41. Government Resolution GAD/No. PD/SPM/1072-P-1, dated 20.10.1972.
42. Government of Maharashtra, Planning Department, Circular No. FFP-1073/P-3, dated 13.4.1973 (Ref. G.R., Finance Department, No. FFP/(V) 1073/P-3, dated 12.5.1972.

22

The District as a Planning Unit: Style and Locus

RAKESH HOOJA

All planning is based on information. Centralized planning without reference to the constituent result in paper plans far removed from reality. The plan formulating decision-centre is thus not the key structure in the planning process; equally important are data collectors, transmitters, 'gate-keeping' information sifters, memory-banks, receptors, and the like (all of which may be considered as minor decision-making centres). Further, with both the work of government, and complexity of life, having vastly increased in the twentieth century and the ensuing need for expert specialization, it has become very difficult for a single decision-centre to cope with all the problems of plan-formulation on a national scale. This problem is naturally accentuated in a large country with a huge population. Therefore, it becomes necessary for advisory-centres or/and parallel decision-centres (with specified sectoral or areal jurisdictions) to evolve so that the planning machinery may prove adequate. Thus, a multi-level approach to planning (with greater say in the hands of decision-centres at various levels) is beginning to be considered more and more suitable.

In India, with its federal structure and commitment to democratic decentralization, the advisory-centres were to be found not only in the national capital, but also at the state levels (where State Planning Departments functioned as information sifters, memory banks, transmitters and—to some extent—

parallel decision-centres, because the planning process was broken up into both sectoral and areal parts (so that information could be handled and processed adequately) with extensions in Panchayat bodies.

Recently, the scope of the State Planning Departments has been broadened by the decision of various State Governments to set up State Planning Boards on the lines of the Planning Commission.[1] It was but natural for lower level sectoral and areal units of planning to simultaneously gain in significance[2] (due to reasons of administrative convenience), even if the plan-formulation decisions continue to be taken at the higher levels and the lower levels remain more implementational as well as data-collection and transmitting units. Hence, we find that the adoption of the multi-level planning framework in India has led to the formation of, among others, National, State, District, Command Area and City Plans.

It is with the sub-state-level units, especially the district and the economic area, that this article is chiefly concerned.

II

Starting with the establishment of 'Sirdars' (or 'Sircars'), each under an 'Amil' or 'Amalguzar' in Moghul times, the revenue district has gradually emerged as the basic administrative unit in India. So much so that the Collector has become the key figure in Indian administration. It was, therefore, but natural that when Independent India went in for planning, Panchayati Raj and Community Development, it decided to base all the three on the district. While the Panchayat structure was always district-based, district Planning (as opposed to the District-wise implementation of national plans) took some time to gain currency. Originally, Panchayat institutions at the district and lower levels used to be asked to make suggestions before a plan was formed, and, after the finalization of the plan, resources were forwarded for utilization to the districts for whom department-wise targets had already been set. But now, with the setting up of State and District Planning Boards, under the guidance of economists, the nature of district planning is undergoing a welcome change.

I intend to discuss in the following pages, the district planning process, as it previously existed, and shall attempt a critique of the present views on the subject. I also intend to question the validity of persisting with historical areal entities (the districts) as basic units of planning. Wouldn't it have been more appropriate to establish new, and, from the planning perspective, more viable administrative units, that is, wouldn't it be more appropriate to re-organize the districts now that planning and developmental activities have become as important as, if not more than, revenue collection and the maintenance of law and order?

III

Y. Raghavaiah[3] feels that the most suitable areal unit of the coordination of developmental and planning activities is the district and goes on to list numerous reasons for his assertion. With an average population of a million (Raghavaiah's figures) and an area of about 4,000 square miles, such a unit is large enough for planning purposes. It has a settled pattern of administration with a high degree of internal consistency and well-established administrative inter-relationships. This, and the long history of district administration, have ensured that the citizen's awareness of administrative processes in a district is adequate (implying that a new administrative or planning unit would need major reorientation as regards mass knowledge and awareness of new administrative procedures). Similarly, people living in an established district have a sense of belonging to that one entity—a community of feeling that takes years to build up. The new centres of political decision-making, the Panchayati Raj organizations, are also district-based, as are several federal, state and quasi-governmental agencies, which set up area or sub-area headquarters in the district town. It would be easier for the few agencies which follow different areal zones to switch to a district-based system than for the opposite to be accomplished. The only alternative (according to Raghavaiah) to retaining the district as the unit, would be a regional body consisting of several districts and this would not only be unwieldy, but also tend to go against the economic, social and political identity-consciousness and feeling of oneness and solidarity of the people. And, lastly, since the district already exists as an administrative unit, to take up planning at the district level would mean that the evaluation of the overall impact on the people of the total administrative effort in the area would become easier.

However, on the other hand, we find economists emphasizing the need to adopt 'mandi areas', or 'Economic Regions' as the basis of planning. Increased urbanization has necessitated the evolution of concepts like 'city feeder regions', 'satellite townships', and 'National Capital Region', thus indicating that towns, with their contiguous, complimentary regions, or the 'city area' may be a more relevant unit for planning. Town planners, who are currently busy preparing Master Plans of the more important urban centres, certainly tend to look upon the city and surrounding areas as a more important unit than the district.

As Nath says, the principal units of administration for planning are the Centre, State, District, Block and the Village and administrative and institutional arrangements exist at these unit-levels for formulation and execution of plans, and for association of popular leaders in planning. "However, they are not adequate for all planning purposes and have to be supplemented by other regions for some purposes of planning, and may even have to be replaced for other purposes."[4] Shri Nath mentions the river-valley system as a unit for the planning of the utilization of water resources, socio-cultural regions and economic areas (following the definition of August Losch, *The Nature of Economic Regions*) as examples and suggests the following three sets of parallel and, perhaps, overlapping regions to facilitate planning: Administrative Regions, Resource Development Regions, and Metropolitan Regions.

I would like to suggest, not proliferation of parallel units of planning, but redrawing of some district boundaries on the basis of geographic, socio-economic and similar criteria, so that we in India can enjoy the best of both worlds. It is definitely not necessary for us to continue with units formed due to chance or the accidents of history if they do not coincide with our developmental needs. We could thus retain the advantages of district administrative set-up while we gain from the formation of viable planning units.

More on this later. Let me digress a bit and move on to an analysis of district planning in practice.

IV

I shall first deal with the form in which it was originally introduced and then move on to the 'new' district planning approach being envisaged by economists today.

The introduction of Panchayati Raj, increased efforts at involving the masses and small communities in the mainstream of the political system, as well as the recognition of the value of increased local flexibility led to the call, originally sounded at the time of the First Five Year Plan, for decentralized grassroots planning.[5]

Thus, in the Third and Fourth Plans, district Panchayati Raj institutions were involved in the planning process.[6]

Panchayat bodies had already been given charge of all community development scheme funds. In addition, a large number of schemes which are being executed by various Government departments are 'transferred' to the Panchayat Samitis, which also receive the necessary financial assistance in the form of grants, grants-in-aid, loans and subsidies. Thus, at the beginning of 1959, developmental functions had been transferred to the Panchayats, the Collector becoming a mere coordinator.[7]

The practice adopted for purposes of district plan formulation was that the various state-level Heads of Departments would, under the supervision of the State Planning Department and in conformity with the Approach Paper to the Plan, draw up a list of the funds available (for a district) under various 'departmental heads', as well as a list of the schemes and projects (situated or proposed in that district) under the jurisdiction of the various departments.

These lists were sent to all Collectors, Zila Parishad Secretaries and Vikas Adhikaris (BDOs). The Vikas Adhikaris were to communicate this information to the Panchayat Samitis. Then the Panchayat Samitis, with the assistance of the Vikas Adhikaris, Samiti or Block (Vikas Khand) were to formulate plans on the basis of the information received. These plans were to be in three parts: (1) in respect to schemes transferred to the Panchayat Samitis, (2) in respect to schemes not transferred to the Samitis (where the Samiti could only make suggestions), and (3) in respect to schemes to be undertaken independently by the Samiti without any assistance from the State Government (which were seldom taken up due to the reluctance of the local bodies to raise their own resources through taxes). These plans were to be discussed and finalized at Gram Sabha and Panchayat Samiti meetings and, after the final approval of the Samiti, forwarded to the Secretary, Zila Parishad (who was also the Deputy District Development Officer by the Vikas Adhikari).

The Secretary, Zila Parishad, with the help of the District Statistical Officer, was to compile the various Samiti plans into a District Plan which would be discussed at a meeting of the Zila Parishad (which was to be attended, in addition to its ordinary members, by senior departmental officials) before transmission to the various Heads of Departments.

The Collector (in his capacity as District Development Officer) was specially instructed to supervise the formulation of the Samiti and District Plans, as also to supervise their implementation later (the Collector is also Chairman of the Zila Parishad in some instance. Similarly, various Heads of Departments were asked not only to supply the samitis with statements of schemes already undertaken as well as envisaged and of the funds available for the purpose but also to instruct subordinate officials to guide and cooperate with the Samitis and Zila Parishads in preparation of local plans. The Zila Parishad approved plans were to be forwarded by the District Development Officers (DDO) to the Heads of Departments, who scrutinized them, consolidated the proposals, added their own comments and proposals and forwarded them on to the State Planning Department, which, after processing, submitted the State Plan Proposals to the Planning Commission.

Later on, after the National Plan had been finalized, various district and samitis targets were to be transmitted by the concerned state-level departments (who would learn of them through the State Planning Department) to the local authorities, who, under the supervision of the DDO and Deputy District Development Officer (DDDO) were charged with the implementation of schemes and fulfilling of targets. Such an exercise was undertaken once in five years on a crash-campaign basis.

A number of problems immediately came to light in the application of this method of plan formulation. The Heads of Departments sent in their information about tentative physical and financial targets to the Samitis late. After that, Vikas Adhikaris and other official at the block level faithfully adhered to the suggestions and instructions received from various departments, as they hurriedly patched together Samiti Plans. (While two meetings of the Panchayat Samiti wre supposed to be held; one to approve a draft plan for circulation among the Gram Sabhas and the other to subsequently finalize the plan, only one meeting could normally be held due to lack of time). In fact, it was found that Pramukhs, Pradhans and non-official members of the Panchayati Raj institutions were rarely consulted[8] and suggestions made by the Heads of Departments dutifully incorporated into the Samiti Plans by the BDO and other extension staff. The transfer of some Vikas Adhikaris during the plan formulation stage also affected, detrimentally, the process, for it was found that most Panchayati Raj non-officials were apathetic and indifferent[9] since they knew that the plans had already been prepared and their views would not amount to much, and thus, freedom would be given fully to the BDOs. In any case Panchayati Raj non-officials were more interested in setting forth demands expressing felt-needs and in making proposals that would gain them popularity and votes, and such proposals were neither desirable, nor feasible considering financial and other guidelines set before the Samitis.[10]

This also leads to the question as to whether grassroots political (elected) figures should be entrusted with plan formulation. For they are liable to attempt and use the plan formulation meetings as a forum for expressing their felt needs and for the transmitting of demands to the government, thus converting the plan into a mere list of demands as perceived from a narrow local perspective. This failing, they are liable to passively accept whatever proposal is set before them even when the needs of the sub-area are being overlooked. In any case, neither Panchayat politicians nor local bureaucrats are adequately qualified to undertake a real exercise in planning and, therefore, local plans have so far tended to be mere financial statements and lists of targets, all based upon instructions and suggestions received from the Heads of Departments.

Another question that arises is whether the preparation of statements of funds available and targets being set is all that planning is supposed to involve. Should not the locating of industries, houses commercial and cultural centres, providing of civic supplies, building of roads, planning of specific education and employment opportunities, etc., all be a part of the District Plan? Can such comprehensive District Plans (something like the Master City and Town Plans but much broader in scope) be prepared by Panchayat Samitis and (transferable) Vikas Adhikaris? Or should a separate, well-qualified District Planning Officer be stationed, either permanently, or for long periods, in each district for this purpose? (Such an officer would have to be attached to the Collector's office and have the same coordinating powers as the Collector. He could perhaps be a member of the Indian Economic or Administrative Service.)

In this context, I would also like to suggest the replacing of economic planning by complete societal planning (so as to lead to economic growth, social change as also political development) with all aspects of life in the district figuring in the plan. Here, I might caution that I am not advocating centralized control, on totalitarian lines, of human life. A societal plan, as envisaged by me, could be in two parts: one complementable and/or enforceable by the government, and the other in the form of suggestions for the people.

Another major problem that arose in district planning during the Third and Fourth Plans was the fact that various departmental officers in the districts are jealous of their rights and powers and tend to look only to their Heads of Departments for instructions thus, making the Collector's coordination task more difficult,[11] and also ensuring that the District Plan is formed in segmented parts on a departmental basis. It is a welcome trend that the Collector's coordinating role is being strengthened, making coordination between various district departmental officers easier and thus making possible the formulation of a fully integrated District Plan.[12]

V

Let me now turn to the newer approaches of economists to District Planning.[13]

It is generally recognized that the district is essentially a local administrative unit and need not have homogeneous economic features. Hence, it is often suggested that each district be subdivided on the basis of economic homogeneity into 'economic areas' or 'Mandi areas', which may be considered to be the lowest units for the integrated provision of socio-economic overheads and services.

Such an economic area may be either: (1) the main centre of marketing and exchange, where the plan must provide for additional services, like technical assistance, and institutionalized economic facilities, like credit, storage and processing, or (2) (in a less farm-dominated area) a centre of growth of industrial (or other) activity which helps to transform the economy of the surrounding area.

Viewed in this context, District Planning involves the proper selection of economic areas and the coordination of the National Plan (and special district) programmes with the needs of the economic areas.[14] Thus, all possible attempts should be made to link the district or one of its economic areas to a national or state project, located in the district so as to ensure that the project implementation is speedier and better, and the infrastructural changes affected by the project are fully made use of. However, this approach also builds up a case for the re-organization of district boundaries so as to coincide with those of the groups of economic areas.

In preparing a plan, the district planner (who has to look to speedy economic growth, integrated and effective utilization of resources—both natural and human—increase in employment, increase in social services and social consumption, redressal of regional imbalances, improving the lot of socially and economically backward sections of the population, and speedy abolition of poverty)[15] has to work at two levels; the District and the Economic Area, with overall frames and strategies being decided at the district level. While details of plans or conservation of natural resources and for production, etc., shall have to be worked out at the economic area level, area-wise and sectoral financial allocation, distribution of employment oriented schemes, and solving of organizational problems are best done at the district level. Coordination and synchronization efforts shall have to be made at both levels while overall integration shall have to be done by the district planner who, as has already been mentioned, shall be conversant with state and national plan priorities.

A district planner must identify his district's resources, extent of their utilization, the nature and extent of the infrastructure needed for optimum utilization, district's social and cultural profile and its relevance with respect to the human factor, pattern of land cultivator relations and their relevance to programmes for increasing production and bettering distribution, nature and extent of social infrastructure (in terms of education, health centres, family planning, nutrition etc.) and its relevance to both economic growth and social justice, employment and production generating infrastructure, and facilities, such as banking, markets, transport, construction, storage, supply of inputs and procedural requirements, and the measures needed to strengthen them.[16] He must also study consumption, requirements for drinking water, housing, and village access road, social stratification, the position of the scheduled castes and tribes, wage levels, unemployment and under-employment and the prevailing income distribution. Only then logical district priorities can be drawn up taking into consideration the existing constraints.[17]

Further, the planner has to learn to anticipate local reactions and responses since plan implementational success shall depend upon the interest aroused among the people and consequent local assistance forthcoming. Here the need for incorporating panchayat bodies in planning becomes obvious. While care should be taken to see that wishful thinking on the part of panchayat non-officials does not lead to over-ambitious plans (which are mere collections of more or less popular demands) being formed, a discussion of plan proposals in panchayat samitis and zila parishads would be very welcome. Cooperative institutions can also be gainfully associated with planning and execution.

Similarly, as has already been mentioned, a district plan should not be a mere collection of various departmental, or sub-departmental proposals. This, besides non-integrated, lop-sided development, may also result in duplication of staff (who have to prepare the various proposals separately without assistance from the personnel of other departments) and breakdown of coordination. Of course, an integrated distinct plan, once prepared, may later be segmented sectorally or even departmentally for implementation purposes. This is because a development plan consists of a bundle of projects, each having a separate sectoral identity, geographic location, time horizon and scheme of estimated costs and benefits, thus, each being in need of separate administrative apparatus within the framework of the district planning machinery. Here, the planner must combine knowledge of local and district conditions with technical knowhow available from the state or national department before indulging in project formulation.

The practice of 'crash programmes', 'campaigns' and the tackling of problems on a 'war footing' are all antithetical to the canons of long-term planning and may even be taken as a symptom of faculty planning. Thus, the planner should be able to anticipate crisis situations and avoid them and the linked need for the adoption of emergency measures.

Given knowledge of Central or State projects in the district (for example large irrigation), famine relief, road building and power projects, fisheries and forest programmes, etc) and their outlay and the employment generated thereby; natural resources (through soil, water and geological surveys, census operations and the like); production—agricultural and industrial—land-use, supply of credit, public expenditure, etc.; and existing transport, communication, educational and health facilities, the district planner has to utilize it giving priority, while making the plan, to the development of socio-economic overheads and resource development, and not to social services which local pressures demand. Plan production targets in their present form should get lower priority than the development of the infrastructure. However, the government has to continue to provide incentives and assistance to individual producers to encourage them to produce goods according to the overall objectives and strategy of development. These incentives also fall within the scope of the district plan.

Thus, we see that the district plan should not be a mere spelling out of targets and financial allocations, but a much more comprehensive document, which, keeping in mind financial restraints, spells out logical relations between sectoral and departmental plans and between various economic areas, and which determines the chronological order in which schemes are to be started and implemented. It is based on calculations of supply and demand, where the need for equipment, trained personnel, buildings, raw materials, unskilled labour, all have been checked against the available supply, and where an attempt has been made to improve the internal organization of the agencies which will

10. Summing up his analysis of the formulation of the (Fourth Plan) Jaipur District Plan in 1966, P.C. Mathur *op. cit.* has highlighted the following eleven points: (Summary mine).
    (*i*) The experience gained during the Third Plan formulation was not put to use and thus *ad hoc* coordination of the plans formulated at various levels had to be resorted to, putting great pressure on the local bodies. A plan coordination and formulation procedure should have been established previously.
    (*ii*) This *adhocism* meant that some departments could not even transmit detailed physical targets and financial allocations to the Samitis since even their overall quota in the State Plan had not been determined in time.
    (*iii*) All detailed instructions about plan preparation were sent to administrative officers after formally consulting only the Panchayati Raj non-officials and that too after the plans had been prepared.
    (*iv*) Some state departments circulated such a detailed set of physical and financial targets that no Samiti could deviate from them without up-setting all state-wide allocations.
    (*v*) Block officials, Samiti and Parishad members all tended to look upon 'approving' the plan as a necessary 'ritual'.
    (*vi*) The consolidation of Samiti plans at the district-level was done with a view to conforming to district targets set by the various departments.
    (*vii*) The District Plan consisted only of 'transferred' schemes with the Samitis. No effort was made to include the schemes to be run by the municipalities in the towns of the district.
    (*viii*) No detailed economic analysis of priorities and the pattern of financing or of the sources of local contributions was made in the District Plan.
    (*ix*) The team of district-level officers, while taking a keen interest in the planning operation, did not attempt to exercise their own initiative and discretion.
    (*x*) All modifications suggested at the local levels were ignored or eliminated at the district or higher level.
    (*xi*) After the plan had been framed, most officials who participated in its making, tended to file away the final documents, and perhaps even to forget its provisions until prodded from above.
11. *See* Haridwar Rai, "Coordination of Development Programmes at the District Level with Special Reference to Role of District Officer in Bihar", *The Indian Journal of Public Administration*, vol. XII, No. 1 (Jan-March, 1966); M. Santaranarayanan, "Role of the District Officer in Changing Administration", *The Indian Journal of Public*

Administration, Vol. XII, No. 4 (Oct.-Dec.) 1966); and M.K. Chaturvedi, "The Elephant and the Tortoise (The District Collector and his Role Identification)", *Journal of the Society for Study of State Governments*, Vol. IV, No. 1 (Jan-March, 1971). Also see C.N. Bhalerao, "Changing Pattern of Development Administration in the District", *The Indian Journal of Public Administration*, Vol, XII, No. 1 (Jan.-March 1966); and Raghavaiah, *op. cit*.

12. *See*, for example, Otima Bordia, "District Administration—Problems of Coordination", Jaipur, H.C. Mathur State Institute of Public Administration, 1970 (Mimeo).
13. I am grateful to Shri Suboth Mathur, Lecturer in the Department of Economics, University of Rajasthan, for suggestions as also for making available to me a note on "District Planning" (unpublished) that he had written for the Collector, Barmer, in Nov.-Dec. 1972. The following section is adapted from that note. It also borrows from D.R. Gadgil's *Kale Memorial Lecture* 1966 delivered at the IIPA Delhi as well as from the unpublished *Report of Indian Mission to Kenya* by Raj Krishna, Government of India, 1972.
14. *See* N.V.A. Narasimhan, "Principles of Integrating of Local and National Plans", *Behavioral Sciences and Community Development*, Vol. 1, March, 1967.
15. V.K.R.V. Rao, "District Planning Concept—Getting to the Grass Roots", *Times of India*, May 23, 1973.
16. V.K.R.V. Rao, *op.cit*.
17. This is in contrast with the previous practice of targets and financial allocations being decided at the national state and departmental levels and being formally approved by Panchayat Samitis and Zila Parishads.
18. K.V. Sundaram in his "Towards a National Urban Policy in India", *Fulbright Newsletters*, March 1973, points out that, while isolated city development plans and urban community development plans were suggested in the Third Plan period, spatial planning started getting attention only in the Fourth Plan. He also emphasizes that a traditional anti-urban bias exists in the minds of our planners and that the problem of integrating urban growth with the development of the surrounding rural areas so as to make the two mutually interdependent is not getting sufficient attention, nor have urbanization and national economic development been linked in the minds of the planners. He thus emphasizes urban regions for planning. *See also* Leo Jacobson and Ved Prakash, "Urbanization and Regional Planning in India", *Urban Affairs Quarterly*, Vol. II, No. 3 (March, 1967).

Also see Sudhir Wanmali and Waheeduddin Khan, "Role of Location in Regional Planning with particular reference to the Provision of Social Facilities", *Behavioural Sciences and Community Development*, Vol. 4, No. 2 (Sept. 1970), where a city-periphery model of planning at the city level is set forth with reference to Nagpur.

19. Town Planning Organization (Rajasthan), *Draft Master Plan for Jaipur*, Jaipur, 1972. District Plans should be similar in approach but have a much wider scope so as to encompass all facets of life.
20. *See* V. Nath, *op cit.*, where he has tentatively set forth a case for urban regions to be adopted for plan purposes. In his six-fold classification, the central places of the different regions are: (1) Metropolitan City, (2) Sub-regional Centre, (3) Multi-District Centre, (4) District Centre, (5) Mandi Centre, and (6) Rural Service Centre. *Also see* V. Nath, "Area Development at District and Block levels", *The Indian Journal of Public Administration,* Vol. XI, No. 2 (April-June, 1965).
For earlier views on Urbanization and Planning and a backgrounder to urbanization problems in India, *see* Roy Turner (ed.,), *India's Urban Future,* Berkeley, University of California Press, 1962.
21. *Also see* Planning Commission, *Research Development Regions and Divisions of India,* New Delhi, Manager of Publications (Government of India), 1964; Planning Commission, *Guidelines for the Formulation of District Plans,* New Delhi, Manager of Publications (Government of India), 1969; and Lalit.K. Sen, *Integrated Area Planning: Concepts and Methods,* New Delhi, Government of India (Training Division, Department of Personnel), Cabinet Secretariat, 1972.

23

District Planning: The Case of Maharashtra

K.V. SUNDARAM

The last few years in Indian planning have seen some experiments in multi-level planning in some States. Among them, the case of Maharashtra is particularly significant for the issues it raises in the methodology and operational procedures for district planning. The purpose of this paper is to set out the present position of district planning in that State, with particular emphasis on how and through what experimentations, the present district planning evolved in the State and how certain particularly knotty issues were solved during the process. Although the solutions may not always be replicable in other situations, it cannot be denied that a case study of district planning in Maharashtra will have many important lessons to offer.

District planning in Maharashtra has essentially emerged through an evolutionary empirical process of political and bureaucratic initiatives, improvisations and interactions. This process is still continuing. District planning was, in the first instance, introduced as a corrective to regionalism[I]. The two main objectives which influenced the State Government to adopt the district as the unit of planning and to take some bold steps in this direction during the Third Plan, were:

(*i*) removal of the inter-district and intra-district imbalances in development; and

(*ii*) desire to ensure that the districts will be given an opportunity to attain full development, having regard to their potential, available manpower and other resources.

The Organisation for District Planning

In 1962, the State Government had set up the Zila Parishads in the State, vesting them with the obligatory function to promote plan development of the districts by utilizing, to the maximum possible extent, local resources and for that to prepare annual and long-term plans giving regard to the plan prepared by the panchayat samitis.[2] In fact, the planning function entrusted to these bodies must be construed as a process of decentralization of economic power complementary to the decentralization of political power. However, the planning function was not seriously taken up by the Zila Parishads. An evaluation committee[3] which studied the performance of the Zila Parishads in 1971 did not find any particular evidence to show that there was any conscious or systematic planning in the local sector. According to the recommendations of this committee, the Zila Parishads were strengthened by vesting larger financial resources in them and transferring to them most of the remaining development schemes which were originally with the State Government. Following this development, the district planning boards were constituted in 1972 for providing a proper planning machinery at the district level and the secretarial responsibility for these boards was entrusted to the chief executive officers of the Zila Parishads. This must be regarded as the first phase of development in district planning.

The District Planning board had the designated minister of the district as it chairman. The membership of the board included:

1. Divisional commissioner as vice-chairman.
2. District collector.
3. Zila parishad president.
4. Mayor of the municipal corporation and/or the president of the largest municipal council.
5. Chief executive officer of the zila parishad.
6. Chairman of the district central cooperative bank.
7. Chairman of the district land mortgage development bank.
8. Regional manager of the lead bank.
9. Three non-officials to be nominated by the State Government.

The District Planning Board was to be assisted by a district planning team consisting of the chief executive officer of the Zila Parishad, the district deputy director of agriculture, the district deputy registrar of cooperative societies, the district statistical officer, the divisional forest officer and the industries officer. The planning officer of the zila parishad was to act as the secretary of the district planning board and as the member-secretary of the district planning team.

One of the criticisms about the composition of the district planning board, as it was constituted then, was that it did not include the representatives of the legislature and Parliament. To fill this gap, the State Government was ultimately persuaded and prevailed upon to constitute a 'district development consultative council', consisting of representatives from the State legislature and Parliament and also persons representing various interests such as industry, trade and commerce, universities and social welfare.[4] At this stage, it should be noted that the district development consultative council was meant only as an advisory body.

The working of these two bodies at the district level was reviewed by the State Government in 1974. It was felt that the elected representatives of the people should be more directly associated in the process of the formulation and implementation of the district plan and it was, therefore, decided to amalgamate the above two bodies and to constitute a new planning body at the district level, known as the 'District Planning and Development Council' (DPDC). The membership of this body did not change, and remained the same as the combined membership of the bodies.[5]

The DPDC is merely expected to offer guidelines to the implementing agencies in the task of plan formulation and ensure coordinated action by the implementing agencies including the Zila Parishad.[6] The day-to-day task of plan formulation and implementation was entrusted to a smaller executive committee consisting of:

(*i*) The designated minister of the district as chairman.
(*ii*) The divisional commissioner.
(*iii*) The president of the zila parishad.
(*iv*) The collector.
(*v*) The chief executive officer, zila parishad.

(*vi*) Two other representatives of the DPDC to be elected by the council. (Later, this was modified as 'to be nominated by a consensus of the DPDC').
(*vii*) The manager, district central cooperative bank.
(*viii*) The manager, lead bank.
(*ix*) The mayor or president of the largest municipal council.
(*x*) The planning officer (secretary).

The executive committee of the council is now required to meet at least once in a month and transact the following business:

(*a*) Consideration of the monthly progress report in the implementation of the district annual plan.
(*b*) Identification of the reasons for shortfall in expenditure as also physical achievements or lack of progress.
(*c*) Suggesting measures for expeditious implementation of the programmes and remedial measures required for the purpose where the progress is found to be tardy.
(*d*) Consideration of new schemes or works for inclusion in the district annual plan by adjustment within the budgeted outlay of the district in case that is found to be very necessary.
(*c*) Consideration of excess requirements/savings indicated by the district implementing officer/agency and propose reappropriation for approval of the Government.

In regard to reappropriation of savings/excess within the approved outlay of the district for the annual plan, the executive committees of the DPDCs have been given certain powers and it has been made incumbent on the heads of departments and their district level implementing officers that decisions of the executive committee are implemented by them and also that no modifications in the annual plan, as approved by the State Government, will be made by them without the prior approval of the DPDC or its executive committee.

At the time of constituting the DPDC, the chief executive officer of the Zila Parishad was designated as member-secretary; but with a view to providing more effective coordination amongst the various developmental agencies, the State Government designated the collector of the district as the member-secretary of the DPDC with effect from December 1975. This must be noted as an important departure[7] in the district planning process as it has tended to shift the focus from the chief executive officer of the Zila Parishad to the District Collector. The reason for this change is the fact that district planning is not merely rural development, but includes several other spheres of activity which are better coordinated by the District Collector who has an overall control in the affairs of the district.

SOME CRITICISMS ABOUT THE PLANNING MACHINERY

The Planning Machinery that has evolved in Maharashtra has certainly some merits; at the same time it has been pointed out that there are certain deficiencies as well. The DPDC, as it is constituted now, is an unwieldy body and it meets only on a few occasions. It is merely devoted to deliberations and its decision-making function is not considered to be very effective by some critics. At the same time, it is claimed that the association of the minister in-charge of the district as the chairman of the DPDC as well as its executive committee, has enabled the district planning bodies not only to have an idea of the thinking and the policy of the State Government on various issues but also to convey to the Government, through their chairman, the aspirations and needs of the district so that, if they did not form part of the State's Plan, an opportunity would be provided to the State Government to modify the plan in the light of the articulations of the district.

Another criticism which is often made is that in the planning process that has emerged at present, the involvement of the panchayati raj institutions below the Zila Parishad level is more indirect than direct. For instance, it is said that the deliberations of the Panchayat and of the Panchayat Samiti in which a larger measure of direct participation by the citizen is possible, get themselves projected as programmes of action by the Zila Parishad which is again reflected in the district plan prepared by the DPDC. Nevertheless, there appears to be a feeling among the representatives of the Panchayati Raj bodies below the district level that they do not have adequate voice in the district planning process.

SCOPE AND FUNCTION OF DISTRICT PLANNING

District planning is not only a real planning, but also a part of the multi-level planning. In fact, district planning calls for a two-way approach—the process of planning from below, lending realism and concrete content, with the downward movement, as well as some measure of guideline and assistance in planning from the State level. The State has to spell out clearly the scope and functions of the district plan by indicating the district level schemes as opposed to the State level schemes.[8] Accordingly, the State Government has specified the State sector schemes and the district sector schemes and this step, more than anything else, has lent a realism to district planning. By and large, the criteria for determining whether a scheme belonged to the State sector or the district sector, were the locations of the programme and the areas which were to benefit by the programmes. Schemes like generation and distribution of power, major irrigation projects costing over Rs. 5 crore, investments in corporate sectors and other institutions, surveys, research and training programmes, administrative and residential buildings, universities including agricultural universities and institutions of professional education like engineering and medical colleges, but excluding arts, science and commerce colleges and polytechnics, the State and national highways and ports, are all considered as State level schemes. On the other hand, programmes like agricultural production, medium and minor irrigation, soil conservation, ayacut development, animal husbandry, dairy development, forest, fisheries, warehosing and marketing, cooperation and community development, small-scale industries, education, social welfare and backward classes, etc., were district level schemes. The district sector is really the residuary sphere and whatever is not specifically included in the State sector belongs to the district sector.

This manner of presentation of schemes into the State sector and the district sector was an important step which enabled the State Government to broadly quantify the total plan outlay on each district. We, therefore, come to the resource allocation aspect of the district planning process.

One of the important measures taken by the Maharashtra State prior to the introduction of district planning in the State was to decide the allocation of funds to district-level schemes and then suitably re-allocate it to the various districts on some rational basis. In order to do this, the State Government took into consideration the policy of balanced development of the districts and the need to accelerate the process in the relatively under-developed districts and adopted a scale of weitghtage[9] with reference to the total population of the district, the urban population, the population of scheduled castes and scheduled tribes, the relative backwardness in the fields of agriculture, industry, irrigation and communications and special problems and special needs of development of the coastal districts, the drought-prone areas and the forest areas. The formula adopted for this purpose is something similar to the Gadgil formula adopted by the Planning Commission. (For details please see Annexure).

The idea of a firm resource ceiling for each district is to be regarded as an important advancement in the technique of sub-State-level planning. It helped in making the entire district planning exercise feasible, realistic and operational. The District Plan now ceased to be a 'shopping list'. The district planners were compelled to think in terms of priorities and were asked to rank their proposals. These were the distinct advantages of the 'resource ceiling approach'. However, this procedure also led to some rigidities in planning. About this, we shall discuss at a later state.

STATE GOVERNMENT MEASURES FOR PLANS WITH DIFFERENT TIME FRAMES

When the Maharashtra Government started it thinking seriously on district planning, the intention was to prepare plans of different time duration—the long-term plan (with a 15 years perspective), the medium term plan (5 years plan), and the short-term plan (annual plan). In fact, some steps were taken during 1968-69 to provide the macro-framework to the 15 year perspective plan. This perspective plan was proposed to be completed in four phases:

(*i*) A data collection and analysis phase including resource inventorying and assessment of levels of development;

(*ii*) A phase of consultation with local people to assess the development needs;

(*iii*) Resource base estimation phase in consultation with the finance department; and

(*iv*) The plan finalization phase.

However, the work was not pursued beyond the first phase. The reasons given are that the State's perspective plan was not ready and that the resource position was very uncertain.

During the first phase, three significant steps were taken by the State Government which are worth mentioning. These are:

(*i*) The Government appointed technical resources survey teams in the major fields of primary production such as agriculture, animal husbandry, dairy, fisheries and forests entrusted with the task of assessing the present position of material production in each district and prospects of growth based on the physical resources of the districts and to make constructive, imaginative and realistic recommendations in this regard. The reports provide a technical framework for formulating projects based on local resources, for inclusion in the district plans and may be regarded as valueable reference documents for local planning.[10]

(*ii*) Efforts were made to collect statistical and economic data for ascertaining the level of development reached in each district, as in 1968-69. A publication called 'District-wise Statistical Information' was published in 1973 by the Planning Department, which provides information on various aspects of development in the districts for *three* time periods—1951, 1961 and 1969-70.

(*iii*) On the basis of the statistical data and the resource surveys, an 'indicative framework' of the proposed perspective for 'district development' was also prepared. This indicative framework provides information on various socio-economic indicators of development, highlighting the position of the district vis-à-vis other districts and the State as a whole. A close analysis of these indicators reveals the degree of backlogs in the different sectors in the district and suggests an ordering of priorities, if the objective is to raise the level of development of the district either to the State average or to the average of the comparatively better developed districts in the State. The preparation of the indicative framework must, therefore, be regarded as a contribution to the methodology in district planning.[11]

The three steps mentioned above must be regarded as valuable preliminary work in the direction of district perspective planning. Although it did not logically lead to the preparation of the perspective plans, nevertheless, it laid the ground work of the formulation of the district five year plans.

PREPARATION OF THE DISTRICT FIVE YEAR PLANS

Before the commencement of the Fifth Plan, steps were taken by the State Government to prepare five year plans for all districts in the State. The following procedures were indicated by the State Government to the district planning bodies as guidelines for the preparation of the Draft Fifth Plan of the Districts:

(*i*) Up-dating of the resource surveys, statistical economic data and socio-economic indictors of development.
(*ii*) Scrutiny of the existing schemes in regard to their relevance and recommendation as to their continuance or withdrawal.
(*iii*) Preparation of a list of schemes and a ranking according to their priorities.
(*iv*) Preparation of a master plan for the district, showing a list of productive and labour intensive works. While some of these works could be included in the district plan, depending upon their priority, the remaining works were kept as 'stand by works' for each block in the district for an emergency situation, *i.e.*, in the event of any natural calamities.
(*v*) Finalisation of the integrated plan of the district.

It is understood that in the light of the guidelines given above, the draft fifth five year plans were prepared by the district planning boards. However, it is stated that in consequence of the national and State five year plans not having been finalized, the district plans also remained as paper exercises only.[12]

FORMULATION OF THE ANNUAL PLANS

It is the annual plan exercises undertaken in Maharashtra since 1974-75 that bring out the multi-level planning procedures that have been established in the State. According to the State Government, during the first year of the Fifth Plan (1974-75), the exercises were not so thorough and full as they commenced being so from the second year.

For the year 1975-76, the State Government, after making an assessment of its resources, decided to embark on an annual plan involving a total outlay of Rs. 350 crore. On the basis of the principles of the distribution of outlays between the State and the district sectors, the districts were informed of their ceilings of outlay and were asked to prepare an annual plan of this order. Some important guidelines about the formulation of the plan were also provided to the districts at the same time in order to enable them to plan in a proper manner. These guidelines laid down the national and State priorities to be observed such as the priorities for the core sector of agriculture, irrigation, power and industries, emphasis on tribal and drought-prone area programmes, provision for the inevitable requirements of on-going schemes which the districts did not desire to discontinue, etc. The districts were also informed that while the ceilings have to be adhered to, they would nevertheless be at liberty to formulate, in the light of the district's needs and aspirations, some other programmes which were beyond the ceiling limits but which could be considered for implementation in case there was any improvement in resources or in case the districts were able to spot out additional resources, institutional or otherwise.

The District Planning and development councils went about the exercise of formulating the annual plans, keeping the above guidelines in view and consulting citizen opinion in as representative a manner as possible. Frequent discussions were held with the various representatives in the DPDC. The representatives of the planning department also attended these discussions with a view to providing information and clarification whenever necessary. The annual plans were finalized after these discussions by the DPDCs and sent to the State Government.

On receipt of the annual plans from the districts and before the finalization of the State Plan, a further round of discussions was arranged between the district planning and development councils and the State Government. The planning minister presided over these discussions which were attended by all the heads of departments or their representatives and by the district minister or ministers who were the chairmen and members of the district planning councils. During these discussions, all the difficult issues relating to the district plan were sorted out. Out of these discussions emerged a State Plan which had a recognizable as well as quantifiable district component and an equally recognizable as well as quantifiable State component.[13]

DISTRICT PLANNING UNIT IN MAHARASHTRA

The planning unit in each district is under the overall charge of the district collector and consists of a planning officer, one statistical assistant and one research assistant. The planning officer is usually a revenue official of the rank of deputy collector. The functions of the planning unit are at present limited to routine functions of preparing the agenda and minutes for the executive committee meetings and of the DPDC, sending returns to the State Government, compiling in district level schemes for preparing the annual plan, etc. No independent studies or analyses are undertaken by this unit. The unit does not also have the necessary technical competence to undertake such studies.

At the Sate level, the planning officers in the planning department have been assigned to a group of districts and they coordinate the work of the districts. They also attend the meetings of the executive committee/DPDC, when necessary.

The State Government is aware of the inadequacies of the staffing pattern at the district level. It has some proposals on hand for inducting more technical staff at this level. It has been proposed that Central assistance should be extended to strengthen the planning machinery at the district-level.

It must be noted in this context that while the State Government has made commendable progress in establishing detailed procedures for district planning, it has not, as yet, developed a technically competent planning machinery at the district level, nor has it made any determined attempt to train and impart skills to the existing personnel on a *regular and continuous* basis.

DISTRICT PLANNING: A CRITICAL APPRAISAL

During the course of this discussion, we have already taken note of the criticism that the Panchayati Raj Institutions below the Zila Parishad level do not have adequate representation in the district planning body. We may now turn to certain other aspects of the district planning process.

District planning in Maharashtra is much more than an exercise, breaking down the State level targets and outlays into district-level targets and outlays. Through trial and error, a process which seeks to build up the State Plan from below, *i.e.*, though district plans, formulated by the DPDC, has emerged. This is undoubtedly some achievement. Yet, what is actually being done today at the district level is only 'district budgeting' within the ceiling of resources allotted to the district. The set of schemes which constitute the district plan are those which are not determined by any objective analysis or study, but have been arrived at by consensus in the meetings of the DPDC and, therefore, are subjective in nature. They are not organized around any inner logic of their own. They mainly rely on an aggregation exercise based upon the proposals or the department agencies. The district plans, therefore, may not answer the rigorous tests of internal consistency, inter-sectoral complementarity, or criteria of efficiency. The district planning staff do not conduct any studies on their own or project alternative plans or do any impact analysis or evaluation of on-going programmes. Thus there is very little analytically informed decision-making in regard to the selection of projects in the district plan.

Another constraint in the district planning process today is the very little scope or manoeuvrability that is left to the district planning bodies for the planning of new schemes. The district plans carry with them the burden of the past—of on-going schemes and committed expenditure—and do not permit of any drastic alteration of priorities and schemes. Some chopping off redundant or irrelevant schemes and pruning of expenditure may be possible in any situation. But to identify these weak spots, and to give effect to any changes in the face of departmental pulls and pressures, require technical competence of an order which is not available today at the district level.

District planning in the State is also characterized by some rigidities. It does no permit of inter-district transfer of funds. This procedure is, no doubt, good, as it ensures that the funds allocated to the district are spent in that area only and are not diverted to other areas. But it also causes some difficulties, particularly in situations where inter-district projects are involved. The command area programme is a case in point. This is classified as a district sector programme, although the project may cut across two or more districts. The funds for the programme are provided in the respective district budgets and inter-district transfers are not possible. The command area authority which has to look at the command area as a whole, has to make adjustments from time to time by accelerating development in some areas and decelerating in certain others for proper sequencing and better management of funds. But since this flexibility does not exist, the command area authority finds it difficult to make suitable adjustments. In a similar way; the departmental heads at the State level, who had previously been exercising tremendous control over the location of investments, find themselves greatly handicapped in the present arrangement. Formerly, they used to concentrate on 'success' projects where better performance was possible and achievements could be shown. But now they find that their tasks is more difficult, as spending in backward areas is more difficult.[14]

The district planning process in Maharashtra has followed certain important procedures in order to make district planning a realistic and effective process. Some of these are in the nature of innovative, administrative procedures and deserve particular mention here:

(*i*) *Reappropriations:* In order to ensure that the financial allocation made available to each district for its five years or annual plan is utilized in the same district, the DPDCs have been given the freedom to recommend reappropriation of savings within the district itself, subject to certain limitations relating to the programmes in the core sector. It has also been laid down that the reappropriations approved by the DPDCs should be given effect to by the heads of departments.

(*ii*) *Release of grants:* A new procedure for release of grants is being followed. According to this, the administrative department concerned with the provisions in the budget voted by the State legislature will directly communicate to the officers, responsible for implementing a scheme at the district level, the budget grants placed at their disposal under intimation to the heads of departments, instead of channelising such releases to the district officers through the heads of departments. This has served to cut down delays in the release of funds to the district-level.

(*iii*) *Accountability of district officers to the DPDC:* Orders have been passed by the State Government specifying that the district level officers are accountable to the DPDC for the implementation of programmes at the district level. The progress of the schemes is constantly being reviewed by the executive committee of the DPDC which meets every month. During these meetings the district officers are given appropriate directions for the better implementation of the schemes. Thus, this procedure has served to improve the performance of the local officials.

SUMMING UP

To sum up, district planning in Maharashtra has several interesting features:

(*i*) A strong DPDC exists, although it has not been given a statutory status.

(*ii*) Various procedures for the effective functioning of the DPDC have been laid down by executive orders of the State Government.

(*iii*) The two major steps taken by the State Government to render district planning a feasible, pragmatic and realistic process are: (*a*) the definition of the district sector schemes which help to define the scope and functions of district planning, and (*b*) inter-district allocations of the divisible portion of the State outlay, which provide the financial parameters to the district plan.

(*iv*) Based on certain time honoured values, pragmatic practices and a trial and error process, a certain form of decentralized planning has emerged in the state. This process, however, has been far from a static phenomenon. In fact, the methodology in district planning has been undergoing continuous modifications and sophistication from time-to-time on the basis of experience gained in the working of the DPDCs and the procedures adopted by them. This great flexibility in the process has imparted great dynamism to the entire process of district planning.

With the measures adopted so far, the State Government has taken some bold steps in the direction of decentralized planning and adoption of multi-level planning procedures.

REFERENCES

1. The shift to district planning in the case of Maharashtra is a significant departure from a 'backlog and problem-oriented concept' according to which the backlog in the plan expenditures during the First and Second Five-Year Plans in the regions of Vidharba and Marathwada was sought to be made good during the Third and subsequent plan periods and the special problems of the scarcity areas, the Konkan region and the Bombay city were to be overcome by evolving special measures. Since this policy accentuated regionalism and affected Sate integration, the idea of district planning to remove inter-district and intra-district disparities was promoted. Thus, district planning served to divert the attention from a 'backlog-cum-problem oriented concept' focused on regions which had political overtones to the 'resource-cum-need based concept' focused on smaller areas (*i.e.*, the districts). This is considered as a 'pragmatic and far-sighted step' and not a mere 'concession or so to satisfy agitators or disgruntled politicians'.
2. Section 100(4) of the State Zila Parishads and Panchayat Samitis Act 1961 (Maharashtra Act V of 1962.)
3. Government of Maharashtra, Rural Development Department, *Report of the Evaluation Committee on Panchayati Raj*, Bombay, 1971, p. 84.
4. However, the taluka representatives had not been included either in the district planning board or in the district development consultative council with the result that they did not have any voice in planning at the district level.
5. The justification for constituting a separate DPDC, although an organization in the form of zila parishads and panchayat samities responsible for planning and implementation of developmental programmes of local character already existed in the State, is stated as follows: The spheres of action of Zila Parishads and Panchayat Samitis were limited to such schemes or programmes which were entrusted to them under the Act. Apart from these activities, some activities were still retained in the State sector which also had direct impact on the development of the district as a whole. Besides, programmes of various financing institutions, urban local bodies and statutory corporations/boards constituted by the State Government have to be coordinated with the development programme of rural areas drawn by Zila Parishads and panchayat

samitis. Thus, there was not single agency which could be entrusted with the function of bringing about close coordination and collaboration between the various agencies responsible for the development of the district.

6. The functions of the district planning and development council are as under:
   (*a*) To ensure coordinated action by the various implementing agencies at the district level including the Zila Parishads.
   (*b*) To give guidance to the various implementing agencies at the district level in regard to preparation and implementation of the perspective five-year and annual plans.
   (*c*) Subject to orders of the State Government, to approve perspective five-year and annual plans of the district.
   (*d*) To review from time to time the implementation of the five-year or annual plans and make recommendations to the State Government in that behalf.
7. This departure is still being criticized by some panchayati raj leaders.
8. During the Third Plan an attempt was made to broadly categorise the schemes into three groups, *viz.*, the State level schemes, the divisional level schemes and the district-level schemes. Basically the State-level schemes were schemes in the nature of external economies benefiting the entire State. The divisional level schemes conferred benefits on the more than one district. This procedure was later given up and the State Government divided the schemes only into two categories, *viz.*, the State-level schemes and the district-level schemes. The divisional level schemes were merged in the district-level schemes and the development outlay was apportioned in the proportion of the benefit to a district.
9. The scale of weightages in terms of percentage of the amount allocable to the districts for the Fifth Plan and the Annual Plans thereunder adopted by the State Government is as under:

Item	*Percentage allocation*
1. Total population	60
2. Urban population	5
3. Population of scheduled castes and scheduled tribes, etc.	5
4. Backwardness in:	
(*a*) agriculture	5
(*b*) irrigation	4
(*c*) communications	5

(*Contd.*)

	(*d*) industries	5
5.	Special problems of:	
	(*a*) drought prone areas	3
	(*b*) coastal districts	1.5
	(*c*) forest areas	1.5
6.	Unallocated amount for meeting special problems	5
	Total	100

10. The reports were prepared in 1969-70. Since then, they have not been up-dated. It has, however, been realised that in many cases further detailed work will have to be done and research in the various fields applied to the specific situations obtaining in the districts has to be undertaken.
11. A critic has pointed out that after the district plan became circumscribed by, or subordinated to, a resource ceiling approach, attention came to be focused more and more on the intra-district sectoral balance, *i.e.*, the backlog in any sectoral development tended to be evaluated only with reference to the other sectors of development of the district economy, and not in relation to the development of the particular sector *vis-à-vis* the other districts or the State as a whole. To what extent this criticisms is valid is open to question, as the tendency for any backward district is always to compare its position with a relatively better off district and with the State as a whole. Pleas see Maharashtra economic development council report, *District Planning: Possibilities and Issues.*
12. It is, however, stated that the strategy contemplated in the Draft Fifth Five-Year Plan of the districts formed the basis of formulating annual plans of the districts.
13. V. Subramanian, "The Citizen and Planning", *Indian Journal of Public Administration,* July-September, 1975.
14. Some have expressed the opinion that this procedure would result in slowing down the rate of growth of the economy. But this is not a valid criticism since district planning is intended to raise the level of development of the backward districts.

Annexure

Indicating the Methodology of Arriving at the Share of the District Under Each Criterion

The total outlay meant for district level schemes is distributed on the following basis:

Criterion I—Population Basis

The benefits of the developments effort should reach the people in general and the weaker sections in particular. In view of this the size of population including that of urban population as well as scheduled castes, *nav-buddhas* and scheduled tribes population is given weightage. Sixty per cent of the district total outlay is thus allocated on population basis.

Criterion 2—Scheduled Castes and Scheduled Tribes

Since Scheduled Tribes, Scheduled Castes (including *nav-buddhas*) are the weakest section of the society, special consideration and weightage is given to enable the district planners to take up special programmes so as to bring them on par with the other sections of the society. In effect this section of the population gets additional weight, since they are also included in the distribution of allocation under criterion 1. Population of Scheduled Castes, Scheduled Tribes and *nav-buddhas* is adopted as revealed in the 1971 census. The Backward Class population of the districts is expressed as a percentage of the Backward Class population of the State and 5 per cent is distributed on this basis.

Criterion 3—Urban Population

Some weightage is necessary because urbanization or concentration of a larger cluster of population in the cities and towns presents some special problems such as housing, sanitation, water supply, slum clearance, power supply, transport, etc. They also throw considerable strain on social services like education, medical, and public health services. As indicated in the 1971 census urban population of the district is considered and is expressed as percentage of the Urban Population of the State. Five per cent is distributed on this basis.

Criterion 4—Agricultural Backwardness

Industrial and agricultural backwardness is the major indicator reflecting the level of economic development. Agricultural backwardness of the districts is decided on the basis of two criteria, namely: (1) value added by agriculture per hectare in the district and (2) value added by agriculture per agricultural worker (cultivators and agricultural labourers).

For working out this criterion, the figures pertaining to the year 1967-68 were taken as this was more or less a normal agricultural year. The value added by agriculture per hectare was worked out by dividing the value added in each district by the gross cropped area in the district and the value added by agriculture per agricultural worker was worked out by dividing the value added by agricultural in each district by the total number of agricultural workers, *i.e.*, the cultivators and agricultural labourers. Since these two independent criteria were worked out, the indicators for each district were pooled by working out the geometric mean of the figures for value added per hectare and value added per agricultural worker. This geometric mean is worked out by multiplying the value of the two factors and working out the square root of the product.

The ratio of the geometric mean of value added per hectare and value added per agricultural worker for the district and the corresponding State average was worked out. For all the districts, the allocation was given in inverse proportion to the ratio for the State. This was because this method gives a proportionately higher allocation to the backward district in proportion to its backwardness as compared with the State average. Thus, the district which has a 10 per cent higher value of its geometric mean than the State average, is given 10 per cent less allocation and on the other hand a district having 10 per cent less value of its geometric mean than the State average is given a 10 per cent larger allocation per agricultural worker. This was worked out by means of a deviation formula.

Criterion 5—Backwardness in Communication

The development of communication is an important aspect of the economic infrastructure and for this purpose 5 per cent was distributed on this basis. For working out backwardness in this sector, the length of railways and the lengths of the national highways, State highways, major district roads and other district roads were considered. Here also, while deciding the district allocation, the geometric mean of the indicators regarding road and railway mileage per 100 sq.km. and per lakh of population has been worked out. The share of each district has been calculated by using the deviation formula as was adopted for working out the distribution under agricultural backwardness.

Criterion 6—Backwardness in Irrigation

Five per cent of the allocable sum is distributed on this basis. Agricultural development to a very large extent depends on development of irrigation. In view of this, five per cent of the allocation was distributed to the districts on the basis of the level of irrigation development in the district. For this purpose, the likely irrigation potential for each district by June 1974 through major, medium and minor projects (State sector) was considered. The percentage of this potential to the gross cropped area in each district was worked out. Similarly, the percentage for the State as a whole was worked out. The allocable sum was distributed to each district by using the deviation formula used in the case of agricultural and communication backwardness.

Criterion 7—Industrial Backwardness

Along with other indicators, the level of industrial development for each district was also considered and on this basis 5 per cent was distributed to the districts in the following manner. The district-wise value added by manufacturing industries as revealed by the Annual Survey of Industries for the year 1969-70 has been used. Per capita value added by the industries is worked out for all districts as well as for the State excluding Greater Bombay. Greater Bombay was excluded since the per capita value is very high as compared to the per capita value in the districts. Moreover, if Greater Bombay is included this will distort the whole picture. The district-wise average worked out to Rs. 55.66. Districts having per capita value added higher than this figure are excluded. These districts are Bombay, Thana, Poona and Nagpur. For the remaining districts, the allocation was made in the inverse proportion of per capita value added by the industries in the districts. For the Nasik District, for example, the value added per capita was Rs. 40.78 which was 26.74 per cent less than the average. Similarly, for the Aurangabad District, the per capita value added was Rs. 2.12 which was 96.17 per cent less than the State average. Thus, the backwardness of the Aurangabad District was 3.6 times compared to that of the Nasik District. Hence, the per capita entitlement of the Aurangabad District too was (Rs. 24.45) 3.6 times that of the Nasik District (Rs. 6.80). This per capita allocation was then multiplied by the 1971 census district population to arrive at the total allocation for each district.

Criterion 8—Special Problems: 5 per cent

(*a*) Two per cent to meet the special problems of drought prone areas. The share of each district is worked out on the basis of the rural population in the drought prone area as identified by the Sukthankar Committee.

(*b*) 1.50 per cent to meet the special problems of coastal districts. Again the share of the district is based on the rural population.

(*c*) 1.5 per cent to meet the special problems of forest area. The amount is distributed in proportion to the area under forests held by the Forests Department in each district.

Index